D1740124

## An improbable midwife

David Stanley Bradford was born 3rd May 1947 a date which, in the Jewish calendar, was a Sabbath designated *Acharei Mot* (after death). By an odd coincidence, that was mere days after ancient scrolls had come to light at Qumran, close to the Dead Sea. David entered an austere, post-war world in Lancaster, in the north-west of England.

The Bradford family described themselves Church of England, and David's early religious education was well supported by a state education system that still valued its Christian heritage. Sunday school and regular church attendance up to his mid-teen years completed the foundation.

David and his Portuguese wife, Ana (married 1972) have one daughter, Natalia.

In adult life, David spent almost 30 years working for British Telecom, where he acquired an understanding of communication theory, and project management principles. A late career change led to a further twelve years in computer programming and data analysis, in a Higher Education setting.

When asked how he came to discover the material for *In the Beginning*, David points to his liking for puzzles and for dabbling in relevant academic subjects like mathematics, the physical sciences and languages. He insists it is his eclectic interests rather than any specialization that made this investigation possible. But the initial impetus arose in late 2002 on the heels of a well-publicised, academic debate concerning something called a Bible Code. With a little lateral thinking, David realised that a genuine Bible Code would not convince a passionately sceptical audience unless it had been backed up with something more persuasive. In that moment the quest was launched.

*To be allowed to assist in the birth of original truth is a singular honour that may never be equalled.*

DSB

Order this book online at www.trafford.com/08-0170
or email orders@trafford.com

Most Trafford titles are also available at major online book retailers.

© Copyright 2008 David S. Bradford.
Cover Design by Alan Taylor.
All rights reserved. No part of this publication may be reproduced, stored in a retrieval
system, or transmitted, in any form or by any means, electronic, mechanical, photocopying,
recording, or otherwise, without the written prior permission of the author.

Note for Librarians: A cataloguing record for this book is available from Library
and Archives Canada at www.collectionscanada.ca/amicus/index-e.html

Printed in Victoria, BC, Canada.

ISBN: 978-1-4251-7071-4

*We at Trafford believe that it is the responsibility of us all, as both individuals
and corporations, to make choices that are environmentally and socially sound.
You, in turn, are supporting this responsible conduct each time you purchase a
Trafford book, or make use of our publishing services. To find out how you are
helping, please visit www.trafford.com/responsiblepublishing.html*

*Our mission is to efficiently provide the world's finest, most comprehensive
book publishing service, enabling every author to experience success.
To find out how to publish your book, your way, and have it available
worldwide, visit us online at www.trafford.com/10510*

 www.trafford.com

**North America & international**
toll-free: 1 888 232 4444 (USA & Canada)
phone: 250 383 6864 ♦ fax: 250 383 6804 ♦ email: info@trafford.com

**The United Kingdom & Europe**
phone: +44 (0)1865 487 395 ♦ local rate: 0845 230 9601
facsimile: +44 (0)1865 481 507 ♦ email: info.uk@trafford.com

10  9  8  7  6  5  4  3  2

# In the Beginning

## (Building the Temple of Zion)

David S. Bradford

In the Beginning

To the memory of my late parents:

Stan and Lily

# ACKNOWLEDGEMENTS

I am extremely grateful to my wife, Ana, for the long-suffering patience she had shown during my preparation and writing of this book. The same goes for my daughter, Natalia, who has also helped me with some of the typing of early drafts, and with her review comments. In one version, Natalia also contributed to a nice cryptic puzzle that, sadly, didn't make it into the final manuscript.

I have also received a wealth of spontaneous comment from many others with whom I have shared my discoveries, analysis and conclusions. Some of my less likely benefactors may be surprised (shocked, even) at how useful their views have been to me. I am keenly aware of how difficult it is to relate to a unique new subject so early in its infancy.

I believe in evidence. I believe in observation, measurement, and reasoning, confirmed by independent observers. I'll believe anything, no matter how wild and ridiculous, if there is evidence for it. The wilder and more ridiculous something is, however, the firmer and more solid the evidence will have to be.

Isaac Asimov
(1920-1992)
*Prolific popular writer*
*and Professor of Biochemistry*

# Contents

# Introduction

In the beginning there was a magnificent plan, a blueprint for everything that would ever come to be. At first, the plan existed only in the head of the Prime Mover. But it was already foreseen that an indelible image of the plan would be left accessible, so that we the created would one day come an important step closer to knowing the mind and the purpose of our Creator.

At the very start of the Hebrew Old Testament there is a short portion of the text that contains a quite staggering amount of additional, encrypted information. The text in question includes the entire first verse of Genesis and most of the second verse, but only seventeen words altogether. The key to unlocking the hidden content is to be found mainly within Genesis 1:1, which includes instructions on how to re-organise itself and the next 10 words. Importantly, the restructuring does not damage or destroy the original text. Yet it allows the same 64 letters to reveal many new words and graphical illustrations, all of which are conceptually related to extended parts of the Bible, even including the Christian New Testament.

Throughout this book I describe the re-organised text as the 'Author's Seal', and suggest that it has a special unifying role in relation to the Bible as a whole. When we examine this Seal, what quickly becomes apparent is that it foresaw important later events in the Judeo-Christian scriptures, and might even have been their blueprint. A more mundane view is that authors of the later biblical books periodically recognised or re-discovered the Author's Seal, and wrote according to what they saw in it. This latter conclusion would have serious repercussions for religious biblical interpretation; although any anxiety in this respect may be tempered with some confidence that the Seal cannot be the product of human ingenuity.

In the chapters that follow you will find my own barely adequate attempt to describe the Seal, an object of surpassing beauty ("They should have sent a poet" : Eleanor Arroway – *Contact*, Warner Bros. Films, 1997). In these pages, my reader will find a rich variety of descriptions for our inheritance, this unique and priceless heirloom that has been handed down, largely-unsuspectingly, through many centuries and countless generations of scribes.

There is no clear consensus as to the age and origin of the first chapter of Genesis. Some Jewish sources would have us believe that the first five books of the so-called Old Testament were all dictated by God to Moses, letter-for-letter. Hence the expression: The Five Books of Moses. After all, that prophet was on the mountain for forty days and nights, just about long enough to take down a text of this length. But modern biblical scholarship envisions a quite different origin, involving a redaction (compilation with judicious editing) from multiple sources of varying ages. For example, the first eleven chapters of Genesis share many features with myths and legends of cultures and civilisations that significantly pre-date Moses. Therefore, those particular chapters could, in principle, have been transmitted first via an oral tradition before being tagged onto the next four and three-quarters books.

In the ongoing debate on origins this, my own book, could be seen to offer a new type of evidence that will partly support, but also challenge the foregoing opinions and others, in varying degrees. This book is not primarily another opinion, but an observation. Its chief purpose is to draw attention to the aforementioned heirloom, so that it may be considered alongside the other evidence for and against divine origin. I certainly think this evidence will prove to be controversial – in different ways to people with alternative world-views. But it would surely be boorish to reject out-of-hand so priceless a gift, coming from a source that is, in other respects, widely worshipped under an assortment of names.

-oOo-

There is another, less-edifying way this subject might be approached. It seems to me that the world of today is obsessed with conspiracies, conspiracy theories, and romantic stories about conspiracies. Many of the more popular offerings in the genre have been those that involve secret codes and ancient mystical knowledge. And some of the more plausible examples are, significantly, bound up in the Judeo-Christian history. I use the word 'plausible' only to emphasise that the Judeo-Christian heritage contains genuine threads of history that many writers have found especially pliable for re-weaving into rich, alternative designs. At the same time, there is a widespread yearning for a truer understanding of the meaning of existence. In light of the Author's Seal, it seems that this hunger is not meant to be left un-sated forever.

I wish to make clear from the outset that the core subject of the present volume is no more another conspiracy theory than an origin theory. It is, however, a new way of looking at the Judeo-Christian scriptures that might be described as the breaking of the Author's Seal, a kind of code analysis stripped of much of the customary conspiracy baggage. It is worth repeating that I do not believe the code or heirloom in question can be of man-made origin. And I describe it as a seal not only because of its position at the very start of the Old Testament but because, when recognised for what it is, this Seal offers a new way of authenticating major parts of the Bible, including the Christian New Testament. By means of copious hidden words and disguised graphical illustrations, this tiny seed of text (only 64 letters) at the very beginning holds the 'genetic' blueprint that describes many of the more important biblical events that span a period of many centuries. Parts of the Bible that are especially recognisable from within this Seal are the Five Books of Moses (also known collectively to Jews as the Torah, and to Christians as Pentateuch), several Old Testament prophets, the Christian gospels and the Book of Revelation. And this particular collection of books, if I may offer a personal opinion, seems to provide evidence that the Author expects them to be viewed as a consistent whole.

The key to recognising the Author's Seal lies in the first seven words of Genesis; as it is written: *In the beginning, God created the heavens and the earth.* (Genesis 1:1). And if you have counted those words and noted that there are more than seven, then you are partway to recognising the correct way to understand the Seal. This is because the verse printed above is not the true beginning of the Bible; it is, rather, an English translation of the original Hebrew text. Throughout this book, the Hebrew word Torah will be used to indicate the all-important original text of the Bible's first five books. It is only by analysing the Hebrew version that the first verse may be recognised for what it really is – a container or frame for the Seal as well as an essential part of it.

The words heirloom, seal and code are not the only ones that could be applied to the Seal phenomenon. When we fill the 7-word frame with further text, we find the Seal is also a window through which we may gaze upon particular parts of the Bible, laid out as a landscape. Indeed, this window is so skilfully conceived that we shall be able to view the same landscape as though from several widely-separated vantage points. And this versatility will in turn allow us to identify alternative landmarks and formations, or to see the same formations in several contrasting ways. Overall, this new multi-dimensional view succeeds in connecting certain familiar biblical events, or symbolic representations of those events, in ways that verify their pre-ordained relationships. That is to say, particular key personalities and major events from throughout the Bible's sixty-six books are clearly depicted within the Seal's various landscapes. But the mere presence of these components within the same Seal is by no means the whole story. Much more important is the fact that each component is represented in a number of alternative ways, and linked to the others with similar rich artifice. Distinctive artefacts that, individually, might easily be dismissed as the product of arbitrary coincidence occur in such rich profusion as to demand an alternative explanation. It will be evident that a skilful designer has been at work, which is only to be expected from a Seal that may be the Creator's own outline plan.

Of course, distinctive structures in the Bible's first creation account have always attracted interest from pious believers and serious academics alike, as well as merely curious observers. An obvious example is the strong emphasis placed on the number 7, including the fact that the whole of the creation account is described in a seven day setting. It has been noted that:

> [Genesis]1:1 consists of 7 [Hebrew] words, 1:2 of 14 (7x2) words, 2:1-3 of 35 (7x5) words. The number seven dominates this opening chapter in a strange way, not only in the number of words in a particular section but in the number of times a specific word or phrase recurs. For example, "God" is mentioned 35 times, "earth" 21 times, "heaven/firmament" 21 times, while the phrases "and it was so" and "God saw that it was good" occur 7 times.
>
> (Wenham, 1987, p6)

The characteristics listed here by Wenham are often mentioned together as a way of demonstrating deliberate intent on the part of the author. There is nothing in this suggestion that could be described as implausible, let alone controversial or threatening either to religious belief or to biblical scholarship. From either position, the dominance of the number seven may be regarded as a simple poetic device that has, nonetheless, probably been responsible for the first creation account being retained as the Bible's opening gambit. A more overtly religious stance might insist that there is a deeper and perhaps mystical meaning than just poetry to be gleaned. But, overall, there is no difficulty in accepting that the 'seven' phenomenon would have been well within the capability of a human author to contrive.

It is here that the Author's Seal will seriously challenge such simple, non-contentious explanations for the origin of the Hebrew Torah. Because the information density in the Seal combined with an amazing degree of internal structural and conceptual integrity certainly do exceed the ability of any human intellect by a seriously large margin. I have more to say on the subject of provenance later.

As to the matter of conspiracy theories, far from introducing any new ones I believe the following chapters will go a long way towards substituting concrete information for the speculations underpinning theories that are already doing the rounds. That may prove to be less pain-free to long-established belief-systems than it sounds. For although this exposition is firmly rooted in the Hebrew Old Testament, that does not mean that it will confirm any existing religious point of view. What it should do – or this is my hope – is to verify the essential core of truth upon which all Judeo-Christian beliefs are based. The corollary is that the Seal may, ultimately, be capable of testing each belief for authenticity, veracity and integrity. The fact that some elements of particular belief-systems appear to be either missing from or especially emphasised by the Seal may prove uncomfortable to the perfectly respectable followers of some 'denominations'. Nor do I have enough knowledge of belief-systems outside Judaism and Christianity to help in recognising aspects of the Seal that may prove helpful to them. But given the present state of this 'new' knowledge, it is inevitable that there are still gaps, many of which will be filled subsequently. Up to now, I have been working alone in this research, and others are sure to extend these findings, in due time. Therefore, the full implications for different faiths cannot yet be foreseen. In this context, it is perhaps appropriate that I should say something about the intended audience for my book.

Quite simply, I hope my topic will be widely read and enjoyed by any and all, as an unconditional bequest from the Creator. But I am not naïve enough to imagine I am writing for a mass audience, or not in the short-term anyway. In fact, I suspect that certain well-established groups, who potentially have much to gain from this knowledge, will initially be the least enthusiastic, for a variety of reasons. The groups I have in mind particularly are Orthodox Jews, practising Christians, Christian scholars and atheists. I expect all of these groups to be far too entrenched in their beliefs and world-views to engage readily with so radical a challenge to the established *status quo*. I would really like to include the followers of other religions in my list, but it would not be practical to list them all separately or reasonable to address them as coherent groups. So I shall limit myself to saying a few words about each of the four groups I have named explicitly.

First, I think that Judaism will be inclined to treat my description of the Seal with disdain, as a trespass on its sovereign territory. Much of my book may be seen as adding little that is acceptable or worthwhile from a Jewish perspective. Some of it is simply confirming what is already accepted as direct divine revelation. And at various points I acknowledge in general terms the existence of Jewish sources that either confirm my own assertions or provide a springboard to what seems to me to be new wisdom. All else will likely be branded the raving of an unqualified upstart, despite the fact that every step in my analysis is easily traceable. But I will be especially interested to hear the Jewish interpretation for aspects of this new knowledge that appear distinctly Christian, since these make up a considerable proportion of the conclusions that follow.

Second, there seem to me to be two particular stumbling blocks in the way of practising Christians seeing this new wisdom as an acceptable revelation of the divine will. First is the source being the Hebrew Old Testament, rather than a neatly sanitised translation. It will soon be realised that the underlying structure beneath the plain Hebrew text confirms only the common, shared truth of Judaism, and of Christianity as its natural outgrowth. It may even force a radical re-think as to whether Christianity has got hold of the right end of the stick in some respects. That is a matter I shall leave for later debate, assuming the relevant parties will engage with the new evidence and bring their views to the table.

The other stumbling-block concerns no less than the role of faith itself. In some Christian circles, faith is held up as a matter only for personal conviction and conscience, albeit within strict doctrinal constraints. One reason for reliance on (blind) faith is a knee-jerk reaction to the unprecedented growth in the status of science in the last few centuries. Before Galileo, Newton and Darwin, to name but a few, the Church was happy to apply a form of rationality to the interpretation of scripture. As long as the earth was at the centre of creation, and we humans were all descended directly from Adam and Eve, logic remained the ally of Christian tradition. But then science came of age, and pulled the rug from under those cosy misconceptions. As a result, logic and imaginative rational thought came to be seen as the preserve of science alone, and have been disowned by many of the faithful. Responding to the troubling fact that science leaves fewer and fewer gaps in which God has a role to play in the world, the argument tends to run something like this: It is asserted that religion and science are ultimately irreconcilable; therefore the tenets of science can no longer be applied to religion; therefore religion and faith cannot be subject to criteria of logic and proof. Since science is founded on logic and evidence and, so it is held, there can be no universally shared proof for religion, therefore blind faith must take the place of evidence in all matters of religious belief and conscience.

But there is an important new factor that must argue against that modern, insular point of view. The strongest possible argument against the evolved status of faith would be the discovery of any form of direct evidence for the existence of the same God to which that faith, without proof, already pledges allegiance. Here, I am referring to a kind of evidence that would be so readily accessible that it could be seen and shared by anyone willing to accept the risk, anywhere and at any time. This could not be just a small local or personal miracle, but a universal Miracle that can be rigorously tested. Here, we are dealing with the sort of proof that is widely assumed cannot exist; but it does exist, hidden in plain sight, and is the subject of this book. What is more, although the Bible appears in places to fly in the face of established scientific principles and fact, the Author's Seal will give us cause to suspect that to be a deliberate avoidance of that particular reality. That would make perfect sense if we accept the Bible first and foremost as a description of evolving morality. But the Seal will soon demonstrate the same Author's limitless understanding of what we call science and mathematics.

As to biblical scholarship, although it is an ostensibly Christian undertaking, I (and I suspect many of its own adherents) see it as a separate and in some ways incompatible undertaking from the actual practice of Christianity. I will go so far as to say that some of the core concepts of mainstream biblical scholarship directly contradict many of the long-held tenets of all three Abrahamic faiths: Judaism, Christianity and Islam. One such victim is the belief described earlier, that the Five Books of Moses (the Jewish Torah) have come down to us from the time of Moses himself. The reason is easy to find; biblical scholarship brings to bear on the scriptures the sort of logical, pseudo-scientific techniques that are anathema to many practising Christians.

Modern biblical scholarship traces its roots to a relatively new brand of analysis first carried out by Julius Wellhausen (1844 to 1918). The earliest modern form of analysis developed by Wellhausen is now known as Source Criticism. And it is that which led to the suggestion that differing styles of writing and choice of vocabulary must, necessarily, be the work of different writers. It is now customary for commentators to assume the Books of Moses have been compiled from a so-called 'E' source, a 'J' source, a 'P' source and a 'D' source[a]. That is, at least four different writers. Since then, many lucrative careers and eminent reputations have been built, standing on the shoulders of Wellhausen. And his methods have blossomed further to include Form Criticism, Literary Criticism and Redaction Criticism. But if one individual can write a book, a shopping list and a letter to the bank, why shouldn't a far more skilful biblical author have written in many styles to suit several overlapping purposes?

---

[a] 'E' = Elohim; 'J' = (J)YHWH; 'P' = priestly; 'D' = Deuteronomy-like

However, the intensely rational mode of analysis is the least of the flaws in the academic pursuit of scholarship, because the true power of logic has, in some ways, been selectively ignored. The paragraph I quoted earlier from Wenham (1987), in which he highlights the dominance of the number seven in the biblical creation account, actually provides evidence of a closed-mind approach. The kind of numerical structural analysis reported by Wenham is only a hint at something much more elaborate, which is the subject of this volume. Every time anyone has noticed the strong focus of Genesis on the number seven, they have been on the threshold of a momentous secret, virtually knocking on the door. As we shall find in Chapter 2, the next steps which ought to flow naturally from that observation are far from being difficult to recognise. Yet until now, in modern times anyway, no one reports having followed the obvious trail. We ought to ask ourselves why that is.

The answer seems to me all too obvious; why would anyone bother to look for something that cannot possibly exist? Modern scholars do not expect to find anything more that is relevant along those lines. If it is assumed that all parts of the Bible were composed by mortal authors, then it would be a pointless waste of effort to search for anything that is beyond the wit of man to conceive. It is quite evident that the scholarly literature is woven around the interplay between history and primitive belief systems that have little practical relevance in our times. It follows automatically that modern biblical scholarship is less a theological pursuit than a branch of anthropology. I do not expect the present generation of mainstream scholars to change direction overnight; but that is, of course, human nature.

It is worth mentioning here that Judaism has its equivalent but much older version of biblical scholarship, which employs an alternative form of analysis known as Midrash. Almost invariably the two kinds of analysis reach totally dissimilar conclusions. It is as though one is looking with the eye and the other listening with the ear. They are both examining the same words, but what each of them sees is quite unlike the other, because followers of the two disciplines hardly ever share their ideas face-to-face. The two points of view reflect totally dissimilar mind-sets.

I can openly declare that this book comes closer to resembling Jewish Midrash than Christian scholarship, not least in its provisional assumption that parts of the Bible are direct revelation from God; yet the midrashic method still manages to validate the identity of the Christian Messiah (to employ a tautological clash). On the face of it, therefore, it appears the Seal may prove kinder to Christianity than to Judaism, by offering more points of contact with their particular creed.

Yet the established churches still face a number of tricky questions concerning the Seal. In particular, there are indications that the Seal has been the foundation for numerous biblical prophecies, including parts of the Book of Revelation. I remarked earlier on the possibility that some parts of the Bible could be literary expansions on what their writers have seen within the Seal. So why, then, does church teaching not already revere the Seal as a favoured, sacred source? Even Jesus taught that he spoke in parables to the ordinary folk, but revealed to his disciples the hidden mysteries (Luke 8:10). As we shall see, the Seal belongs very much to the second category. So why do the surviving gospels recount only the parables? These questions do not constitute a new conspiracy, but merely draw attention to one in particular that is already current: that the early church may, for political reasons, have deliberately purged the original mystical elements from its doctrine. In Chapter 2, I offer an alternative and less conspiratorial explanation, by which the exclusion of the mystical aspects may not have been a wilful act of suppression. But in Chapter 10, we shall see evidence that the western Church once had the perfect opportunity to set the record straight, and failed to act with proper integrity.

The challenge posed to atheism by the Seal may prove to be as severe as anything I have already described. The most respectable form of atheism is based on the undeniable fact that religions in general have their roots in unverifiable belief. Religions are then tolerated only insofar as they codify good moral or ethical standards, and do not impose their more esoteric dogma on the unwilling. But as rational as atheism often appears to be, one wonders how it will respond to the discovery of hard new evidence that supports the blind faith of particular religions. That might be just too big a nut for atheism to swallow, even if it does also force a fundamental reappraisal of doctrine by the three Abrahamic faiths.

-oOo-

The crucial question still remains largely unaddressed, and it concerns the validity and provenance of the Author's Seal. Of course, the appropriate place to give an answer would be at the end of this book, after the best evidence has been presented. At the present stage, I shall confine myself to making just three bold statements concerning the nature of the Seal:

1. Allowing for the latitude that exists in opinions concerning the age of Genesis (ie the basis of the Seal), we can be sure it was written not less than six centuries prior to some of the events that it foresees.

2. It also incorporates knowledge of non-biblical subjects – especially in the realms of science and mathematics – that were unknown until relatively recent times.

3. Over and above the preceding two issues concerning time-stamping, the multi-dimensional structure of the Seal puts its devising far beyond the ability of any mortal intellect, past or present.

By any normal set of standards (maybe including the tools favoured by biblical scholarship), what you will find described in the following chapters cannot possibly exist. So the chief point I intend to demonstrate is that the first 17 words of the Hebrew Bible, as well as having a familiar plain meaning, conceal so much extra information and meaning that it simply must be the product of an omniscient super-intelligence. A great deal of lip-service is paid to the idea of a creator who is omniscient, or all-seeing, without fully grasping what that would mean. The following seven chapters ought to close that gap in understanding.

These are, admittedly, personal views which my reader is at liberty to challenge. And I look forward to a healthy debate, conducted in the light of all the evidence given in the following chapters, served as a fully laid table. Some readers may find the concept of evidence itself an obstacle, due to the way evidence (or proof) has come to be seen in some circles as the polar opposite of faith.

But if the people of Ancient Near Eastern cultures could not have devised the Seal, then there are precious few alternatives. Maybe some observers will prefer to appeal to modern forms of fantasy (the realm of science fiction) for an explanation. But I see no reason to look beyond the explanation given by the Seal itself: *In the beginning God created....*

As far as I can see, the only serious barrier to acceptance of what follows will likely rest in one's pre-disposition to the subject matter. The real challenge is in our willingness to take in the whole cathedral when the sight of its foundation alone may call into question one's prior world-view. Both Judaism and the established Christian Church will find much in these pages to uphold fundamental aspects of their respective doctrines. However, the Church in particular may publicly ignore the rich detail on the grounds that the phenomenon as a whole also supports the 'wrong kind of Christianity'. That is, the Seal may corroborate 1st and 2nd Century versions of Christianity that have been ruthlessly put down and largely expunged from the pages of history, during the last 1850 years. But, if that is what the Author's Seal does, then who could reasonably challenge its authority?

-oOo-

*To readers who have no knowledge of Hebrew* I will add that you need not feel disadvantaged. Although my book is concerned with tightly compact and very elaborate structures designed into the text of the Hebrew Torah (they cannot be seen in translations), the beauty of the Author's Seal is that its features can be seen very easily. When the Seal reveals a Hebrew word, I will indicate its hidden location, write it out, suggest its most likely pronunciation (as an English transliteration) and offer one or more possible translations. Every stage of the process will be traceable, requiring no special skills or knowledge beyond a willingness to think, quite literally, 'outside the box'. Concepts that may be unfamiliar will be discussed as we go along. The same encouragement applies with the meanings of Hebrew words. Readers with a high-enough level of committed interest, may easily check my usage with, say, **The New Strong's Expanded Dictionary of Bible Words**. More casual readers may rest assured that there should soon be plenty of experts more than willing to carry out such checks.

*A special note to readers who are already familiar with Hebrew script.*

In many parts of this book, there are examples of Hebrew text in settings where it appears other than horizontally, comparable to the popular word-search puzzle. Sometimes the text will be seen written vertically, or at an angle of 45°, with either a positive or a negative slope[b]. In every case (including the horizontal), the text may be seen set out in both directions (forwards or backwards); quite often the everyday right-to-left order of Hebrew text will not be observed. Other deviations from present day rules for writing Hebrew script will be rare, but when that happens a rationale will be given in context. Also, differences of both spelling and grammatical rules between ancient and modern Hebrew can be important. Familiarity with modern Hebrew alone will not always be an advantage when assessing the findings presented in the following chapters.

---

[b] The concept of positive and negative slopes comes from mathematics, where a negative line is defined as one which slopes from top-left to bottom-right.

# 1

I pointed out in the Introduction that the first verse of Genesis, which uses ten words in the English King James Version (KJV), derives from only seven words in the original Hebrew. A large part of that difference is found in the six-letter first Hebrew word, which translates to 'In the beginning'. And that single word will serve as the ideal vehicle to introduce the rest of this book, since it demonstrates some early promise of the cryptic skill of the Torah's author. In the Hebrew script of today, this word is בראשׁית, pronounced *B'reishith*. Reading from right-to-left, as with other semitic languages, the names of its six letters are, in order, *beyt* (on the right), *reysh*, *aleph*, *shin*, *yud* and *tav* (on the left).

There are several characteristics of the Hebrew alphabet that distinguish it from our modern Latin version. For one thing, there are only 22 Hebrew letters, compared with 26 Latin and 24 Greek. Incidentally, the first four Hebrew letters are *aleph*, *beyt*, *gimmel* and *delet*; compare with the Greek alpha, beta, gamma and delta, reflecting an evolutionary relationship between the two languages. Although the Greek alphabet is not semitic (a word derived from the name of Shem, the son of Noah), it has inherited some Hebrew features. In fact, the Greek symbol for alpha (ie α) closely resembles the ancient Hebrew aleph (𐤀). In order to honour the greater antiquity of the Hebrew character-set it will, henceforth, be called the alephbeyt.

Another important difference between Hebrew and the Latin alphabet is that each Hebrew letter has an intrinsic symbolic meaning. Thus, *beyt* represents a dwelling (originally a nomadic tent), *reysh* is a man's head, *aleph* is an ox head (see ancient symbol in the next and previous paragraphs), *shin* is a pair of front teeth, *yud* is a closed hand and *tav* is a sign or obelisk.

It is worth noting that the Hebrew letter symbols used today, known as square script, have been in use for a little over 2300 years, but are not the original forms. Just note the difference between the ancient aleph (𐤀) and its current counterpart: א. In the earliest proto-Hebrew script, each written letter was a pictogram designed to resemble the object or concept it symbolised. That 'true' Hebrew script was not immune to change over time; but the Hebrew script in use today did not arise by way of a gradual evolution. Rather, it was adopted wholesale from the later Aramaic language, some time after Aramaic had become the *lingua franca*, the prevalent tongue throughout much of the area we know today as the Middle East.

Another difference between Hebrew and Latin letters is that the former do not have upper- and lower-case forms. In fact ancient texts in the proto-Hebrew script gave little or no indication as to where one word or sentence ended and the next began. Given that there was also no punctuation and precious few spaces to help with reading, that style of writing has become known as *scripta continua*. However, at an uncertain point following introduction of the Aramaic script, a new convention came into use, involving changes made to the form of five particular letters when they occur at the end of a word. The specific letters are: *kaf* (ך,כ), *mem* (ם,מ), *nun* (ן,נ), *peh* (ף,פ) and *tzadee* (ץ,צ). In each case, the bracketed symbols show the normal form (ie initial and medial) on the right, accompanied by its final form on the left. But note carefully that the origin of the Torah pre-dates the use of final letter forms by many centuries, which will be an important fact to keep in mind in the remainder of this book.

Yet another difference is that Hebrew does not employ separate letters to represent vowels. So the letter *heh* (ה), for example, could be pronounced heh, hah, hee, hu or ho; and since the pronunciation can determine the meaning of a word, the only way to know the correct vowel sound may be from the context. An equivalent English example is the pair of words – one a noun, the other a verb – that are both spelled E-N-T-R-A-N-C-E. Since there are no explicit vowels, all 22 Hebrew letters are generally classified as consonants, although two of them: aleph (א) and ayin (ע) are either silent or known by whichever vowel sound they happen to carry in a given context. Another letter, the *vav*[c] (ו) is a vocalised consonant in some situations, but in others is present only to carry an 'o' or a 'u' vowel sound. Those of us who grew up speaking and writing a Latin-based language often have difficulty coming to terms with the lack of visible vowels in Hebrew script. The dearth of explicit vowels in Hebrew will have another

---

[c] *Vav* is the modern pronunciation of the sixth letter, which may have been pronounced *waw* in biblical times.

important consequence for the validity of the subject of this book, which is something I shall discuss in Chapter 2.

A more straightforward difference between Hebrew and Latin script is that letters of the former alephbeyt do not sit on a base line, but hang down from an imaginary shoulder line. The only exception is *lamed* (ל) whose head protrudes above the shoulders. The ancient form of lamed was a shepherd's crook, while the later Aramaic version seen here is reduced to just the head of a crook. Since the symbolic meaning of lamed is teaching and learning, it is most apposite that its written name (spelled *lamed-mem-delet*) can also mean 'to teach' and 'to learn'. Of course, as explained in the previous paragraph, for the same spelling to mean three different things, it has to be pronounced in three different ways. The letter *lamed* will be seen later to have a special place in the context of the Author's Seal; and a very important place it is, too.

One final and very important difference between Hebrew and Latin letters is that each Hebrew letter also has a numeric value, which is something else that Hebrew shares in common with Greek. Whereas the later Latin alphabet has inherited only a vestigial form of numerology (as it is called), in which just seven of its 26 letters (ie IVXLCDM) are utilised for Roman Numerals. Biblical Hebrew language scholar Menahem Mansoor (in BIBLICAL HEBREW Step by Step, Volume 1, 2nd Edition) states that '*This* [numeric] *usage is not biblical. The earliest traces of it are found on Maccabean coins (about the second century B.C.)*'. Of course, if that view was the whole story, then there could be no possibility that the book of Genesis might exhibit an organised numerical structure based of those values. Yet it can and will be shown that the Author's Seal on the start of Genesis does indeed incorporate an underlying numerical dimension which strongly supports the extensive linguistic structures.

But to return to the first word of Genesis, it will now serve to illustrate a convention that I shall use extensively. Observe the way in which three related pieces of information are combined here:

בראשית / B'reishith / In the beginning

The three component parts of this construct are:
i)     the word in modern Hebrew script (on the left),
ii)    a transliteration (in the middle), and
iii)   a translation (on the right).

A few words of explanation are in order. First, the Hebrew word is presented here as a native Hebrew reader would expect to see it. The word or phrase should be read from right-to-left. Next, the transliteration is given mainly as an aid to English pronunciation. I recognise that many who read this book will not be Hebrew speakers nor intend to become so. Therefore, the transliteration will normally be used in my descriptive narrative, and only accompanied by the Hebrew word(s) where its structure is important to the argument. Finally, the translation will, more often than not, be lifted straight from a standard English translation of the Old Testament; which will often be either the KJV or the Revised Standard Version (RSV). However, any translation from one language to another cannot fail to reflect the purpose or agenda of the translator, to some extent. So there will be occasions when I shall offer an alternative translation, or more than one. This is especially likely where the subtleties of biblical Hebrew permit an alternative emphasis that is in keeping with the function of the Author's Seal, perhaps more so than with the plain biblical text. Critics of the Seal hypothesis may suggest that in allowing an alternative emphasis, I am 'tailoring the evidence'. My first response is that it will happen only rarely. More important, though, is the fact that the Seal itself sets the appropriate standard, by means of its internal consistency throughout this and the next six chapters.

In other cases the Hebrew word may be something other than a simple grammatical 'part of speech', such as the name of a person or a month of the year. In such instances, a descriptor (eg The 10th month of the year) may be given instead of a literal translation.

-oOo-

*In the beginning* (note the partial underlining). To anyone acquainted with cryptic clues to crossword puzzles this expression would be an instant invitation to search within its own letters for a shorter hidden word. So, the underlined letters: <u>hebe</u> (the daughter of Jupiter and Juno in Roman mythology) might be the answer to the implied clue of which "In the Beginning" is a part. And part of the special merit of *B'reishith* is indeed to be found in its unrivalled cryptic versatility. As far as composition is concerned, the six letters of B'reishith happen to include the first two letters of the alephbeyt and the last three. Here, there is the merest hint that 'In the beginning' is to be understood in more than one way; that the beginning and the end are somehow bound up together in a way that we may yet discover. We shall find ourselves returning to this possibility at several stages, but especially in Chapter 6.

Next, as has already been mentioned the first two letters of B'reishith symbolise a dwelling (eg a tent) and a man's head. These two letters, isolated from the rest spell בר / *bar* / <u>an heir</u>. We need not wonder too much that the combined images of a head and a family home should represent an heir. Such natural associations are a well-known feature of the way letters combine symbolically in the biblical Hebrew language to form words of conceptually composite meaning. Yet it is quite curious that the word heir should appear at the very instant when God begins his cosmic creation. Especially as we shall be led inexorably to conclude that the Seal has come down to us as a kind of heirloom.

Even more tantalising is the fact that the whole word B'reishith (בראשית) is seen to consist of the full word ראש / *rosh* / <u>head</u> contained within ב י ת / *bayit* / <u>dwelling</u>. Here is a perfect example of the types of cryptic crossword solution just mentioned. And in this case, a suitable clue might have been: *The master is in his home.* To be realistic, isolated associations like this happen all the time in everyday life, and count for little more than their novelty value. In terms of the Seal, however, this is only the start of a much larger phenomenon that is set to assume enormous importance. Again, to start with we need not wonder at 'head' being seen within the first word, as that is the very root of it. It is *rosh* that gives rise to the concept of beginning, like a piece of music that is played or a script that is read 'from the top'. The real surprise is in the way that the necessary prefix and suffix letters that contain this head should happen to spell *bayit*, the Hebrew word for house, and that the whole word repeats the twinned concepts of its first two letters. This first coincident pair of words gives a clue to another, equally significant re-arrangement of letters.

A moment ago, I remarked that B'reishith utilises the first two letters from the alephbeyt and the last three. The first two, in alphabetical order, spell אב / *Av* / <u>Father</u> – a very apt concept when set alongside both a head and an appointed heir, or son. But the same word can also be the name of the 11th month of the Jewish calendar. Then the last three letters of the alephbeyt are also found in their reverse order within *B'reishith*. And together with the yud of B'reishith, they spell תשרי / *Tishrei* / <u>'the first month of the Jewish calendar'</u>; an odd coincidence to say the least. Moreover, the letter *aleph* found in *Av*, is also commonly employed in Jewish dates to mean 'the first day (of) …'. And its second letter, *beyt*, can be prefixed to a month to mean 'of'. So, the first day of Tishrei (written: א״ בתשרי) is the Jewish New Year – known as *Rosh HaShanah* (literally, 'the head of the year'). In this way, the six-letter first word of Genesis also includes a powerful reminder that it signifies the very beginning of time. As though to reinforce this idea, B'reishith also provides the solution to the uncertainty surrounding the choice of which month to mark the start of the Jewish year. Tishrei has come to be accepted as the first month of the year for most purposes, including the religious cycle that determines the order in which the weekly Parshot (Torah portions) are read. However, Tishrei is not the first month for all purposes; it is written:

> *The LORD said to Moses and Aaron in the land of Egypt,*
> *"This month shall be for you the beginning of months. It shall*
> *be the first month of the year for you.*

(Exodus 12:1-2)

The month in question is now known as Nisan, but in biblical times was called Abib. From our point of view, the importance of Abib is that its letters, as well as those of Tishrei, are found within B'reishith (plus the first letter from the Torah's second word). The letters of Abib are spaced evenly as seen in Figure 1.1, and radiate outwards from the middle of B'reishith, so:

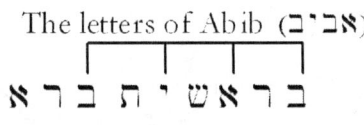

The letters of Abib (אביב)

ברא שית בודתא

Figure 1.1

Later, we shall see further forceful reminders that the first word of Genesis is closely linked to the concept of time.

Next, there is another striking way in which the first word can re-arrange itself – one that has a direct association to the first biblical patriarch, Abraham. So this will be the first example of the Seal – the early text of Genesis – demonstrating an important though modest pre-ordained reference to a later biblical narrative. This time we lift out the middle two letters of B'reishith (בראשית), which spell אש / *esh* / fire. The remainder is a pair of letters at each end which, when we slide them together, form the word ברית / *brit* / a covenant. The biblical narrative corresponding to this metaphor appears to be in Genesis 15 where God begins to make (literally 'cut') his enduring covenant with Abram to give to his descendants all…

> *'this land, from the river of Egypt to the great river, the river*
> *Euphrates'*

(Genesis 15:18, RSV)

## In the Beginning

Immediately prior to this promise, God has instructed Abram to…

> *'Bring me an heifer three years old, a she-goat three years old, a*
> *ram three years old, a turtledove and a young pigeon'*
>
> (Genesis 15:9)

Abram cut the three larger animals down the middle and laid the pieces one against another. Then, later:

> *'When the sun had gone down and it was dark, behold, a*
> *smoking fire pot and a flaming torch passed between these*
> *pieces'*
>
> (Genesis 15:17)

So, here, the "flaming torch" passing between the cut pieces is the narrative fulfilment of the *esh* (fire) that is seen within B'reishith between the two halves, the cut pieces of *brit* (covenant). It is only later, in Genesis 17, that God gives his promise to Abraham to make him the father of many nations. But the two stages are evidently closely connected, as is the following delightful corresponding representation in Genesis 1:1.

To fully appreciate what is going on, or developing within the Seal, we now need to take a step back and widen our focus. The seven words of Genesis 1:1 are composed from 28 letters; and the first three words utilise 14 of them, exactly half. This initial clause reads:

| אלהים | ברא | בראשית |
|---|---|---|
| God | [He] created | In the beginning |

Or, in our adopted convention:

- בראשית / *B'reishith* / <u>In the beginning</u>
- ברא / *bara* / [He] <u>created</u>
- אלהים / *Elohim* / <u>God</u>

Just in passing, we may note that the second word – *[He] created* – is identical to the first half of the first word, although there is no etymological relationship between them.

The next Abraham connection comes from combinations of words 1 and 3, in two ways. We have just seen that B'reishith separates into 'fire' and 'a covenant', which we provisionally linked to Genesis 15. But now consider the rarely mentioned connection between the cutting of the animals in that chapter and the covenant that is described in Genesis 17. In this second stage, the name of Abram is converted to Abraham – significantly by cutting through the shorter name to insert an extra letter *heh* (ה) – and the covenant of circumcision was instituted. The key point here lies in the Jewish expression: מילה ברית / *Brit Milah* / <u>The Covenant of Circumcision</u>. The first part of this expression (ie Brit) we have seen emerge from B'reishith. The second part, Milah, may be obtained from Elohim (the third word, אלהים, meaning God) using just four of its five letters. Note that the letter *mem* (מ) that begins Milah is essentially the same as the final form ם that ends Elohim. Remember that the final forms of five specific letters were introduced long after the Torah was first set down in writing.

A note of caution is in order here, concerning the foregoing proposition that two of the first three words of Torah may foresee the later covenant with Abraham. In fact, the Hebrew word Milah is not to be found in the Hebrew Bible; so the expression Brit Milah is undoubtedly of post-biblical origin. So it is possible that what we have just seen is not part of the evidence of pre-planning we otherwise obtain from the Seal, but a clue that Jewish tradition may already have followed the route we are now taking. That in itself is of great significance, since it would mean that the Seal has been recognised more than once, perhaps repeatedly, as a phenomenon of genuine merit.

The final component of the allusion the Seal makes to Genesis 15/17 also derives from a combination of words 1 and 3. The name of Abram (אברם) may be constructed from the strategically placed first three letters of B'reishith, and the final letter of Elohim. Then the letter *heh* (ה), the middle letter of Elohim will convert Abram to Abraham, but with extraordinary consequences. The three letters that then remain from Elohim are an anagram of איל / *ayil* / <u>a ram</u>, and those that remain from B'reishith spell תיש / *tayish* / <u>a he-goat</u>. Though the details of these fragments do not exactly match the later narrative – the goat being of the wrong gender – the allusion to two of the larger animals in Genesis 15:9 is, nonetheless, unmistakable. And overall, the preceding three cryptic references to Abraham from the same concise text are but a preliminary sample of the rich bounty yet to come. We shall be drawn back to the subjects of Abraham and circumcision at several later stages. In fact, Abraham is set to become one of several persistent themes and motifs throughout most of this book.

# In the Beginning

-oOo-

This is as good a stage as any to mention that the word B'reishith is an *incipit*, having been adopted in Judaism as the name for the book known to others as Genesis. Each of the following four books of the Torah is likewise known in Judaism by its first substantive Hebrew word. Exodus is שמות / *Shemot* / (the) <u>Names</u>; Leviticus is ויקרא / *Vayiqra* / <u>And</u> [the Lord] <u>called</u>; Numbers is במדבר / *Bamidbar* / <u>In the wilderness</u> and Deuteronomy is known as דברים / *Devarim* / <u>Words</u>.

For the moment, we have exhausted the concealed meaning within B'reishith using the tools and information we presently have at our disposal. But substantially more content will become accessible as our skills develop. And, although the first word of the Torah was initially selected for use as a vehicle for describing certain characteristics of the Hebrew language, its obvious versatility confers a more strategic lesson. This is a modest, though important clue to the rich nature of the Author's Seal. This will only be fully appreciated when we recognise that parts of the Torah have been designed to emulate the sort of word-games and puzzles that appeal naturally to the human mind.

Without a doubt the first word of Genesis, overflowing as it is with unsuspected content, is a veritable enigma. But the intrinsic versatility of that word would count for little in isolation. What matters far more, and makes *B'reishith* different from any existing non-biblical construct, is the way its internal structure maps onto extended narrative passages elsewhere in Genesis. It is akin to a tiny seed, the size of which greatly understates its genetic capacity to grow into an elaborate adult form. Or it is a blueprint for a vast, pre-conceived edifice. This is the kind of behaviour we shall discover time and again lurking within the folds of the Author's Seal. And it is the vast extent of this potential that testifies to the super-human origin of, at the very least, the start of Genesis. The versatility of the first word is only a clue to the fabulous treasure that still lies in store - a silver clasp on the entrance to the royal storehouse. Or it is a foretaste of a rich banquet that is already fully laid-out like a wedding feast. Waiting for us there, we shall find fruit and choice meats; vintage wine and freshly-made bread, enough to satisfy any hunger and appetite.

# 2

Before we get too far ahead of ourselves, it is appropriate to ponder the conceptual nature of this enigmatic Seal about which I have said so much but yet so little, because the word seal can conjure up a variety of alternative images. The best analogy I can offer is the sort of wax seal that is, even today, sometimes set on the closure of an important document or envelope. A seal of that type has two principal attributes. First, the impressed design of the seal will often present a recognisable image in relief, to identify the authority of whoever set the seal in place. Second, the seal must be broken in order to gain access to the contents of the document, also proving beyond doubt whether the contents still remain secure or assured.

The Seal of the Author of Genesis will be found to meet both criteria. The image of authority takes at least two different forms: for one thing the Author names himself in the first verse of Genesis, a major component of the Seal. Also, the cunning intricacies hidden within even the first word will testify eloquently to his vast intellect.

Then the breaking of the Seal takes place by adapting the text as it is given, re-organising it according to a simple rule that is also encoded within itself. A well-known adage says that, in order to make an omelette it is first necessary to break eggs. As we shall soon see, the beauty of the Genesis Seal is that the end product gains immeasurably in value after it is re-constituted. The first word of the Torah, already broken and re-made in several ways is, then, a seal within a seal.

What is more, by linking to later clearly recognisable parts of the Bible, this Seal presages a technique that we might otherwise assume had been developed specially for modern electronic communication. This is the concept of an error-detection code, or check-sum that is appended to the start or end of a message block, immediately before it is transmitted. When the message arrives at its destination, it is automatically checked against the error-detection element for calculable evidence of discrepancies. Up to a point errors can not only be recognised but, with a more elaborate error-*correction* tag, also rectified using this technique. Alternatively, automatic background processes may ask for a damaged message block to be re-sent. The key point in this is the fact that an error-detection tag is intimately bound to the content of the message. In an important sense, the message and the tag both 'know' one another. In the case of the Seal, it embodies information about a much wider biblical text, and serves to verify the authenticity of the parts of the Bible that are especially important to its overall message. Therefore, the Seal may allow us to recognise flaws in our understanding, and offer the chance to rectify them. Whether we actually choose to follow up that opportunity is another matter.

-oOo-

In the present Chapter, we shall gain our first clear view of the Author's Seal. But first we must perform some preliminary analysis that will show us how it may be recognised.

The next step in our analysis will call into play the whole of the first verse of Genesis. And the way we proceed depends very much on its own high-level structure; that is, the positions of its word-breaks, and the significance of those positions. This will be an example of the text itself conferring the rule by which it is to be re-structured. The whole first verse is seen below in its native state, to which our adopted convention of word/transliteration/translation is applied vertically to each word. Do remember that the Hebrew text scans from right-to-left, with the result that the English translation given here looks unnatural.

| הארץ ואת | השמים את | אלהים ברא | בראשית |
|---|---|---|---|
| ha eretz v'et | ha shamayim et | Elohim bara | B'reishith |
| the earth and[φ] | the heavens -* | God (He) created | In the beginning |

* The fourth word in Genesis 1:1, known as the Hebrew particle exists only to distinguish nouns that are objects of a sentence from those that are its subjects. It is a language-specific concept, and therefore neither has nor requires an English translation. The sixth word incorporates the particle into the conjunction 'and'.

φ The letter *vav* (ו) used as a prefix and transliterated as 'v' should be pronounced *vuh*.

In this chapter, and at one other place, we shall take an interest in existing knowledge (Wenham, 1987, p35) concerning a superstition that was widespread throughout Mesopotamia, even before the Torah was set down in writing. That was the belief that, within a calendar based on lunar months, the days numbered 7, 14, 19, 21 and 28 were in some way unlucky and fraught with sinister risk. Whether it is just coincidence, we may note anyway that both 7 and 19 are hexagon numbers (see Appendix A(ii)). To set against that superstition and similar beliefs, it can be shown (although it is beyond the scope of this book to do so) that each of the component narratives in Genesis chapters 1 to 11 (often described as the biblical primaeval or pre-history) is a polemic against particular extra-biblical myths and superstitions. Then, Genesis 1-11 as a whole is a sustained protest against all of those other polytheistic traditions. And the biblical pre-history cleverly manages to combine such propaganda with other objectives for which it is better known.

The way in which the first biblical creation account is expressed in a seven-day setting is one facet of just one such polemic. So the fact that Genesis 1:1 contains seven words and has word breaks after 14, 21 and 28 (all multiples of 7) letters contributes to the rejection of any irrational aversion to the number seven. The fear of 19 seems for the moment to be an unexplained exception to a simple rule; yet even this, in its turn, will be addressed by the Seal. But before going any further, I think it is important to be aware that biblical scholarship would see these observations as an end in themselves, merely to add to evidence of the poetic emphasis the first creation account places on the number seven. Needless to say, if that were the end of the matter this book could not have been written.

The presence of word breaks after 14, 21 and 28 letters could by now be accepted as given, leading directly to the next major step in our progress. First, however, I think it is appropriate that for once we recognise some additional intrinsic significance in those numbers. Obviously they are all multiples of 7. But 21 and 28 also have something else in common with the word break after B'reishith, the very first word, at position 6. That is, each of them belongs to the mathematical series of triangular numbers (see Appendix A(ii)). Thus, 6 is the result of 1+2+3; similarly 21 is the result of 1+2+3+4+5+6; and 28 is the result of 1+2+3+4+5+6+7. Triangular numbers will be seen often in these analyses, showing that the Seal has been designed with them in mind, as well as other mathematical principles. So from this point onwards it will be helpful to have available a simple shorthand to assist in referring to specific triangular numbers. The symbol $T_3$ for example, will refer to the third triangular number, which is 1+2+3 (=6). Likewise, $T_6$ will mean 21 and $T_7$ will mean 28.

Furthermore, the number of letters in the first word and the first verse (ie 6 and 28 respectively) are also the first two members of a class of numbers which mathematicians, perhaps with excessive zeal, describe as Perfect. They are called perfect because each is the sum of all its own proper divisors, including 1. Thus, 6 = 1+2+3 (because 1, 2 & 3 all divide into 6, without leaving a remainder); and 28 = 1+2+4+7+14. It turns out that Perfect Numbers are exceedingly rare; the next one after 28 is 496, followed by 8128, 33550336 and 8589869056. It is no small matter, therefore, that 496 will also be recognised by the Seal.

Knowing that some of the word break positions in Genesis 1:1 have several degrees of significance, the question arises, how should we interpret them; what, if anything, is the clue we are meant to recognise and to follow? Perhaps we should separate the 28 letters into four blocks of 7; which will indeed lead to the most prolific outcomes, in terms of the number of ways the text of the Seal may be decoded. That is the path we shall follow in the present Chapter, in two different ways. Although, in due time, we shall also make use of a separation into seven blocks of 4. Without further ado, let me present Figure 2.1, showing the most important general format in which the letters of Genesis 1:1 will reveal their hidden content.

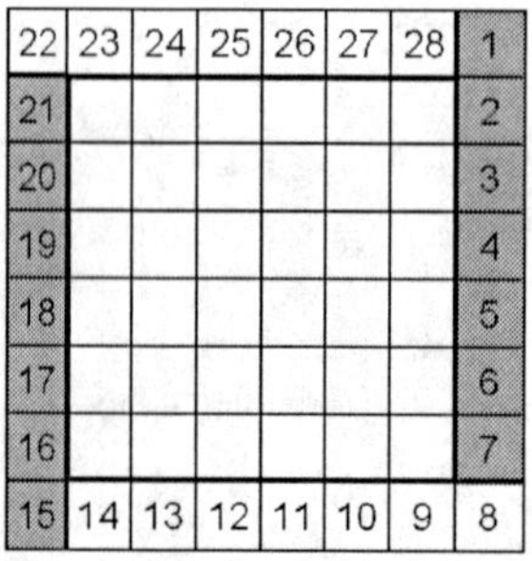

Figure 2.1

Notice that the four blocks of seven letter positions (alternate shading) combined as here lead to an 8×8 chessboard arrangement. Occasionally, it will be helpful to refer to a specific side of the square. When I do so, it will normally be a reference to a sequence of seven letters, not eight. If anything else is intended, that will be made clear at the time.

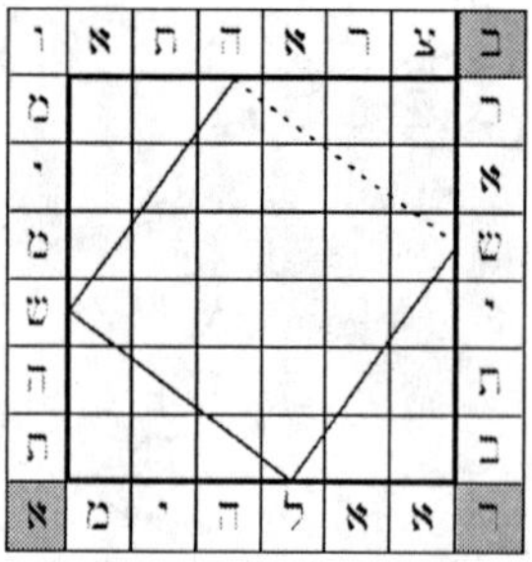

Figure 2.2

At last, we may now see Figure 2.2 depicting the square with the 28 letters of Genesis 1:1 inserted instead of just their position numbers. Here, the text is inserted starting with the shaded letter *beyt* (ב) in the top-right corner, and proceeding downwards initially. The unadulterated 28-letter text of Genesis 1:1 makes one complete circuit of the square.

Figure 2.2 is essentially a transitory stage in our progress, yet contains enough clues to confirm our correct choice of direction. As with many subsequent examples, the clue obviously needed to possess an intrinsic merit of its own (the plain text meaning); but the greater reward is in the consequences that flow from our taking the bait.

Three particular configurations of letters are worthy of special note in the new square setting. In another arena, two of them would be described as Equidistant Letter Sequences, ELS for short. Some researchers, in their quest for evidence of a divine origin for the Hebrew Torah, have been looking for a very specific type of Bible Code. The rationale for the Bible Code is that the Author of the Torah will have arranged the text so that significant words may be found spelled out, not just with adjacent letters, but with letters that occur at other equal intervals – hence ELS. Naturally, in a text of 304,805 letters one would expect to find enormous numbers of ELS words. So the bigger test is not to find isolated words, but to find whole families of words and maybe related dates (especially ones that would originally have been in the future) that occur in localised clusters. Groups of words that cluster together in this way are said to be 'compact', and the degree of compactness can be expressed as a calculated statistical value.

In our own analysis, we will not often expect to find new ELS words, the present stage being the one notable exception. The first eye-catching example is composed from the fourth letter in each side of the square, seen at the corners of the inscribed square in Figure 2.2. So the word that emerges is שלשה / *shelosheh* / <u>three</u>, reading clockwise from the right side of the square. This word for 'three' (masculine form) starts at the fourth letter of Genesis, then proceeds with a skip distance of 7. But let us be quite realistic; when the setting is the normal linear text, the presence of an isolated ELS word would not seem particularly remarkable, except perhaps in the way it extends the emphasis given to the number 7 in the creation account. However, in our new arrangement, the path it traces follows the distinctive outline of the square within a square seen in the above illustration. It thus confers extra legitimacy on the arrangement we have adopted for Genesis 1:1.

To find the second ELS word, recall that the second word of Genesis (ie ברא / *bara* / [He] <u>created</u>) repeats the first three letters of the verse – the first half of the first word. Within our new square, the second word is seen to turn the lower-right corner, symmetrically. But notice that the same sequence of letters also occurs with the same symmetry seen shaded in the first three corner squares; that is, letters 1, 8 and 15. So this ELS word also has a skip distance of 7. And as with the first example, the ELS *bara* would hardly merit a second glance if seen in the regular linear text. Except, of course that it, too, boosts the special emphasise on the number 7. Again, it is the new square setting that emphasises the striking configuration of this ELS word.

| ב | ה | י | שׁ | א | ר | ב |
|---|---|---|---|---|---|---|
| מ | י | ה | ל | א | א | ר |
| מ | י | ם | שׁ | ה | ת | א |
| צ | ר | א | ה | ת | א | ו |

Figure 2.3

If the text of Genesis 1:1 is formatted in an array or matrix, as often employed in Bible Code studies, both of the aforementioned ELS words stand out especially clearly. In Figure 2.3, the first seven letters of Genesis are written right-to-left in the top row. The next seven letters are written right-to-left in the second row, and so on. Both ELS words are seen here as shaded vertical sequences. But notice that the word שלשה / shelosheh / three splits the array symmetrically down the middle. Before very long, the concept of symmetry will become so persistent as to be seen as one of the Author's principal indicators of deliberate design.

This is also a good point at which to take note of a striking configuration of the letter aleph (א) in the right side of the same array. There are only six copies of aleph in Genesis 1:1, and five of them are emphasised in Figure 2.4, where they have assembled into the clear outline of a 45° right-angle triangle, or enough of its outline to make the overall shape evident. Mark well this shape as we shall encounter something remarkably similar, closely related yet more impressive in Chapter 3.

| ב | ה | י | שׁ | א | ר | ב |
|---|---|---|---|---|---|---|
| מ | י | ה | ל | א | א | ר |
| מ | י | ם | שׁ | ה | ת | א |
| צ | ר | א | ה | ת | א | ו |

Figure 2.4

Now that our scope has been widened enough to include the full first verse of Genesis, we may take note of a special sequence of seven consecutive letters which reveal an important alternative meaning when read in reverse. To identify this sequence we take three letters from the start of the fifth word, the whole of the fourth, and two letters at the end of the third word. Together, they give rise to the following expression:

משה תאמי / Moshe ta'owmiy / Moses, my twin (or image)

The grammatical object of the expression is given explicitly – it is Moses. But who is the subject? Well, given the strategic importance and precise meaning of the first verse, it is especially significant that the three letters of Moshe are the reverse spelling of HaShem (literally, 'The Name'). HaShem is a standard Jewish circumlocution for the proper name of The Lord – YHWH – as it was first told to Moses at the burning bush. In a very subtle way, this enigmatic expression is revealing its subject, just as plainly yet just as inscrutably as in the burning bush incident. In fact, the 7-letter text confirms this conclusion if it is extended to an eighth letter. Then, instead of saying just 'Moses, my image', it says 'Moses, image of Yah', where Yah is an abbreviation of the very name told to Moses.

That mysterious reference to both YHWH and Moses as similar faces is, of course, found in the Torah's very first verse. Then, at the extreme end of the Torah, it is said:

> *And there arose not a prophet since in Israel like unto Moses,*
> *whom the Lord knew face to face.*
> (Deuteronomy 34:10)

So here, we have two matched reminders that identical faces are to be expected in many pairs of twins. And the latest allusion in Genesis 1:1 to a corresponding strategic location of the Bible is the first indication that the word 'face' *per se* may have unsuspected importance.

In a veiled way, we have already seen two examples of a geometric metaphor for identical images facing one another. These are the two cases of *bara* (he created) which are placed symmetrically in the 8×8 square. Both are examples of bi-lateral symmetry in which a straight line – the axis of symmetry – divides a plane, or flat shape into identical halves. In fact, although one bara is compact and the other widely spaced, both of them share one common axis of symmetry, which is a diagonal of the square. Therefore the two equal halves (faces) are identical 45° right-angle triangles. Here then is a second allusion to triangles of the same basic shape. To be realistic, at the present stage, an intentional relationship between bi-lateral symmetry and twins facing one another is by no means proven. But a precedent has been set, which will be reinforced by further examples, including the notable arrangement of five alephs fully occupying one half of the 7×4 matrix seen in Figure 2.4. Indeed, Abraham's bi-secting of the three large animals in Genesis 15, and his subsequent spatial arrangement of them, is a particularly arresting, literary example of bi-lateral symmetry.

-oOo-

Thus far, the structure of the Bible's first verse has achieved a very important new purpose. We now understand it is meant to fit around the perimeter of an 8×8 square. Mathematically, a square of these dimensions sits at a unique location within the set of all perfect squares. This follows from a property of triangular numbers (explained in Appendix A(ii)), that any perfect square is a fusion of two consecutive triangular numbers. Our 8×8 square has 64 elements, and these are the sum of 28 and 36 (ie $T_7$ and $T_8$, respectively). But recall that the perimeter itself consists of 28 elements, so that the inner region contains 36. It is this correspondence between the structure of an 8×8 square and its constituent triangular numbers that is unique among all squares. And yet, what is still not immediately obvious is that the enclosed area is meant to be filled with 36 more letters. Of course, having said that, we would be remiss if we did not at least consider it as an option. Therefore, our next and most important step will be to do just that, along with some additional modifications that may sound trivial, but nonetheless have important implications.

The first change I plan to make is to rotate the square through 45° (what else!), so that its diagonals become vertical and horizontal. Second, the text of the first verse will be entered counter-clockwise instead of clockwise, and starting in the right-hand corner. Incidentally, it will be convenient from time to time to identify the corners of the square as the four cardinal compass points (North, South, East and West). So, the new starting point is the Eastern corner, with the text proceeding through North, West and South, and on to a position adjacent to our starting point.

The last of my minor modifications will be to dispense with the use of final forms of letters. The reason being that once all 64 elements of the square have been populated, new words will emerge as in a word-search puzzle, and may be composed from letters that are not normally adjacent in the regular text. In these circumstances, a letter that takes a final form in the regular text could find itself in the middle or at the start of the emergent word. Then the integrity of the emergent word would be compromised unless all 22 letters are standardised as proposed. That is the immediate, practical reason for abandoning final forms of letters. However, a more robust reason is that it takes us a small step closer to the way Hebrew script was written in the earliest biblical times. As a concession to modern Hebrew speakers the final forms of letters will, where appropriate, be shown bracketed alongside the initial/medial form, in our standard convention for definitions.

Example:　　　　　[ם] מ יׁ מ / *mayim* / <u>water</u>

The immediate outcome of these minor modifications, before the insertion of letters 29 to 64, will be seen in Figure 2.5.

In order to regain our bearings, let me point to the positions in this illustration of some of the features we met in the first basic square. The first three words now occupy the top half of the square's perimeter. The symmetrical second word בָּרָא / *bara* / he created in its regular compact form, turns the north corner, while the expanded version occupies the east, north and west corner elements in that order. Then the expression יה תאמ משה // Moses, image of Yah turns the west corner, reading from south to north, against the normal flow of text.

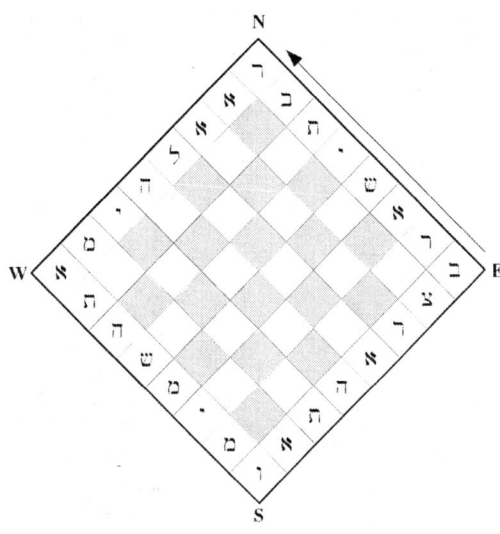

**Figure 2.5**

As has been hinted already, the process for inserting text into the void within the perimeter will follow some very simple, even intuitive rules. For one thing, the required 36 letters will be the first 36 of the second verse, following straight on from Genesis 1:1. And they will be entered in the order they naturally occur; so there is no sleight of hand involved.

The process starts by breaking into the void to a position adjacent to letter #28, to where it will sit on the horizontal diagonal (as did letter #1). Each of the next 19 letters is added adjacent to the one before, proceeding counter-clockwise in the 'onion layer' that is just within the perimeter. After a total of 48 letters have been assigned to their places, the 49th letter again breaks into the next inner layer, once more taking its place on the horizontal diagonal; and so we continue until all 64 elements of the square have been filled.

The full text of Genesis 1:2 using final-form letters, is as follows:

| פְּנֵי | עַל | וְחֹשֶׁךְ | וָבֹהוּ | תֹהוּ | הָיְתָה | וְהָאָרֶץ |
|---|---|---|---|---|---|---|
| *pnei* | *aal* | *v'choshek* | *v'bohu* | *tohu* | *haytah* | *v'ha eretz* |
| the face | was upon | and darkness | and void | without form | was | and the earth |

| המים | פני | על | מרחפת | אלהים | ורוח | תהום |
|---|---|---|---|---|---|---|
| *ha'mayim* | *pnei* | *aal* | *mrachephet* | *Elohim* | *v'ruach* | *t'hom* |
| of the waters | the face | upon | moved | of God | and the spirit | of the deep |

The final outcome is shown in Figure 2.6, with final forms of letters converted to their initial/medial forms for the reason given earlier.

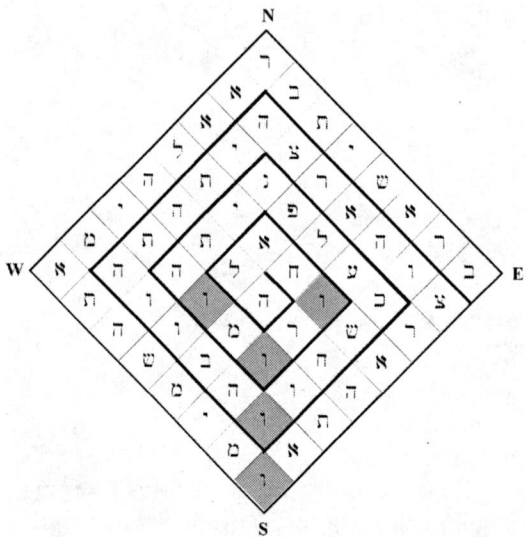

**Figure 2.6**

Overall, the order of the regular text after insertion into the square follows a kind of coiled path that diminishes as it approaches the centre. It is no misreading to suggest that this arrangement of text from the very start of Genesis may be described as a miniature scroll. Ultimately we shall uncover the evidence that we are looking at the same 'small scroll' mentioned both by Ezekiel and in the Book of Revelation.

By far the most stunning component in the completed square is the arrangement of five identical letters that have been highlighted for effect. The letter in question is *vav*; it is the sixth of the alephbeyt and it symbolises a tentpeg. Of topical interest is the symmetry of the positions these five letters have adopted. And their distinctive 'Y' configuration is precisely the shape of the letter vav as it once appeared in the ancient proto-Hebrew script.

Of course, the five highlighted letters are not the only examples of the letter vav in the square, as there are nine altogether. And, if you look closely you will see that all nine are found on or below the horizontal diagonal of the square. It is my own belief that this unusual distribution is unlikely to have arisen by accident; statistically, there is only a 1 in 164 chance that all nine letters should occur in one half of the square, unless by deliberate intent. Although I do also have the advantage of knowing that the same nine letters will assemble themselves into some even more striking configurations in later versions of the Seal. Those arrangements will not only confirm the Author's deliberate intent, but will also show that the sixth letter has been selected for the special role of representing water. Evidently, in our present view of the square all the water has settled into the lowest positions, as water normally tends to do in nature. This is, incidentally, one of the reasons the present orientation of the square suggested itself, backed up by Genesis 1:9: *And God said, Let the waters under the heaven be gathered together unto one place ....* What we see is a distinctly graphical example of the Seal anticipating later biblical narrative.

Given that *vav* is the sixth letter of the alephbeyt, the linear group of three of them in the vertical diagonal immediately gives rise to a further association with the Book of Revelation. There, Chapter 13 begins with the words: *And I saw a beast rising out of the sea ...,* and it ends: *...let him who has understanding reckon the number of the beast, for it is a human number, its number is six hundred and sixty-six.* Evidently, the linear group of three copies of vav represent that number, while all nine collectively represent a sea.

After that most sinister of chapters, there is an immediate change of mood in Revelation, and the very next verse – the start of Chapter 14 – reads: *Then I looked, and lo, on Mount Zion stood the Lamb ....* Which gives rise to the single most important interpretation of the distinctive 'Y' arrangement of the letter *vav*. Given that each vav is symbolically a spike, what we see depicted in the square is the representation of a man being put to death by crucifixion. And each of the five spikes stands for one of the five wounds of Jesus Christ. From a Christian standpoint, this interpretation must have huge implications, since it may replace the need to depend for authority solely on the very Christian reading of certain Old Testament prophesies. Some of those partisan interpretations, numbering in the hundreds, can seem strained and tenuous. And even where a Christian interpretation looks sound, it can be refuted all too easily on the grounds that the same prophetic words apply equally well, if not better, to their contemporary Jewish situations. However, once we become confident in the 'crucified man' interpretation, the square will demonstrate that the events that led to Christianity emerging from Judaism have been foreseen since the very first words of the Hebrew Old Testament.

This Christian connection is eloquently paraphrased at the start of the Gospel of John, thus:

> *In the beginning was the Word; and the Word was with God,*
> *and the Word was God. He was in the beginning with God;*
> *all things were made through him, and without him was not*
> *anything made. In him was life, and the life was the light of*
> *men. The light shines in the darkness, and the darkness has*
> *not overcome it.*

(John 1:1-5).

Notice that in these five self-contained verses each of the concepts 'In the beginning', *made*, *life*, *light* and *darkness* is used twice. Furthermore, each pair comes and goes before the next one makes its first appearance. Very soon, we shall see three of those italicized words mutually linked within the square in a most extraordinary way. The connection with the remaining word of the four will become evident much later; but it will be just as spectacular.

I feel sure it will come as a shock to some readers to learn that John's Gospel contains a barely-guarded reference to the square we are just beginning to analyse. Therefore it is appropriate that we examine straight away one particular family group of emergent words contained in the square. These, it will transpire are capable of interpretation in several ways, each intrinsically unambiguous.

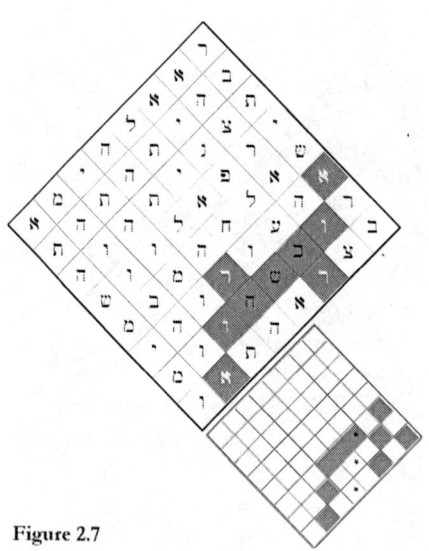

Take a look at Figure 2.7. Once more we see the fully populated square, but now with different letters shaded, and accompanied by an equivalent thumbnail sketch. The smaller sketch also has specific cells shaded or otherwise marked, so that they may draw attention to the letters in the corresponding positions in the larger square. First, we shall focus on the larger square, in which the shaded letters consist of three linear groups of three. The sandwiched group, in which the letters themselves are black, spells [ך] חשׁכ / *khoshek* / <u>darkness</u>. There is nothing surprising about the presence of this word, which comes from the regular text of

**Figure 2.7**

Genesis 1:2, where it says: *And darkness was upon the face of the deep.* Much more interesting are the two adjacent shaded sequences of white letters. These two identical words, one that reads downwards and the other upwards, spell אור / *aur* / <u>light</u>. Both words are composed from letters that are not consecutive in the regular text of Genesis; for example the upper aur consists of letters 3, 29 and 27 in that order. What is particularly striking about this matched pair of emergent words, however, is that they bracket their conceptual opposite, the word 'darkness', with perfect spatial alignment. Moreover, light has the distinction of being the first-named product of the creation, in the very next verse. Again the Seal foresees the later narrative.

*Aur* is the first of many emergent words we shall find in the Seal. And it is even possible to say something meaningful about the likelihood of one or more emergent copies of 'light' occurring in an 8×8 square. As a comparative experiment, I myself have arranged the 304,805 Hebrew letters of the entire Torah into a 553×553 square, as an expanding spiral. Within that square, there are found 937 copies of אור / *aur* / <u>light</u> that emerge from normally non-adjacent letters. That is an average of one *aur* in any square area of 18×18 letters. On this basis, we can say with confidence that, in the absence of deliberate intent, there would be at best a 1 in 5 chance that even one emergent copy of aur will be seen in an 8×8 square; and a 1 in 25 chance that two copies will be seen. And that does not take into account the very low probability that the two lights that do emerge will also be aligned in ways that have several degrees of significance.

The foregoing statistical analysis is more important than may be supposed. As I mentioned in Chapter 1, the relative absence of explicit vowels in Hebrew leads to words that are shorter than in Latin-based languages. It follows that a larger number of valid Hebrew words should be expected to emerge in a letter matrix than would happen with, say, English. So, unless we develop this line of reasoning, the temptation may be to dismiss the above 'light/darkness' effect out of hand.

It is perfectly reasonable to ask if the 8×8 square may also contain irrelevant, non-biblical or modern Hebrew words. In the terms of Information Theory, these extraneous effects could be described as 'noise', a kind of unwanted interference. And I have no doubt that a certain amount of noise is inevitable. But there are two particular factors that show the cryptic, biblical message to be the one that is intended by the Author.

First, there is the statistical evidence. For example, I have already mentioned that statistically we should not expect to find even one copy of *aur* (light) in the square, much less two copies. This argument will apply to just about every emergent word I point out in this book. But there is a much more persuasive, though related indicator of intelligent design[d]. This is the presence of recognisable structure into which the emergent biblical words are incorporated. I remarked earlier that there is only about one chance in 25 that two copies of aur should be seen in the square. But we can take this argument one step further and ask: *Since the relative positions of the two copies of 'aur' seem so important, what are the comparative odds against this having happened by chance alone?* In fact, they are less than 1 in 28,000[e]. The implication is that structure has an especially important role in the Seal. It will not always be possible to calculate statistical odds as I have done here; and neither will it be strictly necessary. From this point onwards, structures of various types will be found to dominate everything we see, so that we can have no doubt that they are deliberately intended. Even if the Seal did reveal words like *cappuccino*, *plastic* or *Internet*, we would know they are only background noise because they do not fit the pattern of structures of their legitimate biblical cousins.

In practice, we shall find that each copy of aur does have its own positional significance, independently of its partner. Clearly, the lower one, which reads upwards, is tightly bound to the vertical part of the 'Y'-shaped group composed of the letter vav. This light is seen ascending with or, more likely, *as* the crucified Christ. Notice, too, that its upper letter *reysh* (ר) is also part of a further linear group of three letters, shaded grey in the thumbnail sketch. Referring to their positions in the larger square, it can be seen that the alternative group spells: עור / *aur* / <u>skin</u>. The transliteration given here is no misprint; this word for skin really is pronounced the same as the word for light. The positional association of these Hebrew homophones within the Seal, along with the fact that skin reads downwards, makes for a most important if, perhaps, astonishing biblical interpretation. The crucifixion of Christ is undoubtedly meant to be understood as the reverse or the undoing of the expulsion from Eden, of which it is recorded:

---

[d] I am trusting that my reader will not confuse this use of the expression 'intelligent design' with the discredited Intelligent Design hypothesis held by creationists to be an acceptable alternative to genuine intelligence in matters of biblical interpretation.

[e] A rationale for the validity of this type of calculation will be found in Appendix C. However, the example given there depends on a comparison of information in both this Chapter and Chapter 7.

*Unto Adam also and to his wife did the Lord God make garments of skins, and clothed them.*

(Genesis 3:21)

The suffering Messiah is exchanging his 'garment of skin' for a new garment of light. Modern day archaeological discoveries and historical research point to the same conclusion in the form of the recently translated Gospel of Judas. Surprisingly, that long-lost text casts Judas in the honoured role of the chosen agent of Jesus, who said to him, "*You will exceed all of them. For you will sacrifice the man that clothes me.*" Our flesh and blood bodies are our garments of skin. Later, we shall encounter further references to the same forward and reverse paths, one employing a more graphical metaphor, and another a mathematical one.

Then the upper, descending light shares its first letter with the middle of the word רֹאשׁ / *rosh* / <u>head</u> (within the longer B'reishith). And it shares its last letter with the middle of the word [ץ] אֶרֶץ / *eretz* / <u>earth</u>, <u>world</u> or <u>land</u>. Overall, therefore, the upper light is seen descending to earth, virtually from the first instant of creation. It is the same Jesus of Nazareth who is credited with saying, "*I have come into the world as a light, so that no one who believes in me should stay in darkness.*" (see John 12:46).

The next two emergent words also belong to a family group that continues one of the Seal's known themes. One of them is a three-letter word substituted by the '*'-character in the thumbnail sketch of Figure 2.7. This word, which shares its first letter with עוֹר (skin) spells: עָשָׂה / *asah* / <u>he made</u>, and could correspond to either of the phrases, *the Lord God* [did] *make garments of skins* (see Genesis 3:21), or to *all things were made through him* (Gospel of John). Notice here, that *asah* (he made) and the two lights form three equally spaced parallel lines. So it may be fair to suppose this juxtaposition is also a reference to the verse:

*And God said Let there be light and there was light.*

(Genesis 1:3)

...in the first day of creation.

Yet another component, shown in the thumbnail of Figure 2.7, is a further three letter word crossing horizontally through the middle of the upper אוֹר (light). Reading from left-to-right in the square, עוֹב / *oob* / <u>deep darkness</u> not only reinforces the adjacent straightforward 'darkness' in the plain text, but again shares its first letter with that of *aur* (skin) and *asah* (he made). In a different context, this deep darkness might be described as stygian – an association that the square will shortly ratify. This too calls to mind the start of the Gospel of John, and the words: *The light shines in the darkness, and the darkness has not overcome it.* Given that three emergent words in the same family group all begin at the same letter and one that is, moreover, unique in the square, we might suspect that the letter ayin is particularly favoured for a reason. And so it will prove to be since, over an extended period, we shall discover that this one letter has multiple pivotal roles in later transformations of the Seal.

We are now at a suitable stage for me to draw attention to the extreme density of the related emergent words we can see in this part of the square. Any attempt to illustrate them all without recourse to a thumbnail supplement would be doomed to result in a cluttered mess. The Author, however, would have no such difficulty. So the density of the encrypted information we find within the Seal must certainly be taken into consideration in our estimation of deliberate design. As must the fact that only 64 letters are involved, taken from perhaps the most iconic text in existence.

-oOo-

Following from the preceding analysis, it is now possible to re-interpret the five verses quoted above from the beginning of the New Testament Gospel of John. In the Christian world, these particular verses are among the best-loved quotations from the entire Bible. Now let me repeat something I remarked upon earlier: that several words and phrases in those particular verses, including 'In the beginning', 'made', 'light' and 'darkness', are pointedly repeated for what has always been assumed to be merely poetic emphasis. Each pair moreover comes and goes before the next begins. But we now know that these same words are all components of a concise family group within the Author's Seal. The confluence of this many related words seems so unlikely that it cannot be allowed to pass without further comment.

With our newfound insight it is but a short step to recognising that the author of John's Gospel was already well acquainted with our Seal. So we need to address the reason why the Author's Seal should now appear to us like a new discovery, when there is ample evidence that it was known in some circles until at least the time the New Testament gospels and the Book of Revelation had been written.

Before going any further, I think it is essential that we attempt to separate identifiable fact from my own speculations, and I suggest we may take as fact the pre-existence of the Seal. If my reader is not already convinced that the Seal is a masterpiece of intelligent design, then I recommend revisiting these paragraphs after reading further chapters. In the present paragraph and the next four, I shall be offering my own opinion as to how the Seal came to be lost for at least seventeen centuries. Unlike some commentators, but in agreement with others, I am prepared to accept that the cause was not entirely a deliberate cover-up by the established Church, but an unfortunate series of historical mishaps.

First, it is well to remember that the early proto-church was no more or less than a new sect of Judaism. Jesus and his disciples were born Jews, circumcised into the covenant and, to varying degrees, lived their lives as pious Jews. Jesus' ministry was, without question, directed towards his fellow Jews, with few exceptions. It is increasingly apparent that one role of the Seal is to keep us mindful of the essential truth of its Hebrew origin. To what extent the Apostles were later expected to preach to gentiles is no longer clear. Paul, once Saul of Tarsus is thought to have been the first to break ranks with Jewish tradition in any meaningful way. But of course he had not been privy to Jesus' original words, and could not have known how complete (or otherwise) his understanding was. Judging by his surviving epistles, what Paul understood made very good sense. But only the contemporary apostles would have known whether what is good sense also made complete sense. The Seal now suggests that it was not. Nonetheless, there was a period of several decades during which the apostles journeyed abroad, almost certainly believing their message to be only for other Jewish ears, but also attracting interest from gentile onlookers.

Given that the early Christian message must have included a strongly Jewish mystical element, of which the Seal is undoubtedly a major component, it is difficult to be sure what the new-style Jews' feelings might have been concerning the outside interest. Also, those were troublesome times, when a careless word in the wrong ear might lead to prison, or worse. That was, after all, how Jesus himself came to be executed. As long as the risk of persecution remained, it made practical sense for members of the new sect to identify one another cautiously, by means of coded signs. And a similar but extended principle must have been employed by one initiate to test the extent of the knowledge of another. Then the first five verses of John's Gospel, quoted above, may prove to be a particularly rich example of the latter test, since it refers to both the source of the Seal (ie In the beginning…) and several of its interrelated components. Anyone 'in the know' would, therefore, instantly recognise that Gospel as coming from an impeccable source. Meanwhile, the uninitiated listener would still see both beauty and relevance in the same verses.

Before long, some of the less cryptic signals would have become widely known, including the ⋙ fish symbol that has been enjoying a resurgence in popularity in recent years. There can now be no doubt that the new sect soon came to include a large contingent of gentiles. Yet the way the Church has developed subsequently would suggest that the deeper mysteries were successfully withheld from all except the pure-born Jews, but even excluding Paul. A proper understanding would, in any case, have depended on detailed knowledge of the Hebrew scriptures. And that in itself would have been as a closed book to the gentiles, both literally and metaphorically.

Then, almost overnight, something quite momentous happened that would set the young Church on an entirely new path. In AD49 the Roman Emperor Claudius decreed that all Jews should be banished from Rome. The gentile Christians at the heart of the Empire were left fully in charge of their own destiny, but isolated from their roots, and blissfully unaware that their faith was lacking one of its principal cornerstones. In the absence of knowledge of the Seal the Church has, ever since, had to be satisfied with little more than Old Testament prophets' supposed cryptic references to their founder, for evidence of legitimacy. Also, the same loss of knowledge and understanding could help to account for the distinctly Christian tenet of 'faith without proof' having been elevated to the status of a virtue. And this may yet prove to be the most difficult obstacle in the way of restoring original truth.

That, then, is my own conspiracy-free suggestion for the way the Author's Seal came to be lost to Christianity. And it also explains why, when Constantine adopted Christianity for the Roman Empire and, later, the Church Fathers met to decide the New Testament Canon, that the gospels of Thomas, Philip, Mary, Judas and others were rejected; they appeared to be too much at odds with the Church's impoverished pauline understanding of its true roots. It explains particularly why the New Testament gospels are heavily loaded with parables, when Jesus himself had told his disciples that the parables were for the ears of the uninitiated; that they themselves were being taught the deeper mysteries (see Luke 8:10). But now that the Seal is back in the public domain, more clearly perhaps than ever before, it could change everything. As I also suggested in the Introduction, the re-emergence of the Seal will not be welcome news for many in comfortably deep-rooted affiliations. If, however, the Seal carries the creator's trustworthy message for the benefit of all mankind then to ignore it would be tantamount to heresy.

The foregoing analysis of Christian history will certainly seem simplistic, not least because it ignores the plain fact that the Church

Fathers were seeking to fashion a religion that would sit comfortably with the political realities of the day. But I am, after all, attempting to be conciliatory.

-oOo-

Turning our attention now back to the re-discovered Seal, it is appropriate to finalise the square's allusion to the crucifixion of Christ by means of further emergent words and references to the Gospels. Take a look at Figure 2.8, which emphasises certain words and the juxtapositions of words (not all emergent) that are especially relevant to events at Golgotha.

Firstly, from the main square we may identify a reference to the following verse:

> *Now from the sixth hour there was darkness over all the land, until the ninth hour.*

(Matthew 27:45)[f]

If this text had said simply 'over the land', then the equivalent in the square would be easy to find; the plain-text word [ה] חשׁכ / *khoshek* / <u>darkness</u> (black letters on a grey background) overlaps the plain-text word [ץ] ארצ / *eretz* / <u>earth</u> or <u>land</u> (hatched background). However, the text pointedly says 'over *all* the land', and the square's allusion to this more comprehensive darkness is only achieved by the presence of the emergent word עוב / *oob* / <u>deep darkness</u> (white letters on a black background), which completes the over-cover of eretz.

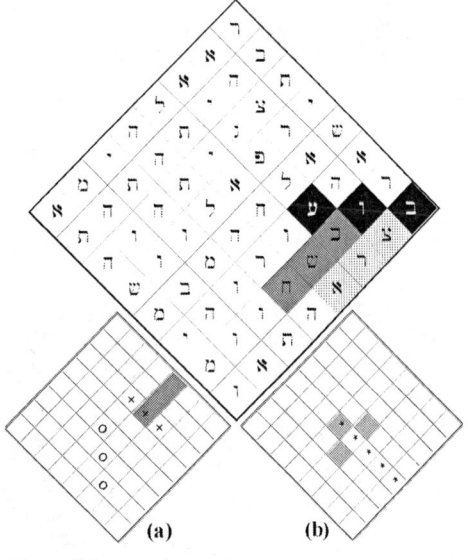

**Figure 2.8**

---

[f] This and the next two quoted verses are not unique to the Gospel of Matthew.

Next, thumbnail (a) indicates three more references to events at Golgotha, which we shall consider in the order in which they occurred. First, the vertical, linear group of letters in the left half of the square spell: למה / *lamah* / <u>Why</u>? Here, we may have a reference to Jesus' plea immediately following the onset of darkness:

> *Eli, Eli, lama sabachthani? That is My God, my God, why hast thou forsaken me?*
>
> (Matthew 27:46)

Whether or not the question was rhetorical at the time, I can declare that the present square does not offer an immediate answer. However, when we come later to the fine adjustment that transforms the present view into a second square, the answer will be perfectly plain to see.

The next biblical reference is seen in the word [ף] עלפ / *alaph* / a <u>veil</u> (or <u>curtain</u>), marked with an 'x'-character in thumbnail (a). These three letters are, in fact, consecutive in the plain text of Genesis 1:2. But they are not a distinct word in that context as they straddle the two words: על פנ י / *aal pnei* / <u>upon the face</u>. Notice, incidentally, the conceptual relationship between the word 'veil' and the expression 'upon the face' in which it is seen. The significance of *alaph* is found in this verse:

> *And behold, the curtain of the temple was torn in two, from top to bottom …*
>
> (Matthew 27:51)

In the fullness of time, it will again be the transformation of the present square into the next by which this metaphor may be properly understood. Meanwhile the presence of the curtain, like the question 'Why?' may serve as a bookmark, that will help us understand the close relationship between the present view of the Seal and its later aspects.

Then the final direct reference to the death of Christ is in the emergent word: שאל / *Sheol* / <u>Realm of the Dead</u>, which is marked in thumbnail (a) using grey shading. Mysteriously, given that the Seal has been unknown to Christians, the *sheol* connection has nevertheless come to be adopted into core articles of the Christian faith – the Creed. And, in the case of the Anglican Church, is an element of the Catechism for Confirmation by which the candidate declares that: … [Jesus Christ] *was crucified, dead and buried. He descended into hell: The third day he rose again from the dead …*.

Next, and still with Figure 2.8, thumbnail sketch (b) indicates the positions of two more closely related words. The linear sequence of letters (asterisks in the thumbnail) spell the compound word לההרחה / *l'harecheh* / to the millstone. Symmetrically placed around the upper end of that expression, the three shaded elements in thumbnail (b) correspond to letters that spell לֹחֶמ [ם] / *lechem* / bread. The letters of this bread are destined to contribute to a truly momentous reconfiguration, with consequences that still ripple through the secular world.

Those, then, are the more direct references made by the present square to the core beliefs of Christianity. Though there is one other which is best understood in terms of a link between the New Testament and the covenant God had made with the children of Israel, at Sinai. In Figure 2.9 (overleaf), the combination of darkness with two emergent copies of light is repeated, along with new thumbnail sketches (a) and (b).

Notice that sketch (b) shows the positions of a 2-letter word (marked 'xx') and a 4-letter word (marked 'oooo') – both emergent. The 2-letter word is לח / *luach* / a tablet, and the 4-letter word is the plural לחות / *luchot* / tables or tablets:

> *And I* [God] *will write on the tables the words that were on the first tables which you broke, and you shall put them in the ark.*
>
> (Deuteronomy 10:2)

Therefore, note carefully that the tablets in the square overlap the plain-text word חשׁך [ך] (darkness), as this is a clue to understanding a pictorial biblical allusion. In the illustration, the main square shows clearly the now familiar two copies of אור (light). Then thumbnail (a) shows each light crossed horizontally by three letters, and we already know that the three letters which cross through the upper light spell עוב (thick darkness). The lower copy of light is also crossed by the valid word, הוה / *havah* / to breath; to exist; ruin (plus several less common meanings). So the overall impression is of two 3×3 squares in which each light and its crossover partner word are the diagonals. Yet, it is not just the presence of two such squares that matters, but more especially their relative positions. Bear in mind that even the presence of two copies of *aur* (light) defied negative odds of 25:1. But their specific positions, relative to each other and to other features, would greatly extend those odds. Assuming the odds are amenable to calculation at all. As the main square of Figure 2.9 shows, and what matters most is that the distance from the middle of one 3×3 square to the middle of the other is a linear sequence of five letters. Therefore,

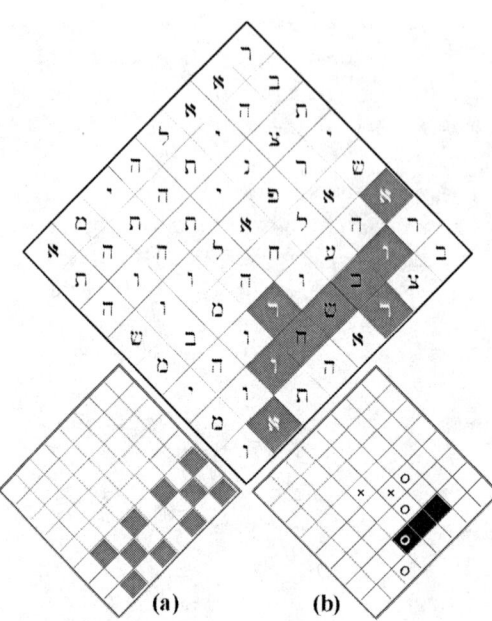

Figure 2.9

the whole is configured like a box shape having dimensions 3×3×5, where these are also the relative dimensions of the Ark of the Covenant. The original Ark made by the Israelites according to God's instructions, had dimensions one-and-a-half cubits, by one-and-a-half cubits, by two-and-a-half cubits; which is 3×3×5 in units of a half cubit. So, what then could be the significance of the emergent word לוחת (tablets) in the square? It is the fact that it passes into the *khoshek* 'darkness' that is within the Ark shape: *and you shall put them in the Ark.* Biblical scholars may like to consider whether the corresponding passages of Exodus and Deuteronomy were written on the strength of the structure of the Seal; or is the Seal an oracle, of which later events at Sinai are the partial fulfilment?

This explicit depiction of the 3×3×5 Ark-shape is not unique, but will be seen at two other places. Thus, it is set to become an important leitmotif that serves to evoke the Ark-theme in a particularly graphic way. Yet the Seal will also succeed in representing the Ark by two other broad methods, one literary and the other more clearly numeric, both of which have multiple, alternative forms.

That brings us to the subject of the 2-letter word, marked 'xx' in thumbnail (a). We have noted that these spell לח / *luach* / table (or tablet) which is the singular of *luchot*. Clearly, in the main square, the single tablet is placed just above the 'Y'-shaped configuration of five copies of the letter vav. Therefore, it is enclosed within a notional square of which three corners, each containing a vav, form the upper

'V' component of the crucified man. If, then, we complete that 3×3 square with its upper fourth corner – a letter *aleph* (**א**) – that would make this overall shape also five small squares in height, and suitable to represent a second Ark shape. Three spectacular and independent confirmations for this proposition will be seen at later stages.

Once again, try to imagine having to represent all of the above content in a single view of the square. And keep in mind that the present Chapter and Chapter 4 are both concerned exclusively with the same 64 letters entered into the square in the same systematic way.

-oOo-

Now we may move on with what will appear to be a shift of emphasis, although in reality it belongs to the same inclusive progression. Take a look at Figure 2.10, because it accentuates two distinct areas of the same square.

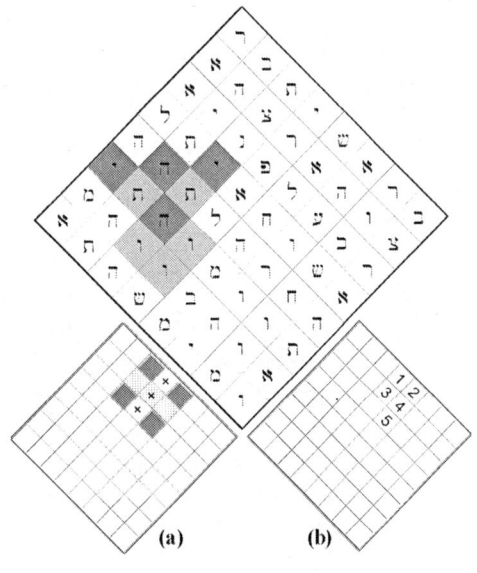

The nine elements that are emphasised in the main square we may gloss over quite quickly, merely noting their overall bi-lateral symmetry in preparation for something else we shall see in Chapter 7. Although it is worth noting here that the word תהו / *tohu* / formless which is best known as belonging in the plain text of Genesis 1:2, is seen twice more in the midst of the same group, in emergent forms that cross through each other. In Chapter 5, the same area will be occupied by a more active

**Figure 2.10**

arrangement of letters that will most emphatically not be formless.

Right away, we may switch our attention to the 3×3 area that is emphasised in thumbnail sketch (a). Notice that the plain-text word ארץ [ץ] / *eretz* / earth (or land) appears here (hatched background) as well as at the end of the first verse: *And the earth was formless and void.* And it is this explicit (ie not emergent) *eretz* that confers relevance to the family group of components in this small area. First of all, note the linear sequence marked 'xxx'. These letters spell פְּרִי / p'riy / <u>fruit</u>, so an 'agricultural' theme is immediately suggested. Then the four corner letters (grey shading), read clockwise spell לְנָתַשׁ / le'natash / <u>for a root</u>. Taken as a whole, this compact group is a delightful example of the way the text of the Seal is enriched in its new square arrangement. Almost certainly, it is also a simultaneous reference to both the third day of creation and to Eden. However, the same 3×3 region contains another highly significant word that is, for a quite different reason, proper to be associated with the word 'land'. In thumbnail (b), the order of the relevant letters is indicated. Then, referring to the same elements in the main square, we see that these five letters spell יִשְׂרָאֵל / Yisrael / <u>Israel</u>. Therefore, this one localised area undoubtedly contains the complete expression: *Land of Israel*.

In its present form, the merit of the hidden word *Yisrael* is not unqualified. It is certainly in its favour that this word is contained entirely within the topical 3×3 zone. And in this respect it sets a precedent that will be amply justified in further aspects of the Seal, in later chapters. Yet there is something a little unsatisfactory, vaguely troubling about its current configuration. It just does not seem properly formed in the same way as other emergent words. And in a most surprising way, it will transpire that the imperfection is a deliberate opening gambit by the Author to demonstrate his wider plan. This is understood in terms of the word יָצַר / yatzar / <u>to form</u> or <u>mould</u>, which may be seen in the square in a triangular formation, spelled with the י and ר of Yisrael, and the צ of *eretz* (land). The verb *yatzar* is seen first in Genesis 2:7, where: *God formed man of the dust of the ground*. More to the point is its use in the passage:

> Yet now hear, O Jacob my servant; and Israel whom I have chosen:
> Thus saith the Lord that made thee, and formed thee from the womb...
>
> (Isaiah 44:1-2)

The Seal, in stages, will show Israel being re-formed into a more perfect shape, within a womb. The second stage will be seen in Chapter 5, but will not be fully understood until Chapter 7

What is more, at the present stage three of the letters of Yisrael correspond to the linear emergent word שְׁאֹל (Sheol) which was highlighted in Figure 2.8. That word means the 'Realm of the Dead', and the fact that the name Israel is so closely linked with it has a significance that also will only be fully understood when we reach Chapter 7.

Now take a look at Figure 2.11, which shows two more emergent words that are certainly related to those in the previous illustration.

The word on a hatched background is רָאָה / *ra'ah* / <u>to look</u> or <u>see</u>; while the word on plain shading is [ץ] חֵפֶץ / *hephetz* / <u>take delight in</u>. These words not only go well together conceptually but, overlapping the topical 3×3 area on four out of their six letters, also draws out extra meaning from fruit and Israel especially. But if the number of emergent words squeezed into this area already seems extreme, the same region will be seen in later chapters to be positively bursting with further, related concepts.

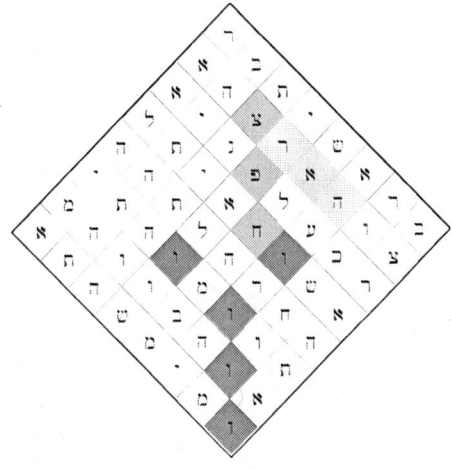

**Figure 2.11**

Finally, for the present Chapter anyway, we turn our attention to the area that is emphasised in Figure 2.12 (overleaf). In the main square of this illustration, the 2×4 rectangular shaded area is quite clearly located at a position of symmetry in the square. Specifically, the longer axis of symmetry of the group is one of only four axes of bilateral symmetry for the whole square. What we shall now find is that this distinct region, along with some other co-located features, has a lot in common with the description of the fourth day of creation. It is useful to remind ourselves of what was accomplished in the fourth day. It is written:

> *And God said, Let there be lights in the firmament of the heaven to divide the day from the night; and let them be for signs, and for seasons, and for days, and years:*
> *And let them be for lights in the firmament of the heaven to give light upon the earth: and it was so.*
> *And God made two great lights; the greater light to rule the day and the lesser light to rule the night: he made the stars also.*

(Genesis 1:14-16)

# In the Beginning

The fact that God made two great lights is especially relevant to the Seal as we now see it, because we already know that the square contains two, and only two emergent copies of the word 'light'. However, the key new points to note are all found within the first of the above verses, of which these are the more obvious components:

1. יהי / y'hiy / <u>let there be</u> or <u>let it be</u>
2. הלילה / ha'laylah / <u>the night</u>
3. לאתת / l'otot / <u>for signs</u>
4. (also אתת / otot / <u>signs</u>)

Especially important is the fact that the first two words in this list are both palindromic, a form of literary symmetry – since they read the

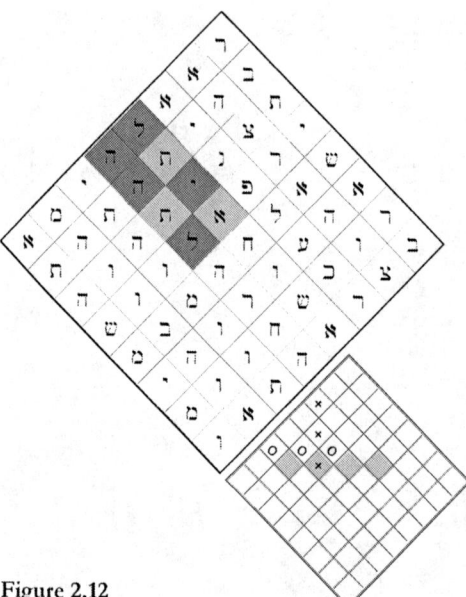

**Figure 2.12**

same forwards and backwards. Indeed, these are the only palindromic words to have occurred in the Torah up to this point which, being the fourth day of creation, marks the mid-point in the seven-day context. There is more to say in Chapter 5 on the subject of symmetry in the creation account.

But all the emergent words in the above list are to be found closely associated with the highlighted area of the main square. In fact, the second and fourth words in the list together make up the entire contents of this highlighted 2×4 area. And both may be read cyclically, either clockwise or counter-clockwise, in that setting.

Next, the first word in the list, יהי (y'hiy) ('ooo' in the thumbnail) contributes to no less than three instances of symmetry. The first is its inherent palindromic form, which then combines with six other letters beneath it (seen in Figure 2.10), all sharing the same vertical axis of symmetry. And third, y'hiy combines with a further emergent אתת / otot / <u>signs</u> ('xxx' in Figure 2.12), hence 'let them be signs'. Together they share the same bi-lateral symmetry as the highlighted cyclic 2×4 group. The longer, horizontal לאתת / l'otot / <u>for signs</u> (four shaded elements in the thumbnail) also passes through the same 2×4 zone and it, too, has a role in the same symmetrical 9-letter group, of which *y'hiy* is the crown. What is more, this *y'hiy* could be combined with either copy of *aur* (light) to complete the expression אוֹר יְהִי / *y'hiy aur* / <u>Let there be light</u>. Significantly, these are the very first words spoken by God, in Genesis 1:3. In reality, only one copy of *aur* is proper to be combined in that way, but the reason cannot be seen until we get to Chapter 4.

It is, at this point, appropriate to draw attention to a special way in which the present incarnation of the Seal emulates the seven-day structure of the first creation account. It does this through a pictorial representation of the Menorah – the seven-branched candlestick of the Temple (a clear allusion to light). See how, in Figure 2.13, the seven branches fit the layers of our square. This results from our choice of orientation for the square, and is another confirmation for our correct decision.

Notice also how groups of digits in the sequence 1-2-3-4-5-6-7, expanding from the central 4, reveal the number of letters found in each layer of the square, thus:

| | | | |
|---|---|---|---|
| Layer 4 (inner) | : | 4 | = 4 |
| Layer 3 | : | 3+4+5 | = 12 |
| Layer 2 | : | 2+3+4+5+6 | = 20 |
| Layer 1 (outer) | : | 1+2+3+4+5+6+7 | = 28 |

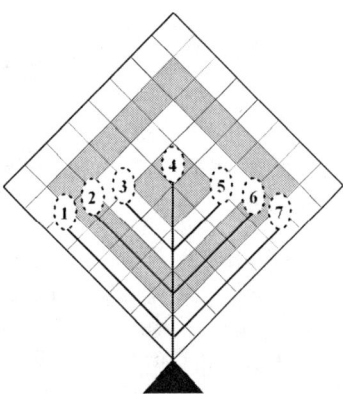

**Figure 2.13**

It is particularly apt that both the Menorah and the Ark of the Covenant started out as original artefacts in the Tabernacle in the desert. Just as they are now seen as artefacts in the Author's Seal, obtained from the first few words of Genesis. So this adds authority to the popular view that the building of the Tabernacle was analogous to the original creation of the universe; they are both built and equipped according to the same blueprint. All-in-all, the Seal is doing an excellent job of emphasising the deeper purpose of the first creation account, mainly through its symmetry.

Before we move on to fresh pastures there are a few remaining emergent words and phrases that either perfect the symmetry of the restructured Seal or set the scene for later restructuring, or both. Figure 2.14 shows the appropriate content.

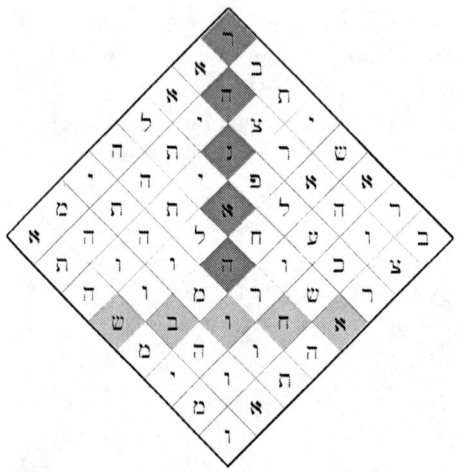

**Figure 2.14**

Firstly, overlapping the central 2×2 square region which contains the single luach (tablet) is the vertical expression נְהַר הֵא / *hey, nahar* / Behold, a river! Of course, the Bible is replete with references to rivers. Almost invariably, descriptions of the crossing of a river are associated with a major leap forward in the history and development of the Israelites. Or the mere mention of a river may mark a significant shift of subject or emphasis in the Bible's narrative. For example:

> *And a river went out of Eden to water the garden …*
> (Genesis 2:10)

What we do not yet see, however, is that the expression 'Behold – a river!' gives notice of something truly momentous that we shall see in Chapter 5. All I can say for now is that the meaning has everything to do with the crucified man, in whom the expression has its source. What matters especially is the presence of five wounds (spikes) rather than four, which indicates that the roman soldier has already pierced the side of the crucified man with his spear. And that was when water was seen to issue from the wound. In Chapter 5 we shall see the true river with perfect clarity.

One river that is only occasionally mentioned in the Bible, and never by name, is the river of Egypt which we know today as the Nile.

That river more than any other has mainly negative connotations in the Bible being, for example, Pharaoh's instrument for the disposal of newly-born, Israelite boys. Later, with poetic irony, the first of the ten plagues visited by God on the Egyptians would be the turning of the Nile waters into blood. Yet there is one episode involving this river which, though tinged with maternal sorrow, is ultimately a positive event. To avoid Pharaoh's genocidal plans, the baby Moses is cast adrift in a basket among the bulrushes at the edge of the river. It is to this episode that the horizontal string of five letters (lighter shading in Figure 2.14) refers. Recall the expression 'Moses, image of Yah', which we found concealed in the first verse. The five highlighted letters overlap at their left-hand end with the middle letter of Moshe (Moses) in that expression. And, when we read three letters horizontally starting from that position, we get the word שבו / *shebu* / <u>sparkling gem</u>. Then, if we read three letters from the right, we get אחו / *achu* / <u>a bulrush</u>. Recalling that all copies of the letter vav in our square are concentrated into the lower half and represent water, the fact that these two emergent words appear horizontally, high in the lower half, indicates that the basket and child were safely buoyed upon the surface of the river.

There is however an alternative interpretation for *shebu*, one that takes us to the extreme end of the Christian Bible. The penultimate chapter of the Book of Revelation describes a second creation (or third if we count the flood), the provision of a new Jerusalem in which its walls are foursquare, its length the same as its breadth. In each wall there will be three gates, and the twelve gates are twelve pearls. And, according to the writer:

> *I saw no temple in the city — for its temple is the Lord God the Almighty and the Lamb. And the city has no need of sun or moon to shine upon it, for the glory of God is its light, and its lamp is the Lamb.*
>
> (Revelation 21:22-23)

Likewise, the Seal is foursquare, and each letter of the word 'three' which we saw in Chapter 1 coincides with the mid-point of each side (the fourth letter in each seven). Also, the third letter of שלשה (three) is the first letter of שבו / *shebu* / <u>sparkling gem</u> corresponding perhaps to the twelve pearls. And the walls of the city are also described as adorned with every jewel, twelve types in all. As to the source of light in the city, as we have seen the square Seal is structurally equivalent to the seven-branched Menorah of the Temple, and contains two copies of אור / *aur* / <u>light</u>. One of these lights is attached to the three lower elements of the crucified man, the Lamb that is sacrificed, and the other emanates from the Torah's first word, the instant of creation.

In the same vein, also consider the following text:

> *Then he showed me the river of the water of life, bright as crystal, flowing from the throne of God and of the Lamb through the middle of the street of the city ...*
>
> (Revelation 22:1-2)

And to correspond to this, the Seal bequeaths the expression: והנ אהר / *v'hey nahar* / <u>And behold – a river!</u> seen in the top of its N-S diagonal. So, there is every reason to suppose that the author of Revelation had been shown a specific vision corresponding to the Seal. And this is an interpretation that will be spectacularly confirmed at a later stage, when further hitherto puzzling biblical passages will become more clearly understood.

Once we have acquired some additional skills and knowledge, we will also be able to go on to relate the perceived symmetry in the biblical creation account to further aspects of the stories of Abraham, Moses and Jesus. For the moment, anyway, we have completed our examination of the first square of text. But that does not mean we should think of it as a completed work. Far from it, as there are many components of the present square which may be viewed from alternative perspectives, and will also interlock with identical locations in other, equally rich squares. All of which means that this and later square aspects of the Author's Seal will endorse, reinforce and, therefore, authenticate one another by means of precisely located points of contact. This is a phenomenon I shall sometimes describe as latching. And, in an important sense, this is the Seal's answer to the natural sceptical question: *Can't we find further valid words in the square – even modern words – that have nothing to do with the Bible?* After all, a conventional word-search puzzle that is supposed to contain, say, ten boys' names would not be taken seriously if it was found to contain twelve by accident, or if several girls' names can also be seen. In the case of the Seal, the key lies not just in the list of words that may be found. It is just as important that emergent words are consistently found in distinctive and meaningful spatial relationships and in compact groups. It is this exceptional degree of organisation that testifies most clearly to deliberate design. Whether that design is also of supernatural origin is a question that should be postponed until the entire scope of the phenomenon is in view. Our pleasant difficulty, as we delve deeper into this miracle will be to keep in mind the full magnitude of what has gone before, to build up a true appreciation of its entire scope.

# 3

In many ways the first square of text has set a pattern and a benchmark that must, by any conventional criteria, seem impossible to sustain. Given the modest seven word length of the first verse of Genesis, it has already delivered up inordinately large amounts of concealed meaning and references to other parts of the Bible. So, it is worth taking a moment to try to appreciate the wide-ranging role of Genesis 1:1. Our impetus is the surprising quantity of encoded literary content in just the first verse, although this brief review will be much more strategic than a list of our findings to date.

With reference to the topics of Chapter 2, our discovery that Genesis 1:1 may correctly be re-organised into a square frame for the insertion of further text represents only one of two ways in which that verse could be described as a container.

The other containing role of Genesis 1:1 calls to mind the modern concept of a project. The literal meaning of the first verse is all-embracing; it sums up very concisely everything else that follows, not only in the first creation account, but even the whole Bible, and perhaps the whole of existence. If the complete Bible is considered the documented progress of a formal project – which indeed it closely resembles – then the first verse would be a very succinct 'Client Requirement Definition' of all that is to be achieved. It is surprisingly easy to extend this metaphor, to relate specific parts of the Bible to four other, standard project components, thus:

1. Genesis 1:2 to 1:31 (the active phase of the first creation account) is a stage-by-stage overview of the Client's plan to achieve his strategic aims. At the start of the Introduction, I had in mind this component (along with the Client Requirement Definition) when I referred to a 'magnificent plan',

2. Genesis 2 and 3 (the second so-called creation account, up to man's expulsion from Eden) is a partial description of 'the problem' that the project is designed to address, and also an

early stage of the sixth day where the creation of man is still a very long way from complete,

3. Genesis 4 to 11 (the remainder of the biblical pre-history) is a much more detailed description of the problem, in which just about every negative aspect of the human condition, our flaws and frailties, is encapsulated, and

4. Genesis 12 onwards (the history of Abraham and the Hebrew people) is the documented progress report corresponding to every important step in the preliminary plan of man's education, so that he may become worthy to cooperate actively in the wider plan. That is, to achieve his majestic destiny *in the image of God* (Gen 1:26).

The fourth of these components is the practical expansion of Day 6 of the first creation account. Taken to its logical conclusion, this implies that the sixth day is still an ongoing work in progress. It also has to be said that the progress described from Genesis 12 onwards starts from a very low point, with many descriptions of behaviour which to modern western eyes seem brutal, callous and uncivilised. And subsequent progress in man's education throughout the rest of the Bible is very slow indeed and punctuated with many setbacks.

-oOo-

As we have seen in Chapters 1 and 2, the first two verses of Genesis have already been busy and productive, in the extreme. On the other hand, I have given notice of equally impressive alternative versions of the Author's Seal, using the same source text. And the next way to appreciate some of that further potential is by means of a review of the same territory as seen in the previous two chapters. This time, however, we will perceive our surroundings as though through a different eye. How can that be possible? By way of an analogy, astronomers are now able to analyse the composition and deduce the inner processes of distant stars using more than just visible light. In the case of the nearest of all stars, our Sun, photographs taken in ultra-violet and x-ray wavelengths reveal previously unsuspected aspects of its structure and behaviour that are invisible in ordinary light. Similarly, the Author's Seal, as a square of letters, may be likened to its appearance in 'ordinary' light. Then the view of the same Seal in this and the next Chapter could be considered its appearance as if in light of a different wavelength.

In Chapter 1, I claimed not only that the letters of the Hebrew alephbeyt have numeric values (which is a simple matter of everyday experience in the modern Jewish world), but also that the Author's

Seal on the Torah has 'an underlying numerical dimension that supports its extensive linguistic structures'. Notice that I have not yet suggested that every part of the Torah demonstrates the same phenomenon. That prospect must be left for others to determine; although we shall very soon discover a good reason for suspecting that the whole Torah will exhibit at least some of the special qualities of its first 64 letters. What I can demonstrate quite quickly is that the language of the first 64 letters incorporates a high degree of numerical coherence, including allusions to numerous mathematical concepts, some of which were unknown to the peoples of the Ancient Near East.

For the remainder of the present Chapter, we shall draw heavily on aspects of Hebrew numerology – or gematria as it is called. So it is important that we first put to rest a certain superstition that obsesses many who encounter topics of this kind. It is often wrongly assumed or suggested that gematria is expressly forbidden by the Bible. In fact, the prohibition is not applicable to numerology in its entirety, but only to its specific misuse for the purpose of divination, or fortune telling. It is not even certain that Hebrew numerology is capable of being used in that way; but even to attempt to foresee the future is judged to be a sin. Therefore, let me make clear at the outset that the use of gematria in this book will be limited to the recognition of the intrinsic beauty of the sacred Torah text. Nothing within these pages will even remotely resemble divination.

The rules of Hebrew numerology – or gematria – are not so rigid as those of formal mathematics. For example, suppose an emergent string of digits in the Seal just happen to make a notable number such as 31415 (ie the first five digits of Pi[g]). Then we may find that, because of the context, that might be just as important as when the division of 22 by 7 is used as a practical approximation to Pi. In other words gematria may, along with its other functions, evoke established mathematical concepts using non-mathematical means.

But the numerical dimension of the Seal, and of the Torah text beyond the Seal, is not limited to the letters of the alephbeyt having numerical values. As we saw in Chapter 1, the positions of word breaks in Genesis 1:1 expressed as numbers are a non-gematria way in

---

[g] *Pi* is the name of the Greek letter ($\pi$) that is adopted in mathematics to represent the ratio of the circumference of any circle to its diameter. This ratio is identical for every circle that exists and, in decimal notation, is the whole number '3.' followed by a fractional part consisting of an infinitely long, non-repeating string of digits. A value that will be sufficient for our purposes is 3.1415926 (truncated to 7 decimal places).

which the text has already begun to hint at a numerical dimension. Another non-gematria concept that will prove fruitful is the position at which each letter of the alephbeyt first occurs in the Torah. As a fairly mundane example, Genesis 1:1 utilises 11 different letters, or just half of the alephbeyt. And the last of the eleven to make its first appearance is *tzadee* (צ) at position 28. We shall also discover unsuspected meaning in the relative frequencies of letter values, especially in the Bible's first verse.

These are no more than hints as to the flexibility we may allow ourselves in the search for an underlying structure to the biblical text. But let me sound a note of caution here. The latitude we allow ourselves extends only as far as the range of subjects and concepts we may contemplate. But that only means that we need to be very rigorous when it comes to deciding if a particular finding is significant. When a line of enquiry leads to an unclear or ambiguous conclusion, it must be abandoned. Here, I am describing limitations that I have previously imposed on myself; so the content of this book reflects the final outcome after rejecting 'findings' that fall short of those robust criteria. But, if any finding shows intrinsic merit, or a marked degree of correlation to others, then I shall describe it and show clearly how it fits with or maps onto other characteristics of the Seal. Since we are investigating a phenomenon that shows signs of having come from an intellect that far surpasses the most impressive human abilities, we need to be open to the presence of structural relationships that do not fit with our common experience of literature. Nothing will be exempt from our scrutiny; but that does not mean we may be sloppy in our discriminatory standards.

Those of my descriptions that *are* based on letters having an assigned numerical value (ie numerology) will relate to one of three different types, which are seldom mixed. These three types are known as Ordinal, Standard and *qatan* (Hebrew for 'small') letter values, and they are set out in Table 3.1 (overleaf). The 'Ord.' entries in the table are the ordinal positions of the letters within the alephbeyt – a number from 1 to 22. Incidentally, if the order of the 22 letters had not already been fixed before the assignment of numerical values, then it certainly would be from that point forward. The way that values are assigned is fairly self-evident, though there is good reason for now describing it explicitly.

Apart from the ordinal values, the whole schema is based on the ascending sequence of digits from 1 to 9. This is seen most clearly in the *qatan* values, which reflect two full cycles (ie 18 letters), followed by an incomplete cycle to account for the last four letters of the alephbeyt. Therefore, the qatan values 1, 2, 3 and 4 are each shared by three letters, and the values 5, 6, 7, 8 and 9 are shared by only two letters each. The standard values are derived from the qatan values by the addition of nought, one or two zeros. The qatan values in the first 1 to 9 cycle are left unchanged. So the standard values of these letters are the same as their qatan values. Then the qatan values of the second cycle are augmented with a single zero to generate the Std values. And the qatan values of the last four letters are augmented with two zeros.

Table 3.1

| Ord. | Symbol | Name | Std. | Qatan | Ord. | Symbol | Name | Std. | Qatan |
|------|--------|------|------|-------|------|--------|------|------|-------|
| 1 | א | Aleph | 1 | 1 | 12 | ל | Lamed | 30 | 3 |
| 2 | ב | Beyt | 2 | 2 | 13 | מ,ם | Mem° | 40 | 4 |
| 3 | ג | Gimmel | 3 | 3 | 14 | נ,ן | Nun° | 50 | 5 |
| 4 | ד | Delet | 4 | 4 | 15 | ס | Samech | 60 | 6 |
| 5 | ה | Heh | 5 | 5 | 16 | ע | Ayin | 70 | 7 |
| 6 | ו | Vav | 6 | 6 | 17 | פ,ף | Peh° | 80 | 8 |
| 7 | ז | Zayin | 7 | 7 | 18 | צ,ץ | Tzadee° | 90 | 9 |
| 8 | ח | Chet* | 8 | 8 | 19 | ק | Qof | 100 | 1 |
| 9 | ט | Tet | 9 | 9 | 20 | ר | Reysh | 200 | 2 |
| 10 | י | Yud | 10 | 1 | 21 | ש | Shin | 300 | 3 |
| 11 | כ,ך | Kaf° | 20 | 2 | 22 | ת | Tav | 400 | 4 |

\* This 'ch' is pronounced rather as in the Scottish loch, not as in church. The use of a letter h rather than a plain 'h' indicates the deeper guttural sound.

o These are the five letters which have both normal and final forms. Some schemes of numerology assign different values to the alternative forms.

The information in Table 3.1 will be needed often throughout most of the remainder of this book. So an easy to locate duplicate copy is provided as Appendix D.

The Hebrew standard letter values in particular have a very practical application that would, in biblical times, have been useful in day-to-day life. Using the standard values, it is possible to write all of the decimal numbers from 1 to 499 using no more than three letters to represent hundreds, tens and units. Larger numbers may, within practical limits, be composed using combinations of the letters representing hundreds. This is indeed how standard letter values were used in everyday life for several hundred years; so it should not be supposed that the use of Hebrew numerology is a mainly esoteric pastime. However, once we have seen some of the unexpectedly profound effects of gematria in the Seal, an important question will arise. Are the adopted letter values just a late, practical add-on to the alephbeyt, or does the Hebrew language from the earliest times have an inherent, numerical dimension? After reading the following chapters, arguments that try to discount numerology will, I suspect, tie themselves in knots.

As a general rule, standard (Std.) values of letters seem to be intended for adding together to give the gematria total for a whole word, or a whole verse. Qatan values may occasionally be used in that way, but will more often be treated as individual digits that (as in the 31415 example above) come together sequentially to create meaningful, multi-digit decimal numbers. To repeat, the possibilities open to investigation are quite flexible, but the outcomes that merit our serious attention will only be those that are found to have a clear structure and purpose.

As to the itinerary of our tour, the present Chapter will follow the same route as Chapter 1, and focus on numerical characteristics of Genesis 1:1 only. So I shall start by looking at the simplest case, the sequence of qatan values of the first verse alone, as shown in Figure 3.1.:

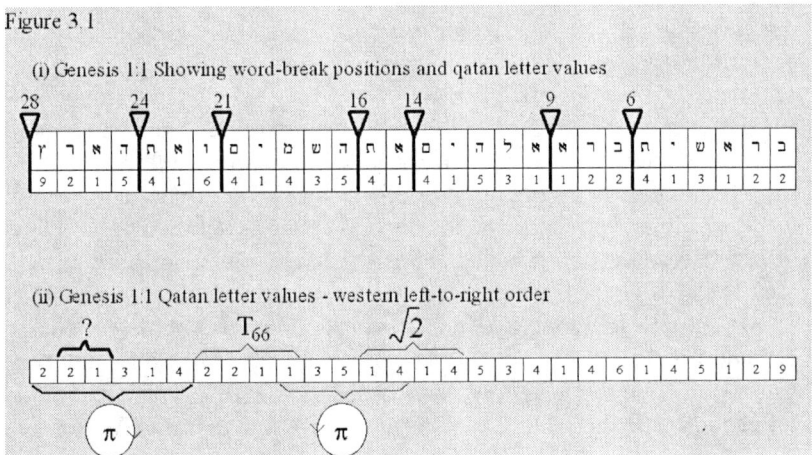

Figure 3.1

(i) Genesis 1:1 Showing word-break positions and qatan letter values

(ii) Genesis 1:1 Qatan letter values - western left-to-right order

The degree of flexibility I have stressed means that groups of digits may be viewed sometimes forwards or at other times in reverse. Also, we shall find ourselves dealing with number-art as much as with mathematics, so a degree of artistic license is to be expected. In the case of the sequence of qatan values associated with the first verse of Genesis I have chosen, in part (ii) of the diagram, to re-write them in traditional western left-to-right order. It is very important to be aware that our modern, decimal method of writing numbers using strings of digits from the range 0 to 9 was not available in biblical times. Therefore, any decimal numbers put there must have been intended for recognition in a distant future. Having said that, the qatan letter values do not include a zero, and that also sets a practical limit on the decimal numbers they may represent.

Even within the first sixteen letters seen above, it is possible to identify five special sequences either overlapping or distinct, most of which have both mathematical and biblical significance. These sequences are not all linear of which two are, for everyday purposes, reasonably good approximations for Pi (symbol $\pi$ in the diagram). Naturally, the qatan values in the diagram cannot provide an explicit decimal point; but it is, nonetheless, easy to recognise the digits of Pi, and the intended location of the decimal point. Take the digits that are derived from B'reishith. Although it is possible to see a linear sequence of 3142, these would overlap two words. So I suggest that we are meant to read letters 4, 5, 6 & 1 of B'reishith cyclically, in that order. Note that reading values cyclically like this is similar to the way that, in Chapter 2, we read the word הלילה / ha'laylah / the night in the letter square. And night is an inherent aspect of cyclic time. For most practical purposes, 3.142 is about as good an estimate for Pi as can be obtained using hand-eye measurements of the diameter and circumference of any circular object. Note that this value shows rounding to three decimal places.

The second approximation to Pi is even better and uses the qatan values obtained from all five letters of the third word, Elohim. In this case, the five values certainly do need to be written cyclically because the initial digit derives from the second letter of Elohim. The value obtained reading counter-clockwise is 3.1415, which is Pi truncated after the fifth digit.

Those are the first two mathematical references within Genesis 1:1; and note carefully that both copies of Pi come from the same two words which previously bequeathed the name of Abraham, and a reference to Brit Milah, the Covenant of Circumcision. Therefore, words one and three now provide a parallel numerical correlation with circumcision.

Another surprisingly important sequence of digits within Genesis 1:1 is 2211, which I have labelled $T_{66}$ in the diagram. In this case, 2211 is the sixty-sixth triangular number (where 66 is itself triangular). The significance of $T_{66}$ is not to be understood in isolation, but as one member of a group of four consecutive numbers: 2208, 2209, 2210 and 2211. Straight away, let us look at the links between the mathematical and biblical properties of these four numbers. In fact 2209 is $47^2$ (ie $47 \times 47$), giving us a very localised square to go with the triangle.

The other two numbers in this group both have a biblical significance. 2210 happens to be the position of the first occurrence of the letter *samech* (ס) in the Torah. Samech is the last letter of the alephbeyt to make its first appearance and only does so nearly halfway through Genesis Chapter 2. This is an inordinately long delay, completely out of keeping with the overall frequency with which samech occurs in the Torah. If the frequency distribution of samech had been more nearly regular throughout the Torah, then it ought to have been seen at least thirteen times by this stage. The statistical significance of the delay is best appreciated in terms of specific numbers. It is widely accepted that the Torah of today consists of 304,805 Hebrew letters, of which 1833 are *samechs*. On average, therefore, one letter in about every 166 is a samech. In statistical terms, there is a 50% chance (ie 1 in 2) that a samech will occur in the first 166 letters of Genesis. Or, equivalently, that it will not occur. We can easily extend this calculation and say that there is a 1 in 4 (ie $2 \times 2$) chance that samech will not occur within the first 332 (ie $2 \times 166$) letters. Calculating the odds against even longer delays is not an additive process, but multiplicative. Each further delay of 166 letters extends the odds by a factor of 2. Therefore, we can calculate that thirteen such delays are unlikely, to the extent of only one chance in 8192. So there is something seriously unnatural about the location of the first samech squeezed, as it is between $47^2$ and $T_{66}$. Yet there is a rational purpose to its long delay that is to be found in the meaning of the very text where it is first seen. In English it reads:

> *And a river went out of Eden to water the garden; and from*
> *thence it was parted, and became into four heads.*
> *The name of the first is Pison: that is it which compasseth the*
> *whole land of Havilah, where there is gold.*
> (Genesis 2:10-11)

As we saw towards the end of Chapter 2, the Seal viewed as a square of letters depicts the expression: 'Behold, a river!' ascending in the top of the vertical diagonal, and hinting that rivers would have particular importance. As to the river Pison, the very first letter samech is found in the word הסובב / *ha'sovev* / compasseth (ie surrounds or encloses). And this fact provides the clue that explains why 2208 is an important member of the same short group of consecutive numbers. To appreciate the logical connection, we need only think back to the process that led to our creating the 8×8 square of letters. Then, it was Genesis 1:1 that showed us how to form its own 28 letters into the sides of a square. And the four groups of 7 letters led to a square of side 7+1=8. The beauty of 2208 is that, if we follow the same principle and divide it by four (just as the river is divided into four heads), it leads to a square of side 552+1. And it is this larger square of 305,809 elements 'which compasseth the whole land of Havilah'. A 553×553 square is the smallest perfect square that is able to contain the 304,805 letters of the Torah; which is, without a doubt, the very land of Havilah 'where there is gold'. So it is again Genesis 1:1 that has led us to this understanding. Note that it does so through the sequence '2211' of qatan values which overlaps words 2 and 3: 'God created'.

A question we have not yet addressed is why the letter samech in particular should be distinguished with the encompassing role, rather than any other letter. One part of the reason is that samech occurs 1833 (ie 3×611) times in the entire Torah. A quick look at Table 3.1 will show that 611 is the gematria of the word תורה / *Torah* (ie 5+200+6+400). So it is most appropriate that samech has been chosen, by its delayed first occurrence, to represent the length of the Torah. Just consider for a moment the expression: 'the length of the Torah'. The frequency of the letter samech in the Torah is 3×611, thus identifying or establishing its environment. Then the 'length' itself is delimited by the location of the first samech. The overall effect seen here demonstrates that the Torah is conceived as an integral whole.

A second reason for the choice of samech may lie in its symbolic meaning. The proto-Hebrew symbol for samech was a thorn, which represents the idea of 'protection'. The association with protection probably has a lot to do with the common practice among nomadic shepherds in biblical times of constructing small enclosures from readily available thorny briers. Such enclosures would keep the shepherds' small flocks inside, and predators out, allowing the shepherds some freedom to relax, especially at night. This is not unlike the idea of the sacred Torah being protected by the encompassing river Pison. Also there is, here, a clear allusion to the crucified man we saw in the square view of the Seal. Since New Testament accounts tell of a crown of thorns that was placed on the head of Christ, and remained in place throughout his crucifixion. If we accept that the crown of thorns symbolises protection of the lamb of God, then we are led straight to the conclusion that he embodies the spirit of the (encompassed) Torah. As John so succinctly put it: *In the beginning was the word ... and the word was God.*

There is little doubt in my mind that the 553×553 square that contains the whole Torah will reveal some really momentous new knowledge. However, that will be the subject for a different book.

Finally, for the present stage, the first verse also proffers the repeating digits 4141, corresponding to the word *ta'owmiy* (my image), coming from the reverse, or reflected reading of this part of Genesis 1:1. The alternative digits 1414, as 1.414 are a reasonable approximation to √2 (the square root of 2). We have certainly seen several situations that involve √2 in disguise because, in any 45° right-angle triangle, √2 is the ratio of the longer side (the hypotenuse) to either of the two shorter sides. Notably, this is a shape that is seen abundantly in a square with both diagonals drawn, which exhibits symmetrical paired faces of 45° right-angle triangles. However, those situations do not, by themselves, prove that the digits 1414 have that meaning here. To see this proof, along with confirmations for several other things we have already met, we need to look at the qatan values of Genesis 1:1 in another way.

First, take a look at the 4×7 matrix of Figure 3.2, which contains the 28 qatan values of Genesis 1:1. Here, the values obtained from the first four letters are seen written left-to-right in the top row. The next four values are entered left-to-right in the second row, and so on.

The first point to note about this matrix is the way that eight out of nine of the 1-digits have assembled themselves into a visually arresting 45° right-angle triangle. This is the largest such triangle that can fit within a matrix of this size, with a sufficient continuous portion of its outline visible to make clear its total shape. So recall from Chapter 2 that the very same text, arranged as a 7×4 matrix of letters (see feinter lines in Figure 3.3) conferred the same basic shape, but composed from five copies of the letter aleph. Four out of those five now account for half of the eight 1s in this larger triangle. Overall, it is now realistic to accept the 45° right-angle triangle

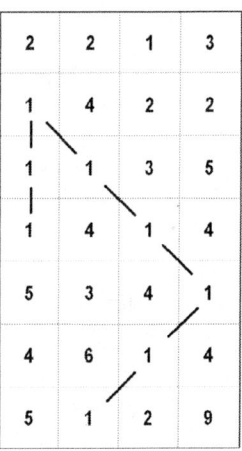

**Figure 3.2**

as another leitmotif (another is the Ark-shapes seen in Chapter 2) that the Author has provided as a watermark in his sacred text.

The second point to note about the new larger triangle is that the central 1414 sequence not only occupies the central row of the matrix (recall that the word 'three' did the same in the earlier 7×4 matrix), but also has both its 1-digits locked into the very triangle it defines as √2. The focus given here to a 1414 sequence will serve to validate something more elaborate we shall see soon.

Now armed with an understanding of qatan letter values, and while our attention is on geometrical shapes, we have a good opportunity to pick up some previously unseen content from the earlier 7×4 matrix. Here it is as Figure 3.3, now completed with qatan letter values.

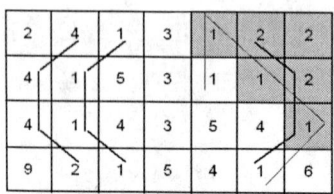

Figure 3.3

Perhaps the most immediately striking feature of this new view is the vertical 333 sequence in the middle column. The significance of this sequence is manifold, starting with the fact that it divides the matrix into equal halves. Secondly, it is composed from the only '3'-digits to be present in Genesis 1:1. And, most surprising of all, all three 3s come from the letters that spell the word שלש / shalosh / three (feminine form).

Over and above the outline of the smaller 45° triangle (feinter lines) there are three meaningful concentric arcs. Any one of these arcs could be interpreted as a symbolic reference to circles generally; but mark closely that the inner arc on the left is composed from every one of the 1-digits that is not already part of the triangle.

The outer arc on the left, as 2444, is notable for being 4×611, which is again the gematria of the word תורה / Torah (see Table 3.1). Especially important is the fact that both 611 and 4 are destined for strategic roles in later descriptions of the Seal. Incidentally, the shaded triangular zone in the upper-right corner of the matrix contains two alternative cyclic sequences of 1222, which are 2×611. And the whole 3x2 group is a cyclic 222111, which has the distinction of being $T_{666}$, the 666th triangular number (see Appendix A(ii)). Also, the arc that overlaps the 45° triangle is 2211 - another copy of $T_{66}$ to add to the one we saw at Figure 3.1, in the linear sequence given by Genesis 1:1. In that earlier diagram, I also put a question mark against a '21' group nearer the start of the verse. Superficially, 21 may be seen as the simple product: 21 = 7×3, which relates two numbers that are widely regarded as important from a biblical point of view. However, by withholding judgement until now, we are able to see that every one of the above family of triangular numbers ($T_6$ = 21; $T_{66}$ = 2211 and $T_{666}$ = 222111) is built-into the composition of Genesis 1:1 in one way or another. Furthermore, the first word of the Torah itself contains the longer sequence 1314, which is half of $T_{72}$, and 72 is widely believed to be the length of one of the names of God.

Another point to note is that the number 333 in the middle column is just part of the 3335 that comes from the masculine form of 'three'. And $3335 = 5 \times 667$, the larger factor being somewhat enigmatic in its own right. This stems from the fact that 667 appears at Nehemiah 7:18 where, ostensibly, he repeats the information found in the second Chapter of Ezra. However, the equivalent number in Ezra is given as 666. Since 666 occurs at three other places in the Bible, including the so-called number of the beast at Revelation 13:18, the discrepancy has long prompted debate among theologians. However, since $T_{666}$ (ie 222111) = 667 × 333, we see that the same 3335 sequence gives rise to both of those factors, and a link to 666. Now at last we have a close affinity between 666 and 667 that is given by the Bible's first verse, because $T_{666}$ derives from the product 333×667. This, and the fact that Ezra and Nehemiah were contemporary suggests that the discrepancy in the plain narrative may have been chosen deliberately to reflect, or represent a legitimate characteristic of the Torah Seal.

In Chapter 6, a tiny modification to the matrix of Figure 3.3 will give rise to a further set of allusions to classical mathematical concepts.

In Figure 3.4, the newer 4×7 matrix has been augmented by the addition of totals for each column, which will now serve to clarify something I remarked on in Chapter 2. Three of these totals (ie 14, 21 and 28) are not only multiples of 7, but also correspond to word-break positions in Genesis 1:1; that is, the very verse from which the matrix is obtained. But recall also that I remarked on a known superstition of ancient Mesopotamia, concerning certain inauspicious days in the months of the lunar calendar. Then the stress given to the number 7 in the first creation account is generally understood to contribute to a biblical polemic against Ancient Near Eastern myths and superstitions. But, in Chapter 2 I also pointed out that the 19th day of a lunar month had been considered equally inauspicious. So, it now seems clear from the inclusion of the 19 total in the matrix, that the Author of Genesis is addressing even that aspect of the same superstition.

| 2 | 2 | 1 | 3 |
|---|---|---|---|
| 1 | 4 | 2 | 2 |
| 1 | 1 | 3 | 5 |
| 1 | 4 | 1 | 4 |
| 5 | 3 | 4 | 1 |
| 4 | 6 | 1 | 4 |
| 5 | 1 | 2 | 9 |
| 19 | 21 | 14 | 28 |

**Figure 3.4**

Now consider the totals of the values in each matrix row, in Figure 3.5. The totals to the right of each row will provide a numerical confirmation for something we could have observed just as clearly in the first square, when it consisted of only a perimeter of letters. It corresponds especially well to something we know about the classical Greek understanding of natural philosophy or, as we know it today, science.

| | | | | |
|---|---|---|---|---|
| 2 | 2 | 1 | 3 | **8** |
| 1 | 4 | 2 | 2 | **9** |
| 1 | 1 | 3 | 5 | **10** |
| 1 | 4 | 1 | 4 | **10** |
| 5 | 3 | 4 | 1 | **13** |
| 4 | 6 | 1 | 4 | **15** |
| 5 | 1 | 2 | 9 | **17** |

Figure 3.5

An early attempt by the Greeks to make sense of the world in which we live led to them assuming that everything is made from combinations of four fundamental 'elements': Fire, Air, Water and Earth. These classical elements are listed here in increasing order of substance – air is more substantial than fire, water is more substantial than air and earth is typically more substantial than water. This archaic classification of substances is by no means spurious. Today, we recognise the four Greek elements as the four phases of matter: solid, liquid, gas and plasma.

We have previously noted that B'reishith, the first word of the Torah in the first side of the square, contains *esh* (fire), within covenant. Also, the fourth side of the square includes the word *eretz* (earth) explicitly. What we may now perceive is that the third side of the square contains [ם] שמים / *shamayim* / heavens, which includes [ם] מים / *mayim* / water. So, the first, third and fourth sides contain the first, third and fourth classical elements, in the correct order. And that is a quite amazing degree of correlation. Clearly, to complete the pattern, the second side of the square ought to contain air, but it does not. We could simply avoid the issue by assuming that air is not seen in the square because air is inherently invisible. This may well be the proper conclusion. But now the row totals in the latest view of the 4×7 matrix come to our aid. Notice that, apart from one point of inflexion (ie no change), the totals increase gradually from the first row to the seventh. What we are witnessing is the numeric equivalent of each row being more substantial than the one before. Even by itself, this progressive sequence of row totals would be eye-catching. But the fact that it also parallels certain literal inclusions in the sides of the square, as well as a real (though primitive) theory about creation, is truly astonishing.

In case it occurs to my reader that the author of Genesis may have understood only primitive science, there are three facts that militate against that view. One is the sheer volume of concealed material in the square and especially in the first verse itself. The second is the number of mathematical concepts we have already seen within that material, which were not known until relatively modern times. The third is the volume of scientific information we have yet to see, including topics that have been at the leading edge of recent research. A better hypothesis is that the Author intends his Seal to be accessible and appreciated in any era. It may even include information that is presently unknown; but to seek it might be construed as divination. More will be said about this prospect in Chapter 8.

-oOo-

The 4×7 matrix seen as any one of Figures 3.2, 3.4 and 3.5 is only our latest way of looking at the first verse of the Torah. Previously, we have examined it in other ways that have been equally productive. But the matrix certainly stands up with those other views in terms of the contribution it has made. So it may seem surprising to hear that the same matrix has another pictorial contribution in store, which links to Eden and events that led to 'the fall', or expulsion. There are two co-related images still to be seen in the matrix. There are also two special clues that steer us towards the correct interpretation; the first being the significant 1414 sequence in the middle row. The presence of this important sequence draws attention to two 2x3 clusters (seen shaded in Figure 3.5) that account for seven out of nine of the 1s and five out of six of the 4s in the whole matrix. The 1414 sequence is especially influential, since one of the 2×3 groups rises from its left half, and the other group descends from its right half. Using five 1s and five 4s in two alternative 1-4-1-4-1-4-1-4-1-4 sequences, it is possible (or, more likely, intended) that we may trace out the two paths seen in Figure 3.6 (overleaf).

Without a doubt, version (b) in this illustration is a classic, if perhaps stylised juvenile depiction of a human phallus. However, it may not be quite so obvious that version (a) is meant to represent a snake, or serpent. Also, the validity of the five-fold '14' sequence is not yet fully established. The ultimate verification will be seen in Chapter 5, which combines information from here and from Chapter 4. So we should mark well the serpent-like configuration, the importance of which will be confirmed spectacularly in Chapter 5. But first, we would like to see some immediate evidence that the two images share a valid connection corresponding to a biblical narrative. And the two associated images are found to relate to a pair of similar Hebrew words that occur close together in the second creation account. In one sense these two words are not just similar but identical.

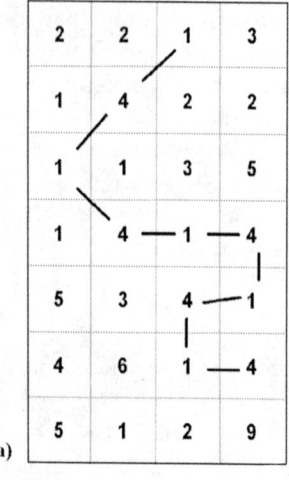
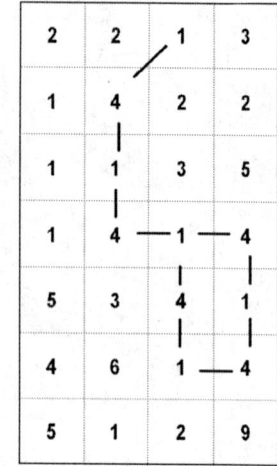

(a)   (b)

**Figure 3.6**

It should now come as little surprise that one of the two significant words is somehow connected with the serpent that tempted the woman in the garden. In Genesis 3:1, we are told that ... *the serpent was more subtle than any beast of the field which the Lord God had made.* The key word here is ערום / *arum* / subtle. However in Genesis 2:25 - the verse immediately preceding this one - we are told that ... *they were both naked, the man and his wife, and were not ashamed.* And the key word here, in its basic form, is ערום / *arom* / naked. The difference between these two words is only in the way they are pronounced, not in their spelling.

I have referred to the basic form of 'naked' here because it is an adjective, and Hebrew adjectives are normally modified by the number and gender of the noun they describe. The basic form of 'naked' I have used is the masculine singular; however, the biblical text uses the masculine plural form, ערומים / *aromiym*. Overall, I feel sure that the minor liberty I have taken will not detract from the Author's intention to link the two pictorial metaphors with the closely associated serpent that is 'subtle' and the phallus that is 'naked'.

-oOo-

Strictly speaking, the form of numerology I have employed so far in this Chapter should not be described as gematria. The term gematria is used properly only when it is applied to a whole-word value, as the sum of its individual 'standard' letter values. When the first verse of the Torah is examined in that way, it exhibits just as much rich content as when viewed either as 28 qatan values or in its native Hebrew letter form. As an introduction to gematria in action, in the next few paragraphs I shall make frequent reference to an extensive Internet website: *The Other Bible Code*, developed by one Vernon Jenkins. In fact, two of the next five illustrations are borrowed directly from pages belonging to that source, the corresponding web address (URL) being given beneath each one. For example, here is how Jenkins introduces the numeric structure of the seven words of Genesis 1:1,

| 7 | 6 | 5 | 4 | 3 | 2 | 1 |
|---|---|---|---|---|---|---|
| :הארץ ואת | השמים | את | אלהים | ברא | בראשית |
| .earth the | and | heavens the | | God | created | beginning the In |
| 296 | 407 | 395 | 401 | 86 | 203 | 913 |

(From: http://homepage.virgin.net/vernon.jenkins/Evidences.htm : Last accessed 8/7/2008)

Note that the Hebrew text in this illustration uses final forms of letters in the third, fifth and seventh words, as is customary with linear text written in the square character set. Also, the font is noticeably different from the Hebrew script I am using in this book.

A quick addition will show that the grand total of the seven word values is 2701, from which several straightforward, though startling consequences follow immediately. Thus,

1. The number 2701 is the product of just two prime factors, viz.
$$2701 = 37 \times 73$$

2. It is the 73rd triangular number ($T_{73}$)

3. The sum of 2701 and its 1072 digit-inverse demonstrates a special coherence, so:
$$2701 + 1072 = 3773$$

3. Pictorially, 2701 may be viewed as the combination of $T_{37}$ (ie 703) surrounded by three copies of $T_{36}$ (ie 666), as shown by Figure 3.7 (overleaf):

Figure 3.7

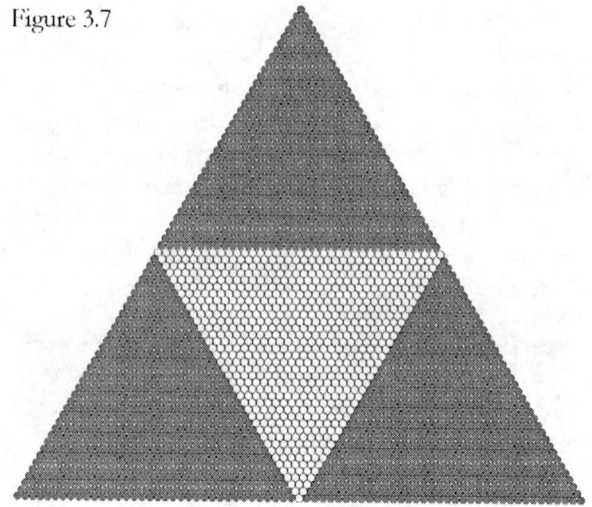

4.       Each of the prime numbers, 37 and 73 is a hexagram or Star of David number (Figure 3.8):

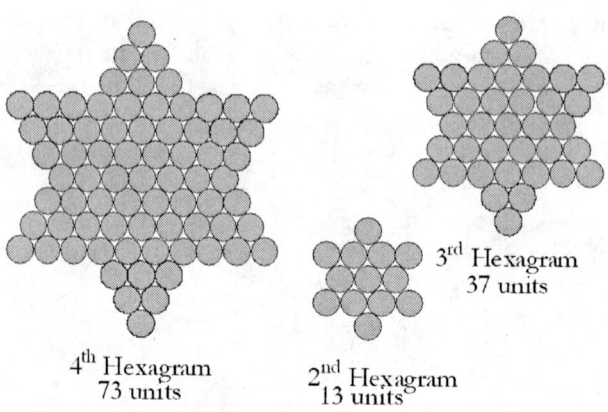

3$^{rd}$ Hexagram
37 units

4$^{th}$ Hexagram
73 units

2$^{nd}$ Hexagram
13 units

Figure 3.8

(The 2nd member of the set of hexagrams is included for background information only, to show that the first three non-trivial members are all prime numbers [The first member (ie 1) is the degenerate member of all figurate number sets (See Appendix A(ii)))

5. Therefore, 2701 may also be viewed as a visually stunning hexagram of hexagrams (star of stars), Figure 3.9.

Figure 3.9

All-in-all, 2701 is inherently a very remarkable number. So we must concede that the above five points are characteristics of the number itself, not of Genesis 1:1 in particular. If and when the number 2701 occurs in any situation, it possesses the aforementioned attributes regardless of whether the context is biblical or otherwise. By itself, the 2701 gematria grand total of Genesis 1:1 might be interpreted as nothing more than a random coincidence.

However, the 2701 total does not stand by itself. For one thing, we already know that the qatan letter values of the same verse also exhibit overlapping mathematical characteristics and biblical metaphors. And we know, from Chapter 2, that the same short text contains an elaborate hidden reference to Moses, and several others to Abraham. From previous experience, therefore, we should expect the 2701 phenomenon to exhibit a lot more than just 'coincidence' value. And it should come as no surprise that the gematria sums of the seven individual words contribute in no small way to an additional, internal structure within the first verse. This is seen most clearly in the next illustration.

|     | A    | B   | C   | D   | E   | F   |     |
| --- | ---- | --- | --- | --- | --- | --- | --- |
| 1.  | 913  | 913 | 913 | 913 | 913 | 913 | 1.  |
| 2.  | 203  | 203 | 203 | 203 | 203 | 203 | 2.  |
| 3.  | 86   | 86  | 86  | 86  | 86  | 86  | 3.  |
| 4.  | 401  | 401 | 401 | 401 | 401 | 401 | 4.  |
| 5.  | 395  | 395 | 395 | 395 | 395 | 395 | 5.  |
| 6.  | 407  | 407 | 407 | 407 | 407 | 407 | 6.  |
| 7.  | 296  | 296 | 296 | 296 | 296 | 296 | 7.  |
|     | 2701 | 703 | 999 | 999 | 777 | 888 |     |

(From: http://homepage.virgin.net/vernon.jenkins/Gen2701.htm :
Last accessed 8/7/2008)

Here then are a few notable facts we may glean from this table of gematria word values:

a) Not only is 2701 divisible by 37, but so are both of the gematria values of words 6 and 7. Their joint sum is 703, which is $T_{37}$ – the same as the central portion of the earlier composite $T_{73}$ triangle (Figure 3.7 above).
(The difference between the values of words 6 and 7 is 111 (ie 3×37), a number that will recur often throughout the rest of this book).

b) These two words map precisely onto the fourth side of the Author's square Seal. Which, as Jenkins points out, corresponds precisely to the expression 'and the earth'. Later we shall see a literary counterpart that also places the earth at the centre of creation.

c) Therefore, sides 1, 2 and 3 of the square are composed from words that give a gematria sum of 3×666 – the three outer zones in Figure 3.7.

d) Four independent combinations of two or three words each give sums that are homogeneous digit triples (ie 777, 888 & 999), where any digit triple is a single-digit multiple of 111 (see (a) above). Also, every one of the seven words takes part in at least one, and as many as three of these triples. Yet none of the first five words is individually divisible by 37.

e) In particular, words 1 and 3 generate 999; and these are the same two words that, previously, both revealed cyclic digits of Pi, and jointly described several major events in the life of the

Hebrew patriarch Abraham. Note, also, that $999 = 27 \times 37$, and that $27 + 37 = 64$ the size of the square that is defined by the structure of Genesis 1:1.

Jenkins has also highlighted a surprising mathematical correspondence between the first verse of Genesis (*In the beginning God created ...*) and the first verse of John (*In the beginning was the word ...*). In the numerology of Hebrew, the decimal digits of Pi can be obtained from Genesis 1:1 to within 0.0012%, from a combination of its letter and word values. The details may be seen in Jenkins' web page: *The evaluation of 'pi' from within Genesis 1:1*, at http://homepage.virgin.net/vernon.jenkins/Pi_File.htm (Last accessed: 14/1/2008). Briefly, the first step is to find the product of all 28 letter values, and multiply this by that letter count; then find the product of the 7 word values, and multiply this by that word count. Finally, the ratio of the two results gives the aforementioned approximation to Pi, scaled up by $10^{17}$.

The Gospel of John was written in Greek before it was translated first into Latin, then other languages. If the Greek scheme of numerology is applied to the Greek text of John 1:1 using the same formula as for the previous case, the result is a very good approximation to the decimal digits of the mathematically important number **e**[h], scaled up by a factor of $10^{40}$. In this case, the discrepancy is a mere 0.0011%. The details of this calculation may be seen in: *The evaluation of 'e' from within John 1:1*, at http://homepage.virgin.net/vernon.jenkins/e_valuation.htm (Last viewed: 14/1/2008).

Not only does the text of John 1:1 emulate the format of Genesis 1:1, but they also share similar mathematical allusions. Then, as we found in Chapter 2, several key words that are poetically repeated in John 1:1-5 are seen as emergent words in the square facet of the Seal. And Genesis 1:1 in qatan letter sequences has revealed two cyclic cases of the digits of Pi, one with an accuracy that is better than 0.003%.

It is clear that the independent findings of Jenkins, or at least the particular parts of his research I have pinpointed here, integrate perfectly with what we already know of the Author's Seal. That is an important conclusion in itself, but I particularly want to move on to

---

[h] The number *e* was found by Leonhard Euler in the 18th Century, and is important in formulae that describe exponential processes and population growth.

develop some further points that follow from the preceding gematria analysis.

First, the gematria of the first word (B'reishith = 913) will lead to some interesting and important associations. Second, the ubiquitous number 37 (and 73 to a lesser extent) will be seen to pop up at several later stages. Third, the appearance of homogeneous triplet numbers (ie small multiples of 111) will have some vital ideas to reveal, mostly in connection with names. To be realistic, these important characteristics of the Seal cannot all be demonstrated at once, and must be developed in stages.

To start with, the digits of 913, the gematria of B'reishith, have two special associations. Consider first the frequency distribution of the 28 qatan letter values in Genesis 1:1, as shown in Table 3.2.

Table 3.2

| Value | Count |
|-------|-------|
| 1 | 9 |
| 2 | 5 |
| 3 | 3 |
| 4 | 6 |
| 5 | 3 |
| 6 | 1 |
| 7 | – |
| 8 | – |
| 9 | 1 |

(One point mentioned only in passing up to now is that there isn't a zero value in Hebrew numerology. Therefore, that sets practical limitations on the use of qatan letter values for communicating decimal numbers).

Notice that the top and bottom rows in the table are inversions of one another. The value 1 occurs nine times in Genesis 1:1, while a 9 occurs only once (notably as the last letter of the verse – the highest value in the highest-numbered position). If, in these two cases, we multiply the value by its frequency, both results are 9. But, as we have found already, the value 3 occurs three times so this, too, gives a product of 9. Recall that all three 3s come from the letters that spell the Hebrew word for 'three', and occupied the central vertical column of Figure 3.3. Therefore, we see an immediate link between the digits 9-1-3 and 3-1-9. That is, 1×9, and 3×3, and 9×1 all give the same result of 9. This reversibility has a quite momentous interpretation when we examine the second mathematical association of 913, next.

Now, recall that 6, the letter length of the first word, is a triangular number, and is also the first member of the set of Perfect Numbers. Then the beauty of the other association of 913 is that it is intimately linked to a distinctive, inherent characteristic of the set of all triangular numbers. To understand the connection, we need to convert each triangular number, in sequence, into what I shall call a 'reduced value' (see Appendix B). And to convert any number to its reduced value, all we do is to add together its separate digits (if there is more than one).

The outcome for the first seventeen triangular numbers is shown in the following table.

Triangle: 1 3 6 10 15 21 28 36 45 55 66 78* 91* 105 120 136* 153
Reduced: 1 3 6 1 6 3 1 9 9 1 3 6 1 6 3 1 9

(* Whenever the addition of digits leads to another multi-digit number, the process is repeated until a single digit is obtained)

No matter how far we extend this process into the triangular number series, the same palindromic set of reduced digits 913 616 319 (underscored in the table) keep repeating endlessly. This recurring sequence could be described as the 'characteristic signature' of the triangular number series (Other mathematical series and sequences also have their own characteristic signatures that emerge only from their reduced values. See Appendix B). Clearly, the 913 with which the recurring group begins, corresponds to the gematria of B'reishith. The 319 with which it ends corresponds to the reversible pattern we found earlier in the frequency distribution table. But the digits 616 in the middle have an altogether different, yet highly significant biblical association. As the number 616, it is known to have once been an alternative to the better known 666, now found at Revelation 13:18 in all modern bibles. Notice, however, that 666 being interchangeable with 616 is a feature of only the New Testament of Christian bibles. In my own copy of the Revised Standard Version, a footnote to Revelation 13:18 reads: "*Other ancient authorities read six hundred and sixteen*".

Without a doubt, the gematria of the 6-letter (T$_3$) first word is alluding to triangular numbers generally. And this fact is mimicked in the last book of the standard Christian Bible, the 66th book (ie T$_{11}$), by the alternative use of 616 and 666 (ie T$_{36}$). The fact that Revelation echoes a key component of the Author's Seal could easily be written off as an isolated, humanly contrived imitation, were it not for certain additional attributes which we shall examine in the next Chapter.

We have, it seems, reached a watershed point in our analysis where multiple, mathematical and pseudo-mathematical associations have converged. The first word of the Hebrew Bible and the full first verse are now seen to link qatan letter values with standard word values; both of these with triangular numbers; and specific triangular numbers with the set generally. In particular, we have now seen a plausible, rational reason why the numbers 616 and 666 should have been alternatives in the Book of Revelation.

What is more, we now know the gematria sum of words #3, #5 and #7 is 777. These are the same words that confer the breaks at 7-letter intervals that led to the formation of the 8×8 aspect of the Seal.

Some of the concepts we have just seen, and some of the linkages between them will undoubtedly seem alien in relation to both conventional mathematics and Christian theology. Most of these concepts were unfamiliar to myself to begin with, and they certainly did not all come to light as a fully-formed package or in the relatively tidy order described here. I have chosen to describe them in the above order so as to draw out their developing interrelationships. But it is quite important to be aware that each component concept has its own inherent merit that can be appreciated in isolation. Then the relationships between them, and with the Seal, can only affirm and greatly boost their separate intrinsic worth. This complex numerical phenomenon will not necessarily be fully appreciated from a single reading. And the foregoing descriptions are as yet far from complete.

-oOo-

Importantly, we are now aware that the meaning of the first verse of the Torah is even more elaborate than could once have been imagined. As a string of 28 single-digit qatan values, we have seen it alluding to several well known yet quite sophisticated mathematical concepts. Some of those concepts also overlay equivalent linguistic biblical messages that we teased out of the first and third words, in Chapter 2. The correspondence between God's covenant of circumcision with Abraham, and the cyclic digits of Pi is especially elegant and indicative of an elaborate coherence of purpose.

Later, we saw that a standard gematria analysis of Genesis 1:1 reveals a large number of further geometrical characteristics, backed up by the remarkably well-tuned values of the seven individual words. Other references to triangular numbers might easily lead to the feeling that triangles, among other geometrical shapes, are key attributes of the Bible's descriptions of creation, perhaps even of the physical creation. But the Seal's particular emphasis on triangles, the number '3' and the word 'three' is only part of a wider picture which will persistently impress itself on our awareness.

Before that we saw the 28 qatan digits of Genesis 1:1 depicting two versions of the geometrical 45° right-angle triangle; then making references to Adam, Eve and the serpent in Eden. The latter two images (Figure 3.6) were found to be pictorial metaphors for two different but identically spelled words (homographs) found in consecutive verses of the relevant biblical narrative. The first of those two verses describes the naked man and woman; while the very next verse depicts the encounter between the woman and the cunning serpent. Therefore, consider how the concept of 'knowing' perfectly links these two expressions: ... *the tree of knowledge of good and evil.* (Genesis 2:17), with *And Adam knew Eve his wife; and she conceived.* (Genesis 4:1).

The effect we are witnessing is a cumulative one; and all along the way, we should be considering not only possible causes but also reasons. Why should the biblical creation account embody so much extra, cryptic knowledge? Perhaps because knowing and cleaving are inseparable concepts, two sides of the same coin. When we cleave to new knowledge, we are preparing to give birth to new understanding; maybe not instantly, but after an indefinite period of gestation. Like grief, this can be a painful process when we are forced to let go of immature 'truths', but necessary to healthy development.

On a purely practical level, our quick review of Genesis 1:1, especially in full standard gematria, has equipped us with new understanding which will permit us immediately to see the complete Seal in a new light.

## 4

Our alternative numerical exploration of the start of Genesis continues in this Chapter, as we extend our scope to the first 64 Hebrew letters. Take a look at Figure 4.1, in which the square we examined linguistically in Chapter 2 has been fully converted to qatan letter values.

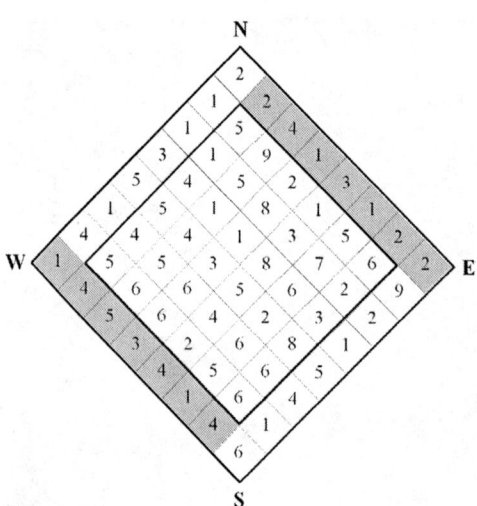

**Figure 4.1**

In this very basic view, it is already possible to see something explicitly that was once mentioned only in passing; that the vertical triple sequence of the letter *vav* (ו) belonging to the image of the crucified man, corresponds to a 666 sequence. This is an important configuration - being one of only three homogeneous digit triples in the complete square - and especially distinctive as it lies at the very foot of the N-S diagonal which divides the square symmetrically.

The first wholly new revelation will, however, be found in the way the square associates this axial 666 with a more elusive 616 — so marrying the two numbers that were alternatives in early manuscripts of Revelation 13:18. We start by looking at the sums of the qatan values in the third and fourth sides of the square. The third side (W to S) is shaded, and its qatan sum is 22. The fourth side (S to E) is un-shaded, and its qatan sum is 28. From these values we obtain the product: 22×28 = 616 as required. Before we move on, there are three important observations to be made about this result, viz.

1. Sides 3 and 4 are the very ones whose angle is bisected by the vertical 666 sequence.
2. The value 22 is also the number of letters in the Hebrew alephbeyt; and 28 is also the number of letters in the first verse of Genesis.
3. The sum of 22 and 28 (ie 50) is the difference between 666 and 616.

That is one way in which the number square generates 616 using its co-factors 22 and 28, but there is one other.

A quick glance at the frequency distribution table for Genesis 1:1 (repeated here from Table 3.2 of the previous Chapter) shows that the higher letter values are relatively scarce. There are no 7s or 8s in the first verse, and there is just one each of 6 and 9. Therefore, the single 6 and single 9 are both first occurrences of the letters from which they derive. Also, they both happen to occur in the fourth side of the square, where the text reads: ... *and the earth*. There are no first occurrences (ie previously unused letters) in side #3, and

Table 3.2

| Value | Count |
|-------|-------|
| 1 | 9 |
| 2 | 5 |
| 3 | 3 |
| 4 | 6 |
| 5 | 3 |
| 6 | 1 |
| 7 | - |
| 8 | - |
| 9 | 1 |

there are no other first occurrences in side #4. Furthermore, the 6 occurs as the first element in that side, and the 9 as its last element; these correspond to letter positions 22 and 28 in the verse. So here, again, we are presented with the same co-factors of 616 as before.

Now the way that 616 was first generated from the sides of the square that are bisected by 666 might have seemed just too good to be true, and a happy co-incidence. So the square provides a second similar example to prove that we are not dealing with a random effect. Recall at the end of Chapter 2, we saw that the top of the N-S diagonal contains the emergent expression הנ רה אה / *hey nahar* / <u>Behold – a river</u>! The letters of the word nahar (river) take gematria values 50, 5 and 200, giving a word total of 255. But check the sums of the qatan values in sides #1 and #2, the sides whose angle is bisected by the word nahar. These are 15 and 17 respectively, giving us the product: 15×17 = 255 as we might expect by now. Notice, too, that the 255 of nahar and the explicit 666 sequence are at opposite ends of the same diagonal.

While still on the subject of the four sides of the square, and their qatan sums, it will prove instructive to find the product of all four sums. But that will be appreciated better in relation to another product, which is an extension of the same principle. Now that the square is fully populated, there is an opportunity to examine its two diagonals in a similar way to its four sides. When the eight values in each diagonal are added, the vertical column comes to 36, and the horizontal row to 37. We know already that 37 is a common factor in all homogeneous triples (eg 111, 666 and 777) and also in the gematria values of both the sixth and seventh words which translate as *and the earth*. And the number 37 was intimately involved in the 2701 gematria sum of the whole first verse. In the previous Chapter, we found that the gematria sum of words 6 and 7 is 703 (ie $T_{37}$), and the balance of 2701 is 3×666, where 666 is $T_{36}$. In fact, 2701 is $T_{73}$, where 73 = 36 + 37. So it is clear that the first verse of the Torah is making a complex statement about the close relationships between all these numbers, even linking them in several independent ways. Thus, we find that the same two numbers are incorporated into the square, as the qatan sums of its diagonals, and therefore independent of those earlier observations. So it is of the greatest significance that 37×36 = 2×666. And now we come to the special way in which the two diagonals relate to the product of the four sides. The latter product is this:

$$15×17×22×28 = 157080$$

...which, as 1.57080, is half of 3.14160; that is, Pi to within about 0.00025%. But note that, where the four sides (a cyclic arrangement incidentally) generate half of Pi, the two diagonals generate double 666. Therefore the overall product of all six components comes to 666π, also to within 0.00025%, after allowing for the proper insertion of the decimal point.

In a quite extraordinary way, the combined qatan and standard gematria characteristics of the square's sides provide yet another alternative emphasis on the number 666. Recall that sides #1, #2, and #3 confer a gematria total of 1998, which is 3×666. In other words, the arithmetic mean value of the first three sides is 666. But now consider the sum of the qatan values of the same three sides. They are 15 + 17 + 22 = 54. Then we observe the following shared attribute:

|  | Cosine(666°) | = | 0.587785252 |
|---|---|---|---|
| And | Cosine( 54°) | = | 0.587785252 |

The two trigonometrical cosines are identical because 666° is exactly 54° less than 2×360°. The same principle holds true for any two numbers A and B, where A is less than 90, and B is a whole number multiple of 360, plus or minus A. What makes this equivalence especially important for the square Seal is the fact that both its perimeter and the cosine function have inherently cyclic characteristics.

We shall recall these results when, in Chapter 8, we examine the number 666 in an altogether different, cyclic setting. Indeed, the word 'recall' and equivalent expressions will occur more and more in these pages, as the Seal finds numerous new ways to repeat and reinforce particular core concepts. Each of the core concepts that are so repeated may be considered a leitmotif, a recurring phrase in a much longer musical score.

That, then, is the first evidence that the sides of the square and its diagonals may function as a coordinated set. Also, the fact that this relationship involves so many geometrical concepts should hint that the ultimate purpose is itself geometrical. Eventually, that impression will indeed be borne out. In fact, as we shall see the fourth side of the square itself bequeaths the early digits of Pi in yet another way. This is at once geometrical and again indicative that the fourth side is unlike the others (in full gematria terms, side #4 is $T_{37}$ while the other three total $3 \times T_{36}$). To begin with, the seven digits of the fourth side (ie 6145129) include all of the first seven fractional digits of Pi (ie 3.<u>1415926</u>). That in itself is surprising; but the bigger wonder is in the way that the fractional digits of Pi map onto the qatan values of the fourth side as shown in Figure 4.2:

| 1 | 4 | 1 | 5 | 9 | 2 | 6 | : Fractional part of Pi |
|---|---|---|---|---|---|---|---|
| 6 | 1 | 4 | 5 | 1 | 2 | 9 | : Side 4 of the square (see Figure 4.1) |

Figure 4.2

Quite clearly, if the ends of the two rows are simultaneously looped around until they meet, then the two 6s will become adjacent, one above the other. At the same time, the positions of all other digits remain aligned as in Figure 4.2. This, then, is one more example of the first verse suggesting the digits of Pi by means of a cyclic rearrangement.

Thus far, the four sides of the square, as qatan sums have revealed only mathematical attributes. However, given the source of the square, not to mention our findings in previous chapters, it would be surprising if they did not also contain some reference to biblical narratives. In fact, the four qatan sums contain a hidden reference to one particular number that occurs at several pivotal points throughout the Bible. Moreover, in following this route we shall be reinforcing an earlier pair of related results.

We start by adding the qatan sums of consecutive pairs of sides of the square, as follows:

$$15 + 17 = 32$$
And
$$22 + 28 = 50$$

In each case, the two numbers we now add were once multiplied giving, respectively, 255 (the gematria of *nahar* (river)) and 616. But now we proceed to multiply these interim results, so:

$$32 \times 50 = 1600$$

Part of the merit of this product is that it is also **40×40**. And these particular factors are most often associated with very dramatic events in the Bible. The rain that fed Noah's flood lasted 40 days and 40 nights; Moses was on the mountain to receive the Law for 40 days and 40 nights; the children of Israel wandered in the wilderness for 40 years; and the Holy Spirit drove Jesus into the wilderness for 40 days and 40 nights. So in this way, too, the qatan values of Genesis 1:1 not only foresee the most dramatic biblical episodes, but they came to be expressed in terms of cyclic time (ie days and years).

Another notable characteristic of 1600 is that it is the product of two squares in three different ways (four if we include $40^2 \times 1^2$). These are: $8^2 \times 5^2$, $10^2 \times 4^2$ and $20^2 \times 2^2$).

-oOo-

When, in Chapter 2, we were examining the square as letters, there were two artefacts that stood out more prominently than any others. One was the juxtaposition of two emergent copies of the word 'light' with the plain-text word 'darkness'. The overall configuration was redolent of a box with relative dimensions 3×3×5; and this was interpreted as an allusion to the biblical Ark of the Covenant, which the Israelites had constructed to God's precise instructions. The allusion was greatly enhanced by the presence of the emergent 4-letter word 'tablets' which passes through the word 'darkness' in the interior of the Ark-image, because God had instructed Moses to place the stone tablets of the Law within the original Ark.

The other especially distinctive artefact was the large 'Y' shape composed entirely of the letter *vav* (וֹ), the whole being interpreted as the outline of a man who is being crucified. We then noted that the upper 'V' portion of the Y could also be viewed as three corners of a 3×3 square; so that the same formation again repeated the 3×3×5 dimensions of the Ark. What is more, an emergent לֻח / *luach* / a tablet is found within the upper 3×3 component. Now, however, we shall see that the latest square of qatan values makes the very same point, in a way that further confirms the Author's knowledge of post-biblical mathematics.

It is quite common for biblical commentators to point out that the shape of the Ark is somewhat reminiscent of a mathematical concept known variously as the Divine Proportion, Divine Ratio, Golden Ratio or Golden Mean, among other names. This number is found extensively in nature, and is so fascinating to mathematicians that it has been assigned a symbol, the Greek letter Phi (Φ), all to itself. The exact value of the Divine Proportion begins 1.618033988 as shown by my pocket calculator but is, in reality, a never-ending decimal number. The ratio 5/3 (being 1.666$^r$) obtained from the dimensions of the Ark is sufficiently close to the value of Phi as to be visually indistinguishable in measured lengths. This leads on to the idea that Phi may be understood through a well-known number sequence. The Fibonacci Sequence is a simple sequence of numbers which, by general consent, begins 1, 1... Then all subsequent terms are obtained by adding together the previous two terms. Thus, the third term will be 1+1 = 2, giving 1, 1, 2 .... The fourth term will then be 1+2 = 3, giving 1, 1, 2, 3... and so on. So the first ten terms in the Fibonacci Sequence are:

$$1, 1, 2, 3, 5, 8, 13, 21, 34, 55$$

The connection between the Fibonacci Sequence, the Ark of the Covenant and the Divine Proportion is that the ratio of any two consecutive terms in the number sequence gets nearer to Phi as the sequence is extended; and two of its adjacent terms, 3 and 5, happen to be the relative dimensions of the Ark. By the tenth term the ratio (ie 55/34) is already 1.6176..., and within 0.025% of the true value of Phi. And even the 5/3 obtained from the Ark is within 3%. But so much for the theory.

The important point for now is that the 1.666... ratio generated by the dimensions of the Ark is the reason sometimes given, not least in sober biblical commentaries, for the Ark of the Covenant to have been specified to the dimensions it was. But these facts in isolation do not confirm that belief or assumption. The evidence that will confirm this intention comes from the Seal as an extensive package, of which Figure 4.3 is just one more stage.

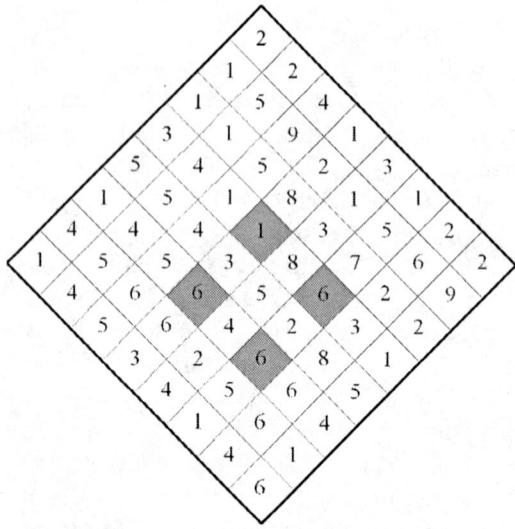

**Figure 4.3**

The four digits that are highlighted here are placed at the four corners of the very same 3×3 square defined by the upper 'V' of the crucified man, suggesting a 5/3 ratio with its height of 5-units. But the Author of the Torah is especially intent on ensuring his meaning is not overlooked or misunderstood. So there are further confirmations designed into his Seal, which we shall encounter in stages.

-oOo-

Now consider the length of the Torah, in terms of the number of Hebrew letters it contains. These days, nobody can be absolutely certain that the current text is a faithful copy of the original. In fact there are different versions that have come down to the present day through alternative branches of Judaism. However, there is one orthodox tradition that was established with one of its central aims being to restore and preserve the integrity of the original Torah. And the text that has come to us via that route is known as the Masoretic Torah.

The term 'Masoretic' derives from the name of a devoutly Orthodox sect of Judaism known as the Masoretes. This sect was established in the middle centuries of the Common Era (AD) to address one aspect of the issue of Jewish persecution. For a time, it was feared that the Orthodox Jewish tradition might be driven out of existence, and the true Torah lost forever. The Masoretes undertook to restore the Torah to its original perfection, by a process of eliminating discrepancies between alternative copies. Note that there is here the implied assumption that there was once a perfect original Torah – the one that was dictated by God to Moses. The restoration process was begun by collecting together copies of the Torah such that each had been handed down through a line of repeated copying that was as independent of the others as possible. The Masoretes then re-compiled a standardised text, eliminating minority discrepancies, unless they had particular reason for thinking the majority were in error.

The work of the Masoretes was meticulous, even to the point of accepting alternative spellings for the same word if the evidence pointed to the difference having existed from the earliest times. For some commentators, the alternative spelling of words is automatically taken as proof of transmission errors. But there is another explanation, more in keeping with the existence of underlying artefacts coded into the text, such as those described in this book. The Masoretic Torah is the one now adopted by Judaism generally, and by researchers into the better known Bible Code. The latter includes an assiduously professional group at the Hebrew University in Jerusalem, who are responsible for the most definitive Bible Code research yet to have been published. It is probably fair to say that many of their findings actually *depend* on the presence of alternatively spelled words. However, there are no alternative spellings within the range of text I describe as the Author's Seal.

For our purposes, the key fact is that the Masoretic Torah contains exactly 304,805 Hebrew letters - a rather large number which, at first sight, does not look at all exceptional. Yet we shall find in stages that 304,805 is just as special as the 2701 gematria of Genesis 1:1, and with a closely related purpose. For the moment, all we need to know is that the larger number is the product of just two prime factors, viz.

$$304805 = 5 \times 60961$$

Given that these factors derive from the Five Books of Moses, they could hardly be more appropriate, one being a 5 and the other a 5-digit number. But these two numbers have much more than transient, superficial appeal on their side.

The larger of the two factors provides a clue to how we are meant to proceed. First we need to remind ourselves of the several ways in which the Seal conferred the number Pi by means of cyclic

In the Beginning

arrangements. Two of them came directly from the qatan values of the first and third Torah words. Another came from the four qatan sums we obtained from the perimeter of the square. And the latest, in the present Chapter, came from the qatan values in just the fourth side of the square. Every one of these has involved turning a linear concept into a cyclic one. Taken together these represent a kind of training programme; so we shall now accept the hint and follow a similar procedure. We first write the number 60961 evenly around the circumference of a circle, forming a regular pentagon. Then we add the two factors together (ie 60961 + 5 = 60966) and do the same with their sum. As can be seen from Figure 4.4, the first arrangement gives rise to a 616 sequence, and the second a 666 in the

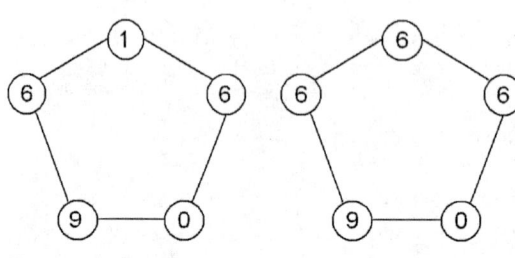

Figure 4.4

identical positions. Therefore, this view of two separate pentagons provides yet another justification for the deliberate New Testament relationship between the numbers 616 and 666. But the two separate pentagons are only the starting point for another three, even more important outcomes. Two of them will not be seen for some time yet. The other is the intersection of the two components, shown by Figure 4.5.

Two points about this overlapping configuration deserve special mention, over and above the fact that it re-emphasises the number pair 616 and 666. One is that the sum of the visible digits is the ubiquitous number 37. The other is the shaded central cluster of digits 1-6-6-6, which are now in the same configuration we saw within the fully populated square (see Figure 4.3) two pages earlier. The main message we should take from this replication of numerical alignment is twofold. First, the group of digits 1666 really must represent the Ark of the Covenant, through the Divine Proportion.

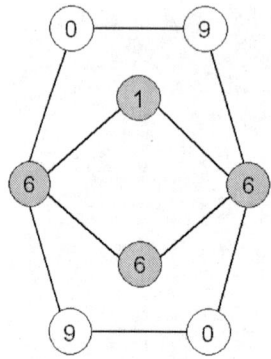

Figure 4.5

More importantly, we are surely expected to recognise that the complete Torah and its beginning are to be considered together as a coherent partnership.

-oOo-

Enough has been said for now concerning the Ark of the Covenant and the Divine Proportion. However, both concepts will continue to re-emerge as we look at the Seal in alternative ways. Right now, I want to move on to consider some aspects of the commandments that go to make up the sum of the Law. Quite often, the word Torah itself is translated directly to the word 'Law'. Yet this English word does not properly capture the real essence of Torah. A better word might be 'instruction', since the Torah is as much a guide as a set of rigid statutes. And this point of view is borne out by the fact that biblical Hebrew does not have a word that means 'to obey'. At one time, the King James Bible used the more appropriate but now obsolete word *hearken*, though *heed* would serve just as well. The point is that man is not an automaton, to follow instructions blindly and to the letter. He is a thinking, feeling being who may one day fulfil his potential and become, by choice, the majestic image of his creator. That calls for wise guidance, judicious encouragement and above all a perfect example, but not for blind obedience.

As to the number of commands in the Torah, I am not referring to the well-known Ten Commandments that God inscribed on two tablets of stone. Rather, the scope we need to apply must be extended to include the 613 that have been identified as applicable to Judaism. Many of the 613 are now obsolete, following the Roman sacking of the Temple in Jerusalem in 70 AD. Instructions that once applied to the now defunct Jewish priesthood, and practices to do with sacrifice, are no longer applicable. Others make such good sense for straightforward reasons of public and personal health, including sensible diet, that it is often assumed that was sufficient reason for their inclusion. However, sensible considerations such as these turn out to be only a part of a much grander vision. But, regardless of which commandments remain valid or current, rabbinic sources have long held that 613 commands of the Sinaitic covenant can be distinguished in the Torah. And that number is not only an important starting point for the following analysis, but will also be justified by it – the sure sign that the Seal embodies a coherent, underlying rationale.

A special point concerning these commands is that the gematria of the word תורה / *Torah* / <u>Torah</u> is 611, while that of ברית / *Brit* / <u>Covenant</u> is 612. This numerical alignment seems particularly apposite once we realise that there are 613 commands contained in the Torah and associated with the covenant that was entered into at Sinai. In the next Chapter we shall see how this sequence of numbers - derived as they are from intimately linked concepts - may be extended to include no less than six consecutive members. So, health and hygiene apart, it appears that 613 was intrinsically an important target number. So, our immediate topic must be the set of 613 commands that Judaism has identified.

Not all of the 613 are concerned with health and hygiene, and some of them are especially distinctive, bizarre even, for one reason or another. There is one in particular that stands out as unique before all the rest. It is written:

> The Lord said unto Moses, "Speak to the Israelites and say to them: 'Throughout the generations to come you are to make tassels on the corners of your garments, with a blue cord on each tassel. You will have these tassels to look at and so you will remember all the commands of the Lord' ... "
>
> (Numbers 15:37-39, NIV)

Two things about this command require our particular style of analytical attention. One is the requirement for a blue cord, rather than any other colour; a point that I shall come back to later. The other is the fact that the very concept of a garment with tassels and a blue cord can be found in the Author's Seal when it is expressed as a square of qatan values. This is best described with a term I used when we first filled the void of the square with the 36 letters that follow the first verse. At that point, I used the word 'layer', comparing the structure of the square to four concentric, inner layers of an onion. After fitting the first verse into the perimeter – the outer layer – we proceeded to break into the next layer inwards. Described in these terms, the square consists of four layers, of which the innermost is a square cluster of just four letters.

Now, to understand the connection between the square of qatan digits and the commandment quoted above, we may disregard the outer layer completely. And the inner layer will play a relatively passive role. Therefore we concentrate almost exclusively on the second and third layers. And what we find is that within that region, the digits that sit exactly on the diagonals act very much like the tassels on a square garment, which is the passive innermost layer. Figure 4.6 highlights with darker shading the positions of digits that are to be understood as tassels. Other features that also contribute to the tassel effect are highlighted in other ways. We may note in advance that each and every one of the four visible tassels is just the kernel of something more elaborate and/or extensive. Symbolically, this 'hidden' complexity seems particularly appropriate for a single command that calls for all commands to be remembered.

Three of the symbolic tassels stand out very clearly as the digit pairs '55', '55' and '66'. Two of these are to be understood straightforwardly: the '66' comes from the stem of the notable 'Y' shape of the crucified man, which is also the outline of a box-like Ark. And one of the '55' pairs is from the נ ה ר / *nahar*/ river in the same diagonal, which has a gematria of 255. The remaining two tassels require more elaborate explanations, and I shall first address the one that is easier to describe.

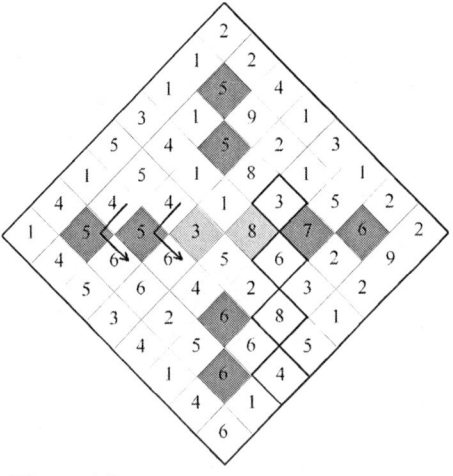

On the right of the horizontal (ie W-E) diagonal, there is a sequence '876', the visual appearance of which commends it as a tassel. Yet it is not especially its appearance that holds the greatest significance, but the fact that the 76 in the second and third layers is

Figure 4.6

exactly double the 38 which precedes it (hold this fact in abeyance for just a moment). In terms of full gematria values, these groups do not just look like 38 and 76; they are, indeed, composed from 30+8 and 70+6 respectively. On top of this simple numerical connection, the 38 comes from the emergent word ל ה / *luach* / tablet which is to the immediate left of the vertical word ל ו ח ת / *luchot* / tablets; and the 76 is to the right of that word (the word *luchot* gives rise to the emphasised vertical 3684 sequence in the illustration). Since the word *luach* is seen nestled within the 1-6-6-6 upper end of the Ark-shaped crucified man, the doubling of 38 to make 76 may well be contrasting this single tablet with the commands that were written on two stone tablets, and placed inside the Ark of the Covenant. That, then, is the third tassel; and later in the present Chapter we shall see compelling confirmation of the importance of the single new tablet.

Regarding the fourth tassel, its rationale is no less elaborate than with the last. The presence of the '55' pair in the left side of the W-E diagonal is merely a signpost to a much more compelling message. First, notice that each 5 belongs to a 456 sequence in the coiled plain text, as it turns the corner in each layer. One of these sequences comes from the word הֹתוּ / *tohu* / <u>formless</u>, while the other derives from the same three letters but as part of the longer word [ם] הֹתוּם / *t'hom* / <u>the deep</u>. Therefore, the two identical sequences are no mere repetition of the same, frequently used word.

Next, when we look for the full gematria value of the 3-letter sequence (a whole word in one case), we find it is not four hundred and fifty-six at all, but 400 + 5 + 6 = 411. And herein lies its biblical meaning and true significance, based on the fact that 411 = 3×137. Granted, we have not previously met 137, but we shall see it again in other contexts. And right here and now, there is a wealth of meaning to be extracted from this number, and especially the fact that we have been shown three lots of 137. This is because the number 137 occurs just three times in the Torah. It occurs only in Genesis and Exodus, and nowhere else in the Bible. Therefore its distribution is not statistically random, but indicates a degree of planning that pervades the entire Bible. However, the immediate significance is in the specific way that 137 is used in the first two books of the Torah. In each case it is given as the age of a notable personality at the time of his death. The first of the three is Ishmael, the illegitimate son of Abram. Of Ishmael, it is written:

> *Altogether, Ishmael lived an hundred and thirty-seven years. He breathed his last and died, and he was gathered to his people.*
>
> (Genesis 25:17)

The next is Levi, son of Jacob and progenitor of the Hebrew priesthood. Of Levi it is written:

> *These were the names of the sons of Levi according to their records: Gershon, Kohath and Merari. Levi lived 137 years.*
>
> (Exodus 6:16)

The last is Amram, of whom it is written:

> *Amram married his father's sister Jochabed, who bare him Aaron, and Moses. Amram lived 137 years.*
>
> (Exodus 6:20)

Almost incidentally, we now have all the components in place to recognise a very special relationship that exists between names and numbers. Recall the way that an analysis of the gematria of Genesis 1:1

as a whole (Jenkins, 2004) highlighted a preponderance of multiples of 111 (ie 777, 888 and 999). But the merit of 111 extends far beyond the first verse, into the realm of biblical names. Take, for example, the gematria of אברהם (Abraham), which is 248, and that of יהוה / YHWH / <u>the four-letter name of God</u>, which is 26. Then we have the following numerical relationships:

$$
\begin{array}{rl}
26 & (\text{יהוה}) \\
+ \ \underline{111} & \\
137 & (\text{the final ages of Ishmael, Levi and Amram}) \\
+ \ \underline{111} & \\
248 & (\text{אברהם})
\end{array}
$$

This compound relationship between people and their ages, together with important names and gematria values within the Seal attest to the Author's strategic purpose and method. Which is, to show that the Seal and the Bible's historical narrative have been designed simultaneously and consistently; and that names have a strangely intimate relationship with numbers. This is a concept that arises often, and on which I elaborate in chapters 5 and 9.

I also suggested earlier that there is a special reason for the tassels on the Israelites' garments to have a blue cord and no other colour. The reason is to be found in the structure of the Hebrew word for blue, and its standard letter values. The word itself is כחול / *cachol* / <u>blue</u>, and its letter values are these:

| ל | ו | ח | כ |
|---|---|---|---|
| 30 | 6 | 8 | 20 |

So we see that the first half gives a sum of 28 and the second half a sum of 36. The relationship between these sub-totals and the square is, of course, that the square has a perimeter of 28 letters (the full first verse), with 36 letters within it. There is no other valid Hebrew word that could convey the same correspondence between the layered structure of the square and the command to put tassels on garments. Therefore, the cord could not have been any colour but blue.

-oOo-

Still with the subject of garments, it seems that the Author's Seal in its present form fulfils a promise that was given in the Bible's description of Noah's post-diluvian life. In Genesis 9 Ham, one of Noah's three sons, finds his father drunken and naked in his tent.

> *Then Shem and Japheth took a garment, laid it upon both their shoulders, and walked backward and covered the nakedness of their father; their faces were turned away, and they did not see the nakedness of their father.*
>
> (Genesis 9:23, RSV)

In Chapter 9 I shall describe an intriguing new way in which we may interpret this episode. But already, in the present Chapter we see that the central 2×2 cluster in the Seal is identified as a garment by its tassels; and it is found precisely over the shoulders of the crucified man. The same metaphor is further enhanced by the fact that three of the central letters spell אהל / *ohel* / <u>a tent</u>. Clearly, a tent is a garment that is not meant for an individual, but for a whole family.

-oOo-

Since we are already focused on the idea of garments, this is a suitable point at which to recall another component of the square that suggests a related topic. In Chapter 2 we found that an emergent word עור / *aur* / <u>skin</u> intersects with its emergent sound-alike אור / *aur* / <u>light</u>. I suggested there that the skin could refer to the following verse:

> *Unto Adam also and to his wife did the Lord God make garments of skins and clothed them.*
>
> (Genesis 3:21)

And I further suggested that the *aur* descending and the *aur* ascending (and closely aligned to the crucified man) might be interpreted as reverse paths. Strangely, this juxtaposition of similar sounding words, along with tassels is probably the strongest available evidence for the veracity of the long lost and recently re-discovered Gnostic Gospel of Judas Iscariot.

Until the 1970s, there were thought to be no surviving copies of the Gospel of Judas. But then a single copy turned up in Egypt, and was restored, translated and finally aired in public in early 2007. And the section of that Gospel's text which connects most directly with the square Seal is the part that is translated so:

> *Jesus said to Judas: "You will exceed all of them. For you will sacrifice the man that clothes me."*
>
> (The Gospel of Judas)

According to this unconventional Gospel, Judas was not the pariah he was long assumed to be, but the most worthy of Jesus' followers to receive the precious mystical knowledge (gnosis). Judas was entrusted with the responsibility not for betraying his Master but for handing over[i] Jesus, so that his soul could be freed from his body in the pre-ordained manner. The Seal's analogy for the same process is the lower copy of light being slightly displaced from, but still parallel to the letters that generate 666 (*'the number of a man'*, Revelation 13:18).

The concept of forward and reverse paths involving the word for skin is delightfully confirmed by a combination of the present square and a later version. Recall that the word skin begins at the sole letter ayin (ע) to be present in the square, and is only one of three emergent words to do so. They are:

עוב / *oob* / <u>thick darkness</u>

עור / *aur* / <u>skin</u>

עשה / *asah* / <u>to make</u>

The gematria sums of the three Hebrew words are 78, 276 and 375 respectively. Notice that the digits of every one of these numbers will reduce (see Appendix B) first to 15 then to 6, and that each of them is independently divisible by 3. But notice especially that their combined sum is 729, and that:

$$729 = 3×3×3×3×3×3$$

In terms of reverse paths, the fact that this result derives from three emergent words that all share the same initial letter, may be described as a 'going out'. Then at Chapter 7 we shall find an equally surprising 'coming in' involving three words that all converge *onto* the same letter *ayin*. This will be an example of a technique that is very solidly programmed into the Author's Seal; that two or more aspects of the Seal often contain components that reinforce one another, whilst also possessing their own independent merit.

---

[i] It is now widely accepted that the Greek word παραδίδωμι (*paradidomi*) that has traditionally been translated as 'betrayed' is better understood as the more neutral 'handed over' or 'delivered'. However, this improved understanding has not yet been prominently announced, or Judas' good reputation acknowledged and restored by the Church.

In the Beginning

Even now, we are far from done with the first square's representation of New Testament matters. The next example derives from the presence in the square of just three homogeneous linear triple digits. We cannot fail to notice this further emphasis on 3, in the form of three triples. These particular digit groups serve to stress the digits 1, 4 and 6. The triple 6 is already familiar to us as a component of the large 'Y' configuration of the letter *vav* (ו). And it is significant that it is placed symmetrically in the lower part of the vertical N-S diagonal. The other two triples, as a cooperating pair, create an alternative symmetry as shown by Figure 4.7.

The distinctive '111' and '444' groups are clearly seen abutting the N-W side of the square, in a way that completes yet another 45° right-angle triangle. There is a strong similarity here, to the larger of the right-angle triangles we saw in Chapter 3, in the 4×7 matrix based on Genesis 1:1. This is not just due to their shapes, but also because the new example is even more obviously associated with several 1 and 4 digits. Using only the two new triples and a decimal point, it is possible to write 1.41414, which is within about 0.005% of √2. And this is the ratio of the hypotenuse of any such triangle to either one of its other sides.

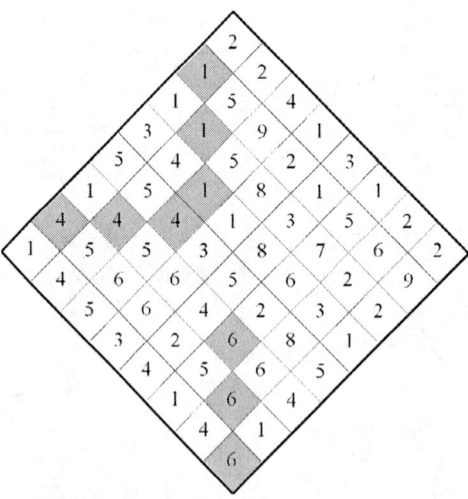

**Figure 4.7**

To return to the subject of symmetry, the 111 and 444 triples have a common axis of bi-lateral symmetry that divides the square into equal 4x8 halves. What is even more striking is that these symmetrical groups overlap with a linguistic group of similar symmetry we examined in Chapter 2. That cluster of letters included the palindromic word הלילה / ha'laylah / the night, the word יהי / y'hiy / let it/there be and two copies of אתת / otot / signs. Now, with the addition of the twin digit triples, the symmetrical group has been expanded to include six components, utilising fourteen numbers or letters. So here again we have significant components of two different views of the Seal, which strongly reinforce one another.

Of course, I did say that the main purpose of the three digit triples is to provide emphasis for the digits 1, 4 and 6. And the particular combination we are encouraged to recognise is 614. This suggestion may come as a surprise when the tasselled garment we examined earlier is supposed to remind us of: ... *all the commands of the* LORD. And each of the digit triples points to a different member of that central 2×2 garment – in fact, the very ones that spell אֹהֶל / *ohel* / <u>a</u> <u>tent</u>. In Judaism the commands are believed to number 613. So it will be time well spent to ponder for a moment the importance of the number 613 in Judaism.

Among the theories as to why exactly 613 commands were given in the Torah, one involves their separation into negative (Thou shalt not...) and positive commands. A thorough analysis has shown that the 613 separates into 248 that are positive and 365 that are negative. It is a straightforward observation that the number of negative commands equates to the number of whole days in a solar year. But it is not so obvious why there should be 248 positive commands. One traditional suggestion is that the human body is composed of that number of components. But that only reflects a very narrow and clearly outdated understanding of the way our bodies work. It is all too easy to adapt that type of 'definition' to correspond to almost any number from 10 billion down to just 6.

A much better and more realistic suggestion is that the number 248 is bequeathed by the gematria of the name of Abraham (אַבְרָהַם). Not only is this verifiably true, but it has the very significant merit that the numbers 248 and 365 both correspond to characteristics we have seen in the word בְּרֵאשִׁית / *B'reishith* / <u>In the beginning</u>. We know that this very first word of the Torah makes multiple references to both Abraham and aspects of cyclic time, including dates and the names of three months. Through this line of reasoning, it is easy to understand the high regard Judaism affords to the number 613.

However, it is evident that the Seal is not emphasising 613 at all, but 614 instead. And the beginning of an explanation for this 'discrepancy' is found in the very lowest part of the square, where a small triangle of just six elements is formed from a 6-1-4-6-1-4 triangular sequence (see Figure 4.8, overleaf).

Without a doubt, this small triangle is the firmest possible foundation for the Y-shaped crucifix. Evidently we should understand the number 614 to be linked to New Testament events, rather than with the Torah alone. A further clue comes from the 'stone' tablets (*luchot*) depicted in this square. Two tablets with ten commandments are seen within the Ark at Sinai; but only one tablet is to be found nestled between the arms of the 'Y'. The crucifixion at Golgotha is the definitive demonstration of just one additional command having been added to the original 613. During his short ministry, Jesus is reported as saying:

> *Do not think that I have come to abolish the Law or the Prophets; I have not come to abolish them but to fulfil them.*
>
> (Matthew 5:17)

But that is only a reference to something more specific. As he also said:

> *But I tell you: Love your enemies and pray for those who persecute you,*
>
> (Matthew 5:44)

The fulfilment came on the point of death, when he was heard to say:

> *Father, forgive them; for they know not what they do.*
>
> (Luke 23:34)

The new command, to love our enemies is the only one that God did not impose on his people without first demonstrating that it is possible. Clearly, we have now identified a 614 to put with the 611, 612 and 613 we already know about. But the promised set of six significant consecutive numbers is still short of two members. And that is something I shall rectify in Chapter 6.

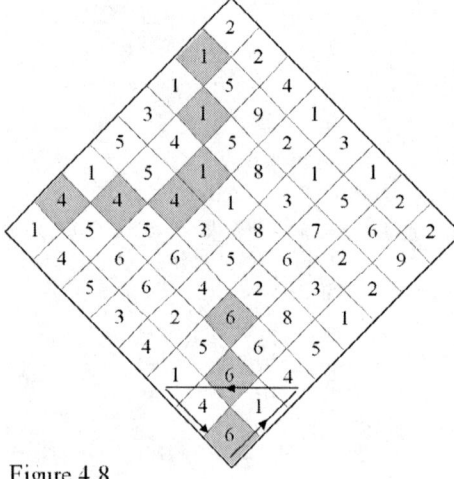

Figure 4.8

While we are still examining the 6-1-4-6-1-4 sequence and the 111 and 444 triples, there is yet another way in which they point to the crucifixion at Golgotha. These numbers and their conjunction within the Seal also provide an explanation for a rather mystifying portion of text found near the end of the Torah. Undoubtedly looking forward to New Testament events are these few enigmatic lines:

*How can one chase a thousand,*
*or two put ten thousand to flight,*
*Unless their rock had sold them*
*and the Lord had given them up*

(Deuteronomy 32:30)

If it could be shown that these lines are referring to the crucifixion of Jesus, then we would see clearly the way in which our rock had not 'sold' us. Quite the contrary, since he has done the very opposite and redeemed his faithful followers. All that is required, therefore, is to show that this text does indeed refer to the crucifixion of Jesus. And I shall complete the connection by demonstrating that the digits that gave us 614 are also capable of generating the ten thousand that were 'put to flight' by the two. The figure of ten thousand is based on two separate results in which one is 10,000 greater than the other.

The first value is obtained from the two upper digit triples, as follows:

$$444 \times 111 \quad = 49284$$

And the other value is obtained from the small triangular 614614 sequence (see Figure 4.8), by pairing digits from the left. This gives us 61, 46 and 14, which we proceed to multiply, so:

$$61 \times 46 \times 14 \quad = 39284$$

Hence the difference between the two results is:

$$49284 - 39284 \quad = 10000 \qquad \text{as intended.}$$

The true merit in this result stems from the fact that the Author's Seal – the first 64 letters of the Torah – contains a coded reference to a distinctive passage near the end of the Torah. So the Seal and that passage together are pointing straight to the New Testament, where the 614th commandment is found to be the fulfilment of the Torah. In fact, that cryptic passage cannot ever be understood in isolation. It requires the Seal on the Torah, as a square of qatan letter values to serve in a role that is comparable to an Enigma machine.

Already the number 614 is prominent enough and influential enough to merit its place in these accounts. The three linear triples: 666, 111 and 444 all make important contributions, either arithmetically or by their alternative symmetries, or both. And the 6-1-4-6-1-4 triangle at the foot of the crucified man has its own parts to play. But we are not yet finished with the enigmatic number 614.

In the Beginning

In the square of letters there is a 3×3 sub-group, placed symmetrically just over the arms of the crucified man, that clinches the matter. In Figure 4.9, the operative region is emphasised by a heavier surrounding border. In the highest position within this region we see the plain-text word פ נ י / *p'nei* / <u>a face</u> in the positions corresponding to 7-9-8 in the accompanying thumbnail sketch. There are also the words הא / *hey* / <u>behold!</u> (positions 1-5) and לח / *luach* / <u>a tablet</u> (positions 3-2) which we have already seen in the central 2×2 cluster. And there is a לאת / *l'ot* / <u>for a sign</u> (positions 4-5-6). Given the rules of biblical Hebrew grammar, the 3×3 region could be saying: *Behold, a face! A tablet for a sign.* So how do we know that these nine letters in particular are meant to convey a self-contained message? It is because the sum of the nine separate standard letter values is 614! And that is an awesome burden to have been placed on one man's shoulders.

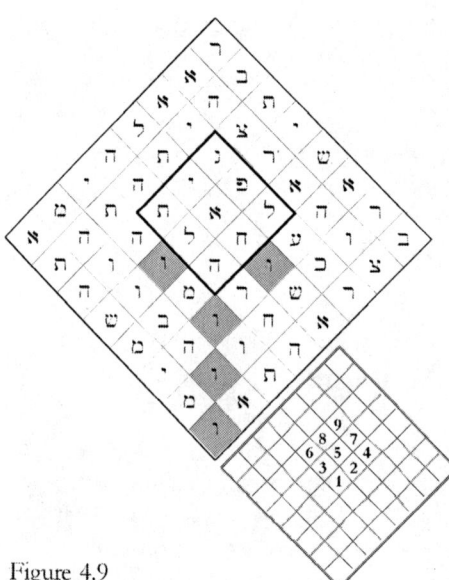

Figure 4.9

The standard letter values will also now start to put some flesh on the skeleton of an idea I mentioned only briefly in Chapter 2. There, I pointed out that the emergent word יהי / *y'hiy* / <u>let there be</u>, could combine with either of the two emergent copies of אור / *aur* / <u>light</u>, to form the first words spoken by God in the Creation. But now we can easily identify the appropriate copy of *aur*, by linking the emergent words to the numeric dimension of the Seal. First, we note that the emergent *y'hiy* (the crown of a 9-letter symmetrical group) sits directly over the 444 sequence we considered above. And the lower, ascending copy of *aur* is squeezed between the vertical 666 sequence and the emergent word לוחת / *luchot* / <u>tablets</u>. So it is of the utmost significance that the gematria of *luchot* is 444. To understand why the expression 'Let there be light' is associated with two copies of 444 will depend on a transformation that takes place in the next Chapter. However, the full explanation will have to wait until Chapter 6.

-oOo-

If there is one clear lesson that we can take from the present Chapter, it is the unerring connection that exists between the Torah and the New Testament. References to the original 613 Torah commands cannot and should not be ignored. These include the tassels on the corners of the inner layer of the square, which is therefore to be seen as a garment. And the number 613 as the sum of 365 and 248 (the gematria of Abraham) was established as a foundation that is evidently foreseen even from the first words of the Hebrew Bible. Yet it is the number 614 that is explicitly emphasised by the present version of the Seal. It is, moreover, emphasised in such a way that it can only be understood as the fulfilment of the 613, and then only through the agency of the crucified man.

To look at it from further back, facets of the Seal seen in these first four chapters all combine to demonstrate a vast strategic plan. There is a high degree of consistency in the way information has been squeezed firstly into the Torah's first six letters, then the first fourteen, the first 28 then the first 64. It is instructive to compare the extreme density of information encrypted within these 64 letters, with the relatively diffuse results that emerge in the better known Bible Code. Yet even those results are offered to the academic community as a discovery of momentous importance, on the basis of their calculated 'compactness'.

## 5

Rivers, we shall find, are a motif that will become our principal guide for a time. And an early herald of this theme came in the first square aspect of the Author's Seal, with the expression וְהֵנ נָהָר / *v'hey nahar* / <u>And behold, a river</u>! We shall tentatively assume that that expression refers to:

> *...the water of life, bright as crystal, flowing from the throne of God and the Lamb through the middle of the street of the city.*
> (Revelation 22:1-2).

And that 6-letter expression was indeed flowing through the middle of the street of the city that is the Seal, in the top of its vertical axis.

We have also seen: *Moses, image of Yah*, the prophet who as an infant was entrusted to the waters of the river of Egypt – the Nile - but at the end of his life was not permitted to cross the River Jordan. The Jordan in particular and one other biblical river play a special joint role in revealing their mutual importance through their gematria values. The other river is the כְּבָר / *Chebar* / <u>Chebar</u>, alongside which the prophet Ezekiel experienced his visions of God's chariot throne and four 'living creatures'. I shall return to the subject of the living creatures in two later chapters. But for now we may simply note that the gematria of Chebar is 222, while that of יַרְדֵן / *Yardan* / <u>Jordan</u> is 264. These two gematria sums can remind us of a property of any square with one or both of its diagonals drawn, by means of this relationship:

$$\frac{264}{222} \times \frac{264}{222} = 1.414171$$

That is:
$$\left(\frac{264}{222}\right)^2 \cong \sqrt{2} \quad \text{(within 0.003\%)}$$

Recall that √2 is the exact result of dividing the length of a diagonal in any square by the length of its side.

The Jordan's biblical importance is that it is the river the Israelites needed to cross to reach their promised land 40 years after leaving Egypt, and the step that Moses was not allowed to make at the end of his life. And Ezekiel's visions took place during the Babylonian exile. So, in effect, we are being confronted with two rivers that are both intimately associated with the two biblical periods of captivity for the Israelites. Furthermore, both 264 and 222 have other links to the Author's square Seal. To begin with, 222 is the square root of the product of the two symmetrical homogeneous triples we found there and examined in the previous Chapter. That is:

$$222^2 = 111 \times 444$$

And we already know that the result of either one of these products (ie 49284) helps in explaining a previously obscure passage near the end of the Torah. So the mathematical square of 222 certainly has wider biblical relevance; but so too does the square of 264, which is 69696. Not only is the latter number palindromic (a form of literary symmetry), but it also happens to be a perfect fit for the 8×8 square in which the Seal reveals its greatest potential. This happens because 264 is exactly divisible by 8, so that 69696 may be distributed evenly throughout the 64 elements of the larger square. But it does so in such a way that each element contains a perfect 33×33 array. That is to say:

$$8 \times 8 \times 33 \times 33 = 264^2 = 69696$$

It is worth noting here that the next nearest numbers that will fit the 8×8 Seal so perfectly are 65536 (below) and 73984 (above). There is a difference of around 4000 in each case, demonstrating that these perfect-fit numbers are quite rare. But 69696 is the only one that also happens to be palindromic.

Nor should we assume that the above description of 'perfect fit' applies only to the Author's Seal. It is surprising to discover that the book of Ezekiel itself (from which we obtained the 222 of Chebar) has, from ancient times, made use of the same phenomenon, a clue to the veracity of the Seal. According to one authority:

> Oddly, a set of sixty-four marble and granite tablets with
> the entire book of Ezekiel carved in raised letters, laid out

in a square grid, and also written in *scripta continua*, was
discovered in Iraq during Israel's War for Independence.

(Satinover, 1997, p54)

Whoever took the time and enormous trouble to carve those 64
stones – and we cannot discount it being Ezekiel himself – was
probably as much aware of the reality of the Seal as we are now. Later,
I shall show spectacular evidence that this is indeed the case. But since
I have now hinted that an Old Testament book might, just might have
been contrived to agree with the Seal, it will surely occur to my reader
sooner-or-later that I did not make the same suggestion in relation to
the New Testament gospels. That is to say, I did not suggest in
Chapter 2 that artefacts in the square of text may have been the direct
inspiration and source for imaginative writers of those books. In fact,
in neither case do I think that is a satisfactory explanation for the
origin of the Judeo-Christian scriptures. I merely avoided the question
until now, because there was still a risk that the Seal itself might have
been assumed to be a human contrivance. Indeed the time of Ezekiel
and the Babylonian exile would have been the perfect opportunity to
perpetrate so cruel a hoax. That was an extended period of about 70
years during which the intelligencia of Jewish society had been
uprooted from their homeland, isolated from their people and
collected together with copious time on their hands. This was, after all,
the same period in which the Babylonian Talmud – the most
important collection of all commentaries on the Torah – was initiated.
But a point comes, either already or in the next chapters, when it is no
longer tenable to suppose
that the Seal is man-made.
There can never have been
a human mind with the
inventive capacity needed
for that task. Therefore, any
biblical writer who was
aware of the Seal would
certainly view it as a divine
revelation, and treat it with
due reverence.

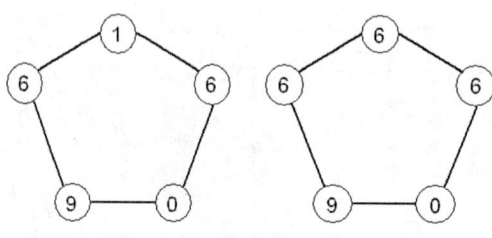

Figure 5.1

Now recall the two pentagonal numbers, which in the previous
Chapter we obtained from the 304,805 letter length of the whole
Torah. The relevant illustration is repeated as Figure 5.1. If we now
combine them into the configuration shown by Figure 5.2, the nodes
that contain numbers reveal a perimeter with a sequence 6-0-9-6-0-9-6,
reading clockwise from the shaded 6. Then, by ignoring the zeros, we

are left with 69696, the square of 264. Notice, by the way, that the sum of these perimeter digits is 36, then the inclusion of the internal 1 increases the overall total to 37. Here again we find the same two numbers that are the qatan sums in the Seal's square diagonals, now bequeathed by the complete Torah. So here we have further evidence that the entire length of the Torah is strongly bound to its first 64 letters (through the perfect fit 69696).

Incidentally, the empty upper and lower nodes in Figure 5.2 have been included only to show the similarity between the result we have obtained from a physical characteristic of the Torah and a diagram known from Jewish Kabbalah (see Figure 5.3, overleaf). The latter is described variously as the Tree of Life or as the Ten Sephirot. Note also the five shaded nodes of the Tree of Life. Not only do these resemble the outline of the crucified man revealed by the Seal, but the one on the left (named Gevurah) represents judgement, and Hesed on the right is mercy. These correspond to Jesus' responses to the two men who were crucified to the left and right of him. Only the one who bore witness to Jesus' innocence was granted the merciful promise of a direct passage to paradise.

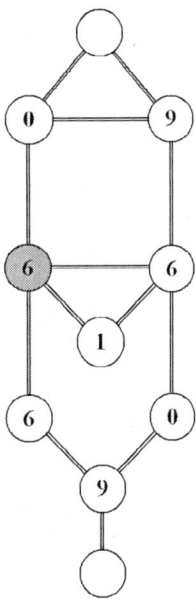

**Figure 5.2**

These references to the Kabbalah are not idle comment, since it will be another of its concepts that will enable us to recognise further content in the Seal.

-oOo-

To create a new view of the Seal, we shall find it necessary to make one tiny but all-important modification. This will be one of those decisive stages where the basic text at the start of Genesis – the intact Seal – must be broken and re-made. The first time we rearranged the same text, the guiding principle came from the very structure of the first verse. On this new occasion, however, the clue has an external origin. Though whether or not that source is truly independent of the Seal as we now know it, may be open to speculation.

It will also be helpful to introduce some new terminology at this point. Up to now we have enjoyed the simplicity of working with a single square arrangement. And although it was first populated with letters, then later with numbers, it was nonetheless the same square.

## In the Beginning

But very soon we will find ourselves looking at a second square, then a third and, eventually, a fourth. So, from here on, I shall refer to the first square as G1 (where G stands for Genesis), the next one as G2, and those that follow as G3 and G4.

From the very start, while I was examining the beginning of Genesis and making fresh discoveries, I found it both interesting and fruitful to learn more about the Jewish perspective on life and the Torah. One thing I recognised very quickly is what seems to be a strange contradiction in the Jewish outlook. On the one hand, an Orthodox Jew will not speak the four-letter name of the Lord (the Tetragrammaton) due to reverence and observance of the third commandment (of the Ten). Yet, on the other hand, the pursuit of relevant mystical knowledge is, if not actually encouraged, then at least accepted freely. And any new knowledge or wisdom that emerges from the search is suitably cherished. The one activity that is, of course, strictly forbidden is divination – the pursuit of knowledge of the future and the power that such knowledge might confer.

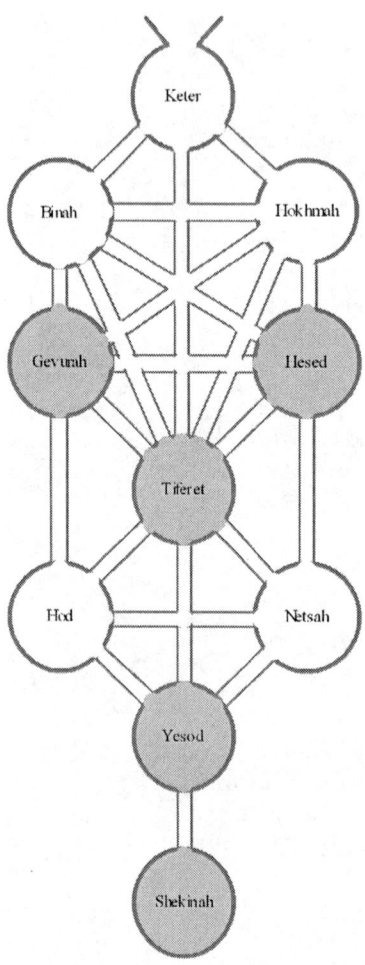

**Figure 5.3**

Jewish Kabbalah is just one branch of mysticism that is widely known about, even if not well understood. And it is one of the tenets of Kabbalah that, for me, opened the door to the second stage of the Seal (G2). Kabbalists believe that, at the very moment of Creation, one aspect of God remained outside, while another entered the created world. The inner aspect is known as Small Face, and the outer one as Vast Face. Each is represented in the Hebrew alephbeyt by one of the two silent letters; the symbol for Small Face is the first letter, *aleph* (א), while that of Vast Face is *ayin* (ע). In one way, the G1 square has already given notice that Small Face will be found within his creation. The letters in its E, S and W corner squares spell בֹּא / *bo* / <u>He entered</u>. And although their distribution looks very similar to בְּרָא / *bara* / <u>He created</u> found in the E, N and W corners, the newer word would not be found by an Equidistant Letter Sequence (ELS) search. Since its letters are at positions 1, 22 and 15 of the plain text, in that order.

There is only one copy of the letter ayin in the Seal; in the G1 square it was located precisely on the W-E diagonal in the right side. Sequentially, this letter is the 49th in the Torah which (as 7×7) seems quite relevant given the seven day context of the creation account, as well as the many other ways the number seven is emphasised. And ayin is also the first letter to enter the third layer of that square, working inwards from the beginning. Also relevant is the contextual position of this letter, as it starts the expression עַל פְּנֵי / *aal pnei* / <u>upon the face</u> (from: *darkness was upon the face of the deep*). It is not completely out of the question that Kabbalah arrived at the term Vast Face for this very reason. Yet it seems to me unlikely that Kabbalah seized on this dualistic vision of the Creator based on the same understanding of the Seal as our own, given its many clear references to the founder of Christianity. But we might entertain the idea that Kabbalists started by looking upon the same Seal from another angle, on the strength of its equally clear links to many Old Testament events. And, as we shall soon see, the Seal seems to indicate that the assumption of Vast Face on the outside of Creation is valid after all, regardless of the route by which it is discovered.

The transition from G1 to G2 begins with the removal of the letter ayin, symbol of Vast Face, to a position just outside the eastern corner of the square – metaphorically outside the created world. There, it takes up a position as prefix to the normally first letter beyt. Then, just as nature abhors a vacuum, the space or hole left by the missing ayin must be filled. This is accomplished by each of the subsequent letters shuffling one place nearer to the beginning. Overall, most letters that move do so within their existing layer, except for letter #61, a *chet* (ח), which jumps out of the fourth layer – the central cluster – into the third. It is surely an intentional metaphor that, as each successive letter in turn moves nearer to the beginning, the hole it leaves moves like a bubble towards the centre of the square. Finally, the reshuffling that takes place within the central cluster leaves one final gap, which is filled by the 65th letter, a *yud* (י) that was originally excluded from G1 by truncation. Now the bubble has reached the surface of the water and burst, leaving the surface smooth again. How

# In the Beginning

odd, yet totally appropriate, that the verse affected by this transformation ends: *and the spirit of God moved upon the face of the waters.*

The new G2 square still contains 64 letters, but that number now includes the 65th letter of the regular Torah text. The net effect is shown in Figure 5.4, in which I have emphasised what I consider to be the most important outcome. Notice that in this new facet of the square, the two outer layers have not changed, but the two inner layers – constituting a perfect 4×4 square - have both been rotated by one letter position. This is not unlike the movement in a combination lock, and the effect is indeed to unlock substantial amounts of new information. The visually arresting new shape (shaded letters) is a case in point. But this is just the first of many new artefacts that occur in this square, many in the same positions as important objects that we saw in its pre-cursor. In effect, we are seeing the outcome of *all things made anew* (from Revelation 21:5).

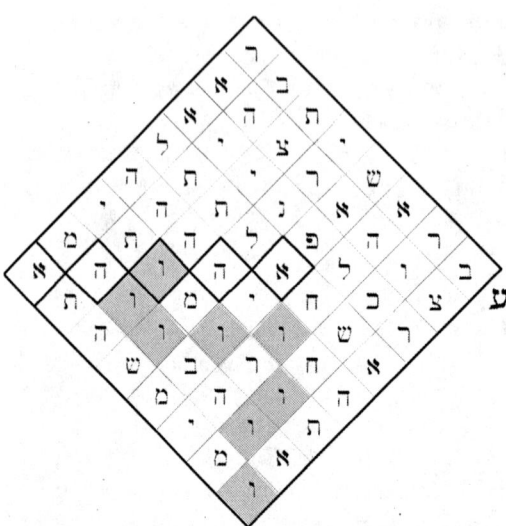

**Figure 5.4**

As in the G1 square, the highlighted winding shape is composed entirely from the letter vav – altogether eight of them from only nine found in this text. It is important to be aware of how the new winding shape came about - that it involved only the 16 letters in the central 4×4 cluster, which included only three copies of vav. These three copies of vav are the only ones that moved during the transformation; the other six stayed in their original locations, waiting to be connected together as we now see them. What is more, since I suggested at an early stage that the letter vav in the Seal might be symbolic of water, there is every reason to suppose this new shape to be a river. And this is the concept I propose to develop first. Obviously the 'sea' we found in the G1 square, and now the river in G2, are both suitable environments in which the suggested bubble might perform its divine ballet.

There is one particular, emergent word in the new square that, from a biblical perspective, explicitly identifies the winding shape as a river. It is a word that did not exist in the G1 aspect of the Seal, but is created by the new transformation. This is אהוה / *Ahavah* / Ahavah from:

> *I gathered them together to the river that runneth to Ahavah,*
> *and there abode we in tents three days.*
>
> (Ezra 8:15)

There is, in the square, a choice of two versions of Ahavah, from a horizontal palindromic sequence אהוהא (heavier borders in Figure 5.4) which may be read in either direction. And since the middle letter of the group is the uppermost letter *vav*, it is in this sense that our river 'runneth to Ahavah'. Observe also that this palindromic sequence shares the same vertical axis of symmetry as was seen in a symmetrical group of nine letters in the G1 square, which I described in Chapter 2. There, I gave notice of further cases of coincident symmetry such as the one we now see. Moreover, the centre of this square now depicts the letters of אהל / *ohel* / a tent in a distinctly tent-like configuration, corresponding to Ezra's: *and there abode we in tents three days.* The duration of Ezra's sojourn may have much to do with the period from Jesus' crucifixion to his subsequent resurrection.

The book of Ezra is one of the select few that are favoured by recognition from within the Seal. It is also among the shortest in the Bible, with only ten chapters. Yet it is one of only four in which, in addition, the number 666 may be found. In Ezra 2, where he describes the return of the first wave of exiles from Babylon to Jerusalem, the heads of families are listed along with the numbers of their kinsmen. One of these is:

> *Adonikam, six hundred and sixty-six*
>
> (Ezra 2:13)

…where, additionally, the word Adonikam means 'my Lord is risen'. I am, of course, suggesting that 666 associated with 'my Lord is risen' is meant to correspond to the 666 sequences in both the G1 and G2 versions of the Seal (ie three copies of the letter vav in linear formations). This could only mean that Ezra may have known of the existence of the Seal, one of very few who, throughout history, have shared this knowledge. But it does not prove that he had any inkling of future New Testament events. Even more tantalizing is the presence, three verses earlier, of the name Bani, which means 'my son'. And three verses before that is one of a most curious pair of entries. The first of them is:

# In the Beginning

*The sons of Elam, one thousand two hundred and fifty-four,*

(Ezra 2:7)

then later:

*The sons of the other Elam, one thousand two hundred and fifty-four,*

(Ezra 2:31)

The listing of two identically named family heads, accompanied by an identical 1254 kinsmen may be custom made to arouse curiosity and invite the reader to seek for a hidden meaning. But the hidden meaning cannot be revealed in this book.

As to the river that flows to Ahavah, the spelling I gave earlier (אהוה) is, naturally, the one seen in the G2 square. It occurs precisely in the W-E diagonal, and of course includes the uppermost letter vav of the winding river. However, for this Ahavah to correspond directly to the text of Ezra, we shall have to resolve a small difficulty, since Ezra does not spell Ahavah in the same way. Happily the explanation is straightforward, since the Ahavah mentioned by Ezra was not originally a Hebrew word. From his point of view, Ahavah is the local name of a river in Babylonia. In describing his geographical location, Ezra's role was limited to providing a Hebrew transliteration (sound-alike) for a foreign word. In fact his options were inhibited to some extent by the fact that Ahavah sounds like the Hebrew word for 'love'; and he would most assuredly have wished to avoid that connotation becoming linked to the abhorrent land of his people's exile. Therefore Ezra opted to spell the name as אהוא. Neither does the Author's Seal spell the name the same as 'love', which is אהבה. If the intention is to avoid using the word 'love', then Ezra did the more thorough job by making two letter changes, where the Seal occupies the medial position. Nonetheless, Ezra has made it clear that he had knowledge of, if not the Seal itself, then the underlying wisdom on which it is based.

The presence of overlapping copies of a word that sounds just like the Hebrew for 'love', combining as they do to form a palindrome, could not be more significant. Especially as the middle letter of that palindrome is also the final element of the ascending river; and Ezra associates the number 666 with the name of Adonikam (*my Lord is risen*). All we need to realise is that the river graphic in the G2 square is derived directly from the prominent 'Y' shape of the crucified man in G1. In fact, the only copies of the letter vav to be affected by the transformation are the three that marked the corners of a central 3×3 square. These are the same three that depict the upper 'V' component of the prominent 'Y' shape. In the G1 aspect of the Seal, the presence of five wounds, rather than four, indicated that the man was already dead. And the six letters ascending vertically from his head: נהור ‏והא / v'*hey nahar* / <u>And behold – a river</u>! gave notice of what was about to happen. For that is what we have just seen in Figure 5.4.

Another reference to rivers in the G2 square will remind us of Genesis Chapter 2, and the river that *went out of Eden to water the garden*. This is the river that was parted into four heads; and in Chapter 3 we found a cryptic reference to the first of those heads named Pison, *which compasseth the whole land of Havilah*. That should call to mind the concept of perfect fit that I described earlier, when we recall that the location where the first letter *samech* (ס) occurs in the Torah (ie letter #2210) gives rise to a perimeter that is the best fit of any perfect square for the entire Torah text. That particular samech is within the word 'compasseth', associated with that first of four rivers. And the fourth of those named rivers is the only one that we can identify today. It is the פרת / *Parot* / <u>Euphrates</u>, which we now see as a vertical sequence of letters in Figure 5.5.

The meaning of the meandering string of eight copies of the letter *vav* is not limited to the concept of rivers. For example, it closely resembles a stylised letter *lamed* (ל). Anyone searching for a Hebrew typeface or font to use with a desktop computer will find plenty to choose from. In this book, the Hebrew font I am using is called SPEzra, and the letter lamed in this font is only slightly different from the highlighted shape in the G2 square. The latter shape could be considered the outcome from merging many of the various characteristics of the letter lamed from the numerous available scripts. It is in this sense that I describe

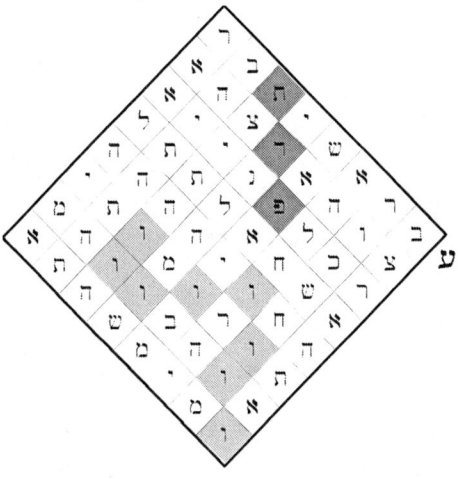

**Figure 5.5**

the shape in the square as stylised. Nor is it accidental that the shape in the square looks like the head of a shepherd's crook. The pictogram for lamed in the ancient, proto-Hebrew alephbeyt was indeed a shepherd's crook. The shepherd uses his crook as either a hook or a goad to keep members of his flock in check. Likewise, the letter lamed is symbolic of teaching and learning, both of which words in Hebrew are spelled the same as the name of the letter (though pronounced differently, of course). And the corresponding meaning of the lamed shape in the square could not be clearer, since it is derived directly from the crucified man in the G1 square; that is he who is both shepherd and Lamb. The teaching and learning being demonstrated here we know corresponds to the invocation:

*Father forgive them for they know not what they do.*

(Luke 23:34)

...and is the perfect fulfilment of the 614th commandment, to 'love those who persecute you'. Also, since the lamed river is a direct adaptation from the 'Y' of the crucified man, it is worth pointing out the most direct interpretation of the removal of the letter ayin to be outside the square. So when, from Golgotha, 'darkness was over all the land', it is written:

*And about the ninth hour Jesus cried with a loud voice, "Eli, Eli, lama sabachthani?" That is, "My God, My God, why hast thou forsaken me?"*

(Matthew 27:46)

If the God that Jesus was addressing is synonymous with the Vast Face of Kabbalah, as now seems likely, this will have two important implications for the New Testament gospels. First, the 'forsaking' to which Jesus was referring is perfectly synonymous with the removal of the letter ayin. Also, when the ayin was still within the G1 square, it was part of the emergent word [ף] עלם / *alaph* / a veil or curtain. Therefore, when the ayin is removed, that would be equivalent to the passage:

*And behold, the curtain of the temple was torn in two from top to bottom ...*

(Matthew 27:51)

The lamed-river shape makes the very same point but in a novel way. Recall in Chapter 2 that I suggested the co-terminal *aur* (light) and *aur* (skin) in the G1 square might represent a reversal of the path of expulsion from Eden. At the time, I said there would be two further ways in which the Seal will confirm this reverse-path hypothesis. The next of them is now visible in the G2 square, in the river-*cum*-lamed shape, and its resemblance to the shape of a serpent we saw in the qatan values of Genesis 1:1. In Figure 5.6, I have simply removed the first and last elements from the original 1-4-1-4-1-4-1-4-1-4 sequence (see Figure 3.6a). Thus leaving a shape that is, despite minimal distortion, unmistakably like the river in G2. The fact that this twinning has been achieved by removing the top and tail links may correspond to the verse:

> *I will put enmity between thee and the woman, and between thy seed and her seed; it shall bruise thy head, and thou shalt bruise his heel.*

(Genesis 3:15)

For the Author of the Torah to replicate the same shape in ways that have completely reverse meanings has a hugely important significance that is easy to understand. One version is composed of the repeating digits '14', and the other entirely of 6s. And, since the new G2 version of this river is the outcome of the man who is crucified in G1, the allusion to the number 614 is unmistakable. This is the same 614th commandment, to love our enemies and those who persecute us.

A closely related interpretation for this lamed is offered by a legend (my assumption) that is closely allied to the Jewish belief in a Messiah. It is said that in every generation there are always thirty-six especially righteous men in the world, any one of whom has the potential to become the Messiah should the right circumstances arise. The formal title of the thirty-six is צדיקים‎ / *Tzaddiqim* / <u>The Righteous Ones</u>. But because there are thirty-six of them, they also go by the colloquialism *The Lamed Vavniks*; the reason being that the standard Jewish method of representing the number 36 employs the letters lamed and vav. The legend of the thirty-six is most definitely a Jewish one. So it is both strange and highly significant that, in the G2 version of the Seal, it is the Christian understanding of Messiah (Greek: *Christos*) that is represented by eight letters vav in the shape of a lamed.

| 2 | 2 | 1 | 3 |
|---|---|---|---|
| 1 | 4 | 2 | 2 |
| 1 | 1 | 3 | 5 |
| 1 | 4 — 1 — 4 |   |   |
| 5 | 3 | 4 — 1 |   |
| 4 | 6 | 1 | 4 |
| 5 | 1 | 2 | 9 |

Figure 5.6

Perhaps the most awesome effect to be seen in the G2 square is the sequence of landmarks encountered by the lamed river as it pursues its journey upwards. In Figure 5.7, I have marked a number of words that further suggest the restoration of the order that had initially existed in Eden.

First, there is a horizontal 3-letter emergent word חרב / *Cherev* / <u>a sword</u> (marked in thumbnail sketch (a) with an 'x' character) placed symmetrically across the N-S diagonal. This corresponds to:

> *and* [the Lord God] *placed at the east of the garden of Eden Cherubims, and a flaming sword which turned every way, to keep the way to the Tree of Life.*

> (Genesis 3:24)

But in what sense can we regard the sword as 'flaming'? For the answer to this, look at the letters in the main square that correspond to the elements coloured black in thumbnail (a). These letters, which enclose the sword, spell אש / *esh* / <u>fire</u>. Given the circumstances which give rise to the G2 image, it is happy news indeed that the lamed river passes through this sword without ever touching it.

Next look at the letters corresponding to the elements I have numbered 1, 2, 3 and 4 in thumbnail (b). Notice firstly that these are the very same positions in which we found the digits 1-6-6-6 in the G1 square of qatan letter values. This is another beautiful example of one square facet of the Seal latching to another on the precise alignment of significant artefacts. When we first saw

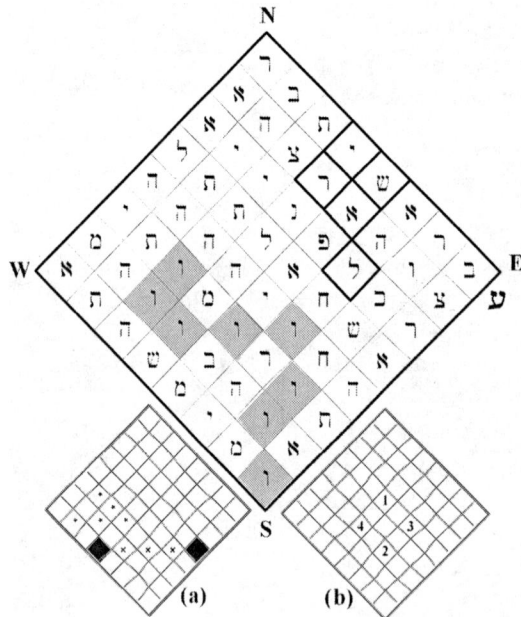

Figure 5.7

beautiful example of one square facet of the Seal latching to another on the precise alignment of significant artefacts. When we first saw those digits they were interpreted as the number 1.666, which is a reasonable approximation to the number Phi (Φ), also known as the divine proportion. That number helped to confirm that the image of the crucified man is meant, among other things, to represent a new Ark (of a new covenant). But now, in our new G2 square, the letters at positions marked 1-3-4 spell לחם / *lechem* / <u>bread</u>. This is not the unleavened bread (*matzah*) associated with the flight of the Israelites from Egypt and with the Ark in the tabernacle, but bread that has been allowed to rise. Incidentally, the square also contains an emergent word יין / *yayin* / <u>wine</u> just above the bread, which Christian readers may find interesting. We shall have reason to return to this yayin in a later Chapter.

The letters that correspond to positions 2-3-4 in the thumbnail spell, רחם [ם] / *racham* / <u>a womb</u>; and the river of living water is seen to flow straight through this womb, passing in two stages between alternative pairs of its letters. This could correspond to the gospel reference to the otherwise bizarre idea of being 'born again'.

We have now reached a point at which we may see important progress in one aspect of the vast strategic plan. This is a trend that began in the G1 square, where we saw the name of ישראל (Israel) spelled within a compact 3×3 zone that also contained *fruit, earth* and *for a root*. In its configuration there, however, 'Israel' seemed less well formed than other emergent words. On the other hand, it was intimately entwined with the letters of יצר / *yatzar* / <u>to form</u> or <u>mould</u>, which remain unchanged and still visible in Figure 5.7. I made a particular comparison between those two words and a passage of text at Isaiah 44:1-2, which speaks of *Israel* being '*formed* as God's special servant, even from the *womb*'. And in the G2 square, it is now possible to see ישראל (Israel) formed into a more perfect symmetrical configuration (letters with heavier borders in Figure 5.7), through a tiny displacement of the letter lamed (ל). It is surely no accident that the symbolic perfecting of Israel is accomplished by the very letter that has replaced the migrated ayin, and is the same letter that is now the headline artefact for the whole square. However, although the present aspect of the Seal now includes a most significant *racham* (womb) through which the headline lamed-river flows, this is not the only womb we seek. An equally important womb will be seen when we reach Chapter 7, along with a remarkable multi-functional artefact in the very same symmetrical configuration in which we now see 'Israel'.

It is quite staggering the number of ways the Seal is designed to bring clarity to passages in the Bible that are otherwise difficult to understand. We should, however, be wary of a real danger that the Seal might be accepted as the sole explanation for certain biblical texts, so that we abandon other, more traditional possibilities. In other words, the biblical authors could be assumed to have composed their works based only on the Seal as a template. As though to stress this warning, we need to be aware that the womb seen in the G2 square does not represent the birth-origin of the crucified man, but a portal through which he is later projected. As we shall find in the third version of the Seal, this womb also has a close affinity with Abraham with whom, incidentally, it shares a gematria of 248. Notice, by the way, how this shared gematria now confers an alternative source of 248 that may be combined with the number of whole days in the solar year, to generate the number of God's commandments in the Torah (ie 248 + 365 = 613). In the final Chapter, we shall see how the G2 womb really has been hijacked by the writers of well-known, post-biblical literature, who have adopted the Seal falsely as their template.

Incidentally, the shared 248 gematria of Abraham and 'womb' is typical of the traditional use of Hebrew numerology, in seeking additional underlying numerical relationships between biblical words and names. In this case, Abraham may be seen as personifying the 'womb' that has given rise to many nations, as promised at Genesis 17:4. And that is the verse that immediately precedes the re-naming of Abram to Abraham, thus changing its gematria from 243 (ie 3×3×3×3×3) to 248. Our own use of gematria in this book is presently less formal, but has the potential to be formalised subsequently.

Even now, it is possible to recognise the evolving role of the womb/bread conjunction. The four letters from which they are composed are at the four corners of a 3×3 square area that was previously defined by the upper part of the crucified man. Yet, in the G1 square, the same four letters were already visible in a more compact arrangement, as the middle positions in the four sides of the same 3×3 area. Earlier in the present Chapter, I described the effect of removing the letter ayin as equivalent to opening a combination lock. And the 'opening' action is easiest to see in the effect that change has had on the womb and bread. The bread has risen to the uppermost part of the topical 3×3 zone; and the womb has been opened to allow the waters of the river of life to pass through.

Now, we already know that the final destination of the lamed river is Ahavah (a cryptic allusion to 'love'). But before it reaches that goal, it has to pass through two identical emergent words that are marked *** in thumbnail (a) of Figure 5.7. This word is מות / *mut* / to die, and it is a direct reference to Eden where the Lord God tells Adam that he may not eat of the tree of knowledge of good and evil,

> *...for in the day that thou eatest thereof thou shalt surely die.*
> (Genesis 2:17)

The key point here is in the precise phrase 'surely die' which, in the original Hebrew, is expressed by the rare use of a repeated verb[j]: מות תמות / *mut t'mut* / dying, you shall die. Therefore, the double encounter of the river with *mut*, who's middle letter vav (a spike) they share is again alluding to the expulsion of Adam and Eve from paradise, which we now see being undone.

Finally, the river arrives at Ahavah. And, as we noted earlier, Ezra also sojourned at this place for 'three days in tents' (a tent being a garment for a whole family), just as the New Testament describes Jesus' resurrection on the third day. Bear in mind that it is inconceivable that Ezra could have known how his merely factual report would one day be re-enacted in a cosmic purpose; even to the extent of the 666 kinsmen of Adonikam (*my Lord is risen*) becoming associated with a crucified man, as seen in the G1 square.

We now move on from the G2 square's allusions to New Testament events. But there are numerous other relevant artefacts still to be described in this square. For example, observe the shaded region in Figure 5.8 (overleaf). The more-deeply shaded elements with thicker borders have three especially important characteristics.

1. They include a remarkable linear sequence of four copies of the letter *heh* (ה),
2. The whole group has bi-lateral symmetry, and
3. It includes a 2×4 area that coincides with an area in the G1 square which contained the cyclic words *ha'laylah* (the night) and *otot* (signs). Here we see another example of one aspect of the Seal latching to another on a precisely defined location.

At the moment, that symmetrical configuration may simply serve to maintain our interest in this very important region of the Seal. But its full significance will only become apparent when we come to

---

[j] There are only 77 cases of such double words in the Torah.

examine the G3 version. One more point is worth mentioning specifically. There is a square group of letters (marked 'x' in the thumbnail sketch) that spell יהוה (YHWH), the Tetragrammaton. This group overlaps with one letter of the 'ההההה' sequence, and with two letters of אהוהא, from which we obtain two alternative copies of Ahavah. And, just as the palindromic הלילה / ha'laylah / the night

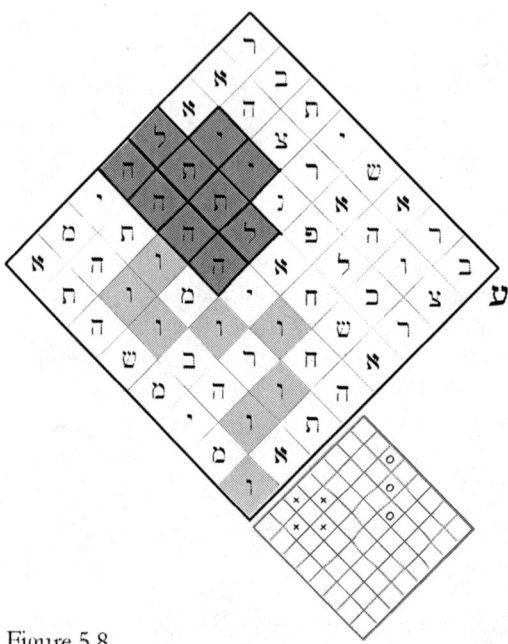

could be read cyclically in the earlier 2×4 group, so YHWH can be read cyclically in both directions here. Given that the four-letter name of God is spelled with three of the most commonly used Hebrew letters, it is perhaps surprising that we have not yet seen it spelled out as a linear sequence in his Seal. That is an omission which will be rectified by the G3 square, where the positions of the current cyclic group will be found to adopt another splendid latching role.

Figure 5.8

One last notable cluster of letters within the G2 square remains to be discussed. A little earlier, we noted the presence of פרת / Parot / Euphrates flowing vertically in the direction of the N-E side. This word also coincides with a position which, in the G1 square, was seen to contain the emergent words 'fruit' and 'for a root' associated with the word 'earth' (or 'land') of the regular text. All of this was within a 3×3 square cluster of letters, and the new Euphrates is now the diagonal of the exact same positions in the new square – yet another example of latching. In the G1 square, we also found the letters that spell Yisrael (Israel), therefore completing the expression 'Land of Israel'. So it is very significant that the name [ן] פאר / Paran / Paran is now found squeezed into a 2×2 section of the same 3×3 group. Paran is the name of the first place in the desert to which the Israelites marched, with the Ark at their head, after leaving the mountain at Sinai. The precise position of Paran, already noteworthy here, will become even more significant at two subsequent stages, including the next. What is more, the tiny mutation in the text that generates the name Paran is the same that transforms the original compressed Israel into its latest, symmetrical metamorphosis as described earlier.

-oOo-

At this point, our focus shifts away from structures in the square that are created by the migration of the letter ayin. Instead, we shall spend some productive time looking at the localised effect of that letter's new position. In particular, as prefix to the Torah the ayin combines with the letters of the first word בראשית / B'reishith / <u>In the beginning</u> in two especially meaningful ways.

First, we should cast our minds back to Chapter 1 and the rich allusions to Abraham contained in the first word, as well as in tandem with the third word. One that is especially important is the word ברית / *brit* / <u>covenant</u> formed of letters 1, 2, 5 and 6. This is the result of lifting out the middle two letters which spell אש / *esh* / <u>fire</u>, corresponding to:

> *a smoking furnace and a burning lamp that passed between those pieces*

> (Genesis 15:17)

And, as we know, this covenant combines with מילה / *Milah* from the third word to generate the expression Brit Milah, the Jewish Covenant of Circumcision.

Now, when the letter ayin (ע) is prefixed to the word 'covenant', an entirely new word is created, viz. עברית / *Ivrit* / <u>Hebrew</u> (the language). So here we see a two-pronged reminder: first that Hebrew is part of the cultural heritage of the heirs of the first patriarch. But equally that language *per se* is the medium of creation, and that Hebrew in particular is the language of the Torah. By now, of course, there will be no doubt in anyone's mind concerning the crucial, multi-layered role of Hebrew in the structure of the Torah, since it would be totally unrealistic to imagine the Pentateuch in any other language revealing the amount of underlying structure we have seen.

The other immediate effect of the ayin as prefix is that, when viewed as a suffix to the first three letters of Torah (which independently would mean 'he created'), the four letters together spell ארבע / *arba* / <u>four</u> (feminine case). Up to now there has been little indication that the number four is in any way special. But that gap in our understanding is about to change dramatically. If we wish to understand the unique importance of 'four', we shall be obliged to take a rather lengthy detour that will take up most of the rest of the present Chapter. This is necessary to help us understand a curious emphasis the Bible places on a relationship between names and numbers.

Of course, we know the four-letter name of God, the Tetragrammaton, is highly revered in Judaism, and it is the one used most extensively throughout the Torah wherever man encounters God personally. In fact, the way in which this name is introduced in Genesis is strange enough to warrant some close attention. For example, it is subject to an overarching pattern of gradual revelation. The first Chapter of Genesis does not declare the four-letter name at all; the name used there is Elohim (God), emphasising majestic power, omnipotence. More especially, there is no direct interplay at a personal level between man and this rather aloof God. The four-letter name – the LORD - is first seen explicitly in Genesis 2:4, at the very end of the first creation account. Here, it is attached to 'God' as the composite *YHWH Elohim* – the LORD God. The same dual format continues throughout the next two and a half chapters (mostly events in the garden of Eden) until, in Genesis 4:1, we see the personal name, YHWH, unencumbered for the first time. This is the precise moment when Adam and Eve have just been expelled from the garden in their new 'garments of skin'. That much is plain to see in the Torah text, even in translations. From this point, the LORD is very active with his human charges, in a world that is more recognisably like our own.

What is not so easily noticed, even in the original Hebrew, is a related underpinning structure that runs parallel to the first creation account, from its first verse to its last. One thing we *have* already seen is that the first verse includes an 8-letter sequence which, in reverse, spells משה תאם יה / *Moshe ta'am yah* / <u>Moses, image</u> (or <u>twin</u>) <u>of</u> <u>Yah</u>. More importantly, the name Moshe is the reverse spelling of the word *HaShem* – literally 'The Name' – which is a standard Jewish circumlocution for the explicit four-letter name. And this may be a deliberate veiled reference to the Lord, as opposed to God the omnipotent. Then, as already mentioned, at the opposite end of the creation account YHWH is seen explicitly for the first time. Oddly, but very significantly, the letters of YHWH also come together (albeit overlapping two words) for the first time in Genesis 1:14. And one of those two words is the first occurrence of the palindromic word

הַלַּיְלָה / *halaylah* / the night[k]. This is, of course, the word seen in the G1 square, in a compact cyclic arrangement directly over one of that square's axes of symmetry. And symmetry now becomes profoundly important for two reasons:

1. Genesis 1:14 begins the description of the mid-stage of creation (ie the fourth day), and

2. It is followed in the very next verse by the start of a special sequence of verses that span the remainder of the creation account – its entire second half.

The first of these two points draws attention to a polemic function of the plain biblical text. In the fourth day, God creates two great lights, which are unmistakably the sun and the moon. In contemporary, neighbouring cultures the Sun and Moon were often names of gods in their own right; whereas Genesis pointedly avoids naming them. In the same place, however, the four-letter name is present in disguise.

However, it is the second point especially that calls for an extended explanation, as it has a strong bearing on the importance of the number 4. But before we proceed to that explanation, let me reiterate three observations that constitute a conceptual family.

First, in Genesis 1:1 the four-letter name is no more than implied by the circumlocution HaShem (literally 'The Name'). Then, at the mid-point in the creation account the name itself is spelled out, but concealed by the darkness of 'night' which God is about to subdue. The appropriate context is ...הַלַּיְלָה וְהָיוּ... / *halaylah v'hayv* / ...the night, and let them be (for signs, and for seasons etc). Finally, the name is revealed plainly for the first time in the very sentence that brings the creation account to a close.

Now we may proceed to examine the six special verses with something resembling a meaningful purpose. In the Hebrew Torah, it is easily seen that Genesis 1:15 is composed from 37 letters (a number the Torah and its Seal have already given clear emphasis); and subsequent verses at intervals of four verses each contain 22, 22, 50, 50 and 50 letters respectively. The complete sequence of verses is 1:15, 1:19, 1:23, 1:27, 1:31 and 2:4. Clearly, the last of them is the very one in which the four-letter name is seen explicitly for the first time. Does this evident sub-structure really matter? Well, a proper answer to this would have to address some more specific questions, such as:

---

[k] The four letter word 'night', without the definite article (ה) occurs in Genesis 1:5.

# In the Beginning

1. Is there a connection between the four-letter name and any of these letter counts?
2. Do those counts possess any important properties beyond their superficial charm?
3. Can we in any case trust the division of verses in Genesis to reflect the purpose of the underlying structures?

Straight away, let me dispose of the third of these questions. The way the Bible is now divided into chapters and verses is a relatively recent adaptation, designed to allow easy cross-referencing in, for example, biblical commentaries. In fact, original Torah manuscripts written in *scripta continua* had no punctuation and precious few spaces in the text, even between words. Texts in that format were meant to be read only by priests and scribes who knew them intimately and, therefore, knew where the word-breaks are meant to be. If the later division into verses somehow came to reflect the underlying structures, that could mean one of two things. Either it was done specifically with those structures in mind, or the agent was acting under 'divine inspiration'. At one level, it does not matter much which of the two explanations is correct, although the possibility of divine inspiration would tend to support the widespread Jewish belief that the entire Torah is of supernatural origin.

Speaking for myself, the mere mention of divine inspiration smacks of 'faith without proof', which for one simple reason would normally be enough for me to reject a proposition out of hand. All too often divine inspiration is offered not as an answer to something that is difficult to explain, but as a way to supplant an obvious explanation with a preferred surrogate. However, in the case of verse divisions in the first creation account, there does appear to be a rather clever clue that points to divine inspiration having been at work there.

Throughout the first Chapter of Genesis, the verb 'to divide' occurs five times, and only as far as verse 18. After that, it does not re-appear within the range of verses we are presently examining. At the same time, the verb 'to multiply' is not seen at all until all five divisions have come and gone. And then 'multiply' occurs only in verses 22 and 28. Each of these numbers has its own intrinsic merit, one as the number of letters in the Hebrew alephbeyt and the other the number of letters in Genesis 1:1, the frame of the Seal. If we accept this as a clue to the Author's deeper intention, and multiply these two verse numbers, we get $22 \times 28 = 616$. And this result is identical to the calculation prompted by the G1 square in two alternative ways. This case of post-biblical fine-tuning seems to me a far more satisfactory example of possible divine inspiration than the usual suspects proffered with no supporting evidence whatsoever.

Assuming we now trust the division of the relevant verses, we still would like to know if the six notable letter-counts have any important properties. In fact they do, and at a number of levels. For example, if they are treated as a T₃ triangular arrangement, they take on the form illustrated in Figure 5.9, demonstrating a remarkable consistency in its layering.

We know, of course, that the 37 apex is one of the two prime co-factors in the product 37×73 = 2701, which is the gematria total of Genesis 1:1 and itself a triangular number. This observation may be moderately interesting but is not terribly momentous by itself.

Then each of the 22s reflects the number of letters in the Hebrew alephbeyt. And they are also both found in the G1 square of qatan values, both as the sum of the third side, and explicitly at opposite ends of its first side. That is, if we allow ourselves to include the eighth letter value for its visual appeal. Moreover, their sum of 44 is also the gematria of the 2×2 central cluster of the G1 square – the garment. But again, by itself, these isolated observations would count for little.

Figure 5.9

As for the three 50s; well in the above number pyramid, they are the foundation for the other three numbers. Very soon, we shall be able to treat them as a special case to answer the earlier question: Is there a connection between the four-letter name (of God) and any of these letter counts? But until we properly make that connection these numbers too, by themselves, reveal little beyond their superficial charm.

Those then are the rather nondescript, immediate qualities of the six numbers; and they signally fail to live up to the spectacular standards we have come to expect. So what about their shared characteristics? Here, at last we appear to strike gold, because the obvious case (the sum of all six of them) is 231, which happens to be the triangular number T₂₁ (where 21 is itself T₆, 6 is T₃ and 3 is T₂). There is also a very special relationship between the 37 apex and the sum of the middle layer, so:

$$\frac{44}{37} \times \frac{44}{37} = 1.414171$$

**That is:**
$$\left(\frac{44}{37}\right)^2 \cong \sqrt{2} \quad \text{(within 0.003\%)}$$

But, wait a minute, haven't we already seen this result!? Indeed we have, and as recently as the start of the present Chapter, where it was bequeathed by the gematria values of the rivers Jordan (ie 264) and Chebar (ie 222). And the reason becomes clear as soon as we realise that:

$$44 \times 6 = 264$$
and
$$37 \times 6 = 222$$

However, it is not yet clear that, apart from their regular spacing, the six special letter-counts have any other particular connection with the number 4. So we really need to look into that possibility.

There is a branch of mathematics known as Graph Theory, which describes the ways in which discrete objects may be joined together by connecting lines (normally straight). At the theoretical level, an object is called a vertex (*pl.* vertices) and the joining lines are called edges. One particular type of graph is the 'complete' graph, in which each vertex is joined to each of the others by exactly one edge. Since we are looking for a connection between (the number) 4 and 6 (letter-counts), we should note the stylised format of the complete 4-graph ($K_4$) (see Figure 5.10).

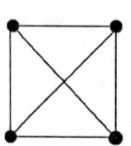

In $K_4$, the four vertices (dots) are all joined to each other using exactly six edges altogether. It is no accident that this is the precise form of all the square identities of the

Figure 5.10

Seal. In fact, the G1 view of the Seal populated with qatan values shares some important characteristics with our six notable letter-counts, as may be gleaned from the merged representation shown in Figure 5.11. The 37 at the start of the sequence is found

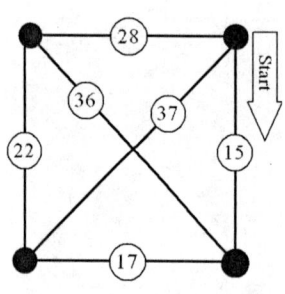

Figure 5.11

explicitly in one diagonal of G1. It is also the sum of the two side totals 15 and 22. The 22 in the third side of course corresponds to either of the 22s in the special sequence. In fact, another 22 is obtained from Side#1, when it is supplemented with the 7 of the migrated *ayin*. Finally, the sum of the totals in the third and fourth sides (ie 22 and 28) is the 50 that is repeated three times in the strange sequence of letter-counts obtained from equally spaced verses.

It is an important fact that the $K_4$ graph also conveys one visual aspect of the solid shape known as a tetrahedron. This shape is a kind of three-sided pyramid, which has four vertices, six edges and four faces. A regular tetrahedron is one in which the six edges are all the same length, and the four faces are, therefore, all equilateral triangles. The $K_4$ graph happens to show a regular tetrahedron presenting its maximum profile or silhouette. It is perhaps no longer surprising that the first divinely anointed king of Israel should be named דוד / *David.* The standard letter values of this name are 4, 6, 4, and this is an accepted, standard notation for expressing the characteristics of a tetrahedron. Some special roles of tetrahedra are addressed more thoroughly in Chapter 8.

Already we can see that the six notable letter counts do, indeed, possess a number of important properties – the answer to the second of the earlier three diagnostic questions. But we are not yet finished with that answer.

Now at last we come to the first of those three questions, and the connection between the name(s) of God and the three repeated 50s. For example, it is recognised in Judaism that:

> [This (ie 50) is] an interval specifically referred to in the more elaborate descriptions of the naming traditions.
>
> (Satinover, 1997, p28)

Without ever explaining what is meant by a 'naming tradition', Dr. Satinover goes on to offer an example of the famous ELS Bible Code, to illustrate the connection between names and the number 50. The letter array in Figure 5.12 shows text taken from Genesis 1:22-26, entered right-to-left, row-by-row from top to bottom.

| | | | | | | | | | | | | | | | | | | | | | | | | |
|---|---|---|---|---|---|---|---|---|---|---|---|---|---|---|---|---|---|---|---|---|---|---|---|---|
| ו | ו | ב | ר | ו | ו | ר | פ | ר | מ | א | ל | מ | י | ה | ל | א | מ | ת | א | כ | ר | ב | י | ו |
| א | ב | ב | ר | י | פ | ו | ע | ה | ו | מ | י | מ | י | ב | מ | י | מ | ה | ת | א | ו | א | ל | מ |
| ו | י | ש | י | מ | ח | מ | ו | י | ר | ק | ב | י | ה | י | ו | ב | ר | ע | י | ה | י | ו | צ | ר |
| מ | ל | ה | י | ח | ש | פ | נ | צ | ר | א | ה | א | צ | ו | ת | מ | י | ה | ל | א | ר | מ | א | י |
| ו | ה | נ | י | מ | ל | צ | ר | א | ו | ת | י | ח | ו | ש | מ | ר | ו | ה | מ | ה | ב | ה | נ | י |
| מ | ל | צ | ר | א | ה | ת | י | ח | ת | א | מ | י | ה | ל | א | ש | ע | י | ו | נ | כ | י | ה | י |
| ה | ש | מ | ר | ל | כ | ת | א | ו | ה | נ | י | מ | ל | ה | מ | ה | ב | ה | ת | א | ו | ה | נ | י |
| ו | ב | ו | ט | י | כ | מ | י | ה | ל | א | א | ר | י | ו | ו | ה | נ | י | מ | ל | ה | מ | ד | א |
| מ | ד | כ | ו | נ | מ | ל | צ | ב | מ | ד | א | ה | ש | ע | נ | מ | י | ה | ל | א | ר | מ | א | י |

**Figure 5.12**

Here, the vertical letters of אברהמ (Abraham) are emphasised by heavier borders and, because the array consists of 25 columns, those letters are seen to occur in alternate rows at regular intervals of 50 letters. That is a very obvious link between the number 50 and a biblically important name. Dr. Satinover then points out (incorrectly as it happens) that between each letter of Abraham and the next, there is exactly one occurrence of אלהי‬ם (Elohim), thus reflecting the change of name Abram to Abraham (see Genesis 17) by the insertion of a letter *heh* (ה) from the divine four-letter Name. By a happy chance, a small error in Dr. Satinover's array obscures a fifth copy of Elohim, and a very important juxtaposition of the two names. In the above corrected array it can be seen that:

- the first letter of the first Elohim coincides with the first letter of Abraham,
- the last letter of the last Elohim coincides with the last letter of Abraham, and
- the middle three copies of Elohim are separated from one another by 50 intervening letters.

The degree of integration evident here is undoubtedly the result of deliberate design. Although we must concede that when dealing with such an extended portion of text that design process would be relatively easy to accomplish. This explains, in part anyway, why the Author has taken the trouble to provide the Seal. Since the immensely greater information density in the Seal could not be the result of human ingenuity, it must have been provided to vouchsafe for the Author's holy word.

There are several further ELS indicators in the Torah, which conspire to affirm the significance of 50. Indeed, the word תורה (Torah) itself is found in ELS form at the start of Genesis, Exodus, Numbers and Deuteronomy. Dr. Satinover attributes many discoveries of this type to Rabbi Michael dov ber Weissmandl, in a period that encompassed the Second World War of the 20th Century. In the first two books of the Torah, 'Torah' is spelled out at intervals of 50 letters, starting with the first occurrence of a *tav* (ת) in each case. In Figure 5.13, we see an array based on the start of Genesis, showing 'Torah' spelled out at 50 letter intervals.

| ה | ה | א | ו | מ | י | מ | ש | ה | ה | א | מ | י | ה | ל | א | א | ר | ב | **ה** | י | ש | א | ר | ב |
|---|---|---|---|---|---|---|---|---|---|---|---|---|---|---|---|---|---|---|---|---|---|---|---|---|
| ל | ע | כ | ש | ה | ו | ו | ה | ב | ו | ו | ה | ה | ה | ה | י | ה | צ | ר | א | ה | ו | צ | ר | א |
| נ | פ | ל | ע | ה | פ | ה | ר | מ | מ | י | ה | ל | א | ה | ו | ר | ו | מ | **ו** | ה | ה | י | נ | פ |
| י | ה | י | ו | ר | ו | א | י | ה | י | מ | י | ה | ל | א | ה | מ | א | י | ו | מ | י | מ | ה | י |
| י | ו | ב | ו | ט | י | כ | ה | ו | א | ה | ה | א | מ | י | ה | ל | א | א | **ר** | י | ו | ר | ו | א |
| י | ו | כ | ש | ה | ה | נ | י | כ | ו | ר | ו | א | ה | נ | י | כ | מ | י | ה | ל | א | ל | ה | ב |
| י | ל | א | ר | ק | כ | ש | ח | ל | ו | מ | ו | י | ר | ו | א | ל | מ | י | **ה** | ל | א | א | ר | ק |

Figure 5.13

Here again, the text has been separated into rows of 25 letters each, so as to emphasise the vertical word תורה. However, a different phenomenon is revealed if we divide the same text into shorter 22-letter rows, as shown in Figure 5.14. In this modified arrangement the letters of 'Torah' (still marked by heavier borders), which were previously aligned vertically, are now much less conspicuous.

| | | | | | | | | | | | | | | | | | | | | | |
|---|---|---|---|---|---|---|---|---|---|---|---|---|---|---|---|---|---|---|---|---|---|
| ו | מ | י | מ | ש | ה | ת | א | מ | י | ה | ל | א | א | ר | ב | ת | י | ש | א | ר | ב |
| ו | ה | ב | ו | ו | ה | ת | ה | ת | י | ה | צ | ר | א | ה | ו | צ | ר | א | ה | ת | א |
| מ | י | ה | ל | א | ח | ו | ר | ו | מ | ו | ה | ת | י | נ | פ | ל | ע | כ | ש | ח | ו |
| ה | ל | א | ר | מ | א | י | ו | מ | י | מ | ה | י | נ | פ | ל | ע | ת | פ | ח | ר | מ |
| ה | ל | א | א | ר | י | ו | ר | ו | א | י | ה | י | ו | ר | ו | א | י | ה | י | מ | י |
| י | ה | ל | א | ל | ד | ב | י | ו | ב | ו | ט | י | כ | ר | ו | א | ה | ת | א | מ | י |
| א | א | ר | ק | י | ו | כ | ש | ח | ה | נ | י | ב | ו | ר | ו | א | ה | נ | י | ב | מ |
| ל | י | ל | א | ר | ק | כ | ש | ח | ל | ו | מ | ו | י | ר | ו | א | ל | מ | י | ה | ל |

**Figure 5.14**

On the other hand, in this reorganisation we find that four out of five copies of the word אור / *aur* / light are now stacked vertically, as are two out of three copies of [ך] חשב / *khoshek* / darkness. This further emphasis on *aur*, at the noteworthy interval of 22 letters, is especially significant. It shows that a single section of text, at the very start of the Torah has been designed to emphasise, through ELS-like features, both the numbers 50 and 22. And, of course, these are both numbers that feature strongly in the topical sequence of letter-counts.

In passing, we may also note that Jewish Kabbalah posits the existence of a 72-letter name of God. And, since the topical sequence contains two copies of 22 and three of 50 (the number associated with names), that makes six alternative ways to add them to make 72.

I mentioned a little earlier that four of the Five Books of Moses include an ELS presence of 'Torah' at their beginnings. The exception is the middle book – Leviticus – which instead incorporates an ELS copy of the four-letter Name – יהוה, as shown by Figure 5.15 (overleaf). Note that here, the ELS version of YHWH overlaps with a plain-text copy of itself (shaded), and also with the name of משה / *Moshe* / Moses. The name of Moshe starts at the letter *mem* (מ) in the top left corner of this array. Also recall that the Hebrew *Moshe* happens to be the spelling of HaShem (literally 'The Name') when read in reverse.

It is particularly relevant that the first letter of the ELS version of YHWH at the start of Leviticus comes from the word ו י ק ר א / *Vayiqra* / And [He] called. This word incorporates the root word י ק ר (*yaqar*) which has two seemingly different meanings that are, nonetheless, deeply meaningful. On the one hand yaqar means 'to call', as in: *And the Lord called to Moses* …, which is its use here at the start of

Figure 5.15

Leviticus. But yaqar also means 'precious', giving a clear indication of the high regard in which names are held in the Torah. The same conjunction of concepts gives rise to the notion that the Torah is, or represents, the Book of Life – a record of the names of all the elect souls - which exists simultaneously in heaven and earth.

The fact that it is in the middle book of the Torah that the four-letter name replaces the more common ELS 'Torah' highlights another key characteristic of the other four books. As previously mentioned, in Genesis and Exodus 'Torah' is spelled out forwards at intervals of 50 letters. But in Numbers and Deuteronomy, the same word is spelled backwards. So that, in all four cases, the ELS Torah is written in the direction that points toward the central ELS *YHWH* in Leviticus. Also, predictably, the letters of the ELS Torah in Numbers are spaced at intervals of 50 letters each (technically *minus* 50, since the sequence is found in reverse). However, in Deuteronomy the skip distance is only 49 (or, technically, -49). In the context of the present Chapter, there is a nice correspondence between this discrepancy and the removal of the letter ayin from within the Seal to its prefix position. Whilst within the Seal the ayin was the 49th letter, but once it is moved outside the distance between its old and new locations spans 50 letter positions.

A few more miscellaneous facts about the ELS 'Torah' in some of its component books are worth mentioning. One is that, in Exodus the first letter of the ELS word comes from the plain-text word ש מ ו ת / *Shemot* / Names. In Numbers, the last letter of Torah (ie the *heh* (ה) nearest the start of the book) comes from the name 'Moshe'. And in Deuteronomy, the same last letter of the ELS word coincides with the first letter of ה ת ו ר ה / *HaTorah* / The Torah in the plain text. We cannot escape the conclusion that all five books of the Torah have been designed in a consistent way to emphasise the great importance of names, and its own enigmatic role in that purpose. This is a form of coherence that is hardly considered in Christian theology or in biblical scholarship.

We started this lengthy detour beyond the Seal, ostensibly to find an independent reason why the Seal might favour the word 'four'. Along the way we have found in the Torah numerous encoded references to the word 'Torah' itself, and also to the four-letter name of God (YHWH). However, through the notable letter-counts in six regularly-spaced verses, we have accidentally found a much more persistent emphasis on names generally. And the strategic locations of the six verses have also done a lot to emphasise the number 4.

What is more, the fact that there are six of those verses led us to combine them into the four-pointed, four-faced tetrahedron seen as the complete $K_4$ graph. This graph is, we saw, structurally identical to the G1 square when the latter is seen with its four corners fully connected. When the qatan letter totals of the square's sides and diagonals are attached to the edges of the graph, the correspondence with the six verses' letter counts becomes all the more evident. It seems safe to conclude, therefore, that the $K_4$ graph and the G1 view of the Seal are intentional counterparts. So we now have exactly four corresponding concepts:

1. The Author's Seal
2. The $K_4$ graph.
3. A sequence of six verses with letter-counts related to 1. and 2.
4. Rivers (based on the fact that the same ratio (ie $\sqrt{2}$) is generated both by the gematria values of Jordan and Chebar, and by the first three notable letter-counts).

Therefore, note that it is just six more verses after the end of the first creation account that we see the verse:

*And a river went out of Eden to water the garden; and from thence it was parted and became unto four heads*

(Genesis 2:10)

The emphasis the Torah places on 'four' is not only subtle but is also entangled with many other concepts. Even now we are still not finished tracing the clues based on 'four' that might explain the importance of names. Earlier in the Chapter, a certain conceptual progression was observed. At first, the four-letter name is merely implied in Genesis 1:1, with the expression השם / *HaShem* / <u>The Name</u>, which is also the reverse spelling of the name Moshe (or Moses). Later, at the mid-point of the creation account – the fourth day – the name itself makes a first guarded appearance as consecutive letters that overlap two words. That is, in Genesis 1:14 the name is concealed within the Hebrew two-word expression: ...וֹיְהִי הַלַּיְלָה... / *halaylah v'hayv* / ...the night, and let them be (for signs, and for seasons etc). Finally, as we know, in Genesis 2:4 (the very last verse of this creation account) the four-letter name is seen explicitly for the first time.

Now recall from Chapter 1, all the various references – both direct and more subtle - to Abraham and circumcision that we found hidden in the first and third words. This theme now resumes its importance because, against any reasonable expectation, the name of Abraham is also to be found alongside YHWH in Genesis 2:4. It will not be seen in any translation, however, because it is an anagram of בְּהִבָּרְאָם / *b'hibaram* / when they were created. A simple rearrangement of these letters will produce בְּאַבְרָהָם / *b'Avraham* / with Abraham. Two particular points are to be noted here. First, we have the critically important conjunction of the very first YHWH *with* Abraham. Also, the literal translation 'when they were created' looks forward to the crucial future role of Abraham as 'father of nations' and progenitor of the people that would ensure the safe transmission of the Torah for the benefit of all those nations.

To repeat something I mentioned at the start of our detour, until this Chapter there did not seem to have been any emphasis at all on the number 4. In fact, until now the numbers 37 and 3 (which is seen as an ELS word in the first verse) have been far more prominent. However, the configuration of the ELS 'three', viewed as a square-within-a-square could be seen as an early hint to the latent importance of 'four'. And that impression looks even more likely given that this 'three' is composed from the fourth letter in each of the four sides of the square.

It is no exaggeration to suggest that from this point onwards, it is going to be 'four' that will take centre-stage. For one thing, those of its letters that come from within the G2 square spell *bara* (to create). *Arba* (four) also starts and ends with the two silent Hebrew letters. So this further binding of symbolic Vast Face and Small Face, in association with letters of the word 'to create' may serve to verify an essential role of 'four' in creation. Yet an awful lot is still resting on the assumed importance of a concept for which we have, admittedly, been depending on circumstantial evidence.

We are also about to discover that there is an intimate link between (i)the ayin, (ii) the Bible's first word, (iii) creation and (iv) time. If the moment of biblical creation is synonymous with the Big Bang of cosmology, then they both must indicate the beginning of time – the moment when the clock of our universe started ticking. We have already seen that the first word separates into the names of two months of the Hebrew calendar: *Ab* and *Tishrei*. The first is composed of the first two Hebrew letters written forwards, while the latter includes the last three letters written backwards. In fact the two letters of Ab, combined in an alternative way with Tishrei to make "בתשרי א", meaning the first day of Tishrei, the Jewish New Year or *Rosh HaShanah*. Note particularly that we are dealing here with the twin cyclic concepts of *day* and *year*, both suggested by the Torah's first word, which has previously revealed the value of Pi in a cyclic formation. And this convergence of concepts may be confirmed beautifully through the concept of 'four' and the gematria of the same B'reishith (ie 913). See the result of multiplying them together, thus:

$$913 \times 4 = 3652$$

The point to note here is the correspondence with the length of a solar year, which is only slightly over 365.2 days. The discrepancy is only about 0.01%, or one hour over the entire length of a year.

It is no trivial coincidence that time is often likened to the unceasing flow of a river.

-oOo-

The migration of the letter ayin (ע), the forty-ninth letter of Genesis, to become its prefix was initially a speculative move prompted by one of the tenets of Jewish Kabbalah. Yet we are already accumulating a sizable body of new corroborating evidence that flows automatically from that simple experiment. That does not mean just the circumstantial evidence we discovered during the course of our extended foray beyond the normal confines of the Seal, but more especially the evidence seen within the Seal in the early part of this Chapter. We now find ourselves on a path that will inexorably demonstrate that the physical creation and its symbolic description at the start of Genesis are conceived together, as one. Much of that additional evidence will be seen when we come to analyse the G2 facet of the Author's Seal as qatan letter values, in the next pages, but also in relation to the physical world in Chapter 8.

# 6

Once we start to re-examine the whole G2 square, populated by qatan letter values, the numerical characteristics of *arba* (four) will completely dominate. Take a look at Figure 6.1, which shows an unembellished view of the numerical transformation.

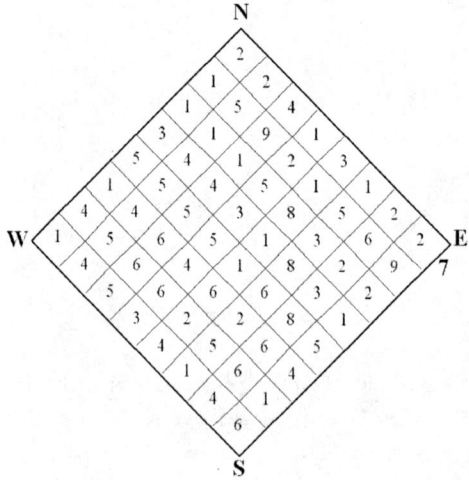

Figure 6.1

Straight away we may make two simple observations. First, there are no '7' digits whatsoever within this square. The other is that the external 7 of the migrated letter *ayin* is now closely aligned with the initial 22 of the regular text. This allows us to make a straightforward modification to an earlier view of Genesis 1:1, as a qatan sequence. It is now evident in Figure 6.2 that the '7' prefix serves to generate the best known and most widely used approximation for Pi. That is:

$$22 \div 7 = 3.142857^r$$

I shall mention that this useful ratio is within 0.04% of the true value of Pi, only so that the greater accuracy of other references to Pi will stand out. Later, we shall consider a possible meaning for the Seal showing us not just another approximation to Pi, but in particular one that overlaps the very beginning of creation.

The new placement of the ayin prefix gives rise to an intriguing similarity between the first and fourth sides of the G2 square (ie E-to-

N and S-to-E). The qatan sum of the fourth side is still 28, and this is the product of prime factors 7×2×2, while the first side now begins 722. So there is a striking, though superficial similarity between the new start of Genesis 1:1 and its end. But more especially, the presence of the new 7 gives rise to an additional tranche of references to the

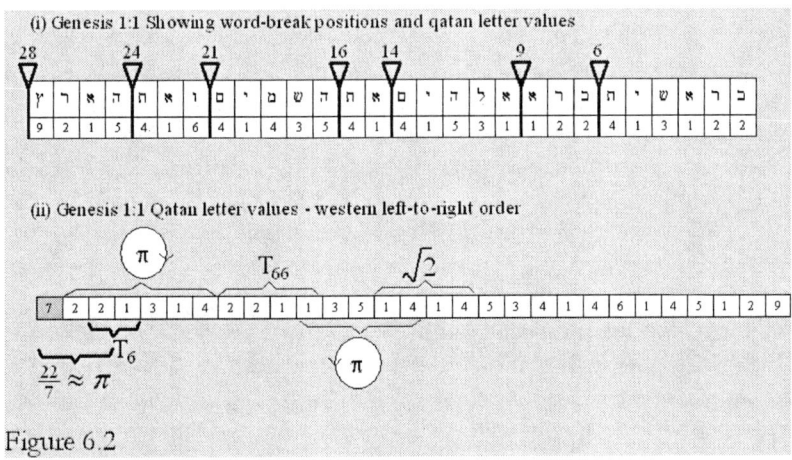

Figure 6.2

concept of names, some of which derive from the digits at each end of side #1. Previously, the initial two digits were 22, which we know is a co-factor of 616 with 28, the qatan sum of side #4. And we also know that 616 is associated with the expression:

> ...*the number of the beast, or the number of its name.*
> (Revelation 13:18)

But once the 7 prefix is in place, the initial digits are now 72, another number that Jewish Kabbalah associates with names, including the length of one of God's names. Could it be that the main purpose of the migrated letter ayin is to enhance the three-way relationship between Torah, numbers and names?

To be realistic, this last observation would have no standing in these analyses, unless it could be supported by other internal testimony. And there are no less that four other facts in the G2 square which serve to endorse the link with names. First is the presence of the word *arba* (four) itself, which is easily associated with God's better known four-letter name. This connection is entirely dependent on the presence of the 7 from the ayin of Vast Face. Second is the presence of the digit pair 42 at the other end of the same side, which is the length of another of the creator's names (by definition the end of the first side of the square is the seventh letter of the normal text). Finally, the prefixed 7 augments the qatan sum of Side #1 from 15 to 22, which may be associated with Side #4 in two ways. First, the new qatan total of sides 1 and 4 together changes from a meaningless 43 to the more significant number 50. And this number, so we are told, *is specifically referred to in the more elaborate descriptions of the naming traditions.* (Satinover, 1997). The new qatan total for Side #1 is, of course the same as two of the special letter-counts we examined in Chapter 5, which ran parallel to the development of the names of YHWH and Abraham. And the 50 total of sides 1 and 4 together is the same as another three of those six letter-counts. Also, when the qatan sum of Side #4 is multiplied by the new sum of Side #1, their product is 28×22 = 616. We know that 616 is closely associated with 666 both in the G1 square, and in the book of Revelation where, as alternatives, they are linked to the 'name of the beast'.

However, we should be mindful in these analyses that we may yet only be re-tracing the thought process that has already led to the development of the so-called naming traditions. But it is still worth repeating that the original and new locations of the migrated ayin span 50 letter positions.

A related consequence of the new location of ayin is that, in the context of the G2 square, it is also obliquely adjacent to the last letter of the first verse. Together, these letters spell [ץ] עץ / *etz* / a tree. Which calls to mind a popular Jewish belief that the Tree of Life of Genesis 2 is synonymous with the Book of Life and the Torah, all of which are said to record the names of the elect.

-oOo-

We shall now consider the relative merits of viewing the word 'four' as the qatan sequence 7221 (the way the regular text reads) or as 1227 (the way the word itself reads). We shall consider each possibility in the order shown here.

So what could possibly make 7221 more important for the Seal than any other number of similar size? The answer becomes blindingly obvious once it is pointed out; after which it may be taken as another fundamental, underlying relationship between the Seal and the natural world of numbers.

There should be little need to go over in too much detail the importance of the homogeneous digit triples we found in the G1 square, except perhaps to recall the symmetry of 666 by itself, and an alternative symmetry of the 111 and 444 seen there together. And, of course, the three of them in combination were our guide to the existence of a 614th commandment, conferred by the crucified man. We also saw evidence from other research (Jenkins, 2004) of the underlying prevalence of multiples of 111 in combinations of the standard gematria values of the seven words of Genesis 1:1. And it is the concept of symmetry along with a simple multiple of 111 that will establish the significance of the 7221 obtained from the word 'four'. We are about to see that 7221 is at a pivotal position between two other numbers which are otherwise quite unrelated, apart from both having a strong affinity for the number 6. One of these numbers is 7776, and its dependence on 6 is that :

$$7776 \quad = 6 \times 6 \times 6 \times 6 \times 6$$

And: $\qquad\qquad 7776 \quad = 7221 + 555$

The other number is 6666, which is more obviously related to the digit 6. But also:

$$6666 \quad = 7221 - 555$$

To be realistic, the twin results we see here will not be judged to have any important mathematical significance. We may note that the full difference between the upper and lower sixophile numbers is 1110, which looks unimportant now but will soon be seen in a different light. For the moment we shall have to be content just being aware that 6666 and 7776 demonstrate the favoured position of the word for 'four' in the design of the Hebrew alephbeyt, language and Torah. There is, however, an immediate implication of this observation that is truly stunning. Contrary to the normal assumption, the Torah cannot be just a skilful literary composition using a language that had developed freely, in the way that languages generally do. Rather, the multi-layered richness (linguistic and numeric) built into the Torah must depend on a language and alephbeyt that have been custom-designed for this purpose. Consequently, the normal assumptions of linguists, as to how Hebrew has evolved, will require a complete overhaul.

Also, the numerical relationship we have just seen is only one of three functions of the 7221 sequence obtained from the word 'four'. Another is a sum that is obtained from all the homogeneous linear groups in G2, of three or more elements. There is a 111 group, a 666, an 888 and a 5555. The fourth one comes from the 'הההה' we saw in the equivalent square of letters. And it is only this group and the 666 sequence that come from homogeneous letter sequences (666 comes from a '١١١' group). The other two sequences both derive from combinations of two letters. So it is more than a little strange that the sum of just these two comes to 6221, which is exactly 1000 less than the 7221 group. But the sum of all four homogeneous groups is:

$$5555 + 888 + 666 + 111 = 7220$$

… which differs by only one. So it is likely that we are now seeing the explanation for the first line of the following Torah passage:

> *How can one chase a thousand,*
> *or two put ten thousand to flight,*
> *Unless their rock had sold them*
> *and the Lord had given them up*
> (Deuteronomy 32:30)

In fact, this is only the first of two ways in which the Seal links one and one thousand with the number 888. So it is of the utmost significance that the latter number happens to be the total that derives from the word Ιησους (ie Jesus) in Greek numerology. It was the other three lines of the same passage for which we found an explanation in Chapter 4, based on the Seal's numerical references to the crucified man. If my reader feels that the suggested link from the G2 square to Greek numerology is out of place, it is well to recall that most New Testament books were first written in Greek, which was the *lingua franca* for educated communication in those times. Also, we now have clear evidence that the Author of the Seal was well able to see across all ages, including the early centuries of the Christian era. So the fact that the Seal is derived from the older Hebrew scriptures would not preclude it containing knowledge of a later event or language. In any case, Hebrew and Greek are related through an evolutionary line.

This is a suitable place to highlight two other ways in which the Seal emphasises numbers that consist only of 8s. As we saw in Chapter 5, the conspicuous *lamed* shaped river of G2 consists of 8 out of the 9 letters *vav* that belong to the Seal. And the fraction 8/9 evaluates to the infinitely recurring decimal 0.8888…. Recall also from Chapter 3 that the 4×7 matrix of qatan letter values obtained from Genesis 1:1 revealed a large 45° right-angle triangle. The outline of that triangle consisted of 8 out of the 9 qatan values of 1 in that verse, thus generating the same infinitely long decimal fraction. It is extraordinary that the Seal should reveal such strikingly recognisable shapes at all.

What is really mind-boggling, however, is that it does so with alternative letters, with equal 0.8888... ratios, and with opposite symbolism. By which I mean that the matrix based on Genesis 1:1 also included the image of the serpent that tempted the woman, leading to expulsion from the garden of Eden, whereas the visually similar lamed-shaped river represents the reverse path pioneered by the crucified man.

The alternative 1227 sequence obtained from *arba* has even more biblical consequence than its reverse self. And the most significant will be its relationship to an inherently important sequence of six consecutive numbers. It was noted at one point that the gematria of the word Torah is 611, and that of brit (covenant) is 612. It is also widely recognised that the Torah contains 613 commandments that are applicable to Judaism; and we saw in Chapter 4 that the crucifixion of Jesus, or more properly his feelings about it conferred a 614th commandment. That gives us a sequence of four consecutive numbers of some intrinsic worth. It is also easy to see 616 as a member of the set – this being the number that the G1 square generated in two alternative ways, and is associated with the 'name of the beast' in Revelation 13:18. But a more pertinent reason to include 616 in the growing list is that this is the gematria of הַתּוֹרָה / *HaTorah* / The Torah (including the definite article). Here we should recall from the last Chapter how, in the ELS copy of 'Torah' at the start of Deuteronomy, its final letter coincides with the first letter, the definite article, of HaTorah in the regular text.

A sequence of six consecutive numbers is now defined by its end-points: 611 (Torah) and 616 (*The* Torah). And we have most of its intermediate members. But we are missing a 615, which we shall address in just a moment. First, we need to establish a pattern which will, at once, relate the six numbers to the topical number 1227, and also point us in the right direction to find the missing 615 needed to fill the gap. Two observations will suffice. First, it is possible to generate 1227 by adding pairs of numbers from the sequence, so:

$$611 + 616 = 1227$$
and
$$613 + 614 = 1227$$

The second observation is that the members of each of these pairs are conceptually related. Thus, Torah is Law (or instruction) and HaTorah is, literally *The* Law, the definitive finished article. Also there were originally 613 commands in Torah, but it takes the New

Testament gospels to make this number up to 614. In each case, the higher number of the pair represents completion of what the lower one began. And that is enough of a clue.

We now have both a template for determining the missing number, and a test for veracity. The template is the 1227 total the missing number will make with its 612 partner. And we know the 615 must, in some way be the completion of the 612 obtained from the word 'covenant'. Something else we already know is that we obtained the word 'covenant' from the very first word of the Torah. And that is, of course, the beginning of the creation. So, maybe the 615 we seek will be found at a place that represents the end of what the first word began. And so it is, if we are careful to limit our scope, and exclude the seventh 'day', the Sabbath that follows the active phase of creation. In the biblical creation account, all seems to have been accomplished by the end of the first Chapter, at Genesis 1:31 (notice that this verse is among the ones that contain the six special letter-counts we analysed in Chapter 5). In the Hebrew text of this verse, its very last word is הַשִּׁשִׁי / *ha shishiy* / the sixth, which has a gematria of 615, as required. So now we have all three of the numbers that represent completion, to go with their 'initiation' counterparts; and we can also complete the third sum,

$$612 + 615 = 1227$$

It is also worth noting that the word *ha shishiy*, because it includes the grammatical definite article, is unique among endings of the six days. The previous five days are all rounded off with a number that does not include the definite article. This is a prime example of the kind of deliberate subtlety that is lost in translations. Bearing in mind that the 616 contribution comes from The Torah, we cannot escape the conclusion that the inner pair of numbers must demonstrate the 614th commandment, and Jesus' statement:

> *Do not think that I have come to abolish the Law or the*
> *Prophets; I have not come to abolish them but to fulfil them.*
> (Matthew 5:17)

Speaking for myself, I find the latest set of results extraordinary to the point of spectacular, yet beautifully elegant. The irresistible convergence of several otherwise unrelated pieces of information from divers sources is hard to comprehend by any familiar yardstick. In fact, the only possible explanation is that it was pre-planned from the moment any part of the book we now know as the Bible came into existence. Its fulfilment has also required the unwitting co-operation of religions that might prefer not to see their labours contributing to this phenomenon. By which I mean most particularly the meticulous analysis that led to a definitive count of the 613 commandments of Judaism. This analysis is attributed to Rabbi Moshe ben Maimon (Maimonides) (1135 to 1204).

Finding six consecutive 3-digit numbers with such coherent purpose is amazing enough. Yet the sequence may be extended by two more members at its lower end; though the purpose of the two extra numbers seems to be quite different. We start by noting that the six are all connected in various ways with the name of the Torah, or the content of the Torah as a covenant or its constituent commands. So it is most apposite that the extra two members of the set come from the length of the Torah, in terms of the number of letters it contains. The length of today's standard Torah, the masoretic text, is 304,805 Hebrew letters. When this number is doubled it becomes 609,610. There is a delightful aesthetic balance at the heart of this process, in which the given number is doubled to produce near-equal left and right halves. The two halves of this number do not participate in the pairings that generate 1227 (the qatan sequence of the word for 'four'). They do, however, underpin the six in two important ways. Numerically, 609 and 610 are the foundation upon which the others are stacked. And this is a metaphor for their other meaning: that the letters of the Torah are its raw materials, the stuff from which the covenants and the constituent commands of covenants are all built. In a subtle way, the eight consecutive numbers tell us that there is a purposeful progression of **numbers** → **letters** → **language** → **commands** → **covenant** → **Torah**. They are all created as a coherent set. But 'number' is the most fundamental material from which everything else emerges systemically - the whole is greater than the sum of the parts. And, although the Torah is the end-product of a five-stage evolution, every one of the underlying building blocks is still perceptible, including number. The ultimate consequence of this observation will become apparent in Chapter 8.

With hindsight, the model of six paired numbers just examined also confers extra legitimacy on the six verses with special letter counts which we examined in Chapter 5. Five of the six are found in Genesis 1, at verses 15, 19, 23, 27 and 31; and the sixth, with minimal creative license may be numbered 35. Given that the final three letter counts were 50, 50 and 50, it is notable that verse numbers paired from the two ends towards the middle (ie 15 + 35; 19 + 31 and 23 + 27) also make 50, 50 and 50. It is especially telling that verses 19, 23 and 31 of Genesis 1 all mark transitions from one day of creation to the next. In fact, they complete the fourth, fifth and sixth days, which some authorities believe represent a stage of populating the domains created in days 1, 2 and 3 respectively.

The last of the day-day transition points (ie verse 31) culminates in the word ‏הַשִּׁשִּׁי‏ / *ha shishiy* / <u>the sixth</u>, with its gematria of 615; so it is noteworthy that the inclusion of the definite article (the letter ‏ה‏) found there, is what creates a letter count of 50 for that verse, from what would otherwise be only 49. This is the third place where we find a 50 is derived from a 49, or vice versa. The first was the removal of the letter *ayin* (position 49) to become a prefix on the Torah. The second was the ELS encrypted four-letter word 'Torah' composed from letters at intervals of 50 in Genesis, Exodus and Numbers, but at intervals of only 49 in Deuteronomy. Both of those earlier examples were described in Chapter 5. But note that the six special consecutive numbers described above, when augmented with 609 and 610 from the length of the Torah, reinforce the same concept. When all eight numbers are paired as before we obtain:

$$609 + 616 = 1225$$
$$610 + 615 = 1225$$
$$611 + 614 = 1225$$
$$612 + 613 = 1225$$

Now, 1225 may be expressed in several ways. It is $35^2$ (or 35×35); it is $5^2 \times 7^2$ (or 25×49); and it is $T_{49}$. The product 25×49 is especially meaningful as it calls to mind some of the ELS arrays discussed in Chapter 5. There, using 25-letter segments of text from the start of Genesis and Exodus, we saw the word 'Torah' spelled with letters at regular intervals of 50 letters each. In the book of Numbers, 'Torah' is spelled in reverse at intervals of -50 letters. And in Deuteronomy, the interval is -49. A significant degree of careful design is at work here.

Especially surprising is the realisation that many of the effects we are studying – and more yet to come – have been the result of a tiny mutation in the Bible's early text. And, although the migration of the letter *ayin* is clearly a crucial step in a wider plan, I am still quite certain that some readers will find the concept distasteful. Yet how can anyone be offended by a priceless heirloom that is bequeathed to us as an illustration of the Creator's handiwork. Many of the world's most intractable social problems are the result of alternative religious interpretations. But we now have sight of the Author's coherent, fully-dependable Seal to demonstrate which parts of his creation are trustworthy.

One possibility we have not yet considered, apart from the ratio 22/7 as an approximation to Pi, is whether the same three letters that confer those digits might have a significant meaning in their own right. In fact they do, as רבע / *raba* / <u>a square</u>. This is not too surprising, since this is the root of the word 'four'. But the shorter word does offer one confirmation that our decision to read the early Torah text in the setting of an 8×8 square is the right one. The same numbers have another nice way to reinforce the same conclusion, so:

$$722 - 111 = 611$$

…where 111 is a ubiquitous value underpinning many characteristics of the early Torah, and 611 is the gematria of the word Torah itself.

oOo-

Adjusting our focus now, to take in the whole panorama of the G2 square, we may identify many important features in Figure 6.3. For example, the highlighted number 888 is important as the focal point for several purposes. When 888 is combined with the 2 above it, we obtain the following effect:

$$2888 \div 4 = 722$$

(the topical digits that now overlap the start of the Torah).

Then the 888 combined with the 4 below it, reveals this:

$$4888 = 611 \times 8$$

(611 being the gematria of 'Torah', and 8 the dimension of the Seal).

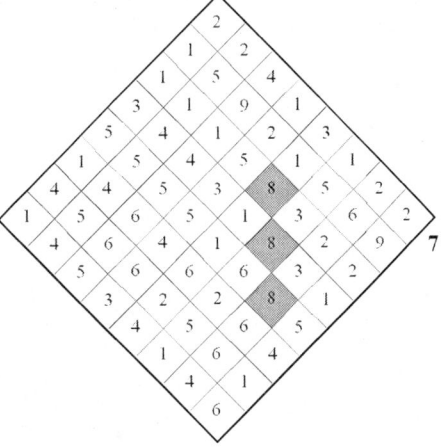

**Figure 6.3**

What makes the latest result especially exciting is that the four digits of 4888 coincide exactly with what was the location of the word לוחת / *luchot* / <u>tablets</u> in the G1 square, having a strong association with the giving of the Law at Sinai. And, moreover, we know that the full gematria of *luchot* itself is 444.

It is here, finally, that we may complete a complex metaphor we have watched develop through chapters 2 and 4. In Chapter 2, we noted that the emergent יהי / *y'hiy* / <u>Let there be</u>, could be combined with either of the two emergent copies of אור / *aur* / <u>light</u>, to generate the first words uttered by God in the Creation. Then, in Chapter 4 we found that the word *y'hiy* sits directly over a qatan 444 sequence, and the ascending *aur* is squeezed between the vertical 666 sequence and the emergent לוחת / *luchot* / <u>tablets</u>, with its gematria of 444. But the new G2 aspect of the Seal is, of course, the outcome of the crucifixion seen in G1. And although the original 444 sequence and the word *luchot* have both now been destroyed, the two separate 444s have been replaced by an 888. What is more, this new emergent number coincides with positions of three of the letters of *luchot* in G1. Clearly, if there had been more that three 8-digits in the Seal, then these associations would be somewhat de-valued. As it is, there *are* only three qatan 8s altogether in the G2 view of the Seal. So we are witnessing a construct of spectacularly high quality.

Still on the subject of *luchot*, we know there were two of those tablets placed inside the Ark of the Covenant, evidently suggesting that the product 444×2 = 888 symbolises a three way relationship between (i) the Ark at Sinai, (ii) its G1 representation and (iii) the identity of Jesus of Nazareth. This association also contains echoes of the numerical tassel we examined in Chapter 4. There, the two central horizontal letters of *luach* (a tablet) conferred a gematria of 38, separated from an adjacent 76 (ie 2×38) by the vertical emergent word *luchot* (tablets). Right now we may appreciate another purpose to the two separated halves of that tassel, so:

$$38 \times 76 = 2888$$

Here, we see a new type of latching, in which distinctive characteristics of one square 'reserve a place' for equally distinctive characteristic of the other. Notice also that the horizontal 5136 which replaces the original 3876 now combines with the 2888 through which it crosses in the special way seen here:

$$\left(\frac{5136}{2888}\right)^4 \cong 10 \qquad \text{(within 0.0064\%)}$$

Finally, for the number 4888 anyway, we may easily spot that the full gematria of the four letters from which it derives (though not a *bona fide* word) is 496. And 496 is not only $T_{31}$ and third member of the set of Perfect Numbers, it is also twice the gematria of 'Abraham', and of רחם / *racham* / <u>a womb</u>.

Another important, one might say extraordinary combination which features the 888 group is a complete 28884, incorporating an extra digit at each end of the homogeneous triple. The beauty of this number is that:

$$28884 = 7221 \times 4$$

Notice especially here that the 7221 qatan sequence derived from the Hebrew word for 'four' is multiplied by the nominal value of that very word.

The next two numerical inclusions in the G2 gem are both references to important numbers in nature that we have met before. Both are highlighted in Figure 6.4, one in the main square and the other in the accompanying thumbnail sketch.

Referring first to the thumbnail, the letters inserted there merely indicate the order in which qatan values in the main square are to be read. Thus, the sequence a-b-c-d-e-f-g in the thumbnail corresponds to the digits 3141592 in the main square. These digits evidently refer to the value of Pi, as a decimal 3.141592 truncated to seven digits of accuracy. That is, within 0.000021% of the true value of Pi. Compare this level of accuracy with the modest 0.04% of the ratio 22/7. And the fact that these seven digits are placed symmetrically in the G2 square again testifies to the role of careful design.

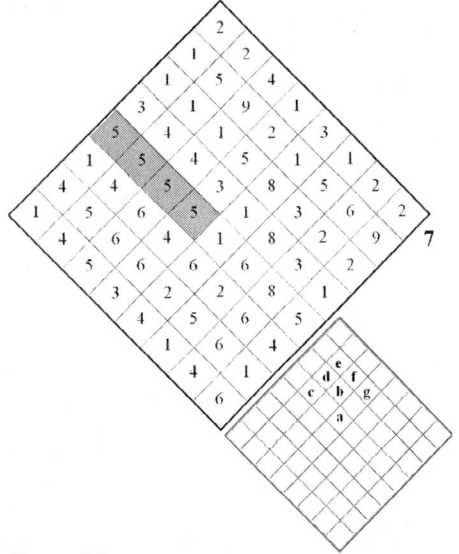

**Figure 6.4**

The other encoded number from nature is built into the now familiar 5555 sequence. This time, the square is able to provide a direct reference to the exact value of the number known as the Divine Proportion, or Phi (Φ). Recall that previously we have been shown only approximations to Phi, in situations that are, at the very least, redolent of the Ark of the Covenant. But now we have the exact equality:

$$\Phi = 5\wedge.5\times.5 + .5$$

The expression on the right of this equality is just an alternative way to write:

$$\frac{1+\sqrt{5}}{2}$$

And when this expression is evaluated, the result is 1.61803398815 according to my own pocket calculator. But, in reality, the decimal part of this result goes on forever, without repetition.

To complete this observation, the location of the 5555 sequence in G2 will soon be found to be at least as important as the precise value it generates. But this will only be seen in a later incarnation of the Seal.

The last of the numerical inclusions in the G2 square provides a three-way association between very widely separated parts of the Bible. These are: (i) the very beginning of the Torah, (ii) the book of Ezra (once again) and (iii) the New Testament gospel of Matthew. The link in question comes from the four qatan values at the very centre of the G2 square seen shaded in Figure 6.5.

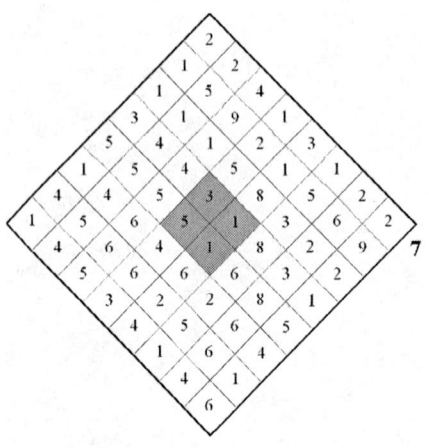

Reading these digits counter-clockwise from, and to, the top we obtain the number 35113. And this number has some quite remarkable properties. First, it is the 76th hexagram number, which I shall designate $H_{76}$. We recall from Chapter 3 that a hexagram number is one from which a 2-dimensional Star of David shape may be physically constructed using the given number of equal size objects (usually small discs).

**Figure 6.5**

In that Chapter, we saw that two early hexagram numbers (ie $H_2 = 37$ and $H_3 = 73$) are the co-factors of 2701. And the latter product is the gematria of Genesis 1:1, which is now the perimeter of the Seal. But, in the very centre within that perimeter, we may see the following even more remarkable product:

$$35113 \quad = \quad 13 \times 37 \times 73$$

...where 13 is itself $H_1$. And, whereas the gematria of Genesis 1:1 conferred the splendid star of stars (repeated as Figure 6.6), because 13 is also a hexagram number, the centre of the G2 square could be represented by a similar design in which each of the tiniest elements is also an $H_1$ Star of David. That is, stars within stars, within stars, to three levels. In other words, the number 35113 is not only a hexagram number itself, but its three prime factors are all also consecutive hexagrams. This relationship, in which the product of three consecutive hexagrams is also a hexagram is quite unique.

Figure 6.6

As to the Ezra and Matthew connections, these are mutually dependent. Where Ezra describes the first wave of captives returning from exile in Babylon, we see this verse:

> *The children of Bethlehem, an hundred twenty and three.*
> (Ezra 2:21)

By quoting the number 123 in close association with Bethlehem Ezra, perhaps unknowingly, foresees the sighting of the so-called Star of Bethlehem (see Matthew 2:7-8), since 123 = 13 + 37 + 73. Now, given that these are the same three hexagram factors of the 35113 hexagram, they may well account for the common assumption that there were three wise men bringing the three gifts to the Christ-child. A more realistic conclusion is that the 'sighting' of a significant star was an early discovery either of the nature of the number 35113, or its central presence in the sacred Seal, and Ezra's geographic interpretation.

Those, then, are the purely numeric pointers to New Testament events at Bethlehem. But there are also two linguistic indicators that we met in the previous Chapter. In the same part of the G2 square, in a most distinctive formation, we find the letters of [מ] רחם / *racham* / a womb, and [מ] לחם / *lechem* / bread. The womb undoubtedly represents the so-called virgin birth. While *lechem* is a key part of לחם בית / *Beyt lechem* / Bethlehem.

-oOo-

Now we come full circle in more ways than one. We have completed the analysis of items included wholly within the G2 square of qatan values, and some that extend outside it, but only as far as the new ayin prefix. But at the start of the present Chapter, I suggested there might be a deliberate rationale for the approximation to Pi (ie 22/7) which now overlaps the beginning of Genesis. Where the remainder of the present Chapter differs from the first part and most of this book is that it is not so much pure observation as a speculation on my part, albeit built upon a foundation of hard facts.

Consider for a moment some of the specific findings I have already described, this time looking for persistent underlying themes. For example, we have seen numerous cases of the digits of Pi, four of which come from cyclic sources. With this mechanism, it is possible the Seal is urging us to look, or think, more extensively in cyclic terms.

Then there have been at least two cryptic indicators that what we see in the Seal (and maybe in the Bible itself) may show a reverse path or process, related to the expulsion from Eden at Genesis 3/4. One is the shape of a letter lamed in the G2 square, which is remarkably similar to the serpent depicted in a 4×7 matrix obtained from the letters of Genesis 1:1. The other is the descending *aur* (skin) in the G1 square, which is co-terminal with the ascending *aur* (light). Chapter 7 will also reveal a three-part effect that could be described as a 'coming in', corresponding to a 'going out' we saw in Chapter 4. We may also contemplate whether the reverse-path effect is also being emphasised by several meaningful names and expressions that may be read backwards in the regular Torah text. One very early example is the expression *Moses, image of Yah...*, consisting of eight consecutive letters within Genesis 1:1. Another is the four-letter name of God, detectable for the first time in Genesis 1:14. Here, the hidden name spelled in reverse overlaps two words, which include the noteworthy palindromic *halaylah* (the night) at the central point in the creation account. More recently, we have been examining the reverse-written word arba (four), created at the very start of the Torah by the migration of the letter ayin.

Finally there are several instances (not previously described) of strategically placed words and phrases that are similar to one another, and are presented as mirror images. A rather striking example is in Genesis 2:4, which starts with an expression involving 'the heavens and the earth', then ends with 'earth and heaven'. In fact, the latter phrase at the very end of the biblical creation account also reverses 'the heavens and the earth' as it appears in the first verse, like a pair of matched book-ends. Another especially important case of book-ends involves the extreme limits of the Torah. The second verse of Genesis includes two uses of the word face; there is the 'face of the deep' found within the Seal, and the 'face of the waters' excluded from the Seal. Here, we could be seeing another allusion to the Small Face and Vast Face duality of God, espoused by Kabbalah, one within and the other without. Then, only two verses from the very end of the Torah we see this:

> *And there arose not a prophet since in Israel like unto Moses,*
> *whom the Lord knew face to face.*

(Deuteronomy 34:10)

So, we have a number of distinctive literary constructs, many of which are of known relevance to the Seal, and are either:

- **cyclic**, or
- **reversals** (backward text), or
- **inversions** (strategically placed combinations of whole words presented in reverse order), or
- **enclosures**.

The third and fourth of these concepts may also point to what is intended in the special paired numbers: 611+616; 612+615 and 613+614 in which the larger number in each pair represents completion of what the smaller member began. But, overall, these are four very persistent and all-pervading themes, which surely require more than just tacit recognition. It may be we are expected to derive some higher significance from what are merely clues. Whether that is the intention or not, there can be no harm in testing the temperature of the water. And it seems to me there is only one way in which the whole Torah can be made to obey every one of these clues. That would be if its end is forced to loop back to its beginning, perhaps with the ayin prefix interposed; with Vast Face at the interface, so to speak.

This interpretation would also help to explain the expression *I am the Alpha and the Omega* repeated three times in the final book of the

Bible - the book of Revelation - with increasing emphasis, or urgency. Notice here the use of the first and last letters of the Greek alphabet, giving the clearest hint that the last letter is coincident and synonymous with the first. In that case, the cyclic Torah may even be just a primer to what is intended for the message of the complete Bible. And that would be the perfect explanation for the restoration of the Holy City at the end of Revelation – a new home to replace the lost Eden, where God and man may live side by side. This idea is by no means spurious, since the Seal itself shows ample evidence of being a template for all biblical temples. It even bequeaths all the more important temple artefacts, like the menorah and the Ark of the covenant.

There have in fact been two previous examples of an encircling effect, which we could accept as prompts to think along similar lines. One was, of course, the way the 28 letters of Genesis 1:1 became the perimeter for the first two square views of the Author's Seal. And just look at the richness of the consequences still flowing from that one simple act. Then we followed clues that led us to form the first 2208 letters of the Torah into a similar square perimeter. That turned out to be the smallest perfect square capable of containing the 304,805 letters of the Hebrew Torah. The rationale for that was the position (ie 2210) of the last of the Hebrew letters (ie *samech*) to make its first appearance. And, significantly, that was within the word 'compasseth'. So, by now forming the whole Torah into a closed loop we are following a prosperous, tried-and-tested route.

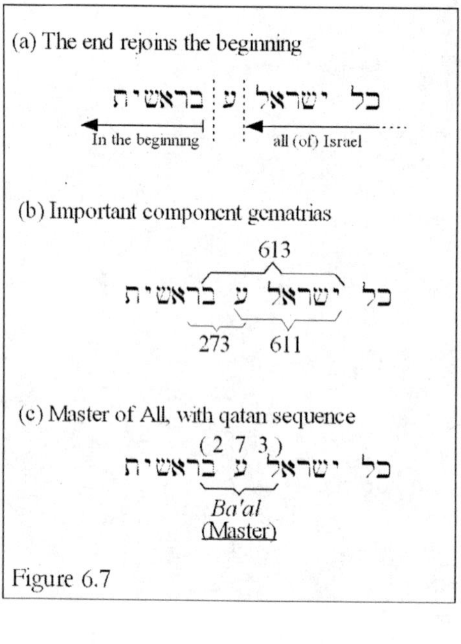

(a) The end rejoins the beginning

כל ישראל  ע  בראשית

In the beginning  |  all (of) Israel

(b) Important component gematrias

613

כל ישראל ע בראשית

273     611

(c) Master of All, with qatan sequence

( 2  7  3 )

כל ישראל ע בראשית

Ba'al
(Master)

Figure 6.7

Now, if the end of the Torah is meant to join onto its beginning in the way I suggest, then previous experience tells us we should expect some significant outcomes to emerge as revealed confirmation. So it is incumbent on us to check for meaningful consequences at the new interface. In Figure 6.7, part (a) shows the migrated ayin (ע) prefix at the centre of the relevant text. The beginning of the Torah is seen to the left of the *ayin*. Then the end of the Torah re-enters from the right, to end alongside the interposed ayin. The beginning shown here consists of just the first word B'reishith (In the beginning), while the end consists of כל ישראל / *kal Yisrael* / <u>all of Israel</u>, taken from:

> *and for all the mighty power and all the great and terrible deeds which Moses wrought in the sight of all Israel.*
> (Deuteronomy 34:12)

Within Figure 6.7, we may readily see sequences of letters (and their qatan values) that are known to be of special importance. This assessment applies particularly to the words *four* and *square*, and their corresponding sequences 1227 (or 7221) and 722. We should also note that the three letters of *raba* (square) are an anagram of ערב / *erev* / <u>evening</u>. This matters because of the way the biblical creation account marks the transition from one cyclic day to the next not with the word night, but with the words evening and morning. In fact, it is verses containing such transitions that conferred three of the special letter-counts we analysed in Chapter 5. Clearly, the calculation, 722 – 111 = 611 applies equally to the case of 'evening' as it did to 'square'. And why stop there when a second stage leads to another distinctive number, so:

$$611 - 111 = 500$$

So, to proceed now to the new content in the join from end to beginning, there is one especially important emergent word at the interface. This is בעל / *Ba'al* / <u>master</u>, which combines the Torah's very last letter (from Israel) with its first, along with the interposed ayin. Converting the right-to-left Hebrew letters of *Ba'al* to the western left-to-right qatan values we obtain the sequence 273, which significantly is also the gematria of the overlapping *arba*. There is more to be said about this number in due course.

On the right side of the divide, the gematria of ישראל (Israel) is 541. But when this is augmented by the adjacent letter *ayin* it becomes the ubiquitous 611 gematria of 'Torah'.

Next, there are three surprising consecutive groups of three letters each, spanning the section of text from the *shin* (ש) of Israel, to the *shin* of B'reishith. The central three are, of course, Ba'al (master), often in the sense of a husband and head of the family. Very appropriately, to the immediate left of Ba'al in Figure 6.7 is the word רֹאשׁ / *rosh* / <u>head</u> itself, within B'reishith. And to the right are the same three letters reordered as ארשׂ / *aras* / <u>to betroth</u>. Given this juxtaposition of the words husband, head and betroth, it is easy to understand why Judaism casts the heirs of Abraham in the role of a bride to the Lord God husband. And the word heir is also clearly visible in the letters בר (Bar) at the very start of B'reishith.

Finally, returning to the comfortable world of hard facts, we should not be too surprised to find there is a special relationship between the four-letter name of God, and the extent of his Torah. The connection is found in the gematria values of the two halves of the divine name, which are 15 (from י ה) and 11 (from ו ה). Observe the following effect defined by those two values as upper and lower limits:

$$11 \times 12 \times 13 \times 14 \times 15 \qquad = 360360$$

... and the next relationship between this result and the length of the Torah in terms of the number of letters it contains:

$$360360 - 304805 \qquad = 55555$$

But note now the product of the gematria values of B'reishith and the overlapping arba (four):

$$913 \times 273 \qquad = 249249$$

And that

$$304805 - 249249 \qquad = 55556$$

Comparing the first stage of each result, we quickly find that:

$$360360 - 249249 \qquad = 111111$$

What is especially significant about the above effect is that:

- the first number is derived from the *four*-letter name, by a left-right separation that is reminiscent of the way 609 and 610 were recently obtained from the length of the Torah,
- the second derives from the word *four* and the Torah's first word, and
- the length of the Torah is at the exact half-way position between the two numbers.

Nor should we forget a result we saw earlier, that the very busy 'four' combines with the gematria of B'reishith in the following striking alternative way ...

$$913 \times 4 = 3652$$

... thus giving the digits of the length of the solar year (ie 365.2 days) to an accuracy that is within about one hour over the full year. The key concept demonstrated here is of time (days and years) as a cyclic phenomenon.

-oOo-

Without a doubt, the migration of the sole letter ayin to its new position as prefix to the Torah confers an amazing degree of benefit on the Seal. And there is one more effect that is the equal of any.

In Chapter 2, we examined the first verse of Genesis as a 7×4 matrix and found two words that are spelled in the manner of the famous Bible Code with letters that occur at intervals of 7 letters in the normal text. One in particular, the word (ה)שלש / *shelosh(eh)* / <u>three</u> divided the matrix symmetrically into equal left and right halves. However, if the same matrix is now re-drawn with the ayin prefix in place, as in Figure 6.8(a), a new and quite astonishing effect comes to light. It is an effect that again combines language and mathematics in a remarkable way.

Referring to the shaded elements in the illustration, we find that the horizontal word for 'four' is juxtaposed to the word for 'three' with a right-angle between them. What comes to mind most naturally is that this alliance must represent the well-known standard right-angle triangle, having sides in the ratio 3:4:5. How do we know that this shape is even feasible? It is because of the famous Theorem of Pythagoras (c.575BC to c.495BC), which states:

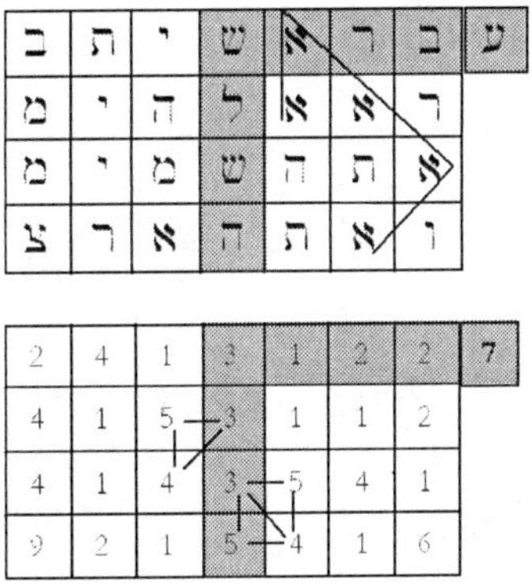

Figure 6.8

> *In any right-angle triangle, the square constructed on the hypotenuse is equal in area to the sum of the squares on the other two sides.*

This theorem is applicable to *all* right-angle triangles, not just to the minority that happen to have sides with lengths in whole number ratios. However, a triangle whose sides are in the ratio 3:4:5 is one of the minority, because of the equality $3^2 + 4^2 = 5^2$ (ie $9 + 16 = 25$). And this triangle has a right-angle between the sides of relative length 3 and 4; that is, exactly like the words 'three' and 'four' in the matrix of Figure 6.8(a).

That is already a delightful visual effect, if only we could be confident that it is deliberate. So it would be nice to have just a little more evidence. For one thing, only the names of three and four are made plain in the matrix, so we need some proof that 5, too, has a planned role. There are two ways in which the number 5 is related to the word for 'three' in particular.

First, in Figure 6.8(b), it is seen that the matrix of qatan values contains only three copies of the number 5 which, significantly, are found in columns 3, 4 and 5. Also, it can be seen that each 5 combines with adjacent 3 and 4 digits in a triangular group, in such a way that the 5 is at the right-angle position. This configuration corresponds to the fact that in all triangles, the largest angle is always opposite to the longest side; and in a right-angle triangle, the longest side is the hypotenuse, opposite to the right-angle.

Next, there is a powerful indicator we have seen before, but only now have reason to associate it with the Theorem of Pythagoras. We know that the reason the word for 'three' perfectly bisects the 7×4 matrix of Genesis 1:1 is because its first letter is the fourth in the verse, and its other letters occur at regular intervals of 7 in the plain-text. And in Chapter 2, when we first formed Genesis 1:1 into the perimeter of a 8×8 square, that was also the reason why the same four letters took up the corner positions of a square-within-a-square. Then Figure 6.9 shows vividly how the Author of the Seal intends the word 'three' to relate to the Theorem of Pythagoras. Part (a) of this illustration is repeated, so we may see the amazing similarity between it and part (b). Part (c) will help in demonstrating the truth of Pythagoras' Theorem.

The square outlines of Figure 6.9(b)&(c) are drawn to be of equal size; and the eight shaded triangles (four in each) are all identical to one another in shape and size (it would not matter whether the eight triangles are slim or stubby, as long as they are all identical). Therefore, the two un-shaded squares in (c) together must equal the area of the single un-shaded square in (b). Also, it can be seen that the latter square is defined by the lengths of the hypotenuse of the four triangles, and the two smaller squares are defined by the lengths of the identical triangles' two shorter sides. This description is widely known as a *proof by rearrangement* of the Theorem given above in words.

For our purpose the key fact is, of course, that the square-within-a-square in Figure 6.9(a) is a very simple rearrangement of the 7×4 matrix of Figure 6.8(a). The letters at the four corners of the inscribed square are the same letters that occupy the middle column in the matrix. They spell the word שלשה / *shelosheh* / three which, in the matrix, is juxtaposed to ארבע / *arba* / four, in the same way as the two shorter sides in a 3:4:5 right-angle triangle. That, then, is the second proof of how the Author intends us to recognise this close association between the use of Hebrew in the Seal and simple mathematics.

Figure 6.9  (a)

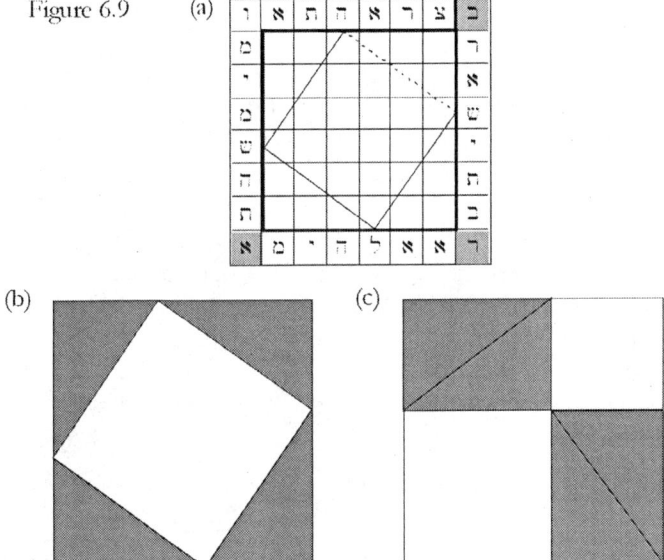

(b)    (c)

Next, we may observe a rich numerical aspect to the word for 'three', which at once depends on the reticent '5' and also renews the persistent theme of triangular numbers. Here, we note the number 3335, which is bequeathed as a qatan sequence from שלשה (shelosheh) seen in the earlier matrix of Figure 6.8(b). It is self-evident that 3335 is divisible by 5; and performing the division reveals the other factor to be 667. That is derived from the masculine form of shelosheh. However, the feminine case - שלש (shalosh) – bequeaths a 333 sequence directly. And there is a very important connection between 333 and 667, which follows from the fact that 333 = 666 ÷ 2, and $667 = 666 + 1$. These essential factors lead directly to $T_{666}$ (ie 222111), since $333 \times 667 = 222111$ (see Appendix A(iii) and the formula for calculating $T_n$). Note particularly that 667 and 333 come from the masculine and feminine forms of 'three' respectively. So $T_{666}$ is a union of the two.

Now a quick glance at the top-right corner of the topical matrix (Figure 6.8(b)) shows that the digits of 222111 are indeed present in triangular form. Notably, the linear '111' component itself belongs to a 45° right-angle triangle suggested by the letter *aleph*. But its presence here has the added purpose of forming the hypotenuse of the 222111 triangle. What is more, each 1 in the 111 sequence belongs to a different version of the word ברא / *bara* / He created:

- the middle 1 comes from the explicit *bara* in the plain text,
- the upper 1 comes from the same three letters as the first half of the first word, and
- the lower 1 comes from the emergent ELS *bara* spelled with letters spaced at 7-letter intervals in the plain text (these were at the first three corner positions in the G1 square).

Clearly, the existence of this triangular $T_{666}$ is independent of the ayin prefix, although three of its components also contribute to the word *arba* (four) when the ayin prefix is in place.

The last mathematical exhibit in the augmented matrix depends on the qatan sequences of both 'three' and 'four', each understood as a four-digit decimal number. But the effect we see is not something that could have been known and understood by any extant culture of biblical times. The two topical words confer the following essential ratio:

$$\frac{3335}{1227} = 2.71801 \quad \text{(to 6 significant figures)}$$

This value is very close to the mathematically important number **e**, underestimating the actual value by a mere 0.01%. If this ratio had been the only shared effect of 'three' and 'four', it could reasonably be dismissed as a simple happenstance. However, it is not an isolated effect but one of several. It, therefore, deserves to be taken seriously as a deliberate inclusion on the part of the Author of the Torah.

It is perhaps also significant that **e** is central to calculations of compound interest and, therefore, mathematical models (formulae) that describe population growth. And the same is true of the Fibonacci Sequence that is implied by every one of the numerical references the Seal makes to the Ark of the Covenant. This connection is certainly in keeping with the importance the Bible attaches to the increase in the seed of Abraham, marked particularly by the divine census in the book of Numbers, and many counts of family members recorded elsewhere in the Bible.

-oOo-

To conclude the present Chapter, I simply want to summarise four numerical relationships that appear most improbable yet nonetheless do exist. Each of them has its own intrinsic merit, but as a family group possess the systemic property that the whole is greater than the sum of the parts. Three of these relationships are recent discoveries in this Chapter. The other from Chapter 4, relates the gematria values of the Tetragrammaton and the name of Abraham and is repeated here:

$$
\begin{array}{r}
248 \\
-\ \underline{111} \\
137 \\
-\ \underline{111} \\
26
\end{array}
$$

    248       Gematria of Abraham (אברהם)

-  111

  137       (the final ages of Ishmael, Levi and Amram)

-  111

   26       Gematria of YHWH (יהוה)

This result is one of many demonstrating that a clear bond exists between names and numbers in the Bible.

A more recent discovery is that 304,805 (ie the number of letters in the Torah) is at the precise mid-point between 360,360 and 249,249, a span of exactly 111,111. The upper and lower limits here are themselves by no means random. The first was obtained from the gematria of YHWH, by the product of the range of integers defined by its first and second halves (ie 11 and 15 respectively). This name especially is inseparable from numerical considerations. The other number is the product of the gematrias of the overlapping B'reishith and arba. Thus, every part of the above calculation is intimately related to the Tetragrammaton, or the Seal or the whole Torah.

Before that, we found that the notable sequence of numbers 500, 611 and 722 also differ by increments of 111. Admittedly, the first of the three is just a nice round number; whereas the others have a definite biblical significance. 611 is the gematria of the word 'Torah', and 722 is the digit sequence that starts the Torah once its 49th letter, the first ayin (ע) has been moved to become its prefix. It derives from the word 'square'.

Earlier still, we discovered that 7221 (a digit sequence obtained from arba) is found precisely at the mid-point between 6666 and 7666 (ie 6×6×6×6×6), a span of 1110, or 10×111. So, clearly, the word 'four' and the four-letter Name of God are both intimately tied to an underlying numerical foundation to the Torah.

Overall, therefore, our investigations have led us to find four strikingly similar numerical relationships in which a number that is of great biblical importance is at the mid-point of a significant number range. And in each case the operative range is defined by numbers that are also biblically important or mathematically distinctive. Moreover, the ranges concerned are also all distinctive multiples of 111; those multiples all being 2, 10 or 1001.

We may also note here that the 248 gematria of Abraham used in the first of the above calculations is its value following the modification from Abram (see Genesis 17:5). Since the gematria of [ם] רחם / racham / a womb is also 248, we find that the union of Abraham and a womb generates 496 (ie T$_{31}$ and third Perfect Number). But before the name of Abraham was modified its gematria had been 243, which is 3×3×3×3×3. The fact that both a 3×3×3×3×3 and a 6×6×6×6×6 are active in these descriptions leads to another, corresponding observation. The ELS word *shalosh* (three) in the 7×4 matrix of Figure 6.9(b) gives rise to a 333 sequence that symmetrically divides the matrix in its vertical axis. And in the G1 aspect of the Seal, it was a 666 sequence that divided *it* symmetrically in *its* vertical axis.

In conclusion, I suggest it is untenable to suppose these four separate results are unplanned and unknown to the omniscient Author of the Torah. Yet, for them to be deliberately intended would force a total rethink concerning the origins of the Torah, its coherent structure and the names it contains. Even the language in which the Torah is written can no longer be assumed to have evolved independently of a vast, elaborate strategic plan. And the Hebrew alephbeyt is now seen to embody far more internally-consistent structure than could have come about accidentally. These interrelated design features are crying out for a proper explanation, be that rational by our normal standards or not. That will inevitably call for a closer partnership between modern biblical scholarship and traditional, Jewish thought. Yet the copious evidence for supernatural design is surely enough to overwhelm these normally daunting obstacles.

# 7

In all of human history there can never have been a more skilfully woven text than the start of the Hebrew Torah, which manages to say so much with only its first 65 letters. It is almost as though the plain words we read at the start of the Bible are mere meta-data, when the real content is to be found only in deeply embedded sub-structures that cannot be seen or comprehended all at once. Yet the ability to see every facet simultaneously is the only way to explain how this phenomenon could have been conceived. Living, as we do, in three perceptible dimensions, the only accessible approach to the Seal on the Torah text is by looking at a series of 2-dimensional slices. Our difficulty is similar to the problem of two observers who are asked to describe a certain shape that they can both see simultaneously. Paradoxically, one says it looks like a rectangle, while the other says it is a circle. In reality, they are both equally correct because the object they see is a cylinder seen from alternative perspectives. And their limited perspectives may be something over which they have no control.

A number of biblical prophets seem to have been aware, perhaps only dimly, of particular aspects of this Seal; though not the same features in every case. Evidently the collection of features that each prophet recognised appears to have been influenced by his immediate circumstances, limited by the social and philosophical stage reached at the time. For example, none of the prophets would have recognised the decimal digits of Pi, not least because the decimal number system was not developed until post-biblical times. And even after decimal arithmetic became the norm, it would be several more centuries before Pi became known to better than the popular 22/7 approximation. On the other hand, knowledge of triangular and hexagram (ie Star of David) numbers goes back at least as far as Ancient Near Eastern civilisations. That was possible because figurate numbers[1] such as these

---

[1] see Appendix A(ii)

may be represented pictorially and do not depend on the number system in which they are expressed.

Ezra, too, although not normally counted among the prophets, must be seen as having knowledge of some aspects of the Seal. In fact, Ezra seems to have been particularly aware of the importance of triangular numbers such as 666 (see Ezra 2:13) and Star of David numbers like 13, 37 and 73, the sum of which is 123 (see Ezra 2:21). Ezra even links the latter number with Bethlehem – City of David; hence the later New Testament association between Bethlehem and a star worthy to be followed by wise men. By the end of the present Chapter, we will have added the names of Isaiah, Daniel and Amos to the list of knowing prophets. We already have some evidence that Ezekiel and the author of Revelation were aware of diverse aspects of the Seal. And we are about to see another example from those two books. Eventually I shall prove that certain features were known independently by these two specific prophets. Some of the knowledge they shared must wait a while longer for an explanation; but there is one part that will now lead naturally to both the third and fourth re-making of the Seal. These two new facets will be known as G3 and G4 respectively. Here are the passages from those two widely separated books, which show they are describing the same phenomenon:

*"But thou, son of man, hear what I say unto thee; be not thou rebellious like that rebellious house: open thy mouth and eat what I give thee."*

*And when I looked, behold an hand was sent unto me; and, lo, a roll of a book was therein;*

*And he spread it before me; and it was written within and without: and there was written therein lamentations, and mourning, and woe.*

(Ezekiel 2:8-10, KJV)

*Then I saw in the right hand of him who was seated on the throne a scroll written within and on the back, sealed with seven seals.*

(Revelation 5:1, RSV)

*Then [another mighty angel] was holding a little scroll, which lay open in his hand. He planted his right foot on the sea and his left foot on the land.*

*So I went to the angel and asked him to give me the little scroll. He said to me, "Take it and eat it. It will turn your stomach sour, but in your mouth it will be sweet as honey."*

(Revelation 10:2, 9, NIV)

Of course, it is not yet obvious that the later book is fully independent of the earlier one. In fact, we may safely assume that the author of Revelation was entirely familiar with Ezekiel's writing. But in the next Chapter, I shall provide compelling evidence for their independence (where that matters) using differences in their descriptions of another vision they share in common. The differences will show that neither author completely understood what he saw; but the same differences will allow us to determine one consistent, overarching explanation for both. We shall find the conclusion they would undoubtedly have reached for themselves, had they been contemporaries and able to discuss their experiences.

Right now, we have enough of a clue to proceed to the next stage in deciphering the Author's Seal. The only hint we need is the knowledge that a scroll of enormous importance, and probably a small scroll, is written on both sides. Coupled to this knowledge is our familiarity with the Seal, which is very small indeed, and rolled up in the manner of a scroll with only one line of text on it. So, in Figure 7.1, the text that was seen in the G2 square (the letter ayin already migrated to become its prefix), is entered into the square in reverse order. The ayin (ע) prefix is now seen at the centre, where the 65th Torah letter was previously placed. Then the next 63 letters follow the familiar, clockwise coiled path, only in reverse, so that the last letter is now found in the eastern corner. Symbolically, we are now looking at the reverse side of the same small scroll, G3 version. The G4

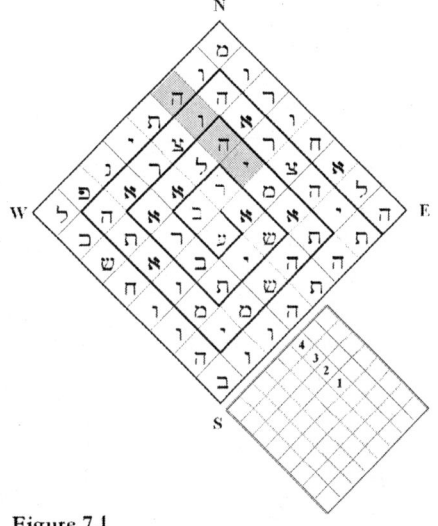

**Figure 7.1**

version will depend on one more tiny modification; yet the effect of making that adjustment is so considerable that the details will have to be described separately.

In the illustrated G3 aspect, the only feature I have chosen to mark is יהוה / YHWH / the four-letter Name of God, or Tetragrammaton. Its position here is the only one in any aspect of the Seal where it appears in linear form. It has been seen in G2 in a tight square configuration (see Figure 5.8), and it is always visible by allusion in the text: [ם] םשה / *HaShem* / <u>The Name</u>, as part of [ם] םימשה / *hashamayim* / <u>the heavens</u> in Genesis 1:1.

One thing that is especially notable about the four-letter name seen in Figure 7.1 is its location; since the same four elements of the square have held other special words within the two previous aspects. These are best described by reference to the numbers in the same locations in the thumbnail sketch. In the G2 square, positions 3-2-1 contained the word [ן] ן י י / *yayin* / <u>wine</u>. In G1, positions 4-3-2 held [ן] ן יא / *ayin* / <u>Where?</u>, <u>without</u> or <u>to be nothing</u>. The variety of alternative meanings for the latter word is itself revealing. Since the four-letter name is generally absent from square versions of the Seal, the 'Where?' interrogative seems particularly apposite. It brings to mind especially the words of the man being crucified: *"Eloi, Eloi, lama sabachthani?"* – *"My God, My God, why hast thou forsaken me?"* Recall that the word *lama* ('why') was also seen in the G1 square, in Figure 2.8. The other two meanings follow naturally, as they both relate to something that is missing. Equally important is the pronunciation of the word ayin in G1. Since it sounds just like the name of the letter that was removed to generate G2.

Something I normally do at an early stage, after introducing a new version of the Seal, is to draw attention to the positions of all the letters *vav* (ו). The theme we have been tracing up to now is that of 'water', because in previous squares these letters have behaved the way that water normally does. So, in the G1 square, all the water was found in the lower half; that is in addition to five of those letters taking up symmetrical positions in the 'Y' shape of the crucified man. In the second square, eight out of nine of the same letters assembled into a continuous string in the shape of the Hebrew letter *lamed* (ל) or a river.

In our latest G3 square, the same nine letters have become distributed in yet another improbable way. This time, five of them are found in the lower five horizontal rows, and the other four in the uppermost four rows. Therefore the six longest rows in the middle (ie just over 60% of the square) are totally devoid of the letter *vav*. If the distribution of the letter *vav* in the latest square had been totally unplanned, there would be about one chance in 1925 that these letters should be found only in the nine shorter rows where they are now seen. And the odds against chance alone being the agent in both the present distribution and that seen in the G1 and G2 square are only 1 in 163971. The way I have calculated this number is set out in full as a case study at Appendix C. Also, in case it is thought that the latest outcome is a direct consequence of previous distributions, it is not. In the absence of deliberate design, reversing the order of the text in the square should not create any predictable pattern.

The obvious next question is how to interpret this unlikely new distribution of water, for which there are two particularly obvious candidate answers. One is the parting of the waters of the Red Sea, which allowed the Israelites escaping Egypt to pass through. And, there are other aspects of the G3 square that also point to the Exodus as a major theme.

The other candidate for an explanation is the second day of creation, of which it is written:

*And God made the firmament, and divided the waters which were under the firmament from the waters which were above the firmament: and it was so.*

(Genesis 1:7)

Later, we shall see pictorial evidence that this verse is an intended answer, and that the Seal is once more demonstrating its seemingly endless versatility. Or it could be that the second day of creation was always looking forward to the later event.

One direct reference to Egypt made by the new square again involves Abraham, though only by reference, rather than by name. There are three parts of the square which relate the story of the patriarch from the moment he first becomes fully the focus of the Torah, until he and Sarah go down into Egypt to escape famine. Take a look at Figure 7.2 (overleaf), as it shows the route taken.

First of all, in the bottom of the square we see the emergent word בּיִת / *bayit* / <u>house</u> ascending in the vertical diagonal. These are the same three positions which, in the G1 square, contained the triple letter vav and its 666 alter-ego. The newly created house, we may assume, corresponds to the text:

*Now the Lord had said unto Abram, Get thee out of thy country, and from thy kindred, and from thy father's house, unto a land that I will shew thee:*

(Genesis 12:1)

Soon we shall see a numeric partner to the house, which will identify the whole 3×3 lower corner region as of special importance.

In the Beginning

Within the present square, the word bayit terminates just short of the central cluster. And that 2×2 group in now filled with the word arba (four), which includes the letter ayin prefix. Now recall that the word *Ivrit* (ie Hebrew – the language) is spelled with the letter ayin,

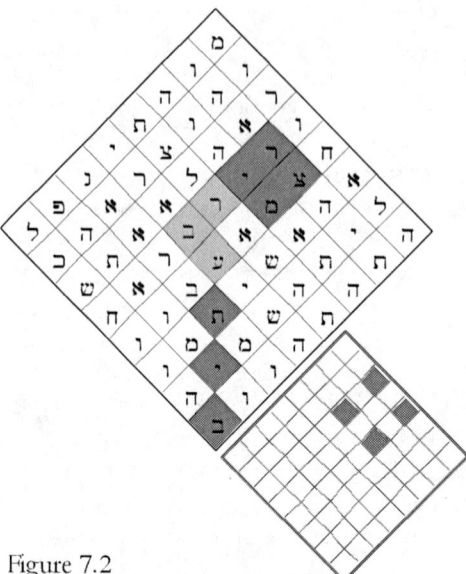

Figure 7.2

followed by four letters of the word B'reishith, the first word of the Torah. However, the route of Abraham's journey does not trace all the way through the whole first word. The journey certainly does continue with the letter ayin just above the house, and it follows three of the letters of arba in reverse (lighter shading), but it then breaks out into the letter *yud* (ʾ) of the darker shaded square zone. In this way, the route of Abraham traces the word עברי / *Ivri* / Hebrew (the ethnic identity), from which he was descended. It is here we should recall that the area of the square through which the patriarch is now seen to pass was once (see G2) the location of the word [ם] רחם / *racham* / a womb, which shares the same 248 gematria as the name Abraham. The letters of racham were then in the same positions as the upper 'V' formation of the crucified man in G1.

But note particularly the letters in positions represented in the thumbnail sketch. These spell [ם] הרחם / *ha racham* / the womb. This is a quite different womb; but notice that these letters are in the very same location where, in G1, we once saw ל נתש / *l'natash* / for a root. They also enclosed the word [ץ] ארץ / *eretz* / land, or earth there, and eretz is always found in the same position in every aspect of the Seal. Since we have noted earlier that *racham* (womb) has the same gematria as Abraham, we should also recognise that Abram was promised all the land from the river of Egypt to the great river, the river Euphrates (See Genesis 15:18). And in the G2 square, in Figure 5.2, we saw פרת / *Parot* / Euphrates occupying the vertical diagonal of the very same 3×3 zone. Also, Genesis 15:18 is the very next verse after the one we saw represented by the Torah's first word (*B'reishith*). That was when *esh* (fire) is lifted out of the midst of that word leaving *brit* (a covenant). Yet again we find that a precise location in three different views of the Seal is a blueprint for an important event later in the Torah.

Next, the 2×2 shaded group containing the letter yud of Ivri (Hebrew) traces the all-important cyclic word [מ] מצרים / *Mitzraim* / Egypt, by utilising the same letter mem at both the beginning and the end. Therefore, we have traced the journey of Abraham that is described in the first ten verses of Genesis 12. Also, typically of the consistency designed into the Seal, the final 2×2 group containing the name of Egypt, is the very same location that contained [ן] פראן / *Paran* / Paran in the G2 square. That is the place to which the Israelites would one day travel, the Ark at their head, after leaving Sinai. It was also seen to overlap on three of the letters of ישראל / *Yisrael* / Israel found in G1. So there is a three-way geographical latching on this compact zone between all the three square aspects of the Seal we have seen so far.

What is more, the expression [מ] הרחם / *ha racham* / the womb serves now to complete a progressive three-stage development that corresponds to the biblical passage:

> *Yet now hear, O Jacob my servant; and Israel whom I have chosen:*
> *Thus saith the Lord that made thee, and formed thee from the womb…*
>
> (Isaiah 44:1-2)

Since this text links the name of Israel with the verb *yatzar* (to form) and *the womb*, we should note that:

- In G1, both Israel and *yatzar* were found within a single 3×3 zone, but the letters of Israel were in a relatively nondescript configuration.
- In G2, *yatzar* was unchanged within the 3×3 zone, but Israel had been transformed into a more pleasing, symmetrical arrangement. The new shape was, incidentally, identical to something else that we shall examine later in the present Chapter.
- In G3, the very same 3×3 zone contains the 4-letter expression 'the womb' in its corner elements. These are the same four elements that held the expression 'for a root' in G1.

The same 3×3 group now also completes in a literal sense another metaphor that was begun numerically in Chapter 3. At that early stage, the gematria of Genesis 1:1 (ie 2701) was seen to consist of the $T_{37}$ triangular number (ie 703) surrounded by three copies of $T_{36}$ (ie 666). The central 703 equated precisely with the last two words of that opening verse, meaning 'and the earth'. This made the point very graphically that the earth is to be regarded as the centre of creation, from the biblical perspective. But the opening two verses of Genesis, in the context of the G1, G2 and G3 squares makes the same point in a way that might easily be overlooked. Each of these squares emphasise a particular 3×3 area in three ways. Firstly, where one includes the emergent three-letter word *p'riy* (fruit), the second includes the word *Parot* (Euphrates). Secondly, where one includes the name of Israel, the second includes *Paran*, and the third has the name *Mitzraim* (Egypt). And thirdly, they all include the same three-letter word [ץ] ארץ / *eretz* / <u>earth</u> or <u>land</u>. But note that, for obvious reasons the third copy of eretz (letters 31, 32 and 33 of the regular text) is in reverse direction compared with the previous two squares; the whole text in the G3 square is the reverse of the text in G1 and G2. In principle, however, the word eretz should not be so precisely coincident as it is, because its odd number of letters cannot be centred precisely in a text with an even number of letters. In fact, the latching that we now observe is possible only because of the presence of the letter ayin prefix in the centre of G3. So this fine-tuning was no doubt pre-conceived to put the earth at the centre of creation.

-oOo-

The journey of Abraham described above may be thought of as both a theme and a trend. It is a theme in its own right, having an integrity and consistency within the present version of the Seal. The theme implied here is the life of Abraham, and his evident importance to the plan the Torah represents. But a trend is also developing in a way that can only be seen after two or more aspects of the Seal are available to compare. Every new view of the Seal incorporates one or more themes and motifs that have their own internal integrity. Motifs may include sets of related words that occur together to define a distinct portion of a square, such as the combination of 'fruit' and 'for a root' seen in G1. These sub-sections usually have the form of a recognisable geometric pattern. Even in isolation, such motifs and themes undoubtedly call for recognition. However, when one view after another of the same seventeen and a half consecutive words keep repeating the same themes and motifs, then we have a whole raft of trends needing to be explained consistently. That is to say, there must be a single, inclusive principle that is capable of explaining the extraordinary behaviour of this one short text. The simplest explanation is that the Seal is the product of an omniscient intelligence.

In the G3 square, the Egypt theme continues with a number of references to the events at Sinai which followed the start of the exodus. Notice in Figure 7.3 the emergent word מההר / *m'ha har* / from the mountain, which reads downwards in the top of the vertical diagonal, and is diametrically opposite the bayit (house) of Abraham. And crossing through the new word is ההר / *ha har* / the mountain, thus delineating the uppermost 3×3 group. What we see here is the start of a theme that is about to propel us into a veritable roller-coaster ride, with additional components that follow in quick succession.

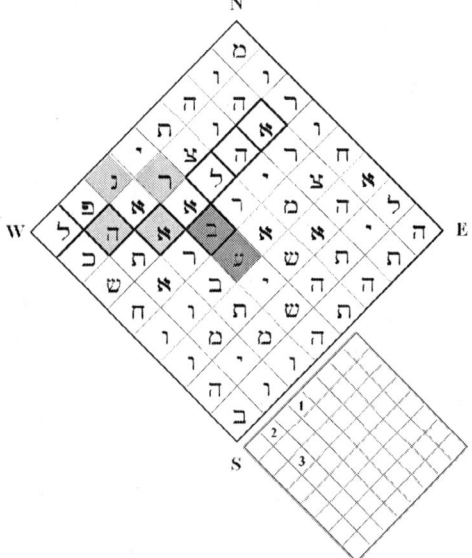

**Figure 7.3**

In the same illustration, we see the word אהל / *ohel* / tent (heavier borders) crossing through the expression 'from the mountain', and through the four-letter Name of God, so that all three share the same letter *heh* (ה). Also, in the left end of the horizontal diagonal is the one-word expression באהל / *b'ohel* / in a tent. If we remember that the Ark of the Covenant was kept in the Tent of Meeting in the Tabernacle, this opens up the possibility for some extensive new understanding. That is, firstly, because the Tent of Meeting (the Holy of Holies) was literally אהל באהל / *ohel b'ohel* / a tent within a tent. Also, the Ark in the Tent of Meeting was where יהוה / *YHWH* / The Lord made his dwelling among men, for the first time since the expulsion from Eden. So this must be the implication we are meant to draw from 'a tent', YHWH and 'from the mountain' all sharing one common letter. Next, whenever the Lord's presence was over the Ark, the Tent of Meeting was always shrouded in a dense cloud or mist.

The appropriate word in the square is עב / *owb* / <u>a thick cloud</u>, found in the centre (deeper shading). Also, the word *owb* has a gematria of 72, the known length of another of God's names. And, if we look closely, we will be able to see the Ark itself in two very different but closely and delightfully aligned forms. The Ark has become a more persistent theme or leitmotif than any other, as our knowledge and understanding of the Author's Seal develops. As such, it is more worthy than most to be recognised also as a trend.

First, we find the letters of the word [ן] ןראה / *ha aron* / <u>the Ark</u> in a small square formation (lighter shading) where, in the G2 square, was seen the four-letter Name of God. This is a particularly stunning example of latching between two aspects of the Seal. It also recalls the fact that the Presence of God in the Tabernacle was always seen over the Mercy Seal, the cover on the Ark – coincident yet in alternative realities.

The other occurrence of the Ark is a pictorial one in the likeness of the one we once saw composed of light and darkness. The new one, too, is formed from two properly spaced 3×3 clusters of letters, one of which is actually defined by the letters of ןראה (the Ark) which we have just examined. Those four letters are at the mid-points of the four sides of the required 3×3 cluster. Then three of its corner squares are occupied by the letters of תפי / *Yapheth* / <u>Japheth</u>, the name of one of the sons of Noah (positions 1-2-3 in the thumbnail sketch). The letters of Japheth pass through the horizontal word באהל (in a tent), reminding us of the text:

> God shall enlarge Japheth, and he shall dwell in the tents of Shem[m]...
>
> (Genesis 9:27)

We shall encounter Japheth again in Chapter 9 in his more familiar setting.

The other end of the new Ark is another distinctive 3×3 group set high in the top of the square. This is where 'the mountain', 'a tent' and the four-letter name of God are all found either within the same area or at least overlapping it on the maximum possible three letters. However, to fully appreciate the Ark metaphor, it is necessary to look at the same square in qatan letter values, as Figure 7.4.

---

[m] The Hebrew word *Shem* literally means 'name'.

Now it is possible to see a new 1666 group in this 3×3 area, in an identical configuration to the expression הֵאָרֹ֣ן (the Ark) in the lower group. These digits are undoubtedly set out in a similar fashion to something we saw in Chapter 4, both at the centre of the G1 version of the Seal, and within the overlapping pentagonal numbers we obtained from the number of letters contained in the Torah. So, the digits 1666 now found in this new square formation (albeit rotated by 135°) may also be understood as the number 616 overlapping 666. However, the same digits interpreted as the decimal number 1.666 have more immediate relevance. We already know that 1.666 is the truncated result of the ratio 5/3 and a reasonable approximation to the Divine Proportion (Φ). The

**Figure 7.4**

proposition that the 3×3×5 dimensions of the Ark of the Covenant may allude to the Divine Proportion is by no means new. The same suggestion has been made by others many times in the past, without any realistic hope of finding confirmation. Yet, against all reasonable expectation, abundant proof of this intention is now at our fingertips. I shall address later the perpendicular 511 and 512 digit groups highlighted in Figure 7.4.

To complete our recognition of the Ark, note that the two 3×3 groups we have just identified span five positions from the centre of one to the centre of the other along a common middle line. That is just as we found in G1 with the emergent copies of *aur* (light). Therefore, once more the Seal reveals the identical 3×3×5 box shape as before. Finally, whereas the Ark seen in G1 was found to contain the four-letter word 'tablets', the latest view of the Ark is blessed with the four-letter Name of God in the same capacity. This is a similarity I shall revisit later with a numeric equivalent.

A related theme requires that we switch our attention back to the 3×3 group containing the word [ן] הֵאָרֹ / *ha aron* / the Ark. Now, we may note that the same four letters can spell [ן] אַהֲרֹ / *Aharon* /

**Aaron**, the brother of Moses and first Chief Priest of the Israelites. We know that the brothers also had a sister, the prophetess Miriam; and it is possible to see not only Aaron in the G3 square, but all three siblings. After Aaron, Moses is the easier to identify, since the lightly-disguised expression משה תאמי / *Moshe ta'amiy* / <u>Moses, my twin</u> is ever-present in the plain text of Genesis 1:1. This expression may be seen ascending, shaded in Figure 7.5, where its last letter coincides

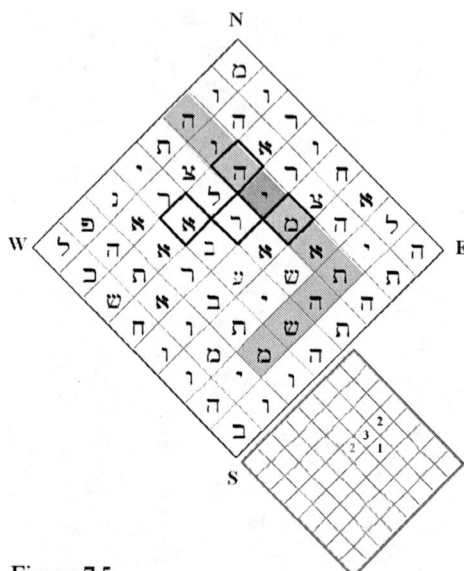

with the first letter of the linear four-letter Name of God. In fact, the expression is here complete for the first time, and now reads יהוה תאמם משה / *Moshe ta'owm YHWH* / <u>Moses, image of the Lord</u>. It is almost certain that we are meant to understand this as a reflected image, since the three letters of Moshe in reverse spell HaShem, meaning 'The Name' (ie YHWH). But there is another and more persuasive reason.

We know, of course, that Moses (my image) is celebrated as the only prophet *whom the Lord knew face to face* (see Deuteronomy 34:10). So, very appropriately, the four letters with heavier borders in Figure 7.5 spell מראה / *mareh* / <u>a mirror</u> or <u>vision</u>. It is by no means trivial that this mirror is represented by the Seal in its vertical axis of symmetry as a horizontal line, or base, with a central vertical component. Notice particularly that the vertical component spells הר / *har* / <u>mountain</u>, since that is precisely where Moses and the Lord did first meet face-to-face. The similarity between this configuration and basic school physics experiments in the reflection of light is also interesting. A mirror fixed vertically to a flat base is commonly used in demonstrating the symmetry of incident and reflected beams of light, at a plane reflective surface. So it is in the G3 square that Moses may be found twinned, like a reflected image of the Lord. And even the *mareh* (mirror) is locked into the symmetry of the square.

**Figure 7.5**

The presence of מרים [ם] (Miriam) is no less surprising, as she is composed from three of the same letters as מצרים [ם] / *Mitzraim* / Egypt. The letters of Miriam are represented as black numbers 1-2-3 in the thumbnail sketch. In fact, her name is read in the same counterclockwise direction as Mitzraim, even starting and ending at the same letter as the other name, omitting only the letter *tzadee* (צ). Symbolically, it is not surprising that the name of Miriam is fully contained within Mitzraim since, until the exodus, she was the only one of the three siblings not to have travelled beyond the country of her birth. She also shares one letter each with 'my twin', 'mirror' and the four-letter Name. Notice the alternative letter *mem* (מ), the grey 2 in the thumbnail that could be used in forming Miriam. Therefore, Miriam also has the potential to be seen in the same configuration as mareh (mirror).

From our point of view, it is also pertinent that the first three letters of Miriam spell מרי / *meriy* / <u>rebellious</u>, for two reasons. First, because this word occurs most often in the book of Ezekiel, including twice in Ezekiel 2:8 where it is aligned with the word 'house' and followed closely by: *a roll of a book … written within and without …* And that is, of course, the clue that first led us to construct the present G3 square. Also, at one stage Miriam did conspire with Aaron, to rebel against Moses. For which all three were summoned to the presence of the Lord within the Tent of Meeting. That was the only time a woman was ever allowed into the inner sanctum of the Tabernacle. And here they are, all four within the G3 replica of the Tabernacle.

While the G3 square of qatan values is still fresh in our minds, it is worth spending a moment examining some structured numerical features in the very top and bottom of the same view of the Seal, as highlighted in Figure 7.6. At the top, where the digits 1666 define the 3×3 end of the Ark, we earlier saw the horizontal word ההר / *ha har* / <u>the mountain</u>, now revealed as a 552 sequence. This number forms the hypotenuse of a 45° right-angle triangle, in which the other two sides each have their own intrinsic merit. But recall that we were once

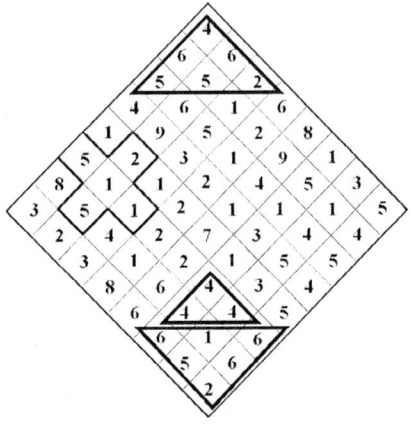

**Figure 7.6**

directed to the same number 552 by the position of the first occurrence of the letter *samech*, the last of all letters to make its first appearance in the Torah. That led to the construction of a square of side 552+1, which is the smallest that may contain all the 304,805 letters of the Torah.

The 264 seen ascending to the very pinnacle of the square is the familiar gematria of [ן] ירדן / *Yardan* / Jordan. And this has been found to be partner of 222 in a ratio that defines the sides of any 45° right-angle triangle. An example of 222 itself is seen in the present square, though we would not count it significant were it not for the fact that it has several other roles, which I will come to later.

Then, descending in the other side of the upper triangle there is a 465 sequence. The chief merit of this number is that it is $T_{30}$. This has an interesting implication, which depends on the best known formula for calculating triangular numbers (see Appendix A(ii)), thus:

$$T_n = \tfrac{1}{2}n \times (n+1)$$

In plain words, the n[th] triangular number (whichever that happens to be) may be calculated as the product of (i) half of n, and (ii) n plus 1. Since either n or n+1 will be an even number, the outcome is always a whole number, despite the ½ factor. In the case of n=30 (ie $T_{30}$), ½n is 15, and n+1 is 31, both of which numbers have associations with names of God. The first of them is the gematria of יה / *yah* / (an abbreviation for the four-letter name), and the second is the gematria of אל / *El* / (an abbreviation for Elohim). Both of these abbreviations appeared together as the central 2×2 cluster in G2. And they are now present as a 2×2 cluster within the eastern 3×3 corner group of the current G3 square. We shall accept this as the first of two prompts to examine the eastern corner more closely, not least because it is the only corner area that has not yet disclosed some important information. It is also worth noting that these two two-letter abbreviated names combine to make אליה / *Eliyah* / Elijah the prophet who was famously taken up to heaven in a chariot of fire (see 2nd Kings 2:11). Elijah therefore occupied the whole central cluster in G2 but, significantly, there is a complete column of five letters in the same square that are an anagram of אלישה / *Elishah* / Elisha, the prophet who inherited the mantle of Elijah. This is a rare example of the Seal recognising the prophets of God, rather than the other way about.

-oOo-

Turning our attention now to the bottom of the vertical diagonal, where the letters previously revealed the word *bayit* (house), there is now a 616 that crosses horizontally through the same 3×3 zone. Since the 'house' occupies the same letter positions as the 666 in G1, we now have a new association between 666 and 616, which were once used interchangeably in early manuscripts of the book of Revelation. Since I have not already declared it plainly, let me say here that the number of ways in which early Genesis and the Seal in particular, keep emphasising these two numbers is the real reason they came to be used interchangeably in Revelation 13:18. Though whether John the author was aware of this remains a matter for conjecture.

Undoubtedly, in the same 3×3 zone there is a degree of symmetry, which includes the 616 sequence and a 444-triangle surmounting it, as emphasised in the illustration. Also, the three lower digits may be read cyclically as either 256 or 625. Where,

$$256 = 2×2×2×2×2×2×2×2 \quad \text{(ie } 2^8)$$

and

$$625 = 5×5×5×5 \quad \text{(ie } 5^4)$$

Powers of 2 and 5 are not seen only in the bottom of the G3 square, but also in the lower face of the new Ark shape. There, the gematria of [ן] ןֹרָאֹה / *ha aron* / the Ark, or Aharon (Aaron) is also 256. And the sequential qatan letter values of the first of these words are 5125, which is 512 overlapping 125 (ie $5^3$). These digits have been highlighted in both Figure 7.6 and Figure 7.4. Now, we can recognise the relevance of one further presence of a 512, which coincides with the longitudinal axis of the new Ark. But the same configuration also draws attention to a 511 sequence, which otherwise might be assumed to have little meaning. There are, in fact, two additional meanings to this 511, one numeric and the other as a signpost.

Numerically, 511 is 7×73, two prime numbers that both have close associations with the Seal. Recall that Genesis 1:1 consists of 7 words, and has word breaks after 14, 21 and 28 letters. Also, 73 is both a Star of David number and co-factor with 37 (another Star of David) in the gematria of this crucial first verse. In a later Chapter, we shall find that both 37 and 73 are intimately bound to the Hebrew word for wisdom.

The same 511 digit sequence also directs us towards two further copies of itself in the eastern corner of the square. And this is the second of the two prompts that lead us to examine that part of the square more closely. Here, the two copies of 511 take up the same diagonal positions of the 3×3 cluster, which in G1 revealed the emergent words 'light' and 'deep darkness'. In the present square, each sequence comes from an identical word היא / *hiy* / <u>she</u>. Incidentally, the gematria of *hiy* is 16 (ie $2^4$), so two of them total 32 (or $2^5$). What is more, the presence in the same small area of the cyclic word ל ההתה / *l'hatat* / <u>to break in upon</u> is of the utmost importance in relating the G3 square to a section of the Torah's narrative text. The complete 3×3 group in the eastern corner seems to be saying 'to break in upon her', implying some kind of incursion into the Seal itself. The eastern corner of the Seal is, after all, a gateway where the entered text either starts or ends, depending which version of the Seal we are considering. In the part of the Torah where the construction of the Tabernacle is described, we find the following strange verse:

> *And he made the laver[n] of brass, and the foot of it of brass,*
> *and the lookingglasses of the women assembling, which*
> *assembled at the door of the Tabernacle of the congregation.*
> (Exodus 38:8)

Of course, these women did not themselves enter the Tabernacle; although their looking-glasses evidently did, since the word looking-glass, or mirror, occurs at only this one place in the entire Torah, and also within the G3 square.

In view of the previous observation, it is now almost certain that the overall structure of the Seal is designed to represent one or more aspects of the Temple of God. Notice I do not refer specifically to Solomon's Temple. The reason being a point I think the Seal makes better than any idle speculation. By its very nature, the Temple built by Solomon was a fixed structure and, as such, did not embody one of the key attributes of other forms. The Tabernacle in the desert was the forerunner of Solomon's Temple, but had the essential property that it was portable. It should also be noted that the portability of the Tabernacle was ordained by divine decree. It is only now that we can begin to appreciate the subtle nuance in the word משכן / *Mishkan*, which is sometimes used in the Torah to mean the portable Tabernacle. This usage emphasises the role of the Tabernacle as the dwelling place of the Presence of God. The 'Presence' came to be known later as the Shekhinah, from the root 'Mishkan'. But Shekhinah is particularly understood to be a feminine attribute of God and,

---

[n] a hand-washing basin

hence, the unexpected significance of the expression 'to break in upon her', which we have identified in the eastern 3×3 group of letters. Christians also point out that when their founder announced that he would re-build the shattered temple in three days, he was not referring to the stone edifice in which he was standing, but to his mortal body. Christians also often refer to aspects of the New Testament gospels that seem to imply that Jesus embodied all the essential attributes of the Tabernacle as a place where the Lord could dwell among men. In this sense, Christians are indulging in the process of *eisogesis* – reading into the Old Testament text only that which supports their established point of view. Except now that we have a clearer understanding of the Seal, it does seem to confirm their assumption.

Now consider the number of ways the Seal has revealed, and implied, the Ark of the Covenant. To begin with, in Chapter 2 we found that a special configuration of the letter *vav* (ו) depicted not only the outline of a man being crucified (supported by several other New Testament allusions), but superimposed on him the shape of another Ark. In the same Chapter, we saw how the Seal, in the orientation I have elected to draw it, also incorporates the seven-branched Menorah of the Temple, both structurally and numerically. It does so in such a way that branches 3 and 5 (dimensions of the Ark) coincide with the outstretched arms of the crucified man. And the fourth and middle branch falls within the central area where, in the G3 square, the word 'four' is found. Indeed, the G1 view of the Seal also implied the reversing of the path of expulsion from Eden, through the co-terminal, homophonic words for skin (descending) and light (ascending). Then a tiny modification to the same text gave us the G2 view of the Seal, which illustrated the same reverse path concept in even more emphatic and colourful terms – the river that flows to Ahavah. So the Christian reading of Old Testament events may not be as fanciful as it first seems; at least, not with respect to the prophetic nature of the Tabernacle and Temple, presaging the one who would one day complete the Law.

It is also appropriate to consider other biblical temples, especially two mentioned in the book of Revelation that are easily overlooked. First it is written:

> *Then God's temple in heaven was opened, and the Ark of his covenant was seen within his temple...*

(Revelation 11:19).

Then later we find:

> *And I saw no temple in the city, for its temple is the Lord God the Almighty and the Lamb, and the city has no need of sun and moon to shine upon it, for the glory of God is its light, and its lamp is the Lamb.*

(Revelation 21:22-23)

Even the final phrase of the latter quotation suggests that the author of Revelation was writing to a plan defined by the Seal, with its menorah structure superimposed on the crucified man. He is the Lamb and the lamp. Admittedly, being aware of the Seal does not automatically confer legitimacy to the text on which it is based. But it does demonstrate that the Seal has been understood down the ages.

It is quite easy to recognise a progression in the Bible that begins with the garden of Eden, moves on to the Tabernacle, then to the Temple of Solomon, to Jesus Christ, God's temple in heaven and, finally, the holy city on earth. With our new-found insight, it is also possible to follow the same progression depicted by the Seal. This is one topic on which the book of Revelation is clearly independent of the model begun by Ezekiel, and other Old Testament prophets. For it takes the temple metaphor much further than any of its predecessors, in fact to its ultimate conclusion.

The Hebrew prophets, with the best interests of their people in mind, do seem to have followed the same progression. In a moment, I shall show how we may know that Amos was adhering to the plan set out in the Author's Seal. First note how the current G3 view of the Seal shows three of the nations that have been neighbours of Israel and Judah, and always potential threats to their stability and security. In Figure 7.7, [ם] מצרים / *Mitzraim* / Egypt is again seen in tight square formation with darker shading. There is also [ם] ארם / *Aram* / Syria, shown with heavy borders. This word utilises the three horizontal letters of *mareh* (a mirror). Lastly, there is בבל / *Bavel* / Babylon, shown with lighter shading.

Amos begins his prophesy with a diatribe against the neighbours of Israel. He then draws attention to the dire consequences that would result if Israel does not do much better than its neighbours, in the application of justice and social standards. As with many of the prophets, Amos describes the consequences almost as though they are inevitable; although there are always alternative paths, options and outcomes. But look at the following part of the prophet's description of the fate that might befall God's chosen:

*As if a man did flee from a lion, and a bear met him; or went into the house, and leaned his hand on the wall, and a serpent bit him.*

(Amos 5:19)

There is no mistaking the plain message of Amos' warning here; if the [elite of the] Kingdom of Israel do not mend their ways, there will be nowhere to hide from God's judgement. But this is a rather strange way in which to phrase so simple a concept. For one thing, the Old Testament does not often equate a bear with raw aggression or danger, except for the notable exception of two she-bears that tore forty-two boys who had mocked the bald-head tonsure of Elisha (2 Kings 2:23-24). In the Bible, this animal is more usually synonymous with ponderous slowness. If we really wish to understand Amos' inspiration, we should look to the Seal on the start of the Torah.

In Figure 7.7, I have numbered a linear sequence of elements 1 to 7 in the thumbnail sketch. The letters in the main square that correspond to 4-3-2-1 spell בארי / *b'ariy* / <u>with a lion</u>. Those corresponding to 4-5-6-7 spell בעיש / *b'ayish* / <u>with a bear</u>, in this case the astronomical constellation of the Great Bear. There is nowhere between the lion and the bear to hide. Notice also that the 'lion' reference is latched precisely to the הההה/5555 sequence that was seen in G2. As important as this latching may appear, it is not yet the most significant, as we shall see later.

As to the serpent concealed in the wall of a house, this can only be a reference to the first verse of the Torah. That is where we saw the image of a serpent as a 1-4-1-4-1-4-1-4-1-4 sequence, in a 7×4 array of the qatan values (Figure 3.6(a)). And when, in the G2 square, we again saw its likeness (interpreted as a meandering river) the very same verse was the perimeter of that square, like a bounding wall. Amos is speaking in metaphors (*As if a man did flee …*) to convey a message that is deeply rooted in the Torah. It is only natural that he

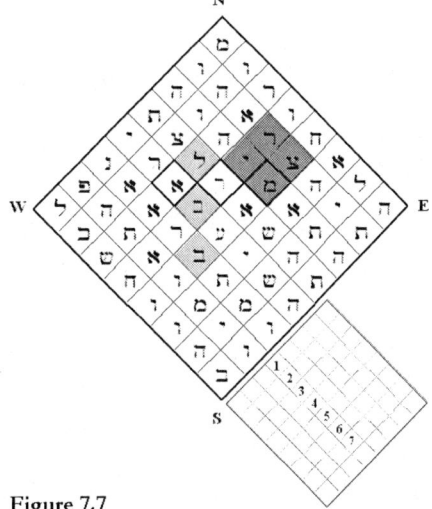

**Figure 7.7**

should be guided by its enigmatic, prophetic opening words – the Author's Seal.

One further observation involving the G3 aspect of the Seal concerns the way a number of components come together to magnify the number 888. We first saw this number in the combined gematria values of the third, fifth and sixth words of Genesis 1:1. That is:

$$86 + 395 + 407 = 888$$

Then we found the same number on plain view in G2, superimposed on the location where the word לוחת / *luchot* / <u>tablets</u> had been seen in G1. Also, the gematria of *luchot* is 444 and, because there had been two such tablets placed in the original Ark by Moses, that square implied the doubling of 444. These last few facts are crucial to the observations that now follow.

The fact that the *luchot* in G1 crossed into the interior of the Ark shape composed from 'darkness' and two emergent copies of 'light' now takes on additional significance. To begin with, it draws attention to the similar role of the linear four-letter Name now seen in G3. Here it, too, crosses into the interior of the newer, equally distinct Ark shape. A further key characteristic of the two four-letter words is in their gematria values of 444 and 26. What we shall do next is to bind these words and their gematria values with the letters that are found in the four corners of G3. In the order the text is entered, the letters found in those positions are: *beyt* (ב), *lamed* (ל), *mem* (מ) and *heh* (ה). As a qatan sequence, they are 2-3-4-5, a sure sign of their sentinel roles; but their greater worth is in the sum of their standard values, which is 77. The strategic locations and numeric attributes of these four letters demonstrate that the Seal is indeed in the form of a temple, through the following product:

$$444 \times 26 \times 77 = 888,888$$

This number is 1000+1 times the 888 value of the word Ιησους (ie Jesus) in Greek numerology. And we are now witnessing a second way in which the Seal presages the mysterious passage near the end of the Torah, where it is written:

> *How can one chase a thousand, or two put ten thousand to flight, Unless their rock had sold them and the Lord had given them up*
>
> (Deuteronomy 32:30)

One explanation for the ten thousand mentioned in this verse was discovered in Chapter 4, where the connection with the crucified man was unmistakable. Then, in Chapter 6, we found a first explanation for the one/one thousand reference; and that involved the 888 which was seen explicitly in the G2 square. And now we have this further effect involving the arks in both G1 and G3, which again links the number 888 with 1000 and 1. The Seal is surely not lacking in the many independent means it employs to demonstrate its priceless underlying themes and concepts.

-oOo-

From earliest infancy, the ability to recognise another human face, friendly or otherwise, is pre-programmed in our brains. We are not only able to recognise faces; we have a deeply ingrained need to do so. In the absence of a real face to focus on, it is quite normal to imagine faces in cloud formations, in the random patterns of marble, or in photographs of the surface of the planet Mars. Occasionally, individuals are born who lack this important ability, but such cases are rare.

The prophet Ezekiel has described seeing *chayot* or living creatures with faces, during his visions by the River Chebar. He wrote that each of the chayot had four faces; one was a man's face, another a lion's, a third was the face of an ox, and the last one an eagle. The writer of the book of Revelation describes experiencing a similar vision; although in his case, there were exactly four living creatures, and each had only one face. However, the four separate faces were the same as those Ezekiel had ascribed to a single chayah. Was the later author just copying from the earlier example? If so, it is hard to understand why the two descriptions should differ in so many details, not just the number of faces. The explanation for the differences will be given in the next Chapter. But both authors are, potentially, open to the criticism that the human mind will see faces even where there are none. This is where the Seal on the beginning of the Torah comes to the aid of these prophets, with the definitive explanation for the origin of the faces they saw. This is also where we must proceed to the final re-making of the Seal, in order to recognise the prophets' source.

We have already examined three square versions of the Seal, re-made from the original Hebrew text of Genesis 1:1-2. Up to now, every time we modified the Seal, it has been with a clear rationale that was perceived as a prompt from one of three alternative sources. The first was the structure of the Torah's first verse. The second was one of the core principles of Jewish Kabbalah, notably the concept of God in the twin guises of Small Face within his creation, and Vast Face on the outside. The third was a selection of passages, also from Ezekiel and the book of Revelation that make sense only in relation to the Author's Seal. Vitally, every adjustment we made to the Seal has led to a rich harvest of new discoveries, which over and above their own intrinsic merit, demonstrate a planned progression in the elucidation of familiar biblical references. That is, events and episodes in the regular biblical narrative are often re-visited and re-interpreted from alternative perspectives.

However, the rationale for a fourth re-making of the Seal will be different, and less obvious. It is as though the Author is saying, 'You have seen the evolution so far, and enough of the method. Now follow your own instinct and judgement.' To be sure, we now have good reason to trust the Author's ability and intentions; he evidently knows our minds and abilities better than we know ourselves. And it is true that there has been a helpful pattern to the route that led to the present point. The next step will, however, require a small 'leap of faith', with only the outcome to act as our assurance.

To put it simply, the best hint so far has been the way the Seal has repeatedly insinuated the concept of an outward path and a return. Since we have already reversed the text in the transition from the G2 square to G3 that cannot also be the final step. That reversal of the text is the most radical adjustment we have made so far, and seems to represent a major turning point (no pun intended). If the entire process is meant to be in left-right reflection (another clue), then the natural next step would be to re-insert the letter *ayin* to its original sequential position. The overall sequence will then have been:

i) Text forwards, with ayin (G1),
ii) Text forwards, ayin removed (G2),
iii) Text backwards, ayin still removed (G3),
iv) Text backwards, ayin restored (G4).

With the text still entered in the tilted square, as in G3, the proper location for the letter ayin would be the corner square at the western end of the horizontal diagonal. Notice that this diagonal is the same one on which that letter was seen in G1.

There is an obvious difficulty to making the change just described, since there will then be two copies of ayin in the new view. A provisional justification stems from the idea that we are moving step-by-step towards a condition of restoration or fulfilment. And that could mean we are looking at the completion of the sixth day, in which the creation of man, in the image of his creator is at last fulfilled. Then it is understandable that two indistinguishable copies of the symbol of

Vast Face are now seen together, symbolically depicting Man as majestic co-creator. But this is only a provisional reasoning. As promised, we shall soon find that the new G4 square will demonstrate its credentials with a clearer explanation for Ezekiel's vision of chayot, or so-called living creatures. First, a more obvious outcome is seen in Figure 7.8.

Superficially, the effect of re-inserting the letter ayin (ע) has been simply to shift all 15 letters in the upper two sides one place to the right, with the consequential loss of the letter heh, middle letter of Elohim (God) from the right-hand corner. And although the larger 7×7 area beneath the two upper sides remains unaltered, even this tiny change is enough to destroy many artefacts seen in the G3 square, including the four-letter Name and the distinctive Ark shape.

One 'constructive' effect of the re-inserted ayin is the redistribution of three of the upper letters *vav* (ו). In terms of the metaphor of water, this shifts the intended interpretation very firmly in

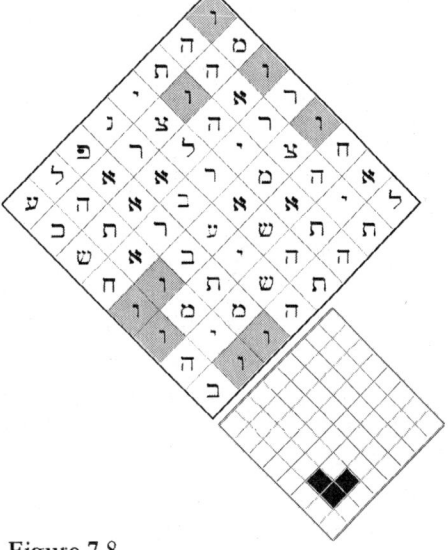

**Figure 7.8**

favour of the second and third days of creation. In the second day, the waters above and below the firmament of heaven were created. Then, in the third day:

> *God said, Let the waters under the heaven be gathered together unto one place …*

(Genesis 1:9)

What the re-insertion of ayin has achieved is to create a clear contrast between the appearance of the waters above and below. The waters above are now fully separated, no longer touching even at their corners, whereas the waters below are (still) gathered together into two clumps. This arrangement does not yet look like the 'one place' described by Genesis; but look closely and it can be seen that the two clumps are connected by the three letters of [ם] מים / *mayim* / <u>water</u>

(positions highlighted in the thumbnail sketch). Overall, this bridge connects two contiguous 2×2 blocks into a single area. Incidentally, the letters of mayim come from the longer word shamayim (heavens), perhaps as a reminder that the firmament that separated the waters had been named 'heaven'.

Another important difference between G3 and G4 is in their four corner squares, the sentinel positions so to speak. Recall that in G3, their qatan values gave a sequence 2-3-4-5, and their standard gematria total of 77 contributed to the generation of the number 888888. It is also worth remembering that in G1 and G2, the letters in three corner squares read clockwise (as an Equidistant Latter Sequence) spelled ברא / *bara* / <u>he created</u>; but reading three corners in the counter-clockwise direction spelled בוא / *bo* / <u>he entered</u>. In retrospect, we now see that those two words taken together offered a fore-taste of the Small Face/ Vast Face concept that was to come, and a more plausible reason for Jewish Kabbalah to settle on that concept.

In the final version of the Seal, the four corner letters confer an altogether different set of messages of which perhaps the most important is their identities. They are *beyt* (ב), *ayin* (ע), *vav* (ו) and *lamed* (ל), and these have been just about the most influential letters in our very extensive exploration. Among other things, these four include the Torah's first and its last letters. In fact, three of them came together when, following numerous clues, we looped the end of the Torah onto its beginning. The ayin prefix then became interposed and participated in the emergent word בעל / *ba'al* / <u>master</u>. Now, the more complete set of four sentinel letters makes the expression בעלו / *ba'alu* / <u>your master</u>.

There is also a numeric dimension to the four corner elements that supports several previous observations. Taking these letters in the order they occur in the plain text of Genesis, the first two have a gematria total of 72, while the last two give 36. Clearly, the first is double the second, and the length of one of the names of God. And notice that the first pair of letters are also now found together in the centre of the square Seal. The number 36 is, of course, always the number of letters enclosed by the outer layer of every square. It also reminds us of the so-called lamed-Vavniks – the thirty-six Tzadiqim (righteous men), any one of whom could become the promised Messiah. And the headline lamed shape in G2, composed entirely of the letter vav, represents one particular righteous man who did become Messiah.

Now we come to the important subject of Ezekiel's vision of chayot, a word that has been persistently translated as living creatures. And we note that the re-inserted letter ayin restores the plain-text phrase ‏על פנ י‎ / *aal pnei* / <u>upon the face</u>. This face has a pivotal role in the explanation of the four faces, which can be explained using Figure 7.9. In the main square, there is an incredibly important, distinctive 'Y' shape which incorporates fully half of all the eight letters *aleph* (‏א‎) within the Seal. Despite its importance, I shall postpone describing it's meaning until we have established the roles of the letters shown by the numbers 1 to 6 in the thumbnail sketch.

To begin with, the letters at positions 1-2-3 are none other than the word ‏פנ י‎ / *pnei* / <u>face</u>. And we shall discover that each one of its three component letters contributes to the identity of one of the faces on Ezekiel's chayot. Taking the letters in order, the *peh* (‏פ‎) begins the horizontal word ‏פר‎ / *par* / <u>an ox</u>. The letter *nun* (‏נ‎) begins the horizontal word ‏נצ‎ [‏ץ‎] / *netz* / <u>a bird of prey</u> (eg eagle). And the letter *yud* (‏י‎) is the last letter of the vertical word ‏ארי‎ / *ariy* / <u>a lion</u>.

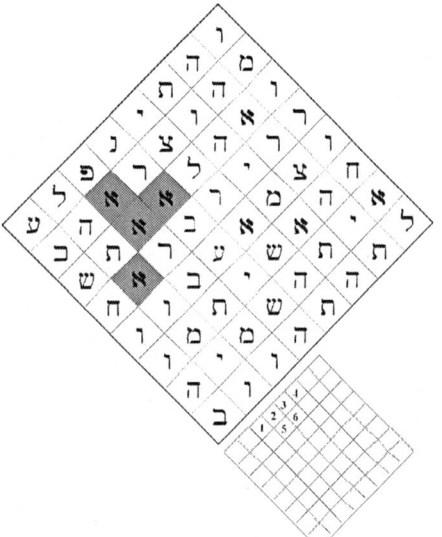

**Figure 7.9**

Note that this is not the same lion as the one I attributed to Amos, since the letter yud is now in a different position. But notice that now, the locations which previously contained *b'ariy* (with a lion), now contains [‏ן‎] ‏בארן‎ / *b'aron* / <u>in an Ark</u>. These are, moreover, the same four linear elements where we once saw ‏הההה‎ in G2. And, as a 5555 group, that led to our finding the exact value of the so-called Divine Proportion (Φ) implied by the dimensions of the Ark of the Covenant. The formula suggested by that group was:

$$\Phi = 5\char`\^.5 \times .5 + .5$$

(this is not an approximation, but an exact equality)
Never have so many pivotal concepts been summed up in just one short paragraph.

So, although the clear outline of an Ark seen in this part of the G3 square has been destroyed by the restoration of the letter ayin, it has left behind a clear literary echo of itself. As if to reinforce this observation, two of the letters of *b'aron* (ie ר and נ) now combine with two adjacent letters in a tight square group that spells [ן] פָּארָן / *Paran* / (the name of a desert). That was the place to which the Israelites first journeyed, with the Ark at their head, after leaving Sinai. And an identical square group was seen in G2, where the present square now has 'Egypt' and G1 showed 'Israel' overlapping.

As to the face of a man seen by Ezekiel, this is where we need to consider the meaning of the new 'Y' shape which was, incidentally, already visible in G3. When we realise its numerous roles in the Seal, it will become clear that we are witnessing the surviving essence of the earlier 'Y' shape, the crucified man. However, I shall henceforth use a very different epithet which was coined by the prophet Daniel as here:

> *The man clothed in linen, who was above the waters of the river, lifted his right hand and his left hand toward heaven, and I heard him swear by him who lives forever, saying, "It will be for a time, times and half a time. When the power of the holy people has been finally broken, all these things will be completed."*
>
> (Daniel 12:7).

Looking back at Figure 7.9 it is not difficult to recognise in the 'Y' shape the 'man clothed in linen' with both hands raised to heaven, this time in exaltation. Each of the upper elements is adjacent to a letter *lamed* (the shape of the river in G2), forming two copies of the word אֵל / *El* / God. But the precise positioning of the man clothed in linen could not be more symbolic. First, note that the lowest element of the 'Y' is resting on the uppermost component of the waters that are below the firmament of the heaven. Moreover, the *two* lowest elements also coincide with the positions of two of the components of the aforementioned meandering river that flows to Ahavah, in the form of the letter lamed. The location of the man clothed in linen will repay closer examination.

Simultaneous knowledge of all square versions of the Seal now becomes essential, because we are examining a leitmotif that persists in this part of the square, like a watermark throughout every version. The first hint of these things to come was seen in the G1 square, where we found a cluster of nine elements that exhibited bi-lateral symmetry.

They included the crowning word יְהִי / *y'hiy* / <u>let there be</u>, crossing symmetrically through אֹתֹת / *otot* / <u>signs</u>. In the G2 square, the same area was crossed by the palindromic group אֹהֵוֹהֵא with identical symmetry, from which we could read אֵהֵוֹהֵ (Ahavah) in either direction. That was the same Ahavah to which the lamed-shaped river flowed, as crucially recorded in Ezra 8:15. And now, in both G3 and G4 we find the Y-shaped man clothed in linen sharing the very same symmetry! I suggest that the face of a man seen by Ezekiel is non-other than the one belonging to the man clothed in linen. I shall return to this man at intervals to describe a number of additional cryptic associations.

Another motif implied by the new Y-shaped man clothed in linen relates to the re-formed name of Israel we saw in the G2 square. If we include the letter reysh (ר) (symbolically a head) above the new Y, then we have an identical shape to the five letters of Israel that we recognised in Chapter 5. In the original square view of the Seal, the name of Israel had been wholly contained within a 3×3 zone that was already notable for other reasons. However, the nondescript configuration of Israel seen there seemed unsatisfactory. Then the tiny modification that transformed the G1 square into G2 also transformed the name of Israel into a much more pleasing, symmetrical configuration, exactly like the man clothed in linen we now see in G3/4, in Figure 7.9.

In principle, the three-stage transformation of 'Israel' into a pleasing 'Y' shape in association with a womb is remarkably similar to the transformation of the crucified man, but in reverse. The large, distinctive, symmetrical Y-shape in G1 was transformed in G2 into the equally distinctive lamed (ל)-shaped river that flowed in and out of another womb. By considering the two transformations together, it is now easy to recognise God's promise to Abraham:

> *Unto thy seed have I given this land, from the river of Egypt unto the great river, the river Euphrates.*
>
> (Genesis 15:18)

The 3×3 zone of the Seal that first contained 'Israel' in G1, now contains *Mitzraim* (Egypt) in G3/4, and had פָרֹת / *Parot* / <u>Euphrates</u> as its diagonal in G2. Also in G1, the same zone contained both the plain-text 'land' and an emergent 'fruit' (synonymous with 'seed'). The degree of correspondence between the Seal and the plain biblical narrative, including the New Testament, is quite extraordinary, demonstrating that the Seal is the blueprint for the entire Bible. And recall once more that the 248 gematria of Abraham is exactly the same as that of *racham* (a womb) – one male and the other female. Either of them could represent the number of positive commandments given to the children of Israel within the Torah. And their sum (ie 248 + 248 = 496) is the 31st triangular number and third perfect number.

Before we lose sight of Daniel, there is one further characteristic of the present square that will help clarify another of the prophet's mystical visions. Daniel wrote:

> *And four great beasts came up from the sea, diverse one from another …*
> *The first was like a lion, and had an eagle's wings …*
> *And behold another beast, a second, like to a bear …*
>
> (Daniel 7:3-5)

Here we see two animal associations that are familiar to us from the Seal. One is lion with eagle; reminding us of the two faces seen by Ezekiel. The other is lion with bear, reminding us of the prophesy of Amos. In the case of Amos, there was also a third component in the appropriate verse. That was a serpent concealed within the wall that is Genesis 1:1. But with Daniel the third component is the Y-shaped man clothed in linen, who is seen above the waters. Therefore the fact that the two lower components of that man coincide with two elements of the river that was seen in G2 becomes doubly significant, since the river had the same general shape as the serpent. We may note once again that the serpent and the river of similar shape represent opposing paths. The serpent is synonymous with the expulsion of the first man and woman from the garden; while the river is the reverse path of restoration, accomplished by the crucified man. I reiterate this example of a reversal only because the same two lower elements of the man clothed in linen give rise to another equivalent effect. This is a 'coming in' that corresponds to a 'going out' we saw in the first square.

First of all, recall that the word *arba* (four) that includes the *ayin* prefix on Genesis now occupies the whole central cluster of the latest square. Now, if we look really closely, it is possible to see two more copies of ארבע /*arba* / <u>four</u>, each emanating from one of the two lower elements of the man clothed in linen. They are not linear arrangements, but each traces three letters in a straight line, before side-stepping into the ayin prefix. In this way, they overlap and combine to trace an outline that is redolent of the Christian ⋈ symbol of a fish, highlighted in Figure 7.10.

A crucial observation here is that three copies of the word 'four' are found to converge on the same all-important letter ayin, in Kabbalah the symbol of Vast Face. The significance of this convergence cannot be over-stated, since it corresponds to an opposite effect we saw in the G1 square. There, the same letter ayin in its regular location was the origin of three emergent words, of which at least two may have associations with the expulsion from Eden. The three emergent words seen in G1 were,

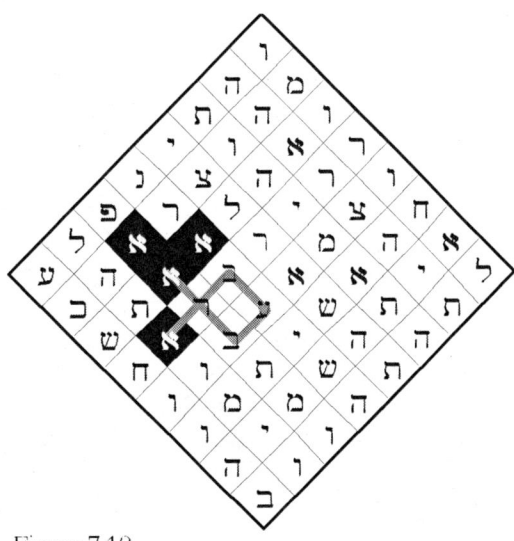

Figure 7.10

| עוב | / oob | / <u>deep darkness</u> | (78) |
| עור | / aur | / <u>skin</u> | (276) |
| עשה | / asah | / <u>he made</u> | (375) |

The gematria value of each word is included above as a reminder not only that they are each independently divisible by 3, but also that their sum is 729, and has the following property:

$$729 \quad = \quad 3{\times}3{\times}3{\times}3{\times}3{\times}3$$

In fact, the average of the three gematria sums is 243, which is the gematria of the name Abram before it was modified to become Abraham. This in itself should alert us to the existence of a vast purpose and a long-term plan in which Abraham and the Seal both figure prominently.

Similarly, the numerical significance of the three copies of 'four' in the G3/G4 squares lies in their product, so:

$$64 \quad = \quad 4{\times}4{\times}4 \quad = \quad 2{\times}2{\times}2{\times}2{\times}2{\times}2$$

I have included the overall product of 64 only to draw attention to an important aspect of the setting in which this revelation is found – a perfect square of 64 elements. The more striking outcome, however, is that all the 3s once seen going out from the letter ayin have been transformed into the same number of 2s that are coming in to that letter. In the next Chapter, we shall consider some of the non-biblical reasons why there needed to be exactly three copies of the word 'four', and why they should overlap and converge on their common letter *ayin*.

The rich variety of both linguistic and numerical concepts that converge here, representing both beginning and end, is hard enough to comprehend. When we also try to visualise the method by which it might have been accomplished, the idea that the Author's Seal can be explained in any familiar terms is simply untenable. We are for sure dealing with an effect that is of supernatural origin.

A moment ago, I observed that the two emergent copies of arba would overlap to make a simple ✕ fish symbol. Apart from the straightforward allusion to Jesus Christ, in his guise as the man clothed in linen, it is possible to draw a rather more cryptic conclusion from the Hebrew word דג / *dag* / <u>fish</u>. The two letters of *dag* are notable for their absence from any view of the Seal. The explanation is that they are among the more reticent letters to make their debut in the Torah. The letter *delet* makes its first appearance as letter #127; and *gimmel* doesn't arrive until position #738. The significance of these numbers is in their difference, so:

$$738 - 127 = 611$$

This result being the gematria of the word Torah; and I shall come back later to the question of numerical content in the G4 square. It is also quite meaningful that the two letters of *dag* combine with a *beyt* (first letter of the Torah) to spell בגד / *beged* / <u>a garment</u>. These letters are consecutive in the alephbeyt, at positions 2, 3 and 4.

Like the concise group of faces seen by Ezekiel, there is another family group of emergent words, which in a similar way to the new Y-shape, also latch to other versions of the Seal in a way that can only be described as spectacular. In the right-hand corner of the square (see Figure 7.11) there is a 3×3 zone which:

- in G1, showed emergent words 'light' and 'deep darkness' crossing through one-another, marking the upper end of the first Ark shape.

- in G3, included two copies of the emergent word הׁיא / *hiy* / <u>she</u> in the same positions.

Here, in the latest G4 version of the Seal, there are yet more emergent words in identical positions. Reading in the same direction as the oob (deep darkness) in G1, we now find איל / *ayil* / <u>a ram</u>. This, by the way, is the same word that is left over from the Torah's third word after its two other letters have been utilised (along with three from the first word) in making the name of Abraham. To go with the new ayil, and reading in the same direction as the original *aur* (light), we now find חׁיה / *chayah* / <u>to live</u>. That is the basic form of

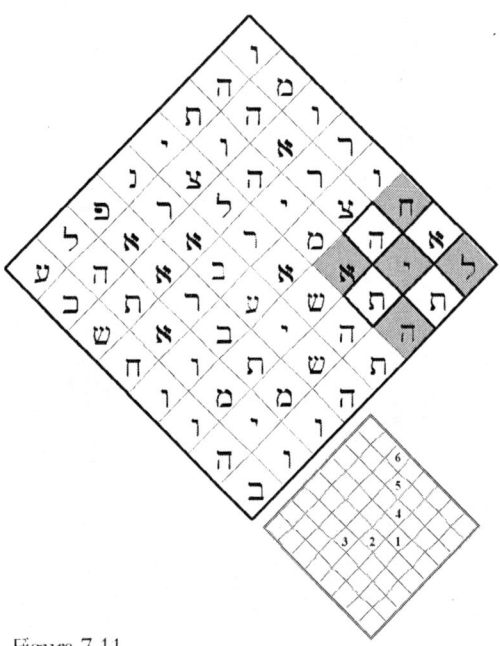

Figure 7.11

the verb, but it is also used to mean to 'bestow life'. That appears to be its meaning in the text:

> *Man doth not live by bread alone, but by every word that proceedeth out of the mouth of the Lord doth man live.*
>
> (Deuteronomy 8:3; Matthew 4:4).

It is also the singular of the chayot described by Ezekiel, the faces of which are also seen in this square.

Comparing the eastern corner of the present square with the G1 version, the relationship between the same 3×3 zones is perfectly remarkable. Over and above the obvious positional latching, there is also a direct conceptual correspondence between the original 'light' and the new verb 'to bestow life'. And there is at least a symbolic correspondence between 'deep darkness' and a ram (as a sacrificial animal). This meaning is intended in Genesis 15, where Abram is instructed to cut three large animals down the middle, including a ram; then:

> *when the sun had gone down and it was dark, behold a*
> *smoking fire pot and a flaming torch passed between these*
> *pieces.*

> (Genesis 15:17)

Those events were given to Abram as a sign that his descendents would receive a land for their inheritance – their promised land. So, in the same 3×3 zone, in the four elements not yet mentioned, we now find האתת / *ha otot* / the signs, binding together the ram and life given.

The letters in Figure 7.11 in positions that correspond to the numbers in the thumbnail sketch make a quite different statement. Those that are in positions 1-2-3 spell שער / *sha'ar* / a gate. And the vertical set, 1-4-5-6 spell שמרו / *shamru* / they guarded. The shared starting point of both words says that they combine to make the expression: *they guarded a gate.* And there are two reasons for thinking this expression must relate to the verse:

> *So he drove out the man; and he placed at the east of the garden*
> *of Eden Cherubims, and a flaming sword which turned every*
> *way, to keep the way of the tree of life.*

> (Genesis 3:24)

For one thing, the three-letter word *sha'ar* (gate) is sitting one place higher than the three positions that revealed the word חרב / *cherev* / a sword in the G2 square. That sword was bracketed by the two letters of *esh* (fire), making it a 'flaming sword'. The gate we now see in the G3 and G4 aspects is, of course, occupying a diagonal of the crucial 3×3 area that was at different stages an Ark and a womb/bread combination. Equally compelling is the Seal's persistent theme of a return path to Eden, in which the centres of all its square aspects have a particularly strong bearing. Recall, particularly, that the G2 view showed the river of living water that passed straight through the sword and the womb on its way to Ahavah.

-oOo-

The 611 gematria of Torah we obtained earlier from the letters of 'fish' is not unique in its association with the man clothed in linen. The distinctive outline of the exalted man, formed from four copies of the letter *aleph* (**א**), is also the focal point for some important effects involving qatan letter values. In Figure 7.12, it is easy to see a further 611 (heavier border) obtained from the lower elements of the Y-shape, along with a 6 belonging to the waters over which he is standing. Apart from anything else, this linear 611 helps to draw attention to a linear 6-1-4-6-1-4 (darker shading). This is the same sequence we saw in G1 in triangular formation, as the foundation of the crucifix. As such, it represents a final commandment to add to the 613 described by the Torah. It was also the sequence from which we obtained the number ten thousand, having associations with Deuteronomy 32:30. Of

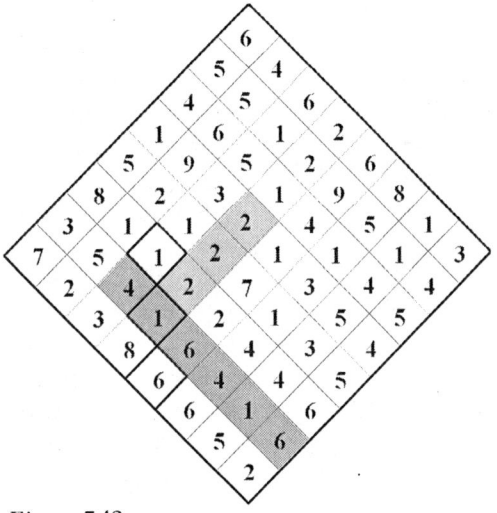

**Figure 7.12**

course, to do so it required the cooperation of the number $222^2$, obtained originally from $111 \times 444$. In the present square the sole 222 sequence (indeed the only 222 sequence in any square) is found abutting the upper 614, where it forms a 1222 group, or $2 \times 611$. Also, parallel to the 614614 there is an unusual 112244, which has two purposes. This is two interleaved copies of 124, making a sum of 248 (the gematria of Abraham and of 'a womb'). Note this use of a union in a representation of male and female attributes. Also, the middle four digits of the six are 1224, which is $2 \times 612$, the gematria of the word ברית / *brit* / covenant.

It is very significant that everything so far described using the latest illustration has incorporated elements of the characteristic 'Y' of the man clothed in linen. We may even go as far as to conclude that the once triangular 6-1-4-6-1-4 replaced by its new linear counterpart corresponds to the words of John the Baptist of whom it is written:

# In the Beginning

*"Behold, I send my messenger before thy face, who shall prepare thy way; the voice on one crying in the wilderness; Prepare the way of the Lord, make his paths straight"*

(Mark 1:2).

Hence, the 614th commandment is undoubtedly to be interpreted as *the way of the Lord*. Notice just above the second 4 in that sequence, a square group of 8125 which come from the letters of Paran, a wilderness region. Notice also the further use of the word 'face', which has particular meaning in the context of the G4 square. The Baptist was, of course, quoting from Isaiah; so there is the prospect that one or both of them was aware of the existence of the Seal. That is by no means out of the question, since John is thought to have been a prominent member of the community of Essenes, which is now widely believed to have had stewardship of the mystical knowledge of the Torah, the so-called Oral Tradition. There is more in Chapter 10 about the Essenes' role in the fate of the Author's Seal.

Another look at the latest illustration reveals that the upper three elements of the man clothed in linen form a triangle that is adjacent to the linear 222 group. A simple observation is that two of those 2s each combine with a pair of elements from the small triangle, to make a 112 sequence. Superficially, this number equates to 4×28, with direct relevance to two important characteristics of the Seal. More important, however, is the fact that the expression יהוה אלהים [ם] / *YHWH Elohim* / The Lord God has that number as its gematria. The expression The Lord God has the distinction of being used of the creator almost to the exclusion of other names, from Genesis 2:4 until the end of Genesis 3. That is, from the end of the creation account until the moment of the expulsion from Eden.

An even more striking effect comes from the fact that the upper 'V' of the man clothed in linen combines with the linear 222 group to form a triangular number. From the six components of this triangle, it is possible to read the number 222111 cyclically, in either direction. And that number happens to be $T_{666}$. So, we have here a quite remarkable reversal of the situation in the G1 version of the Seal. There, the number 666 was seen explicitly while 616, its alter-ego in Revelation 13:18, was concealed in various ways. But their roles are now reversed. In the G3/G4 square, it is 616 that is seen explicitly (twice as it happens), and the larger number is concealed as a triangle. By the same token, the large 'Y' of the crucified man in G1 was associated with an explicit 666, whereas the new, less-substantial 'Y' shape is equally closely associated with a subdued 666.

Notice, too, that the 222 group gives rise to a 1222 sequence (ie 2×611) from either end, just as 222111 may be read within the triangle in both directions. As we have seen one of these sequences begins with the component of the man clothed in linen that is included in the explicit vertical 611.

The present square also contains a numerical confluence that should remind us of something similar seen in G2. To recap, in the earlier version of the Seal, there were four homogeneous, linear digit groups (viz. 5555, 888, 666 and 111). Addition of alternative combinations of those numbers gave results that differed from 7221 (ie a sequence obtained from arba) by either 1 or 1000. And that was interpreted as a reference to Deuteronomy 32:30. In the present square, we now find the homogeneous sequences 1111, 222 and 111. This, too, gives two significant results, as follows:

(i)   **1111 + 111 = 1222**      (ie 2×611)

(ii)   **1111 + 222 + 111 = 1444**      (ie 2×722, also 38²)

The significance of the latter result is compound. First, the number 722 differs from 611 by 111, as first noticed in Chapter 6. Second, the digits 722 also derive from the start of the Torah, when the ayin prefix is in place. And the letters that bequeath this sequence spell רבע / raba / <u>square</u>, no less! Then the other form of this result is 38 squared, where 38 is the gematria of the word לֻח / luach / <u>a tablet</u>, seen in the very centre of G1. So that 38² (or 38×38) would aptly represent the two tablets on which were inscribed the Ten Commandments.

A related observation concerns the numbers 1111 and 5555, which are the only four-digit, homogeneous, linear sequences seen in all square versions of the Seal. Their sum is of course 6666, which was one of the two strategic numbers that enclosed the 7221 sequence obtained from *arba*. Recall that 7221 − 555 = 6666; and 7221 + 555 = 6×6×6×6×6.

The last of the numerical characteristics of the G4 square I want to examine is the 1111 sequence itself, because every one of its elements is at the centre of a notable three-digit number, illustrated in Figure 7.13 (overleaf).

From the top, the first of them is 612 or 216. As 612 it is the now familiar gematria of the word *brit* (a covenant), and a distinctive component of B'reishith, the very first word of the Torah. As 216, it is 6×6×6. Notice, however, that in the G3 aspect of the Seal, the same location contained the ubiquitous number 616.

The second three-digit number is 913 (or 319). As 913 it is the gematria of the entire word B'reishith. But that also combines with 319, at opposite ends of a palindromic number sequence I once called the 'characteristic signature' of all triangular numbers. It is found that, if each member of the triangular number series is reduced to a single digit (see Appendix B), the outcome is an endless repetition of 9-1-3-6-1-6-3-1-9. The central three digits are the enigmatic alternative 'number of the beast' from Revelation 13:18. They have also been generated in several ways by the Seal, and by those verses of Genesis 1 that contain the word 'multiply'.

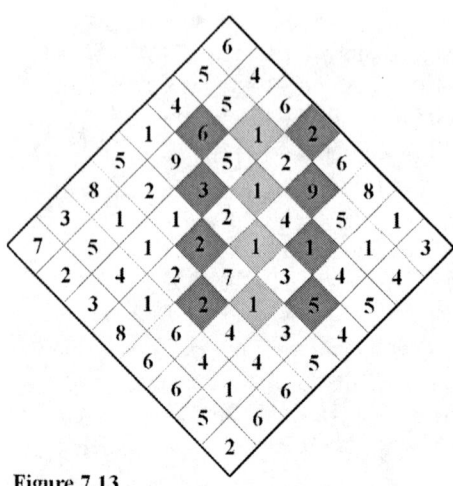

**Figure 7.13**

The third topical group is 112 (or 211). As 112 it is 28×4, combining two values that exemplify the essence of the Seal. It is also the gematria (26+86) of the expression [◻] יהוה אלהים / *YHWH Elohim* / <u>Lord God</u>, the Author of all creation. This is the compound name that is used almost to the exclusion of all others between Genesis 2:4 and the end of Chapter 3. In the Seal, this particular 112 terminates precisely between two others that originate in the man clothed in linen. They do so in such a way that each digit of the linear 222 group participates in one 112 sequence. That is on a par with the remarkable role of 222 when it combined geometrically with 614, as described in Chapter 4.

As 211, the group is related to the length of the Torah in a way that also involves several prominent sequences in the present view of the Seal. And it then leads to a kind of cascade effect. First, notice that this 211 group is the only one to overlap with every one of the 1111, 222 and 111 groups, the sum of which is 1444. Then observe the following product:

$$211 \times 1444 = 304684$$

...which differs from the number of letters in the Torah (ie 304,805) by exactly 121. This difference is rather meaningful; it is not only $11^2$, and fourth Star of David (hexagram) number, but it is also seen as three digit sequences in the G3/4 squares. Every one of these 121 groups has its origin in the man clothed in linen. And two of them, moreover, originate in the same two copies of the letter aleph that start the overlapping copies of *arba* (four) in the fish-shape seen in Figure 7.10. The third 121 sequence is obtained from the letters of אֲרִי / *ariy* / a lion, seen in G4 ascending from the same central element of the man clothed in linen. But note that the gematria of *ariy* is 1+200+10 = 211, the very number that triggered this arithmetic cascade.

It is very easy to be carried away by associations between numbers. But there is another that is so closely related to the last observation that it deserves special mention. Notice the similarity between the following two products using only the numbers just seen:

(i)               **121 × 121 = 14641**      (ie 121 squared)
(And observe that the two copies of 121 that originate from the central element of the man clothed in linen do indeed occupy two sides of a square)

Also,
(ii)               **111 × 222 = 24642**

The difference between these results is 10,001 which again should remind us of Deuteronomy 32:30. But note also that the prime factors of 10,001 are 37 and 137 (ie 37×137 = 10001). Then recall that 37 is itself a Star of David number and also a factor in both 111 and 222. And 137 was the age of Ishmael, and of Levi, and of Amram when each of them died. These are the only occasions when the number 137 occurs anywhere in the Bible.

Finally, the fourth of the notable three-digit numbers centred on the 1111 group is 512, which is $2^9$, or 2×2×2×2×2×2×2×2×2. The same number and other powers of 2 have already helped us tie together some very important structures in the present square (and in G3).

A moment ago we found the emergent word שַׁעַר / *sha'ar* / a gate occupying the diagonal of a 3×3 area that has been incredibly bountiful in all the square facets of the Seal. It is that area which will now repay closer attention. It is also worth repeating that, during a recent short tour of the G4 square, the central element of the 'Y' shaped, exultant man clothed in linen was seen to be the common origin of two copies of 121 (the square of 11 and fourth Star of David number). These are positioned, one vertical and the other horizontal, as two sides of a 3×3 square. His lower element is also the source of another horizontal 121.

Figure 7.14 is a view of G3. The topical central 3×3 zone (not the one bounded by two 121s) is defined by five elements with heavy borders. Obviously, the whole group is centred on the 7 that comes from the ayin prefix to the regular text of Genesis. The next point to note is that the three highlighted horizontal digits and three vertical digits comprise the two consecutive numbers 273 and 274. Both of these numbers have their own intrinsic merit. But note that their configuration is not unlike the consecutive numbers 511 and 512 (grey shading in Figure 7.14). The latter two numbers serve to define the lower end of a 3×3×5 Ark shape, the upper end of which is marked by another similar configuration of the digits 1-6-6-6. And this is really

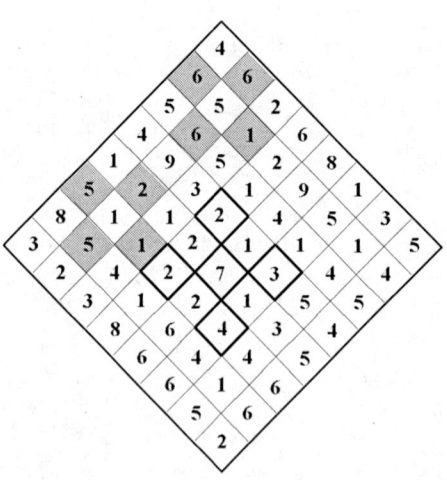

quite extraordinary, since our latest 3×3 central area of focus was once identified in Chapter 4 as the upper end of a 3×3×5 Ark shape. That earlier case was also defined by another 1-6-6-6 set of digits in the G1 square (see Figure 4.3).

Having now seen the clearest hint that the same central area of the G3 and G4 squares is, among other things, continuing the Ark theme, we may also identify a stunningly rich family of numeric attributes in this small central

**Figure 7.14**

area. First, the digits that make 273 come directly from the letters of the word שער / *sha'ar* / <u>a gate</u>. That is no small matter in itself because 273 also happens to be the gematria of the word arba (ie 'four'), and arba is undoubtedly in the position of a gateway to the Torah.

Next, the number 274 = 2×137, where the larger factor occurs only three times in the entire Bible, and always as the age of an important personality at the time of his death. We encountered both 137 and 37 during the aforementioned tour of G4. What is more, the often aligned names of YHWH and Abraham give a gematria sum of 26+248 = 274.

Given that the gematria of Genesis 1:1 is 2701 = 37×73, it seems to me that there ought to be a deep significance to be deduced from the product of 273 (ie 200 + 73) and 137 (ie 100 + 37). And just as 2701 is 73rd triangular number, so the product 273×137 (ie 37401) is $T_{273}$. While its deeper meaning remains elusive, some kind of answer to the riddle may be found in the four other digits of the same 3×3 group. These are bequeathed as two '21' pairs, that were previously seen as part of two horizontal 121 groups that originate in the 'Y' shape of the man clothed in linen. Indeed, their initial elements are the very same ones which give rise to two copies of the word אַרבַע / *arba* / <u>four</u> which, in turn, combine into the stylised shape (✂) of the Christian fish symbol (see Figure 7.10). Naturally, each '21' pair comes from a different 121 sequence (ie 11×11). Within the topical 3×3 square, the four digits of the two 21s occupy positions at the midpoints of its four sides. If we view them as a single set of four digits, they may be read cyclically in four ways, all of which have a certain merit, thus:

1. **2211 = $T_{66}$**
2. **1122 = 2×$T_{33}$**
3. **2112 = 8×264** (where the larger number is the gematria of יַרדֵן / *Yardan* / <u>Jordan</u>, the river)
4. **1221 = 11×111**

In fact, three of these four-digit numbers are also related to important structural characteristics of the Torah. First, 2211 is the position of the first letter *samech* (ס), when the ayin prefix is in place as an additional letter as it is, for example, in the G4 square. Recall that *samech* is the last of all the Hebrew letters to make its first appearance in the Torah after an inordinately long delay.

Next, 1221 = 3×407, where the larger factor is the gematria of the sixth word of the Torah. It is also noteworthy that the qatan sequence of that word is 614, which we now know from Chapter 4 represents completion of the 613 commands conferred by the Torah.

Next, 2112 = 69696 ÷ 33, both of which factors were examined together in Chapter 5. We discovered there that 69696 is a perfect fit for any 8×8 chessboard, and that includes every square aspect of the Author's Seal. And when 69696 elements are distributed evenly throughout a chessboard arrangement, it is found that each of its 64 component squares will contain 33×33. If we then evaluate that product we obtain 33×33 = 1089, which is the same as 121×9. So it is particularly significant that the emergent word תֵשַע / *tesha* / <u>nine</u> is found overlapping the word שַעַר / *sha'ar* / <u>a gate</u> and passing into the narrow space between the two horizontal copies of 121. We also noted in Chapter 5 that the number 69696 may be obtained from the length of the Torah, through the prime factors of 304,805 formed into two intersecting pentagons.

However, we should not lose sight of the original objective, which is to find a clearer understanding for the product: $273 \times 137 = 37401$ (ie $T_{273}$). We may not discover the full meaning all at once, but we can at least take two steps in the right direction. First we should recall that one of the tassels on the centre of the G1 square (see Chapter 4, esp. Figure 4.6) was obtained from a duplicated letter sequence having gematria 411, and that $411 = 3 \times 137$. Next, we should note that the earlier alternative numbers, 1122, 1221, 2112 and 2211 all include a factor of 11. Therefore, bearing in mind that $274 = 2 \times 137$, all nine elements in the topical, central 3×3 group have a role in the following product:

$$11 \times 137 \times 273 \quad = 411411$$

…which is surely the ultimate exaltation of the number 411.

What is more, $273 \times 11 = 3003$. Other research (Jenkins, 2003) has established that 3003 is the gematria of the Torah's first eight words; that is, the whole of the first verse together with the next word, meaning *and the earth*.

All in all, then, the centre of the G3/4 aspects of the Seal drives home very hard its message that it embodies many coherent characteristics. It demonstrates an awareness of several simple mathematical concepts. It shows that these concepts are designed into external aspects of the Torah: its length; the distribution of certain of its letters; and the fact that the Seal and the complete Torah each recognises the presence, the role and the structure of the other. But above all, the rich content within the specified 3×3 area of this square, symmetrically placed on the vertical diagonal, latches precisely with equally eloquent content in the G1 and G2 aspects of the Seal.

The Seal on the start of the Torah is God's temple in heaven – revealed in the only way it can possibly be recognised on earth. This priceless heirloom of surpassing beauty succeeds in describing and illustrating every essential aspect of all the alternative 'temples' mentioned in the 66 books of the standard Christian Bible. It is now crystal clear why God's commandments had to include one that forbids the making of any 'graven image'. Every image we could possibly need is already bequeathed to us in the form of the Seal.

Finally, my reader will surely have noticed one more contrast between the subtly different G3 and G4 squares. Whereas G3 makes many references to the deeds of Moses and his contemporaries, the G4 aspect has so far added nothing new to that particular phase of history. However, the latter version of the Seal, as qatan letter values, has just one more graphical image to impart. In Figure 7.15, observe the indicated sequence of digits 3-1-4-1-5-9-2-6 in a very distinctive configuration. The first point to note is that these are the first eight digits of the number Pi, so represent this important number to an accuracy of about 0.0000017%. While this is not the only continuous sequence of the same eight digits in this square, it is the most important for two related reasons.

First, the path traced by those digits passes twice through the shaded 2×2 group which corresponds to the letters of מצרי מ [ם] / *Mitzraim* / Egypt. We may therefore recognise this as a clue that it represents the entry into Egypt with Joseph, and the later exodus with Moses. But look closely at the overall configuration, and it can be seen to bear a striking resemblance to the northern end of the Red Sea, where the gulfs of Suez and Aqaba contain the Sinai Peninsula. Therefore, not only does this one square depict separated waters (employing the familiar letter vav metaphor), but it makes a

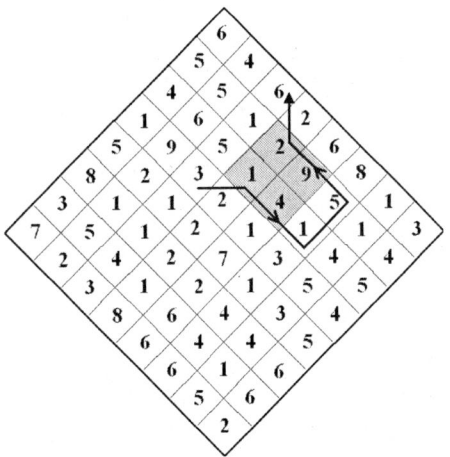

**Figure 7.15**

similar statement with an exceptional degree of geographical aptness to what is, arguably, the most important episode in the Torah. Indeed, the Israelites' forty years wandering around Sinai, after crossing the Red Sea, has been likened to them being exiled in Sheol – Realm of the Dead. And the emergent, linear word 'Sheol' was once seen in just this location where Egypt is now (see Chapter 2, Figure 2.8), and was composed from three of the five letters of 'Israel'. Oddly, the same three elements now depict the number 496, which is $T_{31}$, third perfect number and twice the gematria of Abraham. Equally oddly, of the seven other 3-digit groups parallel to this 496, five of them have either a biblical significance or a merely visual impact, or both.

At the top, the visually distinctive 456 is one of the groups which once, in the G1 square, bequeathed a tassel on the central garment. So that it's standard value is actually $400 + 5 + 6 = 411$; that is, $3 \times 137$, and the ages of Ishmael, Levi and Amram at the times of their deaths. Below this, the same sequence is seen in reverse. Next, the 615 group implies the gematria of הששׁי / *ha shishiy* / the sixth, which is the very last word of Genesis Chapter 1, the active phase of the biblical creation. This number is also a member of the most significant sequence of six consecutive numbers which were analysed in Chapter 6. The two groups on either side of the topical 496 have little obvious merit, apart from 851 being divisible by the ubiquitous 37. However, the 411 (another $3 \times 137$) below the 851 repeats the previous allusions to important biblical personalities. Finally, the bottom group as 543 is not only visually striking, but also three times the fifth Star of David or hexagram number (ie 181).

-oOo-

In an important sense, we are more or less finished with our exploration of the Author's Seal on the Torah, or at least in respect of its elaborate internal structure. I trust that my reader has, by now, reached the same conclusion as myself as to the identity of the Author. In my efforts to describe the indescribable, I have been constantly aware that aspects of the Seal are inevitably meant to be associated with particular biblical events and narratives. And that means some religious beliefs will seem to be favoured and bolstered more than others. I am sure that has always been the Author's intention, and why I am dedicated to placing this information, unabridged, in the public domain. At the same time, I would caution against the followers of any established religious view becoming too smug. It is sometimes said that the greatest achievement of the devil has been to convince us that he does not exist. For myself, that comes a distant second behind his having convinced countless people that each of their contradictory religious beliefs is more true than all others. I do not for one moment believe that any one belief has a monopoly on truth. The message the Seal is trying to impart must be accepted as an integral whole from which we cannot pick and choose as we please. If there is any religion in the world that already embraces this whole edifice to the exclusion of doctrinal issues that muddy the waters, I have yet to find it.

The remaining chapters of this book build on the wisdom the Seal represents, and look outwards and beyond in four distinct ways.

# 8

It is often said that the biblical creation account at the start of Genesis is not a description of the birth of the physical Universe. On the face of it, that seems self-evident, as there are virtually no points of contact between the plain meaning of Genesis and any realistic scientific description of the so-called Big Bang, nor of any standard scientific principles as described by physics, chemistry and biology. However, appearances can be deceptive, and it seems the disparity between scripture and reality may not be quite so clear-cut as first appears. So, given that Genesis Chapter 1 is a somewhat inscrutable description of the way God created the Universe, it is of the greatest significance that he has also made available the means by which we may bridge the conceptual gap between it and our familiar reality.

In Chapter 6, we discovered an important continuous sequence of eight numbers from 609 to 616 that tell of the coherent way the Hebrew Torah is put together. The first two (ie 609 and 610) are bequeathed by the length of the Torah, because doubling its 304,805 letters gives 609,610. By itself, this is no more than a simple curiosity. But the next six numbers, from 611 to 616, add an altogether more important dimension. This is because when we pair them from the middle outwards, that creates a pattern of increasing order, just as the creation account describes the bringing of order from chaos in six days.

The middle two numbers of the six (ie 613 and 614) each represents a number of God's commands. 613 has long been held to be the number of commands within the Torah that are applicable to Judaism. And a 614th command – to love your enemies – was added in the Christian New Testament, to fulfil the Law. These two numbers are essentially just counts; whereas the ones that enclose them reflect a profound relationship that exists in the fundamental nature of number and the Hebrew language (see Appendix A(iii)).

The connection between 612 and 615 is that they are the gematria values of words that may be found at the extreme ends of the active phase of creation. The first word of the Torah בראשית / B'reishith / In the beginning, contains ברית / brit / a covenant; and the last word in Genesis 1 is הששי / ha shishiy / the sixth, from 'the sixth day'. The gematria values of brit and ha shishiy are found to be 612 and 615 respectively. Then 611 and 616 come from the gematria values of תורה / Torah and התורה / HaTorah / The Torah, respectively.

By far the most significant characteristic of the three pairs of numbers is that they are all conceptually related, in an evolution of orderliness. We can see easily that 611 (Torah) contains 612 (Covenant) which, in the case of the Mosaic covenant, contains 613 individual commandments. But considered as pairs, the source or derivation of the larger number can be recognised as the completion or fulfilment of the source of the smaller. This, too, is a kind of evolution.

Each pair also adds up to 1227, which is the qatan sequence obtained from the word ארבע / arba / four, with its intimate connection to the Author's Seal. In Chapter 6, we noted that the presence of 609 and 610 underpin the six main numbers numerically. But as a number of letters, they represent the building blocks of the three more elaborate concepts: (i) commands, (ii) covenant and (iii) Torah. There is, therefore, a multi-faceted relationship between numbers (the language of science) and spoken language (the medium of God's creation – *And God said "Let there be …"*).

In previous chapters, I have often expressed the view that there is a fundamental difference between the incomplete way we see the Seal on the Torah, and the way it is comprehended by its Author and Architect. If it turns out that the Author of the Torah is also the Author and creator of the universe in which we live, then we might expect him to see that differently, too. One point I have already made is that the designer of the Seal must be able to see all its many aspects in a single sweep. From our limited 3-dimensional perspective, we can never hope to achieve the same all-encompassing view, no matter how much proof we accumulate that such a view must exist.

An equivalent dilemma arises when we try to draw 3-dimensional objects on a flat, 2-dimensional page. For example, we may draw a map of a mountainous region using either colour or contour lines to represent differing heights. Or, more pertinent to our topic, we may draw a house in plan view and a selection of elevations. And, although the various aspects of the house may all be visible at the same time, it takes a well trained specialist observer to keep more than one of them fully in mind at once. An even more appropriate example is the 'complete 4-graph (K₄)' we encountered in Chapter 5, which is a 2-dimensional representation of a 3-dimensional tetrahedron. This is akin to seeing a specific profile of the transparent object; but only one from an infinite number of possible profiles. Graphs of that type may be used to show 2-dimensional representations of objects that have even more than three dimensions. However, the more dimensions we try to squeeze onto a flat page, the less satisfactory the model becomes of the real object. In any case, how could we ever hope to understand something that exists mostly, or even partially, outside our familiar reality?

Nonetheless, experts in special effects for movie films have often done a surprisingly effective job of representing this impossibility, in motion, on 2-dimensional celluloid. Then, by watching a rapid sequence of time slices, the viewer has the impression of seeing the changing intersection of a higher-dimensional object with our own three dimensions. If done really well, the effect can be suitably disorienting; the point being that, although we can never have a creator's eye view of our world, he will have no difficulty at all understanding our view of our particular slice of reality. Therefore, the Seal has been designed from the perspective of higher dimensions (higher than three or four), but with the clear objective that we should be able to recognise and to some extent understand its coherent complexity.

Whether the present Chapter of this book is its most important, or least, will be decided only with hindsight. It represents a leap of faith, but by no means a leap in the dark. In the next few pages we step away from the relative comfort and security of the biblical text, and into the cold light of the natural world. However, we do so on the strength of a provident foundation that may have been designed for this very purpose. Out of all the structural artefacts that we have spent the previous seven chapters unravelling, there is a central core that is custom made to lead us in the direction we are about to take. Some of them are almost self-evident clues; others are visible but not yet recognised for what they are. And there will be one further prophetic vision to be explained, which will help draw together some parallel strands that otherwise would never meet. The way to appreciate what follows is to ask often: *How (else) might scientific concepts be portrayed by and artist and poet?*

-oOo-

# In the Beginning

Taken at face value, the first thirty-one verses of Genesis purport to describe the physical creation of our world, our universe. But in the present day and age, nobody would seriously suggest that it does so in terms that are consistent with the way science describes the same phenomena and processes. With good reason it has often been said that early Genesis cannot be compared to a science book or article. And it would be folly to try to do so with the plain Hebrew text, since it is not provided with that as its primary purpose. Rather, like all parts of the Bible, the first creation account exists first and foremost as part of a manual in moral rectitude – often using graphic examples of how not to behave. But that should not preclude the same text concealing additional messages or information.

Take the four square aspects of the Author's Seal, for example. Based on only the first sixty-five Hebrew letters of Genesis, these show quite clearly that the same text may be seen in several alternative, yet equally important ways. Individually, each of those square views demonstrates a wealth of knowledge concerning later parts of the Bible. That includes the rest of the creation account, as well as later parts of the Torah, some if not all of the prophets, and even the Christian New Testament. They also exhibit an inexplicable degree of understanding of clearly defined aspects of mathematics and the physical world. So it is to those last two subjects that the first of our outward-looking chapters is devoted.

As far back as Chapter 3, we found that the first verse of Genesis, in its specific guise as the perimeter of the G1 square, recognises an early philosophical attempt to describe the physical world. It was Aristotle (384 BC to 322 BC) who first suggested that every component of the physical world can be described in terms of combinations of four 'fundamental' elements: Fire, Air, Water and Earth. And we saw that the four sides of the G1 perimeter identify each of these elements in the order given above, with only one readily explicable omission. As Figure 8.1 shows, the similarities between the theories of Aristotle and the structure of the G1 square go well beyond the mere naming of his four elements. The philosopher also imagined that each element embodied a unique pair of characteristics – combining one from each of diametrically opposite pairs: HOT/COLD and WET/DRY. Thus, fire was characterised by the hot:dry combination. But notice particularly the square inscribed within a square, just as we saw with the ELS word שלושה / shelosheh / three, in G1. Evidently, the Author's Seal prefers the concept of number over physical attributes. Or maybe it foresaw something we now take for granted, that mathematics is the true language of science. The deeper we probe into the fundamental workings of our world, the more we have to resort to maths for descriptions and explanations.

Admittedly, we do not see a word for 'air' in its logical place in the second side of the G1 square; but that may be explained on the grounds that air is the only one of Aristotle's elements that is normally invisible. Overall, the inscribed square word for 'three' within G1 is a reasonable facsimile for the theory of Aristotle, and indicates that the Author of the Torah is sensitive to the slow pace and tortuous route by which man's understanding of his world must develop. In Chapter 6, moreover, we saw that the square-within-a-square is also numerically equivalent to the Theorem of Pythagoras, with particular application to a 3:4:5 right-angle triangle. That was just one of many

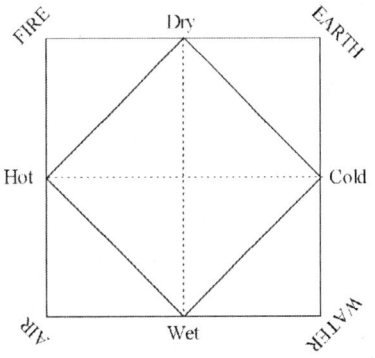

**Figure 8.1**

ways the Seal combines mathematics with geometry and architecture. So, for practical reasons the Seal holds something that is relevant to interest every culture and generation. And, as we have seen, that also goes for our spiritual development, and the extent to which the prophets could recognise and understand the Seal. Not surprisingly, the more mature our understanding of the natural world becomes, the more sophisticated the Author would need to be in fashioning his Seal. Later in this Chapter, we shall go beyond the simple notion that the earlier emphasis on 'four' is a possible allusion to the four states of matter. Almost immediately, it will become possible to relate the three converging copies of arba in the G3 and G4 squares to three tetrad categories of natural phenomena.

In scientific terms, the 'four elements' observation does have its counterpart in the realm of modern physics. As I pointed out in Chapter 3, we now may recognise those elements as the four states, or phases, of matter (ie solid, liquid, gas and plasma) all of which may be observed in just about every kitchen. More to the point, there is a delightful correspondence between their ordered representation in the G1/G2 squares and the progress of creation following the so-called Big Bang. For, although hydrogen and some helium atomic nuclei had already formed by the time the universe was only about three minutes old, for the next 380,000 years the form that matter took remained restricted to plasma. And this corresponds to the first side of the G1 square, with its embedded *esh* (fire). It was only then, when the universe had cooled sufficiently, that those atomic nuclei were able to hold onto a family of electrons. That was when true atoms came into being, as gas rather than plasma. And, incidentally, it was also this sudden binding of free electrons that first enabled light to move around without restriction. Until that point, the universe had been in total darkness. So, in a surprising way, light – the first product of creation in Genesis 1:3 – was closely associated in the early universe with the first ever phase transition. Only after that stage did it become possible for matter to be further transformed into liquid and solid forms (sides #3 and #4 of G1, respectively), and then only following complex transmutation processes within stars.

The overarching sequence is clear enough. From the moment the universe was born, around 13.7 billion years ago, there has been a natural progression towards more substantial forms of matter. That is, plasma gave way to a gaseous form, which was followed by the potential to form liquids then solids. It is a moot point whether, on the cosmic scale, the first liquids were formed before the first solids. But the potential has been for transitions in the order: plasma $\rightarrow$ gas $\rightarrow$ liquid $\rightarrow$ solid, in step with the reduction of background temperatures. So it is highly significant that the square formation of Genesis 1:1 identifies the first, third and fourth phases in its first, third and fourth sides, using the words 'fire', 'water' and 'earth'.

To be slightly pedantic, the phase transitions just described were not directly connected to the passage of time, but to the size of the universe as it expanded. It is the process of expansion that leads to lowering of temperature, which is just as true of the universe as a whole as in the laboratory. The universe began as a super-dense infinitesimal speck and effectively infinite temperature, and it has been expanding ever since. Strictly speaking, science now tells us that the universe did not always expand in the way it does today. There was an initial phase now known as inflation, during which the speed of light limit on velocity did not apply. Then the more familiar expansion took over. And the big surprise is that this two-stage enlargement process is also reflected in the first verse of Genesis in two different ways. First, take a fresh look at Figure 8.2, the familiar 4×7 matrix of the qatan letter values of the Bible's first verse. Here, the first four values are written left-to-right in the top row, then four more left-to-right in the second row, and so on until all seven rows have been filled.

Now notice the totals for each row in the extra column on the right. And it can be seen that there is an overall trend of growth in those totals from the top row to the bottom; that is, from the beginning of the verse to its end. Within the general trend, the first three rows show a smooth increase, and the last four also show a smooth increase, but at a different rate. The two different rates of growth could represent the alternative cosmological inflation and expansion phases. Then the pause (ie no change) between the third to fourth rows would indicate the moment of transition from inflation to expansion. The increasing numbers can equally be interpreted as the trend from plasma (the least substantial form of matter) towards solid.

For obvious reasons, the ongoing increase in the size of the universe causes a reduction in its mean density, even from the moment the infinitely-dense speck came into existence. And that initial condition is reflected in the 913 gematria of the Torah's 6-letter first word – *B'reishith*. This number accounts for more than one third of the gematria of Genesis 1:1, the entire 7-word first verse, and is more than twice the gematria of any other word.

Also, in passing we may note a numerical effect that would not have been recognised the last time we saw the above matrix. First, notice that the familiar diagonal 1111 sequence (the hypotenuse of the 45° triangle) is crossed by a diagonal 2-3-4-5 sequence. And this, too, adds to the sense of a progressive evolution. But notice also just below and parallel to the 1111, there is a 1444 sequence, which we now know to be 2×722. The latter number

| 2 | 2 | 1 | 3 | 8 |
|---|---|---|---|---|
| 1 | 4 | 2 | 2 | 9 |
| 1 | 1 | 3 | 5 | 10 |
| 1 | 4 | 1 | 4 | 10 |
| 5 | 3 | 4 | 1 | 13 |
| 4 | 6 | 1 | 4 | 15 |
| 5 | 1 | 2 | 9 | 17 |

**Figure 8.2**

overlaps the beginning of Genesis when the ayin prefix is in place. Therein exists a persistent link between the two sides of the Big Bang, before and after.

The second allusion of Genesis 1:1 to the same physical process comes from an equally familiar but more literary characteristic of the square. This involves the word בּרא / *bara* / he created, which is the second word of the regular text. But as we know, *bara* is also found concealed as the first half of the first word representing the 'first cause', although there is no etymological connection between the two words. Now recall Figure 2.2, repeated as Figure 8.3 (overleaf), which shows the text of Genesis 1:1, entered clockwise from the top right corner. The first three letters represent the infinitely dense speck from which the Big Bang erupted. The same three letters seen turning the lower right corner are the second word ('he created'), and indicate that creation has begun. We may also surmise that the second word could represent completion of the inflation phase. Then the same three letters seen shaded in the first, second and third corner squares must represent the cosmic expansion, which still continues to this day.

So, although we should never lose sight of the primary function of the Bible (ie the creation of man and his moral education), we are provided with evidence that it can after all say something pertinent about the physical creation as well. But at this stage, the evidence for hidden scientific knowledge in the Bible is still limited to the fields of cosmology and simple physics, where they overlap. However, with this enticement we are, it seems, being beckoned to seek more deeply for some further clue to a meaningful way forward.

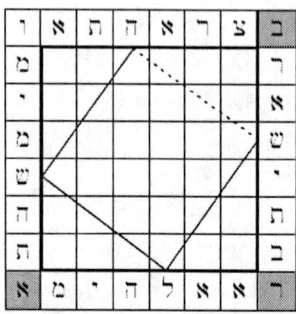

Figure 8.3

It is very telling that all sober descriptions of the Big Bang go back only as far as a short time after its beginning. That may be a very short time indeed – say a billion billion billionth of one second. But scientific descriptions are unlikely ever to go back to Time=0, and certainly not to a condition in which the beginning has not yet happened. Some scientists now refer to the latter state as the prior condition, and readily accept that from our side of the Big Bang we can never have knowledge of that other side. The explanation goes that the Big Bang itself is an information barrier; that any information about the prior condition was inevitably scrambled in that first instant.

Yet the Author's Seal appears to suggest otherwise. For one thing, this short section of text on the very beginning behaves a lot like an error-detection, or error-correction code as used in modern electronic communication. But there is an even more obvious clue to a surviving before-and-after connection. If an aspect if the creator known as Small Face entered his creation while Vast Face remained outside, then that might imply a preserved link. One recent hint of this possibility was seen only four paragraphs ago, in the number 1444 (ie 2×722) in the 4×7 matrix of Genesis 1:1 – a cryptic reference to Vast Face on the outside. Another clue is in the Hebrew word זכר / zakar / <u>to remember</u>, the gematria of which is 227. Clearly, this number also matches the digits that overlap the start of the G2 square which has the letter ayin, symbol of Vast Face, on the outside. The implication is that something exists, other than the natural phenomena with which science is concerned, maintaining a knowing connection between the two sides of the physical creation. In biblical terms, there is a corresponding persistent call to remember, associated with every covenant that God has made with man. For example:

> *I will remember my covenant between me and you and all living creatures of every kind. Never again will the waters become a flood to destroy all life.*
>
> (Genesis 9:15)

Notice here the specific use of the expression 'living creatures', a theme that is closely associated with the books of Ezekiel and Revelation. There, the living creatures have a previously unsuspected meaning that we shall address in the coming pages.

Then we see:

> *God heard their groaning and he remembered his covenant with Abraham, with Isaac and with Jacob.*
>
> (Exodus 2:24)

But covenants are essentially two-sided and, therefore, we also find injunctions like:

> *Remember the Sabbath day and keep it holy.*
>
> (Exodus 20:8)

> *The Lord said unto Moses, "Speak to the Israelites and say to them: 'Throughout the generations to come you are to make tassels on the corners of your garments, with a blue cord on each tassel. You will have these tassels to look at and so you will remember all the commands of the Lord' ..."*
>
> (Numbers 15:37-39)

> *You shall not pervert the justice due to the sojourner or to the fatherless, or take a widow's garment in pledge; but you shall remember that you were slaves in Egypt and the Lord your God redeemed you from there; therefore I commend you to do this.*
>
> (Deuteronomy 24:17-18)

So notice that there are two associations made between a garment and the call to remember. And finally:

> *Remember the days of old; consider the generations long past. Ask your father and he will tell you, your elders, and they will explain to you.*
>
> (Deuteronomy 32:7)

The call to remember is not just addressed to the individual, but is a long-term collective responsibility. And the seriousness of the Jews to abide by the last of these commands in particular is reflected in the passionately obsessive way they copy Torah scrolls. The scribes have elaborate procedures for detecting and correcting transcription errors.

Returning to the 722 gematria of the word 'to remember', two of the corresponding digits at the beginning of the G2 square come from the very first word, B'reishith. And those specific letters are the very same ones which contribute to the word ברית / *brit* / <u>covenant</u>, once the middle two letters of the first word are removed. What better reminder could there be, that God's covenants incorporate the need for both sides to remember? The same point will be made even clearer when, later, we turn to specific scientific knowledge and concepts. And it is no less significant that the two letters we removed from B'reishith to leave brit are אש / *esh* / <u>fire</u>, the first product of the Big Bang.

Ultimately, we shall become aware of other ways in which the Author's Seal and the Torah have been designed consistently to depict aspects of science, including representative topics from physics, chemistry and biology that are especially important to life. In fact, there is one such topic that has everything to do with remembering on a grand scale. The raw materials (information) we need to achieve that understanding are already known to us, but we presently lack the key that will unlock its meaning.

Our next biblical clue, or signpost, to scientific understanding is as elegant as it is complex. It comes in four parts as two pairs, so that none is dispensable. Again, we shall find what we seek only by looking simultaneously at the way the same scene is described by both Ezekiel and the author of Revelation; we shall call the latter John, on the strength of the book's full title: The Revelation to John (The Apocalypse). Again it is their descriptions of 'four living creatures' that contain an astonishing truth. We have already seen one provisional clue from each author, testifying to their common Seal-related inspiration. In the case of Ezekiel, that is the set of sixty-four marble and granite square tablets on which are carved the entire text of his book, in raised letters. These tablets represent all the square identities of the 8×8 Seal. And in Revelation, John describes the new Jerusalem with its twelve gates in four equal sides and a river in its midst. And God and the Lamb are the temple and the light of the city. This is a scene for which the Seal itself is an obvious representation, in ever so many ways. In fact, there is another apposite correspondence between the two prophetic books, in the way they both describe the measuring of a temple, using a reed or a rod (see Ezekiel 40 and Revelation 11). The proportions of the temple in heaven are no doubt represented by the many numerical characteristics of the Seal; as it is written:

> *Then God's temple in heaven was opened, and the ark of his covenant was seen within his temple…*
>
> (Revelation 11:19)

That is, just as we have seen the Ark represented in the Seal in many ways. And since there are numerous similarities between Ezekiel and Revelation in their plain (and maybe not so plain) meaning, we should not be too surprised to find equivalence in the way they unknowingly describe the physical created world.

In their descriptions of four living creatures, there are sufficient similarities to conclude that Ezekiel and John are reporting on the same basic scene. Even though, up to now we have seen no evidence that John was not simply repeating the same basic pattern established by the earlier prophet. But that deficiency cannot be allowed to continue. In a strange yet compelling sense, the way we may know that the descriptions given by Ezekiel and John are independent yet both trustworthy depends not on their similarities, but on some of their differences. In the following table, there is a comparison between the descriptions given by the two prophets of particular attributes of the living creatures.

Table 8.1

| Attribute | Ezekiel | Revelation (John) |
|---|---|---|
| Number of living creatures. | 4 | 4 |
| Number of faces each. | 4 | 1 |
| Number of wings each. | 6 | 4 |
| Intersecting (wheels within-) wheels. | Eze 1:18; 10:10 | No mention |
| Wheels with rims and spokes. | Eze 1:18 | No mention |
| Feet like a calf. | Eze 1:7 | No mention |
| A likeness of hands of a man under the wings. | Eze 1:8; 10:8; 10:21 | No mention |
| The spirit of the living creatures was in the wheels. | Eze 1:12; 10:17 | No mention |
| Appearance like burning coals of fire, or like torches. | Eze 1:13 | No mention |

For some purposes, it is the quantities they mention that are important; for others it is the mystical language that reveals the author's true intent. These things are the key that unlocks the meaning of a wide range of scientific metaphors both in the Seal and in the wider Torah. But before we can recognise that intent, it is essential that we dispense with the linguistic blinkers that have been unwittingly applied in all translations of Ezekiel from the Hebrew.

The word used by Ezekiel, which has been persistently translated as 'living creatures' is חיות (*chayot*). This is a plural form, and there is an undoubted connection with life; but the word 'creature' does not figure explicitly in the original Hebrew text. There is also a clear contrast between Ezekiel's use of chayot, and its use in Genesis 9:15 with which he would have been well acquainted. In the earlier, Torah occurrence, chayot is preceded by נפש / *nephesh* / <u>breath</u> or <u>soul</u>. By omitting nephesh, Ezekiel is highlighting an important point, or difference of emphasis. There is, however, a particularly strong connection between the un-augmented word *chayot* and the verb חיה / *chayah* / <u>to bestow life</u>, which we have seen as an emergent word in the G4 square. That was in precisely the same position where G3 conferred 'she' and G1 revealed 'light', all three-letter words. Once we see the alternative interpretation for Ezekiel's vision, it will become clear that he did not have independent living creatures in mind when he used the word chayot. But the fact that he also used the words hands, feet, wings and faces was guaranteed to steer translations towards that mis-understanding. As we shall soon see, there is an alternative yet fully coherent way to interpret hands, feet and wings, which leads to a totally different conclusion. What we shall find is that the chayot do not themselves possess independent life, but serve to bestow life on mankind. They are not living creatures, but life-giving entities of a type that Ezekiel would not comprehend.

Of the numerous pseudo-anatomical features attributed to the chayot, the faces have already been partially explained in Chapter 7, by reference to the grouped emergent words for ox, eagle and lion, each utilising one letter from the plain-text word 'face'. What is more, all of those words belong to the same G4 square that also conferred the emergent חיה / *chayah* / <u>to bestow life</u>.

It is clear from Table 8.1 that, of the two biblical descriptions, Ezekiel's are the more comprehensive. And we shall seek to find explanations for all the ones in the list. But the germ of an answer comes from the number of faces that each of the prophets saw, and one particular meaning that attaches to the Hebrew word [ף] כּ נ פ / *kanaph* / a wing. Of course, the principal meaning of a wing is an organ of flight. But significantly, the same word can also be used to refer to the edge of, for example, a territory, a garment or (in the present day) a sports field. This should call to mind the use of the word 'face' in descriptions of geometrical shapes and objects, but especially 3-dimensional shapes.

In the descriptions of living creatures given by Ezekiel and John, there is a dominance of the number 4, and a single 6. There is one geometrical object in particular that is commonly described by the numbers 4, 6, 4. This is the three-dimensional tetrahedron, which has four faces, six edges (or wings) and four vertices. The numbers 4, 6 and 4 are listed in that order to reflect a hierarchy of the attributes they represent. Faces have two dimensions, edges have only one dimension, and vertices are dimensionless points. What is more, we have come across this numerical form of description already in Chapter 5, when we were investigating six unusual verses of Genesis 1, spaced regularly at four verses apart. That led to a description of the complete 4-graph ($K_4$), which has the maximum profile or silhouette of a regular tetrahedron. And the $K_4$ graph based on those six special verses had some important numerical similarities to the G1 square of qatan letter values. But before we pursue the biblical aspects of tetrahedra, I want to say a bit more about their natural properties.

The shape of a tetrahedron is quite reminiscent of a pyramid, but with a triangular base. The square base of a traditional pyramid means that that shape is less than perfect, because the square face is an odd-one-out. As long as a pyramid is sat on a flat surface, however, its imperfection is out of sight, and therefore generally ignored. And even the familiar pyramid is capable of resembling any one of the Genesis squares. When seen from directly overhead, a pyramid will look like a square with both diagonals on display. But the tetrahedron is different, at least in the case of a regular tetrahedron (all edges of equal length), because this shape is composed of four identical equilateral triangles. It does not matter which of its four faces sits on a flat surface, because the three visible faces will always be identical. In fact, the regular tetrahedron is one of nature's two most perfect 3-dimensional shapes. In any attempt to explain how the universe works, it would be impossible to do so without mentioning both the tetrahedron and the sphere. As an example, we have already encountered the helium nucleus as an early product of creation, following the Big Bang. The helium nucleus consists of four particles of virtually equal size, which cling tightly together with their centres in the relative positions of the vertices of a regular tetrahedron.

As to why Ezekiel saw the maximum four faces and six wings, this could be due to either his perspective or a subtlety of the objects that he observed. The chayot seen by Ezekiel were either made from a transparent material, or they had an open frame structure. The first is more likely for a reason that will become clear in due course.

On the other hand John reported that he saw only one face on each 'creature', and four wings. For this to happen with a tetrahedron, it is likely that John saw a view such as Figure 8.4.

Here, the perfect triangular outline could be taken for a single face. And the base of the triangle is really three superimposed edges (wings), giving the appearance of only four visible wings. Also, this shape offers an explanation for one of Ezekiel's descriptions of the chayot, in which the soles of their feet were like the soles of a calf's foot. The reason he likens this shape to a calf's foot and not an adult ox, is because the initial cleft triangular shape of a new-born calf's foot soon becomes spread and distorted, from carrying the animal's weight. We

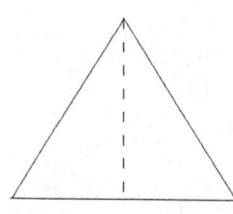

Figure 8.4

have now seen rational explanations for important differences between the two prophets' descriptions of similar visions. In due course, we shall find consistent explanations for all the other mysterious descriptions listed in Table 8.1, using a simple process for constructing a tetrahedron. Before that, it is important that we recognise two even simpler ways in which the Author's Seal may be seen as a tetrahedron.

The simpler of the two constructions comes from the geometrical structure of $T_{73}$, the triangular number that comes to us directly as the 2701 gematria total of the whole first verse of Genesis. It was in Chapter 3 where we found one representation of that number to be a $T_{37}$ triangle (ie 703) surrounded by three $T_{36}$ triangles (ie 666), in the configuration shown in Figure 8.5.

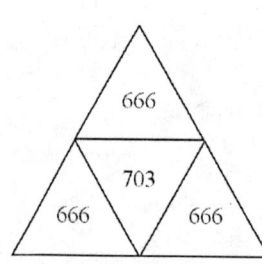

Figure 8.5

It is easy to see that the first verse of the Torah bequeaths four equilateral triangles; and it is a simple step to fold the outer triangles upwards, out of the page, so that their three free vertices come together at a single point. The resulting enclosed, 3-dimensional shape is a tetrahedron, which will be a regular tetrahedron if the three smaller triangles sit upon the 703 base-layer. That is the first tetrahedron. And recall that the fourth side of G1 gave a gematria total of precisely 703, and that 3×666 is the total gematria of its first three sides.

The second tetrahedron has been staring us in the face from every one of the square spiral matrices we have derived from the start of Genesis. Every time we observe the special nature of four perimeter sides and two diagonals we are, of course, observing a regular tetrahedron in its special 2-dimensional guise: a K₄ graph. Each corner is a vertex of the tetrahedron at which three edges meet. The edges are seen as the four sides and two diagonals, making six in all. A difficult property to distinguish in the K₄ view is the equilateral shape of the four triangular faces. Since we see all four faces at the same oblique angle, they all look like 45° right-angle triangles. Every square aspect of the Seal is a tetrahedron seen in maximum profile. To put it another way, if a bright lamp is shone directly down onto a solid regular tetrahedron with a flat screen below, what is the shape of the maximum area of the shadow it may cast? The answer is, a square. Or, if the tetrahedron is not solid but an open-frame structure, the shadow of maximum area will be seen as a square with both diagonals.

Those, then, are the two ways by which the very beginning of the Torah identifies itself as a tetrahedron. But there are two very different ways in which the Torah as a whole does the same, making four independent sources altogether. Earlier, I referred to these as two pairs.

The first of the two larger tetrahedra comes directly from the biblical text. In Genesis 1:2 there are two faces described; one is *the face of the deep*, and the other is *the face of the waters*. Interestingly, the first is included in each and every view of the Seal, while the second is always excluded. This provides an additional explanation for the kabbalistic concept of Small Face within creation, and Vast Face on the outside. Then, at the end of the Torah, with only two further verses to follow, is this verse:

> *And there arose not a prophet since in Israel like unto Moses,*
> *whom the Lord knew face to face.*
> (Deuteronomy 34:10)

Clearly, two faces at the start of Torah and two at its end are sufficient to construct a tetrahedron that may enclose all its five books. And there can be little doubt now of the subtle new nuance in the expression משה האמיה / *Moshe ta'am yah* / <u>Moses, image of God</u> that is found concealed within the very first verse of Genesis. Moreover, the G3 aspect of the Seal extended this expression into:

*Moshe, image of YHWH*, which is 'Moses, image of the Lord'. Both ends of the Torah invoke the name of Moses as a witness, and both intimate that the four faces are in some way equal and identical. This, then, is a vast regular tetrahedron.

The way we acquire the fourth and final tetrahedron represents a departure in principle, as the four faces are not ready-made and pre-existent. There is, in fact, a five-stage procedure to be gone through, which at once explains most of the remaining mysterious observations of Ezekiel's chayot, and also introduces the science of chemistry. The procedure begins with the number of Hebrew letters that make up the complete Torah. That is, 304,805 letters altogether. This number is separated into its two prime factors, which are 5 and 60961 (Stage 1 in Figure 8.6).

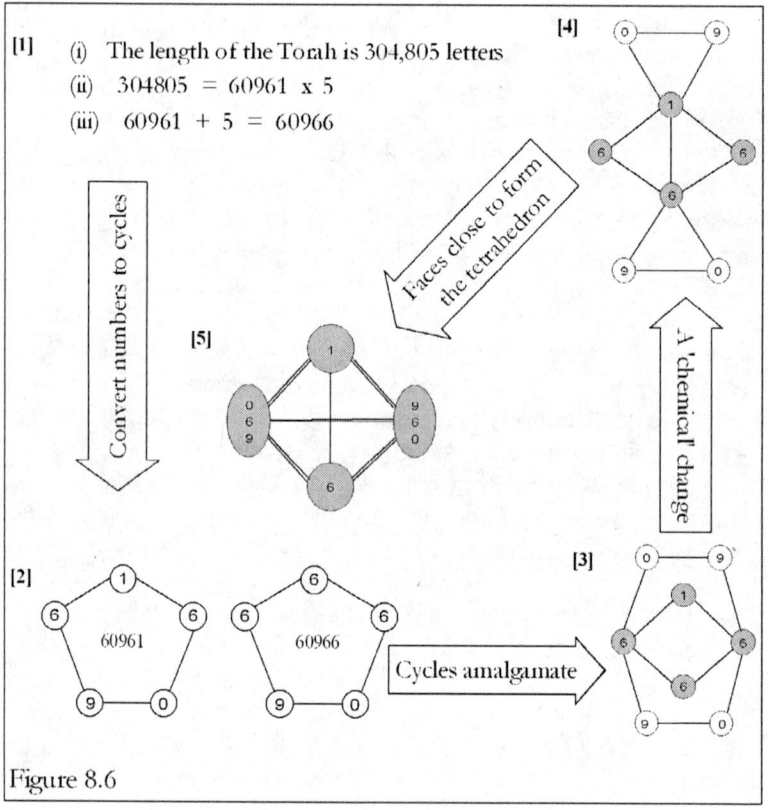

[1]
(i) The length of the Torah is 304,805 letters
(ii) 304805 = 60961 x 5
(iii) 60961 + 5 = 60966

Convert numbers to cycles

Faces close to form the tetrahedron

A 'chemical' change

[5]

[2]
60961

60966

Cycles amalgamate

[3]

[4]

Figure 8.6

Then, as in Chapter 4, the larger factor and the sum of the two factors (ie 60966) are both formed into pentagonal arrangements (Stage 2). At Stage 3, the two pentagons are bonded together, just as we have seen them in Chapter 4, also highlighting the important central 1666 digits in rhombus formation. And this is as much of the process as we have seen up to now because, previously, stages 1, 2 and 3 have been sufficient to demonstrate aspects of the Author's plan in his design of the Seal and the Ark of the Covenant. But notice that the inner rhombus may be interpreted as a cycle, or wheel, within a larger cycle. So, already we have an explanation for the rims of what Ezekiel described as wheels within wheels. What is more, Ezekiel describes the appearance of these wheels as *like unto the colour of a beryl* (or, in RSV, the gleaming of a chrysolite). One way or the other, a clear crystalline appearance is obviously intended, which explains how the prophet had been able to discern all four faces and six edges of the chayot.

After Step 3 in the process, we are stepping into new territory in which the biblical focus gives way to real-world considerations. In the fourth stage of Figure 8.6, a 'chemical' change has taken place, in which chemical bonds are broken and new ones are made. But the nodes to which those bonds are attached have also moved very slightly. In Figure 8.6(4), it will be seen that the internal 1 and 6 digits (atoms) are both now at the centre of five radiating spokes, and these have two important roles, or interpretations. On the one hand, they are the spokes of the wheels seen by Ezekiel; then each is equivalent to five human fingers on the other hand (pun very definitely intended); the central 1 and 6 are each at the centre of five other digits, in both senses of that word. So we are seeing what Ezekiel described as a likeness of hands of a man under the wings. The wings (connecting lines) are the fingers of hands; and the hands are underlying the wings, since hands and wings are here mutually dependent. We are perhaps also witnessing a reminder that the ten numeric digits 0-9 are the basis of our natural, base-10 system of arithmetic, and the vast majority of the numeric artefacts designed into the Author's Seal.

We now have only two more aspects of Ezekiel's descriptions left to explain. And the two explanations are yet again closely related to each other, and to the final step in the process that began with the length of the Torah, and to the subject of life itself.

It will be seen that the fourth stage of the process exhibits four equilateral triangles of equal size. And the final step involves all four of them pivoting in three-dimensions (up and out of the 2-dimensional page in our restricted view) until the three vertices on the right side all meet, and the three vertices on the left side also meet. By that stage the four triangles will completely enclose the form of a tetrahedron, which will have the profile of the fifth and final stage in the above diagram. The edge joining the 1 to the 6 is the only one that has not moved and is, from our perspective, now behind all other parts of the 3-

dimensional shape. Notice especially that, as we should expect, the 2-dimensional representation of this shape takes the form of the $K_4$ graph. So the length of the entire Torah has brought us to the same result as did its first few words. And the mis-translated expression 'living creatures', which both Ezekiel and John have associated with wings and faces, is custom made to get us thinking about how life and the tetrahedron could be related. An expression used only by Ezekiel of the chayot is that...

> *their appearance was like burning coals of fire, and like the*
> *appearance of a lamp ... and the fire was bright, and out of the*
> *fire went forth lightning*

> (Ezekiel 1:13)

We have to wonder, then, why he uses two descriptions – coals and lamps. Is there a difference between them? A similar form of description has been seen elsewhere in a situation that, not surprisingly, is also foreseen by the Author's Seal. That was the episode in which Abram had cut three large animals down the middle, then:

> *when the sun had gone down and it was dark, behold a*
> *smoking furnace, and a burning lamp that passed between those*
> *pieces.*

> (Genesis 15:17).

In a very subtle way, the two unconnected passages are both hinting at two scientific situations (or possibly three) in which the form of a tetrahedron is linked with life itself. Notice that the two texts both refer to a lamp, while one also refers to smoke and the other to coals. Assuming the smoke is akin to soot (which I believe is intended), then this and the coal are both explicit references to carbon, the chemical element. That is the only property that coal and soot share in common. And, as we shall soon see, carbon is intimately associated with life as we know it. Then the lamps may be an alternative form of fire that is altogether hotter.

Earlier in this chapter, I implied a form of fire that is very much more intense than the burning of coal. That is, the thermonuclear conversion of hydrogen into helium in the core of the sun. So it is noteworthy that the passage taken from Genesis 15 actually does mention the sun, though necessarily in a straightforward way that could be understood by anyone in any era. The real point being that the form of helium that is created in the sun is the bare nucleus of four particles. And these particles, two protons and two neutrons, take up relative positions that are at the vertices of a regular tetrahedron. The link between helium and life is slightly indirect, but no less essential. It is the fact that life on earth needs the unfailing energy provided by the sun, as a by-product from the fusion of hydrogen into helium.

The link between carbon and life on earth is much more obvious. In chemical terms, carbon atoms have the happy ability to form four bonds, either with other carbon atoms or with those of certain other elements. It is this gregarious capacity to bond that allows carbon, more than any other chemical element, to form complex molecules, which include sugars, proteins and many other compounds that are essential to life. And another consequence of carbon having a so-called valency of four is that the chemical bonds it forms have a tendency to be oriented towards the vertices of a tetrahedron. Indeed in the gas methane, the simplest of all carbon compounds, one carbon atom is attached to exactly four hydrogen atoms, which immediately settle into a perfect tetrahedral formation. We may even take biblical allusions to carbon chemistry one step further, by noting that Carbon-12 the commonest form (ie isotope) of carbon consists of 6 protons, 6 neutrons and 6 electrons, leading to the most fundamental of all interpretations for the number 666. It is also the case that, when a star like our sun runs out of the hydrogen fuel it needs to make helium, it then starts to convert helium into carbon, a small tetrahedron into a much larger one.

The fact that the length of the Torah can lead to the form of a tetrahedron does not, of itself, mean that it must do so, or that we are expected to follow the procedure described in Figure 8.6. My interpretation of the books of Ezekiel and Revelation is only a hint that we are meant to follow that line of reasoning. And note carefully that we *are* engaged in reasoning, which is a novel approach to the Bible compared with the stance of most established religions. But, since there could still be doubt about the direction of our progress, it is particularly reassuring to find that there is a parallel set of mathematical clues that also derive from the regular pentagon.

A regular pentagon is defined as:
(i)   a plane (ie flat) five-sided figure in which the five straight sides are all of equal length, and
(ii)  the angles subtended by those sides at the centre are all equal (with a value of 72°).

The radial lines that contain those 72° angles combine with the sides of the regular pentagon to form five isosceles triangles in which the other two angles are both 54° (since the three internal angles of a plane triangle always add up to 180°).

The pentagons seen in Figure 8.6 exist only because we formed two 5-digit numbers into that cyclic arrangement, with the initial justification that the number 666 emerges from one of them, and 616 from the other, and because those very numbers are linked by the author of Revelation and by two aspects of the Seal. However, the number 666 has a more fundamental mathematical relationship with the regular pentagon, which can reveal the mind of the artist. This is because the trigonometric cosine of 666° is the same as the cosine of 54°! They are both 0.587785252, to 9 decimal places. The reason they are alike is straightforward: there are 720° in two complete revolutions (ie cycles or circles), and 720 − 666 = 54. The more telling fact is that the pentagon is the only regular polygon that has interior angles of 108° (ie 2×54°). So it is especially relevant that it is the pentagon that serves to convert the length of the Torah into the 666:616 number pair (as seen in the first two stages of Figure 8.6). Thus, the context, the composition and the building blocks all match each other. It may even be noted that the order in which I entered the numbers 60961 and 60966 into their respective pentagons also reveals digit base-pairs of 90. This emergent number matters because 90° is a right-angle, a quarter of a full revolution that is based on a system of 360°.

All-in-all, the way that the two pentagons are formed from the digits of 60961 and 60966 is a delightful artistic composition. It is analogous to a flower vase that is decorated with an herbaceous design rather than, say, random daubs and splodges. The container and its contents are in perfect harmony.

It is at this point we may recall another numeric effect we noticed in Chapter 4. There, the four sides and two diagonals of the G1 square, as sums of qatan values, led to a grand product of 666π, to within about 0.00023% of its true value. In this result, it was the encompassing (cyclic) perimeter that contributed the value of Pi; and we know that the square and diagonals are really the maximum profile of a tetrahedron. Therefore that concise effect bequeathed by the Seal, is the counterpart of the alternative vast tetrahedron seen in Figure 8.6, based on the length of the whole Torah.

To introduce a slightly esoteric tone to these descriptions, we also profit if we extend the regular pentagon into a pentacle. It is to be regretted that the pentacle has suffered a bad press since it was hijacked by followers of dubious areas of activity such as Satanism especially, and Wicca to a lesser degree; but we shall not dwell too long on such matters just now.

Figure 8.7 shows the result of extending the five sides of a regular pentagon until they meet in pairs. The overall effect is of a five-pointed star: the pentacle. Notice that each side of the pentagon is now the base of an external isosceles triangle that has two angles of 72° and one of 36°. And it is these two numbers that provide a two-fold association with the G1 version of the Author's Seal.

The main point of interest is not just in the numbers themselves, but also in the two triangular numbers $T_{36}$ and $T_{72}$. The first of these numbers is 666, seen in the lower part of the vertical diagonal of G1. The second is 2628, which is double the 1314 qatan sequence seen within the Torah's first word. The further association lies with the gematria of Genesis 1:1 (ie 2701 = 37×73), because 666 contains a factor of 37 and 1314 (or 2628) contains a factor of 73. In fact, 2628 = 73 × 36.

Without a doubt, there are multiple inherent properties of both Genesis 1:1 and the whole Torah that are designed to map onto the geometrical pentagon. And there is one other that connects the pentacle with many properties of the Seal. We have noted often the Seal's allusions, both graphical and numeric, to the Ark of the Covenant, and the fact that the relative dimensions of the Ark are consecutive early members of the Fibonacci sequence (ie 3 and 5). Not only is the ratio 5/3 (ie 1.666...) a reasonable approximation to the so-called Divine Proportion, but the Seal has repeatedly disclosed this very number, including the means to calculate its exact value.

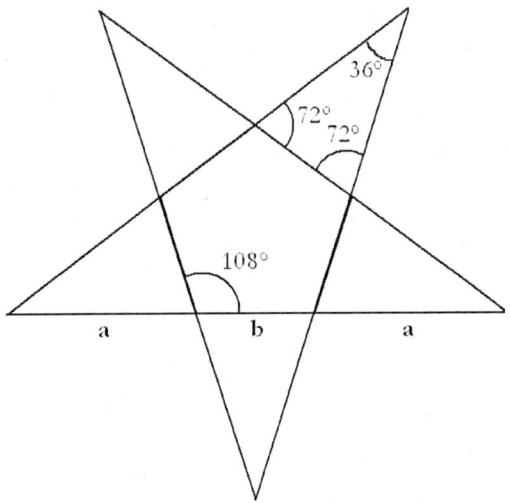

Figure 8.7

The Divine Proportion seems to be particularly important to the Author of the Torah. And it is possible to go one step further with the association. In Figure 8.7, the horizontal member of the pentacle may be considered in three segments, delineated by the two other members that cut through it. These line-segments have been labelled a, b and a (because the two segments labelled a are equal in length). The essential point is that the ratio **a/b** is the Divine Proportion; and so is **(a+b)/a**. This, then, is one more reason why the pentagonal numbers, 60961 and 60966, are the perfect vehicles to demonstrate the vast sweep of the Author's purpose. The Torah cannot be disaggregated into separate sources, but its 304,805 letters must be considered a coherent whole.

These purely mathematical attributes of the regular pentagon and the pentacle are largely over and above the way our pentagonal numbers have combined into a tetrahedron. All-in-all, the additional mathematical attributes of the regular pentagon speak volumes for the validity of the procedure illustrated as Figure 8.6 as a proper way to interpret the Hebrew Torah.

Of course, the visions Ezekiel and John (and Abram) experienced could not have been understood by them as nuclear and chemical processes. But, after two or three millennia, the preserved descriptions of their respective visions now allow us to make proper sense of them for the first time. And I think it is perfectly reasonable for us now to interpret Ezekiel's expression: *the spirit of the living creatures was in the wheels*, as meaning the wheels are an essential stage in one method of constructing the tetrahedra that underpin the science of life.

Thus far, we have taken one huge stride in interpreting what has never before been consistently understood. We can now see that previously mysterious and widely separated passages of the Bible are related cryptic references to important aspects of the science of life, its chemical foundation and the energy that sustains it. Yet one indispensable component of life has not yet been explained. That is the ability to remember, to pass on from one generation to the next the kind of information we now understand as genetic. The genetic code and processes are, together, the collective memory of all life on earth and which, as we shall see, is emulated in the meticulous care with which Judaism makes copies of its sacred Torah Scrolls.

There is no mistaking the deep preoccupation the Torah has for 'generations', and for human reproduction; even from the very first command to man – to be fruitful and multiply. Throughout Genesis 2-11 (the biblical pre-history), there is a frequent review of generations - a listing of names that is often used as a literary technique to introduce a new episode. The same technique continues to be used elsewhere in the Bible, though less frequently. Following the pre-history, Abraham was promised that he would become the father of nations, and that his seed would increase beyond counting, like the stars in the sky. In the first verse of Genesis we have already discovered the naming of Abraham, along with Brit Milah (the Covenant of Circumcision). Also, we know that the gematria of Abraham is the same as that of [ם] רחם / *racham* / a womb. The same verse depicts a human phallus in the 4×7 matrix of its qatan letter values. In fact, the first three letters of

Abraham replicate the second word of the Torah, בּרא / *bara* / <u>he</u> <u>created</u>. The beginning of the Torah is, therefore, especially well imbued with references to human reproduction and the sanctity of life. But the plain text of the Torah gives little hint that its author is aware of the sub-cellular environment in which the information of reproduction is processed and transmitted. As we have so often seen, however, the plain text is rarely the whole story. And the Author's Seal includes many allusions to the details of genetic processes.

The correspondence begins with the classical double-helix structure of DNA (deoxyribonucleic acid), which is represented in the Seal in several ways. For one thing, there are marked similarities between the relative dimensions of the Ark of the Covenant (as terms of the Fibonacci Sequence) and certain characteristics of the double-helix of DNA. For example, the twin strands in DNA are found to be separated by two grooves (a major groove and a minor groove) that have longitudinal separations of 13Å and 21Å (where Å is the tiny Angstrom unit[o] of length). The numbers 13 and 21 are consecutive terms in the Fibonacci sequence, and the ratio 21/13 gives a decimal value that differs from the Divine Proportion ($\Phi$) by less than 0.2%. We know that $\Phi$ is strongly favoured by the Seal in many ways, not just the dimensions of the Ark. Then the double-helix of DNA is 21Å wide, and it completes one full twist after each 34Å of length; again, these are consecutive terms in Fibonacci, and the ratio 34/21 differs from the Divine Proportion by only about 0.06%.

Each full cycle of DNA is composed of exactly ten nucleotide base-pairs – the chemical bases of one strand join 1:1 with those of the other strand like the rungs of a twisting ladder. Seen end-on, one full cycle would resemble a decagon or, more precisely, two superimposed pentagons (see adjacent illustration). That is, not having ten straight sides, but with a marked indentation between each two adjacent nodes. The two pentagons we obtained from the 304,805-letter length of the Torah, and which have previously been seen superimposed in two other ways would serve the purpose. To take this perspective one step further, four full cycles of DNA seen end-on would have an appearance of an inwardly converging spiral, equivalent to the text in the G1 and G2 squares, or diverging like G3 and G4.

Once we look deeper than the superficial structure of DNA, the correspondence to the genetic code, of G3 and G4 especially, becomes even more compelling. The way in which DNA transmits information

---

[o] One Angstrom unit is equal to one ten millionth of a millimetre.

is by use of a 4-letter alphabet. The genetic alphabet of DNA consists of the nucleotide bases: Adenine (A), Cytosine (C), Guanine (G) and Thymine (T). For one thing, nucleotide molecules all contain cyclic components. These consist of either five or six nodes, which are mostly carbon, but nitrogen to a lesser extent. So these pentagonal and hexagonal structures are the real-world pattern that Genesis 1:1 is emulating with the digits of Pi in its first and third words. Recall that the digits of Pi are obtained only when those words are written cyclically as qatan letter values, one a hexagon and the other a pentagon. And these are the same two words whose gematria total is 999, and whose letters combine to spell Abraham, leaving *ayil* (a ram) in the third word and *tayish* (a he-goat) in the first. But there are several other similarities between the four-letter genetic alphabet and the 22-letter Hebrew alephbeyt and language.

Firstly, the genetic code employs 'words', known as codons, spelled with three letters each. And the biblical Hebrew language is also based on 3-letter root words. For example, the root of the Torah's 6-letter first word *B'reishith* is ראש / *rosh* / <u>head</u>.

Next, alphabets of 4 and 22 letters share a numerical characteristic that is far from common. If the Hebrew alephbeyt is separated into a first half and a second half, the gematria values of their last letters are 20 and 400 respectively. It is easy to see that the larger value is the square of the smaller. In the case of a 4-letter alphabet, the equivalent values are 2 and 4, in which the larger is again the square of the smaller. The number of letters in these alphabets differ by 18 (ie 22 − 4), which is the key to their similar numerical behaviour. An alphabet of 40 letters (ie 22 + 18) will have the same property, if its numerical values are allocated by extending the same rule as for Hebrew. Although, in this case the values of the last letter of each half would be 200 and 40,000. Any alphabet in which the number of letters differs from these by a multiple of 18 will exhibit the same property. The choice of a 22-letter alephbeyt for use with the Torah is clearly of great symbolic importance.

A further similarity between the Torah and the genetic code comes from the way the latter is translated. We should be aware that it is possible to construct 64 different 3-letter codon groups from a four-letter alphabet. This is because the first letter position of a group can be filled in any one of four different ways (ie A, C, G or T). Then, for each of those possibilities, the second letter can also be filled in four ways, making 4×4 = 16 ways. Finally, for each of those 16, the third letter position can then be filled in four alternative ways, making 4×4×4 = 64 combinations altogether. So, if a DNA codon is understood as a word, could this perhaps be what is meant by the verse:

*Now the whole earth had one language and few words.*

(Genesis 11:1)

Virtually all forms of life on earth, from the simplest bacteria to the largest mammals, do indeed share the same genetic language. Without knowledge of the Seal, this suggestion might still be offered, but would rightly be seen as an unwarranted flight of fancy. However, knowing the Seal, it would not be too hard to re-interpret the Tower of Babel story as a rich mixture of overlapping metaphors, at least one of which is intended only for our time.

Superficially, there is an obvious correspondence between the 64 genetic codons and the size of the square Seal, which consists of 8×8 = 64 letters. But more compelling still is the presence in G3 and G4 of exactly three copies of the word אַרְבַּע / *arba* / <u>four</u>, all terminating at the same central letter *ayin*. In fact, two of those three 'fours' are unlikely emergent words, which twist around one-another, again in the manner of a short section of DNA. The subtlety of the latter metaphor should not be lost on us, that each 'four' stands for one DNA strand composed from an alphabet of only four different molecular letters.

Now, of all the 64 possible codon spellings, the genetic code requires only 22 different translations (notice that 22 corresponds to the number of letters in the Hebrew alephbeyt). But this does not mean that any of the 64 is not used. What happens in practice is that two or more codons may be interpreted in the same way. For example, the codon combinations TAT and TAC are interpreted identically. These observations bring us to the next important similarity between the two languages, which stems from the fact that 20 of the genetic translations are for the 20 amino acids from which the proteins essential to life are constructed, in chains. And the other two translations represent instructions to indicate where to Start a protein and where it should End. A segment of DNA from a 'Start' codon to the next 'Stop' codon is commonly called a gene. The equivalence here is, on the one hand, between the 20 material amino acids and the 20 Hebrew consonants and, on the other hand, between the more abstract Start/Stop instructions and the two silent letters *aleph* (א) and *ayin* (ע). Remember that the two silent letters are the same ones that represent the twin concepts of Small Face and Vast Face, until now only recognised in Jewish Kabbalah.

That is a very nice correlation because it involves not only the exact partitioning between 2 and 20, but it especially recognises the 2 as being abstract and the 20 being more substantive. Nor is this the end of the matter, because there is a delightful confirmation built-into the structure of the word ארבע / *arba* / <u>four</u>, which has already contributed so much. First, the two outer letters of arba – its start and end, so to speak – are the same two silent letters that match the two genetic *start* and *stop* instructions. Then, the two middle letters of arba spell רב / *bar* / <u>son and heir</u>, highlighting the principal function of the genetic code, which is to transmit the essence of one generation to the next. Finally, the qatan values of the middle pair of its letters are '22'. Given that arba was first seen in G2 overlapping the start of Genesis, it is now evident that the Torah's first two regular letters are meant to draw attention to the number that is shared by the Hebrew alephbeyt and the translations that characterise the genetic code. The crucial role of language in every stage of creation could not be clearer: *And God said … and there was.*

There is another aspect of the Author's Seal that reflects genetics and the chemistry of life. That is, their very similar behaviours with regard to structure. Take the structure of DNA for example. It has an ordered primary structure, which is a very long linear sequence of nucleotide base-pairs. But it also has a very elaborate second-order structure, which is manifest as sets of chromosomes. A chromosome is a neatly wound section of the whole DNA chain, and corresponds to a specific set of genes. In humans, there are 22 pairs of 'X'[p] chromosomes containing genes that are common to both sexes. Then, in females, there is another pair of X-chromosomes, responsible for female sexual attributes. While in males, there is an alternative X-Y pair. Perhaps this will call to mind the preponderance of X- and Y-shaped artefacts that are cunningly designed into the four square views of the Seal. In particular, the two main 'Y'-shaped artefacts are best understood as the 'crucified *man*' and the '*man* clothed in linen'. The first of these incorporated the distinctive 666 group of qatan letter values. And the book of Revelation (KJV) says of 666: '…it is the number of a *man*'.

The main product of DNA (other than new life) is the vast assortment of proteins upon which life depends. Some of these are used as the body's building-blocks while others, such as enzymes, are destined for more of a roving role. All proteins start out as linear

---

[p] The use of the Latin letters X and Y to describe chromosomes derives from the overall shape that they adopt.

sequences of amino acids. But enzymes in particular, and other products such as red blood corpuscles, also have a 'second order' structure. The initial linear proteins in these cases have a built-in preference to fold up into pre-determined 3-dimensional shapes, which give them their specialised properties.

Any description of the genetic process would be neither complete nor realistic if it did not include both the primary and second-order structures of DNA and proteins. And neither would the description of the Author's Seal be complete if it did not describe how it emulates its natural counterparts in two further ways. To begin with, the plain Hebrew text we read at the start of Genesis reflects only the linear, first-order structure of both DNA and proteins. Then the insertion of the same text into any one of the 8×8 squares represents a corresponding second-order structure.

The other similarity has to do with mutation, adaptation and evolution. In the natural world, there would be no physical development of species over time if it were not for occasional accidental mutations at the molecular level. If even a single codon in reproductive DNA becomes damaged, that can lead to a change in the instructions for 'building' a new individual. Earlier in this Chapter, I suggested there are possibly three scientific circumstances in which a tetrahedron is important to life on earth. Two of them are, of course, found in the chemistry of carbon and the formation of helium nuclei by the fusion of hydrogen and, indeed, the nuclear conversion of helium *to* carbon. The third circumstance also involves helium nuclei, but as a by-product of nuclear decay. The radioactive alpha particle is none other than a helium nucleus ejected at enormous velocity from the nucleus of a relatively heavy element. And alpha particles are among the more important agencies of genetic mutation, since they have the capacity to cause damage to DNA. Because this type of damage occurs randomly, many mutations in nature are harmful. Fortunately, a small proportion will confer an advantage to the individual organism that inherits them. The effect of such a change need not be visible or immediate. But a later change in the environment may favour those organisms that have inherited the mutation if, in consequence, they are better able to adapt to their new circumstances than their less favoured contemporaries.

In the course of this book, we have seen two structural changes that broadly meet the definitions of mutation and adaptation. The more obvious mutation was the deliberate removal of the letter ayin from its position as 49th letter of the Torah, to become its prefix. This change directly emulates the removal of a nucleotide base from DNA

– accidentally or otherwise. The effect this had on the Seal (the organism) was quite dramatic, yet essentially and very surprisingly positive. The same text with only one letter displaced immediately changed its second-order appearance, like a chameleon adapting to new surroundings. Many of the emergent words and patterns seen in the G1 square simply dissolved, to be replaced instantly by others that were no less impressive. Clearly, the very first effect was the creation of the word *arba* (four) which, as we have just seen, embodies numerous characteristics of the universal genetic code.

Later, we elected to re-draw the square Seal with the displaced ayin and the start of Genesis at its centre. With that G3 square, the distinction between organism and environment is less clear; but the effect was certainly to bring out the very best from the previous mutation. In particular, three copies of arba (four) then converged at the centre, emulating the linking of three nucleotides into a DNA codon.

-oOo-

Armed with our new recognition of the way the Torah emulates aspects of natural science, it is now again possible to re-interpret the three copies of *arba* (four) found at the centre of both the G3 and G4 squares. The fact that we see three such copies may remind us of three fundamental natural tetrads. One we have already met is the set of four phases of matter: solid, liquid, gas and plasma. Another is the all-encompassing set: space, time, matter and energy. And the third tetrad is the set of all natural forces: gravitational, electro-magnetic, strong nuclear and weak nuclear. It is instructive to be aware that three of these forces (all except gravity) have been at work behind several of the tetrahedral phenomena I have described. The chemical behaviour of carbon is determined by the electro-magnetic force; the fusion of hydrogen nuclei into helium nuclei, and helium into carbon involves the strong nuclear force; and the ejection of alpha particles (helium nuclei) from heavy atomic nuclei depends on the weak nuclear force. Gravity is more often associated with curved orbits and spherical or near-spherical accumulations of matter (eg stars and planets). That is the other 'perfect', 3-dimensional shape.

Each of the preceding natural tetrads has, by definition, four members. But there is also significant degeneracy both within and between the three sets. For example, the four phases of matter all, nevertheless, consist of matter. In certain circumstances, space and time are interchangeable, as are matter and energy. And the four fundamental natural forces are all at the root of alternative forms of energy. Moreover, for a short time following the birth of the universe, the four forces were indistinguishable from one another. So the three sets are not entirely independent of each other. And that, as well as the DNA codon metaphor, would be a good reason why the three copies of arba at the centre of G3 and G4 have been designed to converge.

Incidentally, there is a very nice biblical allusion to the four fundamental natural forces, one that also connects the Torah's beginning to its very end, much like the earlier 2+2 faces of the tetrahedron. In the very first verse the name Elohim may be translated in many ways, of which one is 'force of forces', the omnipotent Prime Mover. Then, at the end of Deuteronomy, with only five further verses to follow, is the following text:

> *And Moses was an hundred and twenty years old when he*
> *died: his eye was not dim, nor his natural force abated.*
>
> ( Deuteronomy 34:7)

Notice here the use of the expression 'natural force' which is an accurate translation, though perhaps more applicable to the natural world than to personal vigour. But note also the specific emphasis on the undimmed eye. The word [ ן ] נ י ע / *ayin* / an eye is the very same as the name of the letter that is responsible for fine-tuning the Author's Seal, through its migration.

Given the elaborate descriptions of genetic metaphors in the previous few pages, it is a natural conclusion that the whole Torah, with special emphasis on it beginning, has been written to demonstrate knowledge of that subject. This conclusion is totally at odds with most traditional assumptions as to the origin of the sacred Hebrew text. The first biblical creation account does, of course, allude tentatively to the subject, with references to fruitfulness and seed within itself. But the extent of the genetic understanding underlying the first 64 letters of the Torah is entirely out of proportion to the plain-text content (In the beginning, etc) and the generally assumed level of its Author's (or authors') education.

At the same time, the transmission of the Torah from generation to generation is surely as reliable as the transmission of genes. Maybe not perfect, but still good enough for the encoded message it contains to have been preserved through more than three millennia. To this extent, Judaism – the vehicle of transmission – has fulfilled an invaluable aspect of the purpose for which it was established. Which is in opposition to the widespread Christian view that around two thousand years ago, Judaism ceased to have any further purpose. We can now see from the dependability of the Seal that the first 65 letters at least are still identical to the original text. And the fact that the whole Torah now consists of 304,805 Hebrew letters leads to enough corroborative outcomes to verify its overall integrity. One letter more or less would be enough to destroy the many numerical effects obtained from its present length. So we may be confident in assuming that any transmission errors that might have affected its length are probably small in number, and that any losses are exactly compensated by gains. Either that, or a change in the length of the Torah over time, leading to its present value, has been part of a long-term plan.

To counter the latter suggestion, it would be very easy (too easy) to appeal to random coincidence as an agency. In other words, the Torah is its present length through nothing more than an accidental convergence of many unplanned changes, both large and small. But then we would also have to account for the remarkable, additional, 'accidental' characteristics in the gematria analysis of Genesis 1:1. Not to mention the hundreds of accidental, emergent properties of the Seal as a whole. How odd it is, then, that the vehicle of this strange coincidence should just happen to be the opening words of the world's most widely recognised sacred text. The possibility of coincidence will undoubtedly be invoked, often. But that is only to side-step the difficult alternative of looking for a proper explanation.

# 9

Our subject in this Chapter is the story of Noah, the flood and the ark in which he preserved a small remnant of humanity and all the animal species that were destined to re-populate the world, once the flood had subsided.

There are many tricky issues surrounding this part of Genesis. For example, did Noah and his family truly exist as a living, breathing family? Was the biblical flood a specific historical event? Did the flood really cover the whole world to a height that engulfed even the highest mountains? And just how big would a boat need to be to contain every known species, even of just the mammals of the world? For my part, I do not think it makes a lot of sense to treat the story of Noah and the flood as recorded history. In fact, the whole of Genesis 1-11 is, in the academic community, generally regarded as a pre-history – one point at least on which scholars and I agree. So I feel that, for the sake of sanity, it is best to treat these eleven chapters of Genesis in the same category as parable.

In an important way, this part of the Bible serves mainly to describe the wayward nature of man, as a generalised problem that needs to be addressed. Then everything that follows in the Bible is, in project management terms, either part of the solution or a progress report. Nor is it helpful to suggest that particular portions of the pre-history have plagiarised earlier ancient Near Eastern myths, such as the creation content of the Enuma Elish, or the flood stories of Atrahasis, or of the Epic of Gilgamesh. There is no denying the overlap of subject matter between those legends and early parts of the Bible. But it is much more enlightening to recognise the underlying mocking tone of the Bible, and to see it as a series of very clever parodies, and a sustained polemic against those other myths and superstitions. Once it is realised what the biblical pre-history is trying to achieve at multiple levels, it becomes much easier to accept its intended underlying message rather than just one more mythical flight of fancy. When we proceed to look at Noah with our vision now trained by the previous eight chapters, he will not be seen as a real person, but as a set of concepts that are both suggested and underpinned by wider biblical considerations.

A clue that the story of Noah may be understood in a non-literal way comes from an analysis using gematria. Other research (Jenkins, 1999) has identified that the eight words of Genesis 8:14 have the same 2701 gematria grand total as Genesis 1:1, and that 'it is only the second to map onto a complete verse'. Notably, that verse reads: *In the second month, on the twenty-seventh day of the month, the earth was dry* (RSV). It is widely accepted that the biblical flood story represents a second creation, a re-creation that mirrors the first in several ways. On completion of an 'un-creation' stage, everywhere is water; then the dry land appears; then God tells Noah to go out of the ark with his wife and family and all the saved animals, so that they all may:

> ... *breed abundantly on the earth, and be fruitful and multiply on the earth*
> (Genesis 8:17, RSV)

Now, to be perfectly honest my own route to a new understanding of Noah as described in the present Chapter was not a straightforward one. I was busy looking elsewhere when I suddenly turned a corner and found myself witnessing the flood, as though by chance. At the time, I was investigating the similarities between the very few texts where the number 666 is seen. One of them is at Ezra 2:13; another is at 2nd Chronicles 9:13 (though this is only a repetition of 1st Kings 10:14); and the only other one is, of course, Revelation 13:18. In 1st Kings and 2nd Chronicles, 666 is reported as the amount of gold, in talents, received in tithe by King Solomon in one year. And it struck me as more than coincidence that Solomon is best remembered for his great wisdom, and that Revelation 13:18 begins, *This calls for wisdom....* It appears that the author of Revelation is subtly trying to say something important either about wisdom, or the number 666, or both. In fact the number 666 serves only as a marker, a tantalising attention grabber. And it is wisdom, naturally, that will lead us towards a proper understanding.

Never wanting to pass over an obvious clue, I looked closely at the Hebrew word חכמה / *chokmah* / wisdom, and noticed that it has some important numerical characteristics. I soon found that the full gematria of chokmah is 73 (ie 8 + 20 + 40 + 5), and the sum of its letters' ordinal positions in the alephbeyt is 37 (ie 8 + 11 + 13 + 5). Remember that the 2701 gematria total of Genesis 1:1 is also the product of these two prime numbers. But I had no idea at the time that Genesis 8:14 shares the same gematria. And it was just as well that I was not distracted by that knowledge, because the route to finding the flood is not nearly so simple and straightforward. The proper route, in fact, depends entirely on being acquainted with two of the four square views of the Author's Seal on the start of Genesis.

The next thing I noticed about the word חכמה (wisdom) is that it has something striking in common with the very centre of the G1 square. The four central letters in G1 also start with a *chet* (ח) and end with a *heh* (ה), just like chokmah, and both are the same length. There was no way of knowing at the time, but I was already halfway to a major new understanding of the biblical flood story. With an eye to now familiar patterns I began to wonder if these two 4-letter words might belong together in a 4×4 square arrangement. In which case, I would have to search for the correct two remaining 4-letter words. I surmised that, if the middle of the G1 square is a proper choice, then why not also the centre of another aspect of the Seal. And the obvious candidate was the integral word ארבע / *arba* / <u>four</u>, found at the centre of both G3 and G4. The addition of this word in particular would also lend a special elegance to the developing pattern. Still not knowing whether I was following a blind alley, or the road to Shangri-la, I knew for certain there could be only one possible choice for the fourth word. It had to be the sacred four-letter Name of God, the Tetragrammaton. Now all that remained was to find the one arrangement of the four words that the Author wanted us to discover.

There are 24 ways to combine four 4-letter words into a 4×4 square; and each result may be rotated to any one of four orientations (assuming the square is to sit horizontally). The challenge was a little like tuning a radio receiver, so that anything other than the correct arrangement produces only static noise. Then, suddenly, I hit the right frequency and witnessed the vision that is illustrated in Figure 9.1. Here, the row I have highlighted spells מבול / *mabul* / <u>a flood</u>; and this one discovery opened the flood-gates to many more, so to speak.

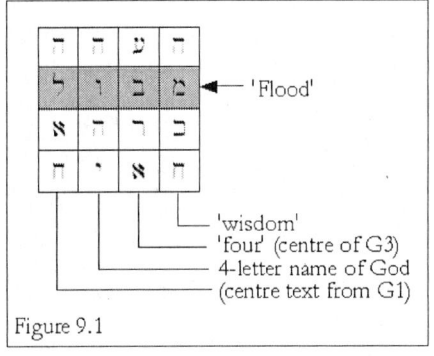

Figure 9.1

When it comes to assessing the veracity of the new 'flood square', the provenance of its component parts will surely prove conclusive.

Two of them are at the heart of the Author's Seal, and another is the very Name of that Author. And, although one group of four letters is not a proper word, it is well to remember that it comes from the overlap of the two-word expression *rwach Elohim* (the spirit of God). Indeed, the word *rwach* may mean both 'spirit' and 'wind', which is surely the same wind that God caused to blow to initiate the process of drying the earth. The last of the four elements (ie wisdom) is, without doubt, closely related to the Seal because two of its numerical characteristics generate the 2701 gematria of Genesis 1:1. Also, the wider Bible consistently associates wisdom with 666; a number that is revealed prominently by the G1 and G2 aspects of the Seal, and more subtly in the G3/4 aspects.

Now, when the Hebrew Bible was being translated into English, a seemingly sloppy 'error' was made. Both the boat that Noah built, and the box the Israelites constructed centuries later to hold the tablets of the Law were given the same name – ark. It would be no more correct to call either one of them an ark. At first it seems unfortunate that they should both now be known by the same name. In the Hebrew, one is called simply 'boat' and the other 'box'. They do not share the same name, but they do share two interesting associations in common. The first is that they are both designed to hold or preserve life, in which respect the case of Noah's ark is relatively obvious. But with the Ark of the Covenant, we may assume that God's presence over its cover – the Mercy Seat – is synonymous with the presence of life *par excellence*. Yet the similarity is even closer than might be supposed. It would be easy to assume that the only occupants of the ark of the flood were Noah, his family and the animals. But, in fact, God himself was present, as implied by two segments of the Torah text. First, it says:

> *And the Lord said unto Noah, Come thou and all thy house into the ark ...*
>
> (Genesis 7:1, KJV)

The operative word here is 'come', not 'go' into the ark. Later, it is written:

> *And God spake unto Noah, saying, Go forth of the ark ...*
>
> (Genesis 8:15-16, KJV)

In one case God and in the other the Lord is speaking as from within the ark. And we see something equivalent in the above 4×4 flood square, which includes both the Name of the Lord and the 'spirit of God'. In this way, the flood square is also demonstrating that the Torah's alternative use of 'God' and 'the Lord' in the context of the flood story is intentional, and not the result of the redaction of two or more inconsistent sources. The redactor in this case is the creator himself, and it is he who has provided all the component texts needed for constructing the flood square.

The other association between the two kinds of ark is through the mathematical Fibonacci sequence, the early terms of which are 1, 1, 2, 3, 5, 8 … We know full well that the relative dimensions of the Ark of the Covenant are 3×3×5; and the Author's Seal has provided copious numerical confirmations for the link between these dimensions and certain mathematical properties of the Fibonacci sequence. Moreover, the prescribed dimensions of Noah's ark – 300 cubits ×50 cubits ×30 cubits – are all obvious multiples of the Fibonacci numbers 3 and 5. But now, we find that the flood square is bracketed by two four-letter groups both of which start and end with letters 8 and 5 of the alephbeyt; thus going one step further into the Fibonacci Sequence. The two 5s and two 8s are, of course, at the corner positions of the flood square.

While we are analysing the literary content of the flood square, it will be evident that the people who occupied the ark in the narrative of Genesis are barely perceptible. Using the 16 letters of the square, the only name that we can construct is that of [ם] חם / *Cham* / <u>Ham</u>, and then only with letters that are not adjacent. If we wish to understand those occupants, we shall have to approach them from another direction, which I shall come to later. Of the biblical flood narrative, it will be especially helpful to have in mind information regarding the construction of the ark, as in these verses:

> *Make me an ark of gopher wood; rooms shalt thou make in*
> *the ark, and shalt pitch it within and without with pitch.*
> *And this is the fashion which thou shalt make it of: The length*
> *of the ark shall be three hundred cubits, the breadth of it fifty*
> *cubits, and the height of it thirty cubits.*
> *A window shalt thou make to the ark, and in a cubit shalt*
> *thou finish it above; and the door of the ark thou shalt set in*
> *the side thereof; with lower, second and third stories shalt thou*
> *make it.*
>
> (Genesis 6:14-16)

The new flood square is brim-full with cryptic artefacts relating mainly to two distinct phases in the life of Noah. There are references to the period of the flood itself; and there are further references to Noah's post-diluvian life. Oddly, there is also a link to a subject that has no direct connection to Noah, but has been found extensively in the Author's Seal. First, take a look at Figure 9.2.

The numbers in the thumbnail sketch show that the current topic is to be found entirely in the middle two rows. And the left and right halves (left half shaded) contain the same digits 1-2-3-4 in the same relative positions, indicating the identical order in which the letters are to be read. Each group of four letters in the main square represents one of the two principal roles of the ark. In the right-hand group, the letters spell מרכב / *merkab* / <u>a chariot</u>. The word 'chariot' is the nearest available in ancient Hebrew to mean a vehicle for transportation which, in an important sense, the ark was. But the idea of a vehicle does not completely capture the overall purpose of the ark which, for many months, also served as a fully provisioned home for all its occupants. Therefore, the four letters of the left-hand group, spell ואהל / *v'ohel* / <u>and a tent</u>. Of course, a tent was the type of home to which Noah was accustomed, at least in later life if not before the flood. To summarise what we have just seen, the two identically structured groups together confer the expression 'a chariot and a tent'; thus encapsulating the twin, utilitarian functions of the ark.

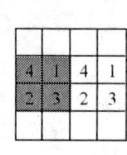

**Figure 9.2**

At the time in which the story of Noah is set, the tent was an essential possession, and the symbol of a family group. The same remained true for the Hebrew people until at least two generations following the time of Abraham. So it is significant that the same two rows we have just examined in one way, may be seen another way that refers to the name and destiny of the first Hebrew Patriarch. The applicable expression here is [ם] וכל אברהם / *v'col Avraham* / <u>and all of Abraham</u>. Notice that all eight letters of the middle two rows are again utilised in the anagram of this expression. No doubt the Torah sees Abraham's seed in a similar role to the ark of the flood, as a way of guarding and preserving life. However, we should probably avoid thinking too literally in terms of physical life (*Man doth not live by bread alone, but by every word that proceedeth out of the mouth of the Lord doth man live*). Instead we should be thinking in terms of the Israelites' role in preserving God's Law throughout the ages, often against an overwhelming current of competing influences. And it is most apposite that this anagram of Abraham is again, as in Genesis 2:4 (see Chapter 5), associated with the four-letter Name, coinciding on the same letter *heh* (ה) which, nine chapters of Genesis later, would convert the name Abram to Abraham. Remember that the often aligned names of YHWH and Abraham give a gematria sum of 26+248 = 274 which, at the centre of G3/4 crosses through 273. The latter number is the gematria of *arba,* which is now a key component of the flood square. Also, the three letters shaded in the main square of Figure 9.2 spell ‏חיה‎ / *chayah* / <u>to bestow life</u>, a word that we have seen in the G4 version of the Seal. In the flood square, this word now terminates at the same letter heh of YHWH that contributes to the name of Abraham.

In the next illustration, Figure 9.3, we are reminded by one special word of the two remarkable 'Y' configurations seen previously in the Seal; and possibly the Y-chromosome found in male human DNA. In previous cases, the 'Y' shapes were associated in one way or another with water; and so it is here, of course. Reading the shaded letters upwards, we first follow three letters of arba (four), but then terminate the new word at one or other of the two letters *heh* (‏ה‎), on either side of the letter ayin (‏ע‎). We therefore see two alternative ways to complete the word ‏ארבה‎ / *arubah* / <u>a window</u>. Now, in the biblical flood narrative there are two types of window described. There is the lattice window mentioned in Genesis 6:16 (quoted above), which God instructed Noah to set in the side of the ark.

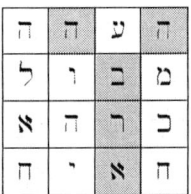

**Figure 9.3**

And there are the windows of heaven through which poured the waters above, to augment the flood waters. The spelling we see in the latest illustration is the one used of the single window in the ark. That is, even though the twin-path spelling in the square (ie left and right arms) suggest the allusion must include the windows of heaven. But either interpretation could be supported by the letter ayin between those arms. The letter ayin normally symbolises an eye, and is believed to be the etymological root of the English word 'eye'; compare this understanding with the normal function of a window, which is to transmit light. But ayin can also symbolise a 'well-spring', a source of water in the form of tears.

The same 'Y' configuration of letters, minus the lower *aleph* (‏א‎), also spells ‏רבה‎ / *rabah* / <u>to increase</u>. The first use of rabah in the Torah is in Genesis 1:22 in the blessing 'be fruitful and multiply'. The same word is also found in:

> *...and the waters increased, and bare up the ark ...*
>
> (Genesis 7:17)

And, just as significantly, the same word is used just three verses before Abram becomes Abraham, to mean 'to multiply' in:

> *And I will make my covenant between me and thee, and will multiply thee exceedingly.*
>
> (Genesis 17:2).

The flood square also depicts the construction of the ark quite nicely, as shown by Figure 9.4. As usual, the numbers in the thumbnail sketch are to be used to refer to letters in corresponding positions in the main square. The following words are easily recognised:

- letters 8-11-16-7 spell מרחב / *merchab* / <u>breadth</u>; this word may also be understood as a large room, as in: *rooms thou shalt make in the ark.*
- letters 16-8-11 spell חמר / *chamar* / <u>bitumen</u> (ie pitch), which Noah applied to the ark, inside and out.

| | | | |
|---|---|---|---|
| ה | ה | ע | ה |
| ל | ו | ב | מ |
| א | ה | ר | כ |
| ח | י | א | ח |

| | | | |
|---|---|---|---|
| 1 | 2 | 3 | 4 |
| 5 | 6 | 7 | 8 |
| 9 | 10 | 11 | 12 |
| 13 | 14 | 15 | 16 |

**Figure 9.4**

In case my reader feels it is unreasonable to accept a non-linear arrangement of letters as an emergent word, it should be borne in mind that the flood square is far more restrictive than was the 8×8 Seal. It contains only eleven different letters, and a maximum of ten linear four-letter sequences and 20 of three letters. But fully half of the possible four-letter sequences are taken up by the four pre-ordained building blocks and the one emergent word mabul (flood). Imagine trying to fit the 5-letter name 'Abraham' into this square without introducing some distortion. It is a practical impossibility.

If anything, the cryptic literary references made by the flood square to the later life of Noah are even more elaborate than its references to the flood itself. It is perhaps useful to remind ourselves of that chapter in the story of Noah. At one stage it is written:

> *And Noah became an husbandman, and he planted a vineyard: And he drank of the wine, and was drunken; and he was uncovered within his tent.*
>
> (Genesis 9:20-21)

Several topical concepts from these two verses are present in the flood square, including the word 'tent' which we saw earlier. There are, in addition:

- The letters at positions 12-11-8 spell [ם] כרמ / *kerem* / <u>a vineyard</u>.
- Letters 16-8-11 spell חמר / *chemer* / <u>fermenting wine</u>[q].
- Letters 3-11-6-8 spell ערומ [ם] / *arom* / <u>naked</u>.
- Letters 11-6-1 spell רוה / *raveh* / <u>drunkenness</u>.

Two symmetrically placed three-letter words then give notice of the family split to which this episode would give rise:

- Letters 15-10-5 spell another copy of אהל / *ohel* / <u>tent</u>, and
- Letters 8-11-14 spell מרי / *meriy* / <u>rebellion</u>.

Further references to the wayward nature of Noah's son Ham will be seen shortly.

-oOo-

If the revealed literary content of the flood square leaves no doubt as to its intended connection to biblical narratives, then the numeric content is hardly less impressive. In Figure 9.5, each letter has been replaced by its ordinal value; that is, its position in the Hebrew alephbeyt. That is the same schema that led to a value of 37 arising from the word *chokmah* (wisdom). Row and column totals

|  | A | B | C | D |  |
|---|---|---|---|---|---|
| (i) | 5 | 5 | 16 | 5 | 31 |
| (ii) | 12 | 6 | 2 | 13 | 33 |
| (iii) | 1 | 5 | 20 | 11 | 37 |
| (iv) | 8 | 10 | 1 | 8 | 27 |
|  | 26 | 26 | 39 | 37 |  |

**Figure 9.5**

have been added, as have row and column labels, to assist in making references to specific elements. The influence of the number 4 in this square will be hard to ignore. It is, after all, a 4×4 square that contains the word arba (four) and the Tetragrammaton. But consider also:

a) the total of all 16 values is $128 = 2 \times 4 \times 4 \times 4$
(Incidentally, written as 2444 this would be $4 \times 611$, where the larger factor is again the gematria of the word Torah),

b) the sum of rows (i) and (ii) is 64; so the sum of rows (iii) and (iv) is also 64; each is therefore $4 \times 4 \times 4$,

c) the sums of the four 2×2 quadrants are 28, 36, 24 and 40, each of which is divisible by 4. Incidentally, each quadrant is

---

[q] Also pronounced as *chamar*, this word was seen earlier, meaning 'to smear with pitch'

consistent in being composed of two even values and two that are odd, and

d) the gematria of the four-letter Name (ie 26) is not only given explicitly in Column B, but is also the sum of column A, and of the four corner values.

Among this list of straightforward facts, there are several subtle references to the G1 square Seal. For example, item (b) implies the 8×8 size of that square. In addition, the upper two quadrant totals (ie 28 and 36) represent firstly the number of letters in Genesis 1:1 and, therefore, the elements in the G1 perimeter, and then the number of elements contained within that perimeter. Those numbers are, as we know, the $T_7$ and $T_8$ triangular numbers. Then the lower two quadrants comprise of rows (iv) and (iii) whose totals are, respectively, 27 and the ubiquitous 37. Recall that the product of these same numbers (ie 27×37 = 999) was the sum of the gematria values of the first and third words of Genesis. And these were the very words which we have seen generate multiple references to Abraham.

Three other sub-group totals that relate to the 8×8 Seal are highlighted in Figure 9.6, along with one I have already mentioned. Notice that the four thumbnail sketches include all 16 elements with no gaps or overlaps. The total I have already mentioned is that of the four corner elements, represented by thumbnail (b). These sum to 26, which is the gematria of YHWH. Notice also that the product of each vertical pair is 5×8 = 40; which reflects the duration of the rains that lasted for the first forty days and forty nights of the flood.

| 5 | 5 | 16 | 5 |
|----|----|----|----|
| 12 | 6 | 2 | 13 |
| 1 | 5 | 20 | 11 |
| 8 | 10 | 1 | 8 |

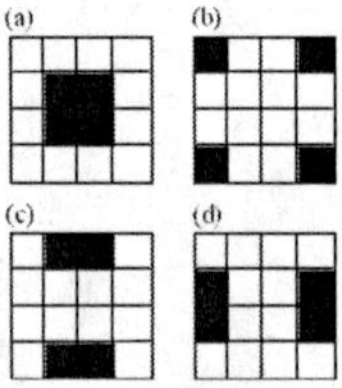

Figure 9.6

The totals illustrated by thumbnails (c) and (d) in the four sides of this square correspond to combinations of pairs of sides in the G1 square. Recall that the qatan sums of its sides were 15, 17, 22 and 28, in that order. So the 32 sum illustrated by thumbnail (c) corresponds to the sum of sides 1 and 2 of G1. Then the 37 sum of thumbnail (d) corresponds to the sum of sides 1 and 3. What is more, these four letters also spell [ה] מלאב / mal'ak / a messenger (or angel).

Lastly, the 33 sum of values represented by thumbnail (a) represents a characteristic of the 8×8 set of marble and granite tablets depicting the full text of Ezekiel (Satinover, 1997, p54). Consideration of those tablets led to our finding the important number 69696 (ie $264^2$), which is a perfect fit for an 8×8 chessboard. That was, incidentally, another association with water, since 264 is the gematria of the name Yardan (ie Jordan), the river. In that arrangement, as in every square aspect of the Author's Seal, each of the 64 tablets will contain exactly 33×33 elements. In Chapter 7, the centre of G3/4 was found to suggest the numbers 69696 and 33 in an altogether different way.

Of course, any reference to the ubiquitous number 4 is also an implied reference to 2, since we have the unique property among numbers that:

$$4 = 2 \times 2$$
$$\text{and} \quad 4 = 2 + 2$$

This is the only instance where a perfect square number is the sum of its positive square roots. And this observation helps to steer us towards an unusual part of the biblical flood narrative. In all cases, the animals to be preserved in the ark were selected in pairs, every male and its mate, a direct application of the number 2. But of all clean animals and fowl of the air, Noah was to preserve seven such pairs. The number 7 is especially blessed in the Bible, but considered inauspicious by certain ancient Near Eastern peoples. The narrative of Genesis 7:2 exalts the numbers 7 and 2, by preserving seven pairs of clean animals. And the same emphasis is reinforced by the flood square. For here, we see that the grand total of all the ordinal letter values in the flood square comes to:

$$128 = 2^7 = 2 \times 2 \times 2 \times 2 \times 2 \times 2 \times 2$$

Other key numbers are emphasised by the names of the principal characters in the flood account. There were eight people went into the ark; four of whom were named, and four others referred to simply as 'their wives'. The named individuals were Noah himself, and his three sons: Shem, Ham and Japheth. All these names have cryptic properties that are directly relevant to their context. For one thing, the name Shem as a Hebrew word literally means 'name'. That alone should alert us to hidden depths of meaning. Second, each of the names Shem and Ham (more properly pronounced Cham) comes from the start of a word that is the name of a number. שם (Shem) is the beginning of שמונה / *shemonah* / eight; while Ham is the beginning of חמש / *chamesh* / five. Notice particularly that the numbers five and eight are consecutive Fibonacci numbers that are now seen at the four corners of the flood square.

Next, the names of Shem and Ham are related to the name of Noah in two very unusual ways. The name of their father is spelled נ ח (Noach), which has a gematria of 58. So Shem (8) and Ham (5) are sons of Noah in a distinctly numerical sense. The other connection involves the spelling of the three names, as shown by Figure 9.7. Here it can be seen that the name of Ham is no more than a figment, based on the names of Noah and Shem. Ham would eventually be cursed because he made light of the nakedness of his drunken father, whereas Shem and Japheth cooperated in covering Noah, while also avoiding looking.

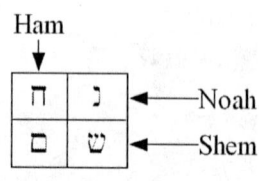

**Figure 9.7**

The name of יפת / *Yapheth* / Japheth continues the association with the numbers 5 and 8 in a rather different way, which involves the standard values of its three letters, thus:

$$10 \xrightarrow{\text{(x8)}} 80 \xrightarrow{\text{(x5)}} 400$$
$$(\text{י}) \qquad\qquad (\text{פ}) \qquad\qquad (\text{ת})$$

Every one of the four named people in the flood biblical story is closely aligned to a number 5 or an 8, or both. Evidently, these personalities are more closely aligned through number than they are by blood. Perhaps number also takes precedence over language more generally in this context since, in the three and a bit chapters of the Bible in which Noah is the principal human character, he utters not a single word.

When Japheth is added to the previous 2×2 letter-matrix, we obtain some further startling effects. The inclusion of the name Japheth as in Figure 9.8 results in two important new emergent words. One of them is שני / *sh'ney* / two (another Fibonacci term), and the other is תחש / *tachash* / a clean animal. As we have seen, in the biblical narrative, all animals went into the ark by 'twos', but the 'clean' animals were especially favoured, there being seven lots of two of each variety. What we now see is that the seven different letters in the latest

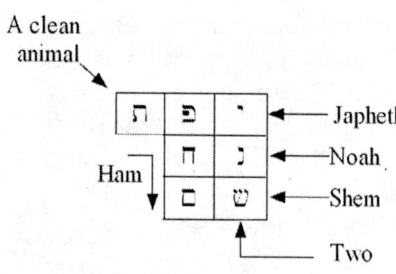

**Figure 9.8**

matrix confer the emergent word two, and the expression 'a clean animal'. In fact, *tachash* and *sh'ney* form two sides of a triangle, with the name Japheth as its third side. And it is rather interesting that the gematria of Japheth (ie 490 = 70×7) also places particular stress on the number 7.

The same seven-letter matrix reveals something equally interesting when it is expressed as standard letter values. That is, the names of all the named personalities except the cursed Ham.

$$58 \quad + \quad 340 \quad + \quad 490 \quad = \quad 888$$

Noah       Shem       Japheth

This result is reminiscent of something we saw explicitly in the G2 square, where all the three 8 digits that are present within the Author's Seal came together as a linear group. And that whole group overlay the position of the word *luchot* (tablets) seen in the G1 square. Luchot has a gematria of 444 and, since there had been two of those tablets within the Ark of the Covenant, 888 was implied.

In light of the above observation, it is notable that the names of Shem and Japheth bequeath an alternative numerical reference to that Ark, as the product:

$$340 \quad x \quad 490 \quad = \quad 166600$$

Shem       Japheth

We may recall several previous occurrences of the digits 1666 and the fact that, as 1.666, it is a good approximation to both the Divine Proportion (which is built into the dimensions of the Ark of the Covenant) and the ratio 8/5. As we now know, the latter two digits have very strong associations with all the personalities named in the biblical flood story.

To understand some further numerical characteristics of Noah's family it is helpful to reflect on the precise description of the way Shem and Japheth covered their father's nakedness. It is written:

> *And Shem and Japheth took a garment, and laid it upon both their shoulders, and went backward, and covered the nakedness of their father; and their faces were backward, and they saw not their father's nakedness.*

> (Genesis 9:23)

Not only is the *modus operandum* employed by the two brothers questionable in terms of rational behaviour (averted eyes would have served just as well), but the word 'backward' is pointedly mentioned twice. If we accept the word backward as a hint at another numerical effect, we obtain some further striking results. The implied action is to write the numerical value of each name backwards; so the 340 of Shem becomes 043, and the 490 of Japheth becomes 094. If we take their sum, we obtain:

$$043 \quad + \quad 094 \quad = \quad 137$$

mehS  htehpaJ

Recall that 137 was the age of Ishmael, of Levi and of Amram at the time each of them died. And recall the following curious relationship:

| | | |
|---|---|---|
| | 26 | (the gematria of הוהי /YHWH) |
| + | 111 | |
| | 137 | (the final ages of Ishmael, Levi and Amram) |
| + | 111 | |
| | 248 | (the gematria of םהרבא / Abraham) |

Now observe the effect when we also introduce the reverse digits of Noah:

$$85 \quad + \quad 043 \quad + \quad 094 \quad = \quad 222$$

haoN  mehS  htehpaJ

This result has four particular points of contact with previously observed effects, as well as the obvious relationships among themselves.

First and foremost, it was the same numbers written forwards that gave a sum of 888. And there is no earthly reason why three numbers should behave in this way, as can be shown by just a single counter-example. So, if the above set had been 75, 048 and 099, these would also have given 222; but their reverse values would be 1905. Also, since subtraction is the reverse of addition, we find that 888 − 222 = 666.

Second, 222 is the full difference between the gematria values of Abraham and YHWH in the above two-stage calculation. And we know that YHWH is an explicit component of the flood square. Also 'and all of Abraham' is an anagram of that square's middle two rows; and the same eight letters, as identical 2×2 clusters, spelled ohel (tent) and merkab (chariot).

Third, 222 is the gematria of Chebar, the river alongside which Ezekiel experienced his so-called 'Chariot' visions. And the word מרכב / *Merkab* / <u>Chariot</u> is found in the flood square as just mentioned. In fact, merkab is also an anagram of מכבר / *m'kebar* / <u>from Chebar</u>. So the cryptic association that is implied by Ezekiel is repeated by the numerical characteristics of Noah, Shem and Japheth.

Fourth, 222 is also related to the jointly symmetrical numbers 111 and 444 seen in the G1 aspect of the Seal. That is,

$$222 \times 222 = 111 \times 444$$

The natural conclusion is that widespread biblical narratives have been composed with underlying structures that favour the numbers 111, 222, 444 and 888.

Another inevitable conclusion of even greater importance is that names and numbers appear to be determinedly linked in many biblical narratives. The biblical flood account might have been composed to make this very point, which seems to subtly pervade the entire Bible. At the start of the book of Numbers, the first divinely ordained census is initiated with these words:

> *Take ye the sum of all the congregation of the children of Israel,*
> *after their families, by the house of their fathers, with the*
> *number of their names, every male by their polls;*
>
> (Numbers 1:2)

Notice particularly the expression: *the number of their names*, and compare that with these verses from the Christian New Testament:

> *Also it causes all, both small and great, both rich and poor,*
> *both free and slave, to be marked on the right hand or the*
> *forehead, so that no one can buy or sell unless he has the mark,*
> *that is, the name of the beast or the number of its name. This*
> *calls for wisdom: let him who has understanding reckon the*
> *number of the beast, for it is a human number, its number is*
> *666.*
>
> (Revelation 13:16-18)

Compare especially the expression *the number of its name*, with earlier *the number of their names*. It is only in the earlier case that the names of the Israelites are considered individually. Also, as we see in Revelation 13, the number 666 in particular is somehow associated with a corrupt attitude to the individuality that is implicit in the concept of a personal name. The same notion is implied by Ezra, who includes the number 666 among a long list of individual names alongside numbers (see Ezra Chapter 2). In our next Chapter, we shall see that Ezra was imbued with more wisdom even than King Solomon who, significantly, is also associated with the number 666.

We began the analytical content of this Chapter with the simple observation that the word chokmah (Wisdom) confers the numbers 73 and 37 from alternative numerical attributes of its four letters. The importance of these two numbers is two-fold; to start with, they are consecutive Star of David or hexagram numbers. And it is surely significant that the number 123 which Ezra associates with Bethlehem (see Ezra 2:21) is the sum of the first three Star of David numbers (ie $13 + 37 + 73 = 123$). Also the product of these same numbers (ie $13 \times 37 \times 73 = 35113$) is found as a cyclic group at the very heart of the G2 square. There the number 35113, itself a hexagram number and quintessential star of stars, is enclosed within the letters of the two most significant words: [ם] מחר / *racham* / a womb, and [ם] לחם / *lechem* / bread. The latter word is, in fact, the second half of the word Bethlehem[r], the city of David.

The other important shared attribute of the numbers 37 and 73 is that they are the prime co-factors of the 2701 gematria of both Genesis 1:1 and Genesis 8:14. The later of these two verses we have noted marks the end of the biblical flood account. These verses are, then, the beginning of the first creation and the transition from the later un-creation to a re-creation. What we have not yet established however, is that *chokmah* shares some essential characteristics with a particular word we examined in Chapter 4.

In Chapter 4, we recognised that the numerical view of the G1 square exhibits 'tassels' in the form of notable combinations of digits in its diagonals. In the main, these tassels are clearly attached to the central 2×2 cluster, except for an 876 sequence which began with the horizontal 38 in the centre. This 38 came directly from the emergent word לח / *luach* / a tablet, and the full 3876 sequence was split into two parts by the emergent word לוחת / *luchot* / tablets (gematria 444), the plural of *luach*. Incidentally, the number 876 which made that tassel conspicuous in the first place is $12 \times 73$ and sits in the diagonal whose qatan letter values total 37. Given that the tassels in G1 are set in the two diagonals of that square, it is particularly significant that the product of the diagonals' qatan sums was $36 \times 37 = 1332$, which is

---

[r] Bethlehem, or *beyt lechem* is, literally, 'house of bread' or bakery.

2×666. Since 666 is biblically allied to wisdom, it turns out that there is a particularly impressive connection between the inner cluster of G1 as a garment with its four tassels, and the biblical commandment to put a specifically blue cord on the tassels (see Numbers 15:37-39). We shall see next that the words *cachol* (blue) and *chokmah* (wisdom) have a strong numerical empathy.

In Chapter 4, we observed that the gematria of *cachol* (blue) is 64, the size of the square defined by Genesis 1:1. In terms of full gematria values, these words collaborate in re-affirming an important aspect of another of the (blue) tassels of G1, so:

$$73 + 64 = 137$$

Recall that 137 was the age of Ishmael and of Levi and of Amram at the times of their deaths. And one tassel conferred two copies of 411 (ie 3×137).

Next, we note that each of these four-letter words produces the same sum of 37 from their letters' ordinal values. From *cachol*, we obtain $11 + 8 + 6 + 12 = 37$; and from *chokmah* we obtain $8 + 11 + 13 + 5 = 37$.

If anything , the internal structures of blue and wisdom are even more illuminating. The right and left halves of *cachol* have separate gematria values of 28 and 36. These numbers are not only consecutive triangular numbers but also important attributes of all square aspects of the Seal, the perimeters of which consist of 28 elements, and contain 36 elements. Clearly, the numbers 37 and 73 obtained from *chokmah* also embody a key attribute of the Seal, being the co-factors of the 2701 gematria of Genesis 1:1. Also, the right and left halves of *chokmah* have gematria values of 28 and 45. Not only is 28 the same as obtained from *cachol* (because they include the same two letters), but 45 is also a triangular number. Between these two words, their various halves have generated the three consecutive triangular numbers $T_7$, $T_8$ and $T_9$. Moreover, the 45 we obtain from the second half of חכמה /*chokmah* / wisdom has an additional significance. It is the sum of all the prime factors of 666, so that:

$$666 = 2×3×3×37$$

and
$$45 = 2 + 3 + 3 + 37$$

Notice, therefore, that the Hebrew for wisdom has this further, in-built affinity for the number 666, the number that the Bible twice associates explicitly with the word wisdom.

-oOo-

Exceptionally, I believe it is worth including a summary of the main points of this Chapter, which embodies a coherence that may be masked by the details. These are the salient points:

♦ The number 666 has three particularly forceful associations:

  • With the Author's Seal, explicitly in the G1 and G2 squares and subtly in G1 and G3/4.

  • With names, in Ezra 2:13 and Revelation 13:18.

  • With wisdom, in 1st Kings 10:14 and Revelation 13:18 (see also next Chapter).

♦ The Hebrew word for wisdom, *chokmah*, shares several numerical features with Genesis 1:1 and with the complete G1 square. Literally, there is a structural likeness between *chokmah* and the centre of the G1 square so that together they point to the existence of a 4×4 flood square. The flood square also contains the words YHWH and *arba* (four).

♦ The flood square reveals many words and phrases that relate directly to the biblical flood account and to the later life of Noah. The same square, as ordinal letter values, possesses a marked degree of coherence (largely founded on the number 4), and links with the perimeter and diagonals of G1. Surprisingly, it does not appear to say anything explicit about Noah or his sons, with the exception of the four corner values of '55' at the top and '88' at the bottom. Together, these hint at the 58 gematria of נ ח (Noah) and sum to the 26 gematria of YHWH.

♦ The flood square again links the names of YHWH and Abraham linguistically. But these two names also give a gematria sum of 26+248 = 274, with two important connections. 274 is twice 137, which was first found in G1 as a tassel on a garment, and links three important biblical personalities who all died at that age. Also, at the centre of the G3/4 aspects of the Seal, 274 was seen to cross through 273, which is the gematria of אַרבע / *arba* / <u>four</u>. But now, the tiny flood square not only includes the name of YHWH explicitly, and Abraham as an emergent word, but of course includes the explicit word *arba*.

♦ The names of Noah and his sons (Shem, Ham and Japheth) demonstrate a marked degree of numerical coherence among themselves, independently of the flood square. Thus:

- The names of Shem and Ham are linguistically allied to the Hebrew words for eight and five respectively. While the name Shem literally means 'name'.

- A particular 2×2 matrix of the names of Noah and Shem already subsumes the name of Ham.

- The same matrix augmented to 7 letters by the name Japheth reveals emergent words for 'two' and 'a clean animal'. Clean animals were brought into the ark as seven pairs.

- Numerically, the names of Noah, Shem and Japheth sum to 888, a number that is seen in the G2 square associated with the river that flows to Ahavah (see Ezra 8:15) and, in Greek numerology, is the value of the name Jesus.

- Genesis 9:23 describes a bizarre episode in which Shem and Japheth walk backwards in a tactic to cover their father's nakedness. When the gematria values of Noah, Shem and Japheth are written backwards, their sum becomes 222. This is also the difference between the gematria values of YHWH and Abraham, both of which are present within the flood square. Also, $888 - 222 = 666$, where subtraction is addition backwards.

- Ezra subsumes the numerical attributes of *chokmah* (wisdom) into an onward pointer to the New Testament. At Ezra 2:13, he links the number 666 with the name Adonikam (lit. 'my Lord is risen'). Then, at verse 21 of the same Chapter he associates 123 with Bethlehem. The number 123 is the sum of 13, 37 and 73, which are the first three Star of David numbers. The product of the same three consecutive stars (ie 35113) is also a Star of David number, which featured in the centre of the G2 square.

It is quite evident that the concepts of wisdom, names and numbers are closely related in the more mystical foundation of the Bible. In particular, all three come together at the end of Revelation 13. It is equally evident that a similar sort of connection links the stories of Noah, Ezra and Jesus of Nazareth. These personalities along with Moses are all, in very different ways, associated with restoring life and hope where it had seemed lost.

# 10

In reaching this stage, I have made a number of claims concerning elaborate sub-structures that underpin the Bible, from its first beginning to its extreme end. The main focus has been a mere 64 Hebrew letters at the start of Genesis. And the very fact that so much (seven chapters) can be written about so short a text says a great deal about its elaborate underlying design. Admittedly, some pages in my descriptions are taken up with the re-iterated details of those structures when, in subsequent stages, additional closely-related items have come to light. But even when we strip away my own repetitions, the fundamental nature of the Author's Seal contains overwhelming evidence of a richly coherent design. In the face of so much evidence, the veracity and integrity of the Seal's structure cannot seriously be doubted. And the identity of the Author-cum-Architect is no less certain, since the Seal reveals knowledge of subjects that were unknown until many centuries after the Torah was first set down in writing. The Author cannot be just super-intelligent, but would have to be omniscient.

I touched upon the concept of omniscience in the Introduction, where I suggested the implications are regularly underestimated. It would be wrong to assume that an all-seeing creator can only see everything that *is* happening. That would, of course, be an awesome ability; but it suffers from one fatal flaw; that kind of seeing is an entirely passive pursuit. Omniscience of that type simply does not live up to its billing. Surely, the only omniscience worthy of the name is the kind that can see every possibility. This alternative definition implies an altogether different, more valuable kind of seeing - an infinite, creative imagination. In fact, the start of the Hebrew Torah, which I call the Author's Seal is the best possible proof that the greater kind of omniscience is not only possible, but actually exists. When all the probabilities of the Seal's myriad interrelated components are taken into account, it will be recognised as the most wonderful text of its length that can possibly exist. To put this more plainly, in order to compose a 64-letter text with the degree of versatility we have witnessed must involve rigorous testing of an almost infinite number of alternatives. Given that the principal aspects of the Seal are all 8×8 squares, the task might be compared to memorising every possible game of chess, from start to finish. But, although there are billions upon billions of possible chess games, even this task fails to capture the scale of the difficulty of designing the Seal.

-oOo-

What I shall do in this final Chapter is look at the evidence that the Seal has been discovered, lost and re-discovered, intermittently throughout history. What that should demonstrate is that my own descriptions are not the unique product of one fevered imagination. There is an English proverb: *You can't make a silk purse out of a sow's ear.* If the purse the artisan produces is of pure silk then, without question, his raw-material was pure silk. For the same reason, the Seal can be described in the terms I use in this book only because it has been designed for the purpose. It is probably safe to assume that there will not be found any extra-biblical text of similar length that can be shown to embody the same degree of meaningful, hidden structure. I mean this as a challenge to anyone who, having read this book, still will not cleave to the evidence of their eyes.

It should come as no surprise that the earliest evidence for knowledge of the Seal is seen throughout the Old Testament: the prophets and other writings. The descendents of Israel (Jacob) are, after all, the appointed guardians of the Hebrew scriptures, especially the sacred Torah. But taking the broader view, it is natural that whenever the Seal has been re-discovered its content should be bent to the beliefs and the circumstances of the finder. So, when the witness was Jewish the message became tailored to the destiny of God's chosen people, and the result is now seen most clearly in books of the Bible, but not just the Old Testament. In every case, we can also work out which of the many aspects of the Seal were recognised at the time. We have already noted particular examples including parts of the books of Ezekiel, Isaiah, Daniel, Ezra, the Christian Gospels and the book of Revelation, as well as descriptions of King Solomon's famed wealth and wisdom. In this respect, the Seal may serve as a latter-day Rosetta Stone, bridging gulfs between the seemingly irreconcilable. It has brought clarity to perplexing biblical narrative and, in due course, will do the same for some mystifying aspects of recorded history where hitherto there has been confusion and apparent contradiction.

Ezra is an interesting case in point, as he is not normally counted among the Hebrew prophets. In Judaism, Ezra is remembered as the priest and scribe who led his people out of exile in Babylonia back to their homeland and Jerusalem. Ezra's role was, therefore, similar to that of Moses in an earlier age; and it has been said that Ezra was sufficiently righteous and wise that he might have merited the earlier prophet's mantle. The Bible does not say outright that Ezra was wise; we are left to reach that conclusion ourselves from the ample evidence. Two examples will serve to make the point, both of them found in Ezra 8.

Back in Chapter 5, we noted a close correspondence between an artefact of the G2 square and the following text:

> *I gathered them together to the river that runneth to Ahavah,*
> *and there abode we in tents three days*
>
> (Ezra 8:15)

The artefact was an unbroken sequence of the letter *vav* (ו), eight in all, that had adopted the outline of a letter *lamed* (ל), or of a meandering river. And the uppermost element of that river was the middle letter of a palindromic linear group אהוהא, from which we may read אהוה (Ahavah) in either direction. To be perfectly realistic, it is impossible to know whether Ezra was aware of the Seal, or it of him. Either he was inherently wise in his decision to pause at the river where, incidentally, he discovered and rectified the absence of any priests of the tribe of Levi, or his wisdom may have resided in his knowledge of the Author's Seal, which he then put into practice.

The other example of the wisdom of Ezra is found in these verses:

> *Then I proclaimed a fast there, at the river of Ahavah, that we*
> *might afflict ourselves before our God, to seek of him a right*
> *way for us, and for our little ones, and for all our substance.*
> *For I was ashamed to acquire of the king a band of soldiers*
> *and horsemen to help us against the enemy in the way: because*
> *we had spoken unto the king, saying, The hand of our God is*
> *upon all them for good that seek him; but his power and his*
> *wrath is against all them that forsake him.*
>
> (Ezra 8:21-22)

To understand these verses properly, we need only look at the Bible's attitude to horses and their role at the high and low points in the history of the Israelites. In the Torah, it had been decreed:

*But he [the king] shall not multiply horses to himself, nor
cause the people to return to Egypt, to the end that he should
multiply horses; for as much as the Lord hath said unto you,
Ye shall henceforth no more return that way.*

(Deuteronomy 17:16)

In conventional terms, the period of King Solomon's rule had
been the highest achievement for the children of Israel. That was the
time when the northern kingdom (Israel) and the southern kingdom
(Judah) were united under one king; when relations with neighbouring
cultures had been stable, yet in Solomon's favour; and building of the
Temple, God's dwelling on earth, had just been completed. But the
root of their doom was already on display when we read:

*And Solomon gathered chariots and horsemen: and he had a
thousand and four hundred chariots, and twelve thousand
horsemen, which he placed in the chariot cities, and with the
king at Jerusalem.*

(2nd Chronicles 1:14)

Also:

*And Solomon had horses brought out of Egypt ...*

(2nd Chronicles 1:16)

From that moment, the fortunes of God's chosen people plunged
into freefall culminating, about five centuries later, in the 70-year
Babylonian exile and the destruction of Solomon's Temple.

At the end of the 70 years, Ezra led his people to freedom without
accepting protection from the horsemen of King Cyrus of Persia. The
contrast could not be more stark. The supposedly wise Solomon
directly flouted an explicit command recorded in the books of the
Law. Whereas Ezra the humble priest and scribe, having understood
the lesson implicit in the 70-year exile, goes to great lengths to comply
with the same command. Who, then, is the wiser? The difference
between Solomon and Ezra is seen in their alternative forms of
wisdom; Solomon's mainly self-serving, and Ezra's dedicated to God
through service to his people. The fact that both descriptions include
the number 666 is especially illuminating. In the case of Solomon (see
2nd Chronicles 9:13 and 1st Kings 10:14), 666 is the weight in talents
of the gold he receives in tithe in one year. But for Ezra, 666 is a
number of souls, the kinsmen of Adonikam who had returned from
Babylon to Jerusalem, metaphorically from death to life. Equally
importantly, the name Adonikam literally means 'my Lord is risen'.

Nor does the role of horses end with the contrasting behaviours of Solomon and Ezra. The word סוס / *sus* / <u>horse</u> confers a qatan sequence of 666, and is the only word of biblical Hebrew to do so! Given the biblical prohibition on horses, it also seems odd that this particular word should start and end with the same letter that is so reticent in the beginning of the Bible. The letter *samech* (ס) is the last of the 22 to make its first appearance, at position 2210. And this is squeezed between $47^2$ and $T_{66}$. Symbolically, the letter samech is a thorn and represents the concept of protection.

The way that Ezra associates the number 666 with 'my Lord is risen' connects beautifully with aspects of the Author's Seal, in the order:

1. G1, the crucified man includes a vertical 666 group,
2. G2, the river is seen that runneth to Ahavah (ie love), and includes a horizontal 666 group, and
3. G3, where we find only an oblique reference to 666 (as a triangular 222111, or $T_{666}$), and the only explicit linear occurrence of the Tetragrammaton, YHWH, the name of the risen Lord.

It remains uncertain whether Ezra was granted fore-knowledge of the New Testament events that would fulfil the prophetic vision of his living experiences; although I expect others to have strong opinions on the subject. My own present purpose it simply to demonstrate that Ezra was more than likely aware of the Seal on the start of the Torah, and that is why his book came to be established in the biblical canon. All the books that show evidence of knowledge of the Seal are suffused with a particular aura of wisdom. Nor is it accidental that the Seal is the quintessential template for all the biblical temples, and that those who returned with Ezra to Jerusalem made it their task to rebuild the destroyed Temple of Solomon.

As we have seen, many allusions to the Seal are built-into the New Testament too, within the Gospels and its final book, the book of Revelation (The Apocalypse). Other references can be found in the so-called Lost Gospels that were not adopted into the New Testament Canon. However, as we shall see next, the fact that the biblical canon is now meant to be closed forever has not prevented the Seal having an influence on subsequent history and literature.

-oOo-

Within the western world, there have been two especially influential, international organisations that may trace their *raison d'être* to the Seal on the start of Genesis. One was the Poor Fellow-Soldiers of Jesus Christ, later known as the Knights Templar. The other is the loose aggregation of confraternities known collectively as Freemasonry. Without ever publishing viable evidence, the Freemasons lay claim to a heritage that goes back to the Templars and beyond, at least as far as the building of Solomon's Temple. And I think it may indeed be possible to connect the origins of both organisations to the Author's Seal on the Hebrew Torah. Although the surviving evidence seems to suggest, at best, that the latter-day organisation may have accidentally happened upon earlier knowledge after a dark-age of several centuries. The fact that freemasons selectively choose to emulate aspects of the Templars' principles is no proof of direct descent. In due course, however, I shall describe a much more certain connection between the historically real Knights Templar and a very well known literary legend. This will be a link for which there is no better explanation than knowledge of the Seal.

In the remainder of this final Chapter, I go on to compare aspects of the Seal with both historical fact and aspects of one popular myth. In the history of conspiracy-busting, I believe this to be new territory. I will go so far as to propose that the Seal may be viewed as a new primary source in those areas of research. And it is the one key that will be able to unlock more puzzling aspects of the historical record than any other – one of its 'Rosetta Stone' functions.

Throughout the history of the Seal, those 'in the know' have been influenced most by the faith, sect, society or other body to which they felt they owed the greatest allegiance. Secrecy is nearly always the chief watchword, because collective ownership demands a high degree of group loyalty. Freemasonry is often described as a secret society but is no more so than either the Knights Templar, or Judaism have been. None of them has been outwardly hidden from the eyes of the world; but all have, in varying degrees, been secretive about a certain kind of knowledge that is assumed, wrongly as it now appears, to have been in their sole keeping. Whenever a new member is born, and/or initiated into one of these organisations (circumcision is a form of initiation), they are introduced into the central, secret knowledge only gradually or with extreme caution, if at all. Only the most able and trustworthy are made privy to the deepest core of the ancient, arcane knowledge. Knowing what we now know about the Seal on the Hebrew Torah, the assumption must have been that it can never be discovered accidentally by anyone who is not already steeped in an unlikely mix of none-too-easy subjects.

# In the Beginning

-oOo-

With our new knowledge and understanding of the Seal, we are in an advantaged position to explain both the early development and ultimate downfall of the Templars. And both of those historical episodes have been linked to a long-standing mystery – Why did the Templars take a sudden close interest in Hebrew texts?

The idea for creating an order of military monks in the Holy Land seems to have been mooted soon after the end of the first Crusade. History records that that campaign had somewhat mixed results. Like all major episodes that have ever taken place in the Holy Land, the initial success – in this case the relief of Jerusalem from Islamic occupation – was followed by subsequent loss of ground, and difficulties in ensuring the safety of Christian pilgrims travelling to the region. Ostensibly, the Poor Fellow-Soldiers of Jesus Christ were established to provide resident protection for civilian Christian pilgrims. And, whatever else may have happened, they came to fulfil that role quite admirably until the eventual overthrow of military Christian activity in Outremer[s].

On their arrival in Jerusalem in 1118, the first nine members of the Order of military monks had been allocated quarters in a palace converted from the Al Aqsa mosque on the Temple Mount. Popular speculation in modern times imagines the 'Templars' unearthing a fabulous treasure in the maze of tunnels that exist beneath the Temple Mount. Some have suggested that their find included accessories and trappings from the once richly endowed Temple, many made from gold or overlaid with gold, some encrusted with precious stones. Perhaps they had found the original seven-branch candlestick – the Menorah – and the Ark of the Covenant, both iconic symbols of Judaism. When the word 'treasure' is mentioned, it is often to a vision of precious metals and jewels that the mind first turns. That, as we shall see, is the mistake that has usually been made in relation to the treasure of the Knights Templar. And even when commentators have tried to suggest a more edifying explanation, their hopeful speculations have always lacked the requisite factual foundation. Some of the wilder speculations have suggested the Templars had (also) discovered a human head, which might have been that of John the Baptist, or even the embalmed head of Christ. In reality, we shall find that the treasure we seek bears little resemblance to King Solomon's annual tithe of 666 talents of gold. Instead it will have more in common with the wealth

---

[s] Outremer (literally 'beyond the sea') was the name by which the territories seized in the first Crusade became known in Europe.

of humanity entrusted to the safe keeping of Ezra, including the 666 kinsmen of Adonikam he describes.

It is on record that the Knights Templar discovered something of great value beneath the Temple in Jerusalem, beyond which all else has necessarily been speculation. In what follows, I make the straightforward substitution that the 'something valuable' is, in fact, the Seal on the start of the Hebrew Torah. After this, all else will fall into place beautifully. If we may now re-interpret the above suggestions in light of the Seal on the Torah, it is much more plausible that the Templars had identified the *image* of the Menorah we have seen within the G1 square (see Chapter 2) and the many references the Seal makes to the Ark – both literal and graphical It is highly unlikely that anyone in those times would have understood the additional mathematical allusions to the Ark which we now recognise. As for the embalmed head, its identity will become clearer when we come to examine the way the Templars were forcibly overthrown.

The fact that the Seal is able to reveal the Menorah, the Ark of the Covenant, the crucified Christ and many graphic depictions of other biblical scenes makes it the new prime candidate to explain the Templar treasure. The fact that it is also dependent on the original Hebrew Torah is especially telling when we consider the roots of the first members of the Order of the Temple. The original idea for the military monastic order was developed jointly by the Abbott Bernard of Clairvaux and Hugh, Count of Champagne. The Order's first Grand Master was Hugh's liege subject Hugh of Payns, born near to the city of Troyes in northern France. So this Hugh was likely to have felt a strong bond of loyalty for his liege Lord. And it is probable that the first Grand Master was chosen for both his loyalty and modest education, to suit the task the Count and Bernard had in mind for him.

Troyes is perhaps best remembered as the venue for one of the western Christian Church's major Councils, held in January 1129. That is, less than eleven years after the founding of the Poor Fellow-Soldiers. It is known that the Council of Troyes was addressed by Hugh, Count of Champagne, but not because he was secular overlord of that region since he has already stepped down from that position. Rather, it was because of his close ties to the Knights Templar that he opted to champion their rights to all the benefits due a properly constituted ordo. We may, however, start to entertain the notion that the Council was called in Troyes *because* of the Templars. Other business could have been conducted just as easily at an alternative venue, but maybe not the subject of the Order of the Temple, for which the Council of Troyes approved no less than seventy-three new rules. Also, while most of the churchmen who attended the Council were French, there was present one Stephen Harding, the English-born Abbott of Molesme. It is said that: 'Stephen Harding was a scholar of the first rank, revising the text of the Latin Bible and calling on Jewish rabbis to help him understand the Hebrew Old Testament'. (Read, 2001, p96). It seems that Troyes, as the seat of the Count of Champagne, had already become the focus for an undercurrent of interest in Hebrew texts.

Harding seems to have been born the right man at the right time. By a stroke of luck, not too many years earlier, Troyes had also been the home of an influential Jewish philosopher known as Rashi – an abbreviation for Rabbi Shlomo Yitzhaki (Solomon ben Isaac) (1040 to 1105). Rashi was a very devout and sober student of the Hebrew Torah who, in later life, produced a thoroughly accessible commentary on both the Torah and the Babylonian Talmud. It is widely acknowledged that the contributions of Rashi in this area of expertise are among the most accurate, incisive and comprehensive available. Even today, they are still consulted by Torah students of all ages and diverse backgrounds. The fact that Rashi lived and worked in Troyes may have been purely coincidental, but it is almost certain that Stephen Harding would, at some stage, have been introduced to his work. And it is surely no coincidence that the Christian scholar best able to make use of the work of Rashi was brought to the Council of Troyes, at a time the fortunes of the Templars were about to improve dramatically. So, what could have been going on in the background in Troyes?

There is one very puzzling aspect of the early history of the Knights Templar. For a period of between ten and twenty years, the original nine members did not increase. Nor did contemporary writers of that period record any Templar activity that would confirm their declared purpose of defending pilgrims throughout the Holy Land. That role would come to the fore only later. It now appears that in the early years, these soldier-monks were kept fully occupied searching the Temple in Jerusalem, and probably despatching anything relevant they found to the court of Champagne. This single channel of communication seems to have been of crucial importance during the Templars' first 20 years or so. In fact, Hugh, Count of Champagne is known to have visited his nine charges in Jerusalem three times, before himself becoming a serving member of the Order.

During those early years, all the known interest in understanding ancient Hebrew texts was concentrated in the European end of the communication channel. The Templars themselves may have been in the dark to some extent, concerning the full import of their work. And that state of affairs appears to have prevailed right up to the time the first Grand Master, Hugh of Payns, died in 1136.

Following the death of Hugh, the Order elected Robert of Craon to be their new Grand Master. And this one development seems to have precipitated a dramatic change of direction and of fortunes for the Order of the Temple. Judging by events over the next few years, it appears likely that Robert's education was far superior to that of his predecessor. It is at this point that the Poor Fellow-Soldiers may have woken up to the magnitude of the secret they had spent nearly twenty years unearthing.

The new Grand Master lost no time in approaching the then Pope and, by means we may now have some hope of explaining:

> [obtained] additional and exceptional privileges from Pope Innocent II in a bull published in 1139 *Omne datum optimum*.
>
> Addressed to 'our dear son Robert', this ruled that the Order of the Temple should be exempt from all intermediary ecclesiastical jurisdiction and be subject only to the Pope. Even the Patriarch of Jerusalem, before whom the founding knights had taken their vows, lost any authority over the Order. The bull allowed the Temple to have its own oratories, and permitted priests to join as chaplains which made the Templars wholly independent of the diocesan bishops both in Outremer and in the West. The Temple was entitled to receive tithes but need not pay them – an exemption that had hitherto only applied to the Cistercian Order; it could have cemeteries attached to its houses and bury travellers in their *confrâtres* – rights with a considerable pecuniary value. They were also entitled to booty taken from the enemy, and were to be answerable only to their Master who must be one of their number and chosen by the chapter without any pressure from secular powers.
>
> What was behind this papal largesse?

> (Read, 2001, p116)

What indeed!? Clearly, the year 1139 marked a major turning point in the Templars' fortunes. It is likely the court at Champagne were none too pleased with the new Grand Master's unprecedented, liberal display of independence. But the cat was well and truly out of the bag. There was nothing to be done about the fact the Church had become a third party to their secret. The Templars could not know it, but their indiscretion was destined to catch up with them more than a century and a half later.

Scholars have puzzled long and hard as to why any Pope should sign away so much of the Church's power. Over the years, there would be several occasions when the western Church might have rued that decision, yet did nothing by way of a retraction. The rights of the Templars would not be seriously challenged until 1307 when King Philip IV (the Fair) of France rose up against them, with the Church's tacit approval. For 168 years, the Church seems to have been hamstrung in its uneasy relationship with the Templars.

By 1139, a new generation of initiates would have been in place at both ends of the Templar communication channel; and the old guard would soon pass away. Maybe the knights were never meant to understand the secret they guarded so carelessly. But over the next decades the channel with Troyes was broken, and the proper understanding of the secret knowledge began to splinter and diverge almost immediately. As we shall discover, it was the Templars alone who would try to uphold the purity of the wisdom.

For their part, the Church has never breathed a word of it. Since the structure of the Seal on the Torah can account for so many of the items reported to have been among the Templars' treasure, we might suspect the Church was troubled by important differences between that knowledge and their own unbending slant on the original Christian message. Consider, for example, the following passage taken from one of the gospels adopted into the New Testament canon:

> ...he [Jesus] *said, "To you it has been given to know the secrets of the kingdom of God; but for others they are in parables, so that seeing they might not see, and hearing they might not understand."*
>
> Luke 8:10

Since the Gospel of Luke tells us that the Apostles were made privy to mystical knowledge, we ought to ask why the adopted Gospels relate only parable at the expense of the mystical alternative.

Needless to say, the original golden Menorah and Ark of the Covenant never did come to light. That is, despite their great size, which would make them difficult to transport and conceal. On the other hand, neither did any hand-written copy of the Seal belonging to the Templars see the light of day; although that might be because it was neither sought nor recognisable. One thing we may now properly appreciate is the *double entendre* implicit in the adopted, unofficial title

'Knights of the Temple'. Given that every 8×8 square facet of the Seal represents aspects of the architecture of diverse biblical temples, it is quite significant that one of the few surviving illustrations of Templar life shows two knights engaged in a game of chess.

Bye and bye, once the Holy Land was permanently lost to the Europeans, it would be impossible for the Templars to justify their continued existence. They would then be surrounded by only those who either could not, or would not want to understand the priceless truth the Templars possessed. And I am not, here, talking about a hypothetical document or manuscript that someone has said they heard probably once existed. I am referring to a sacred text that is very well-known in translation, is found in many ordinary homes, and is described at length in the first seven chapters of this book. Later in the present Chapter, we shall see further evidence that aspects of the Templars' secret knowledge had found its way to the Order's original home-base in northern France and would, after a fashion, outlive its temporary guardians.

The dissolution or forcible overthrow of the Knights Templar starting in 1307 is, if anything, even more rooted in conspiracy than was their initial formation and rise to power. The background is fairly straightforward and well documented. During the 13th Century, crusader forces in the Holy Land waged an ebb and flow struggle against Saracen and other anti-Christian forces. But with ever dwindling reinforcements arriving from Europe, in 1291 the wars for the Holy Land were effectively over. Town by town, castle by castle the entire mainland was finally lost to the advancing Muslims. For the next twelve years, the only military Christian presence was an offshore garrison of Templars on the island of Ruad, two miles from the coast by Tortosa. And even that was abandoned when the enemy began building a causeway that would inevitably lead to its eventual loss. A larger garrison stationed for a few years more on Cyprus hardly counts as a foot in the door. Their presence there had virtually no further military influence in Outremer.

During 184 years in which the knights of the Temple defended Christian interests in the Holy Land, their Order became immensely rich. Not least because the western Church had exempted them from paying tithes, and empowered them to collect tithes of their own. But also, they had received many gifts of land and property from patrons who were at the very least sympathetic to the Templars' mission, and in some cases grateful for their past protection. The Templars are also regarded as having been the first international bankers in ways that we would recognise today. They invented the concept of a 'promissory note', or travellers' cheque, as a way for pilgrims and others to transport their wealth securely. Anyone travelling within Templar influence could deposit a form of security at their place of origin then, on production of a Templar note of credit, draw cash against their deposit at some remote location. For this type of system to work, it is not only necessary for the banker to have large sums of cash on hand at all locations. It is also necessary to have a way to validate a promissory note so it cannot be forged. And that implies a sophisticated form of encryption. The once meagrely educated Poor Fellow-Soldiers had come a long way from the time their official seal showed two knights sharing one horse. Of course, each individual knight was indeed sworn to poverty; but the Order itself became fabulously wealthy, enough to rival the Church and many kings and nobles. At the same time, however, once the Templars had relinquished they outpost of Ruad in 1302, they effectively lost their original *raison d'être*.

While the Templars had been accruing their great wealth, there were others who did not fare so well; in financial markets there are usually both winners and losers. One who had fared particularly badly was King Philip IV (le Bel) of France. Through a mixture of bad judgement, mis-management and sheer profligacy, he had succeeded in borrowing from the Templars (and others) more than he could ever hope to repay. Philip was not a man to give in to the 'inevitable', and so he plotted to turn the situation to his own advantage. The plan he devised was nothing less than the overthrow of the Order of the Temple, simultaneously in all its many preceptories, castles and manors in territories the King controlled. If the plan worked, Philip would not only succeed in wiping out his entire debt, but might stand to gain untold additional wealth, as 'spoils of war'.

The western Church at the time was headed by Pope Clement V, no longer headquartered in Rome but in a series of cities in France, and more or less the puppet of Philip. Also, the Church had already been gathering evidence that the Knights Templar had slipped into the ways of Satan. There was hearsay evidence of heresy and blasphemy, which had come to the ears of the King of France.

King Philip issued sealed orders to his seneschals, to be opened everywhere simultaneously early on 13th October 1307, a Friday. The orders were that the King's own loyal forces should occupy all Templar properties, confiscate their possessions and arrest their more senior members pending trial on charges of blasphemy and heresy. In many places, the plan proceeded like clockwork, and the nett outcome was to Philip a nett income, the solution to all his financial problems.

In some places, however, the Templars had been warned by sympathisers early enough to make their escape. Some senior members of the Order, most notably its last Grand Master, Jacques de Molay, were imprisoned for the next seven years and periodically tortured. It is not altogether clear why King Philip persisted with the torture for so long, unless he was still hoping to lay his hands on the elusive 'fabulous treasure' long ascribed to the Templars. As we know, the treasure was never found because it did not exist in the form anyone except the Templars would have expected. The real treasure we now know is more precious than any amount of gold. And one opinion is that it lay unrecognised in full view of the King, like pearls before swine. However, Read (2001) writes that the treasure did indeed include 'the seven-branch candelabra, seized by the Emperor Titus, the crown of the kingdom of Jerusalem and a shroud'. We have seen the candelabra (Menorah) within the G1 facet of the Seal. The same square contains the word עלם [ף] / *alaph* / <u>a veil</u> or <u>shroud</u>, and four tassels attached to what is crearly meant to be understood as a garment. The horizontal emergent word כתר / *keter* / <u>a crown</u> is also visible in the western quadrant of G3 and G4. Since the Seal itself has the appearance of a temple in various forms this crown would, for some observers, equate to the 'crown of the kingdom of Jerusalem'.

It goes almost without saying that the charges of blasphemy and heresy levelled at the Templars had no foundation. The courts of heresy are invariably conducted in a spirit of blind fanaticism, feeding living flesh to sadistic inquisitors who never tire of hearing their victims' screams. Skilled interrogators know how to pose loaded questions in the style of 'Have you given up beating your wife', leaving no safe way to answer. But even a kangaroo court will benefit from a grain of truth that can be exploited.

The sort of charges levelled at the Templars included all the perennials such as sodomy and other homosexual and perverse sexual practices, Gnostic and magical rites, and devil worship. These are standard fare in most heresy trials. However, for the Templars only, the accusations specifically included the worship of an unspecified head, and this detail deserves some particular attention.

Speculation about the worshipped head has never really gone away, and a number of popular theories have come and gone over the centuries. Among the favourite candidates have been the head of John the Baptist and the embalmed head of Jesus Christ (brought to France by Mary Magdalene, no less!). Others say the head was that of a goat, or that it may have had three faces. Whatever the true nature of the elusive head, it was also reputed to go by the name Baphomet. These last suggestions have remained popular with the 'man in the street', but fell out of favour in scholarly circles long ago. Yet, with the new-found knowledge of the Author's Seal in our armoury, I think it is now realistic to re-open that particular file.

For one thing, recall that the very first word of the Hebrew Torah, בראשית / *B'reishith* / In the beginning includes the words ראש / *rosh* / a head and תיש / *tayish* / a he-goat. If that doesn't count as a clue and a half, then I do not know what might. Also, the suggestion that the worshipped head had three faces would align perfectly with what we know of the G4 aspect of the Seal. There, the three letters of *pnei* (a face) each contributes to the identity of a different one of the faces seen by Ezekiel on his so-called living creatures (a mis-translation of *chayot*). Please hold onto these hard facts while we take a short but important detour.

One matter that often drew attention to the Templars' early activity was of course their particular interest in Hebrew texts. That would help to explain the presence of Abbott Stephen Harding at the Council of Troyes, just ten years after the founding of the Templar Order. And that can also be a reason why the above hypothesis ascribes the name Baphomet to the proposed goat, although the veracity of this part of the theory is less certain than the rest. The argument normally goes as follows:

- The Greek word for wisdom is Sophia;
- When Sophia is transliterated into Hebrew, one possible spelling is שׁוּפִיא (note the unsatisfactory ambiguity),
- In one of the Jewish mystical traditions, the letters of a Hebrew word may be cryptically converted using a technique called atbash. (In this technique, any occurrence of aleph (א), the first letter of the alephbeyt, becomes a *tav* (ת) the last letter, and vice versa; the second letter *beyt* (ב) becomes the second-last, *shin* (ש) and vice versa, and so on. Hence the name of the technique: אתבש = Atbash),
- Finally, the atbash counterpart of שׁוּפִיא (Sophia) is בפומת (Baphomet).

In reality, the word Baphomet has no legitimate existence, and its atbash derivation from Sophia is highly questionable. But it was raised as an accusation, and the fact that it is founded in a known Hebrew mystical tradition at least reminds us that the goat-head hypothesis may have been contrived by someone who knew of the Templars' fascination with Hebrew texts. And herein lies a significant risk to credibility; the atbash conjecture for Baphomet may be a relatively recent addition to a much older piece of historical detail. The very real presence of 'head' and 'he-goat' within the first word of Genesis (see Chapter 1) appears to be the one genuine clear link between the Author's Seal and the accusations of heresy. However, add to that the atbash derivation of Baphomet and, at a stroke, a legitimate piece of material evidence becomes a potential target for derision. The baby is thrown out with the bath-water.

One question that comes to mind immediately is this: If the Templars' accusers already knew about the head and goat in the Seal, just how much else of the Templars' secret was already known to them? The answer seems to be, 'more than we might suppose'. It is on record that a Templar sergeant, one Stephen of Troyes, came forward on behalf of the prosecution. The sergeant gave evidence that the Templars would sometimes conduct ceremonies during which the head they worshipped would be brought in by a priest, preceded by two brothers (presumably soldier-monks) carrying a candelabrum bearing two large candles. For the moment, we may be content just to note that the accuser had his origin in Troyes where the secret knowledge had evolved differently. And the evidence given by the Templar sergeant will soon be seen to be a corruption of the wisdom conferred by the Seal. Also, if the Templars' accusers already knew the proper derivation of the head and the he-goat, there is no reason why their informant could not then go on to acquaint them with more complete information about the Seal. Indeed, he may already have done so, but it suited his new masters to suppress the greater truth.

As appealing as the goat-head hypothesis may be, and it is perfectly realistic, I think it is possible to offer an additional source for the original 'head' accusation. The alternative explanation may seem a little obtuse at first, until we consider the sort of people who might have been spying on the Templars, to inform on what they had seen and overheard. Suppose, for example, a number of Templars had been overheard discussing the rosh (head) we know is contained in B'reishith. If that happened only once or twice, it could create a kind of expectation that would tend to amplify the importance of something else they discussed. Let me be more specific. Bearing in mind the place where the spying took place – mainly or entirely in France – there is a way in which the French word tête (head) could easily have been heard by mistake. Should any Templar have been careless enough to speak about the geometrical properties of the Seal, it is inevitable the word tetrahedron (plural: tetrahedra) would emerge. Not only does this word begin with the syllable that sounds like tête, it also includes a badly pronounced English 'head'. Also, in the plural (tetrahedra) both are followed by a 'ra' that might be construed as a foreign god, namely the Egyptian Sun God. This, in itself, could have set alarm bells ringing in ecclesiastical circles, owing to the Roman Church having once displaced, or absorbed, several versions of sun worship. Incidentally, one of them was Sol Invictus from which Christianity adopted 25th December to celebrate the birth of Christ. That date is very close to the Winter Solstice, the day of shortest daylight, after which the sun moves noticeably higher in the sky with each passing day.

The Templars' accusers would have been pleased with every scrap of additional evidence that came their way. And their would-be witness(es) most certainly knew French, and might know enough English to be misled into thinking they had heard the word 'head' (pronounced *heed*) in an unfamiliar dialect. But it is less likely they would have been familiar enough with the Greek names of geometrical Platonic solids to avoid misunderstanding those. The fact that two and two made five would have suited King Philip all the way to the execution pyres. It gave him just enough plausible evidence of idol-worship on which his interrogators could build their whole case. And all additional talk of sodomy, magical practices and devil-worship were no more than standard window-dressing in those circumstances.

Notice especially that I have not introduced a new conspiracy here. The basic factual skeleton already exists as recorded history, but has lacked the flesh of detail that would bring it to life. The Seal, as we now know it, contains two clear pieces of information that establish the true nature of the Templar secret, and explain the more realistic of the charges levelled against them. One is the combination of head and he-goat, and the other the tetrahedral nature of the Seal (just one of four tetrahedra the Torah manifests).

Almost regardless of how much truth was available to King Philip, he certainly had a streak of theatre in his psychological makeup, choosing the date on which to act to be a Friday the 13th. But why did he then hold the last Templar Grand Master for seven more years before finally putting him to death? The answer may just be found in another characteristic of the Torah's first word. As qatan letter values the same word that provides 'head' and 'he-goat' also converts to a sequence 221314, that is after converting to left to right order. The central 13 (the original arrest date) comes from the letters of אֵשׁ / esh / fire, and 1314 is the year in which Jacques de Molay was finally burned at the stake. By waiting until that year, Philip may have been sending a coded message to the surviving Templars, that he was not completely in the dark about their secret. Recall that 1314 is 73×18, just as 666 is 37×18. In the end, the King did not live long enough to enjoy his 'victory'. The final poetic irony is that King Philip IV (Le Bel) of France and Pope Clement V both died later in the same year.

Before we move on to other topics, it is only fair that I play a small part in setting the record straight about the principal role of the Templar Knights. After all, the popular conception seems to be that their main interests lay in accumulating wealth and guarding a dangerous secret. In truth, the Templars were both pious Christians and honourable soldiers. In military terms, they were clever strategists. Yet when, against their advice, foolish and arrogant crusader leaders chose to leap headlong into senseless battles, the Templars' sworn duty often led to them throwing their weight behind a doomed enterprise. In doing so, they often shed much of their own blood. It is high time the Knights Templar received proper credit for their considerable services to the western Christian world, instead of misplaced suspicions of baser motives. As to their supposed heresy, they were surely only guilty of showing a deep respect for a particularly inspiring example of the handiwork of the God of the three mono-theistic, Abrahamic religions. At any time from 1139 onwards, the Church in Rome could have grasped the nettle and put right its impoverished teaching. Instead, one Pope after another swept the issue under the carpet, until the only way out of their dilemma was the crucifixion of the innocent.

-oOo-

Once a copy of the Author's Seal had become isolated from its proper cultural roots, it soon found expression in non-biblical myths and legends. Again, we are drawn to the French city of Troyes, which had been the home of the Templars' first Grand Master, Hugh of Payns, as well as their chief architect Hugh, Count of Champagne. We have already noted that Troyes had been the home of Rashi, the celebrated Torah commentator, and that the English scholar of Hebrew the Abbot Stephen Harding had attended the Church Council of Troyes.

From the time the Order of the Poor Fellow-Soldiers was formed in 1118, the Count of Champagne is known to have travelled to and from the Holy Land three times. There are many simple reasons why he might have done so. But the varied, long-standing link between Hebrew texts and the city of Troyes gives us grounds for supposing relevant information of this type was being traded constantly between the two centres. The important question is what could have happened to the information after it reached France?

Two generations after Count Hugh, the court in Champagne was graced with the presence of one of the earliest of the great French writers, Chrétien of Troyes (Chrétien = Christian). Chrétien's chief penchant seems to have been for poetry in rhyming, eight-syllable couplets, often consisting of many thousands of lines. He has also been credited with the unofficial title of 'inventer of the modern novel'. The best work of Chrétien is dated between about 1170 and 1191 and includes *Lancelot, the knight of the Cart* and *Perceval, the Story of the Grail,* among others that also cross-refer to the so-called Arthurian legends. The provenance of stories in this vein appears extremely incestuous, drawing on existing material from diverse sources, but mainly from throughout north-western Europe. Likewise, Chrétien's own output has been adapted and extended across the succeeding centuries. Even the two epic poems mentioned above were not actually completed by Chrétien. In the case of 'Perceval', other writers went on to add about six times more material than Chrétien had written himself, in what have been called the Four Continuations. All in all, the Arthurian Legends we know today are a mish-mash of Chinese whispers.

On the other hand, students of the genre have been able to unpick many of the tangled threads in those stories and, to some extent, to work out their provenance. Unfortunately, with the work of Chrétien that has been about the only available recourse, since he was unusually parsimonious with details of his sources. There are, however, certain motifs in the literature, which indicate strongly that his sources include material that came from the Knights Templar, during the time their channel of communication from the Holy Land had been open. That is, material which includes a phenomenon I now describe as the Author's Seal on the Hebrew Torah. The access that Chrétien had to remaining members of the court of Hugh, Count of Champagne probably proved decisive to the survival of the northern European copy of the Seal, though only as a ghostly shadow of its true self.

The literary context is quite straightforward; King Arthur heads a court of the most heroic and chivalrous knights imaginable, not unlike the high ideals of the Poor Fellow-Soldiers of Jesus Christ and the Temple. Into that setting, now introduce some more mystical and esoteric elements: the sword Excalibur, a Fisher King and the Grail, or Graal (not initially described as holy). The fact is that some of these concepts appear to have been drawn straight from the Seal. Take the case of Excalibur. Later elaborations on the legend posit two alternative origins; one being 'the sword in the stone' and the other 'the Lady in the Lake'. Some authorities see these as different swords, and in the 15th century *Morte Arthure*, the second sword is known as Clarent.

The Seal is much clearer than that. In its G2 aspect, the fifth horizontal row from the bottom includes the emergent חרב / *cherev* / a sword (darker shading in Figure 10.1), enclosed between the letters of אש / *esh* / fire. From a biblical perspective, in Chapter 5 we interpreted this conjunction as the 'flaming sword which turned every way, to keep the way of the Tree of Life' (see Genesis 3:24). But in the G1 square, the very same five elements contained two particularly

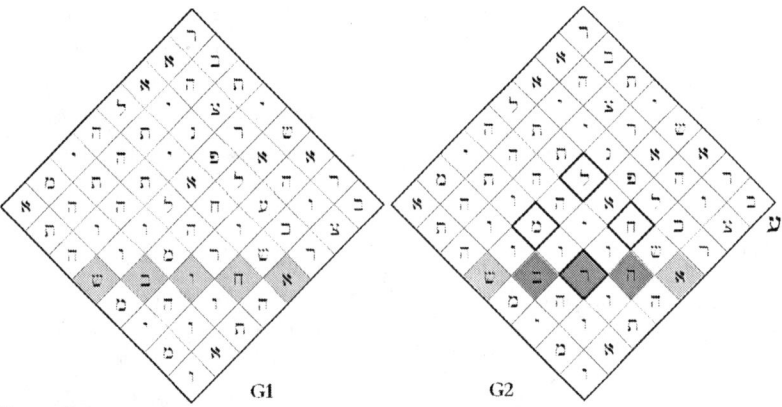

**Figure 10.1**

relevant, mutually overlapping, three-letter words. One was שבו / *shebu* / sparkling gem, and the other אחו / *achu* / a bulrush. Figure 10.1 shows the relevant row highlighted in both G1 and G2.

In the original context we associated both the sparkling gem and the bulrush with the story of Moses. Now, however, we are in a position to recognise an alternative association between these words, and the superimposed sword of G2, relevant to their collective adoption into mediaeval mythology. *Shebu*, the 'sparkling gem' is undoubtedly a gem *stone*, a stone in which the sword is embedded. On the other hand, the bulrush is now supposed to be growing at the edge of a lake in which the sword is concealed, submerged. Recall that, in both the G1 and G2 aspects of the Seal, all the water (letter vav) is confined to their lower halves. Thus, all the Arthurian requirements are in place apart from, perhaps, the identity of the Lady of the Lake. She is explained by the presence of the word רחם / *racham* / a womb just above the sword in G2 (the lower three letters with heavier borders in Figure 10.1). In fact the letter reysh of racham is shared as the middle letter of cherev (sword). The womb we see here is not a linear arrangement, but occupies the same three positions as the upper 'V' portion of the crucified man in G1. This womb (Lady) is also just below the surface of the water (lake).

In the absence of knowledge of the Seal, the concept of the Fisher King has been attributed to a number of possible origins. These include Celtic mythology, Christian symbolism or a French play on words (*pêcheur* = fisher; *pêcheur* = sinner). Clearly the second and third of these suggestions would both fit with the content of the G3/4 facet of the Seal. These two aspects both depict an elevated, exalted man (a second 'Y' shape), standing upon the lower waters and from whom emanates the ⋙ fish shape formed from two entwined copies of the word ארבע / *arba* / <u>four</u> (see Figure 10.2). Without doubt, the fish could represent the reformed sinners who are to be raised out of the waters that are beneath the firmament, up to the waters that are above the firmament of heaven. The view in Figure 10.2 is, of course, the only aspect of the Seal which reveals a linear copy of the four-letter name, יהוה / *YHWH* / <u>The Lord</u>. Notice particularly a group of three letters, רתכ, underlined in the left side. When written in reverse, these spell the emergent word כתר / *keter* / <u>a crown</u> in which the letter *reysh* (ר) is shared with the image of the fish where it is pivotal. It is this combination of fish and crown with the exalted man that must have inspired Chrétien to develop his idea for the Fisher King. Later, the crown will be found to have an additional meaning.

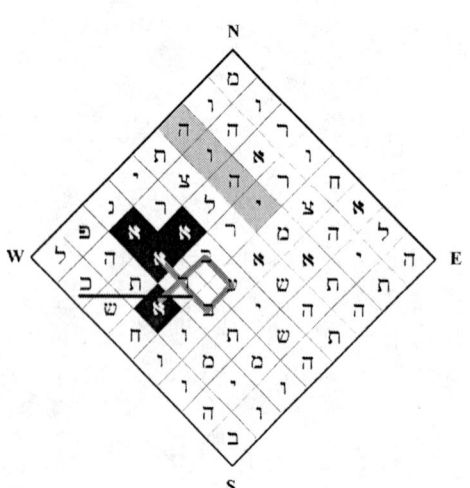

**Figure 10.2**

As for the Grail, it has always eluded a proper explanation, simply because it was not satisfactorily defined at the outset. It was Chrétien who, in Perceval, the Story of the Grail first introduced the word to the growing Arthurian literature. In it, Perceval stays overnight in the castle of the Fisher King where, with each course of a meal, he sees a vision of a ritual procession in which magnificent objects are carried from one chamber to another. First, a young man passes by carrying a bleeding lance then, later, two boys carrying candelabra. Finally, a beautiful young woman passes by carrying an ornately decorated Grail containing a single communion wafer of the holy sacrament that has the power to sustain the wounded father of the Fisher King.

Christian symbolism abounds in this description, notwithstanding the candelabrum which is easily identified in the G1 square as the seven-branched Menorah of the Temple in Jerusalem (see Chapter 2). Its vertical stem originates in the lower 'ו ו ו' or 666 sequence, and two of its branches (nos. 3 and 5) are perfectly superimposed on the outstretched arms of the crucified man. The four outer branches align with the regular order of the inserted text in the two outer layers of the square. As to the reason why Perceval saw two boys carrying candelabra, the G1 square contains exactly two emergent copies of the word אור / *aur* / <u>light</u>. We have already noted that one piece of gossip used against the Templars had been that the head they worshipped would be carried into a ceremony by a priest, preceded by two brothers carrying a candelabrum bearing two large candles. That accusation was brought by a Templar sergeant, one Stephen of Troyes, more than a century after Chrétien. And, while it is not an explicit reference to the Seal, it does appear to link the Templar trials to Chrétien's earlier writing, using known attributes of the Seal. If nothing else, this case of mis-reported information will surely serve as a salutary warning against misuse of the Seal, including its concealment 'under a bushel'.

I have no wish to suggest that Chrétien had any other purpose than to preserve important ideas that would already have been familiar to his immediate audience. He perhaps did not feel it was his responsibility if the original rationale failed to transfer to a wider audience; even though it was this subterfuge that has led to the loss of his true source of inspiration. History will determine whether it was right or decent for Chrétien to subvert sacred texts to a secular mythology. Although we should be alert to the possibility (likelihood even) that he was writing 'to order' and had been sworn to secrecy regarding his principal source. At best, secrecy leads to misunderstandings, and at worst to thoughts of conspiracy and unwarranted persecution.

The bleeding lance in the procession may be understood as the spear of the Roman soldier, who used it to pierce Christ's side. The depiction of the crucified man by the Seal utilises five copies of the letter vav (symbolically a spike), corresponding to the five piercing wounds.

Finally, we come to the ill-defined Grail itself, and the wafer it contained. To demonstrate the inspiration for this, Figure 10.3 repeats information about the G2 aspect of the Seal, which we analysed at Chapter 5.

Here, the operative elements have again been given heavier borders. It is clear that these four letters include positions which, in G1, were the upper 'V' portion of the crucified man. In that setting, the numerical 1-6-6-6 equivalent (the '1' digit at top) made this a 616 over 666. The same digits as 1.666, over and above their arresting configuration, also cooperated in G1 to define the relative dimensions of the Ark of the Covenant, one of the chief artefacts of the Temple. The number 1.666 is, of course, a truncated decimal form of the ratio 5/3, generated by the positions of the Menorah branches that correspond to the arms of the crucified man. Linguistically, in the G2 square shown as Figure 10.3, the same four elements now confer לחם / *lechem* / <u>bread</u>

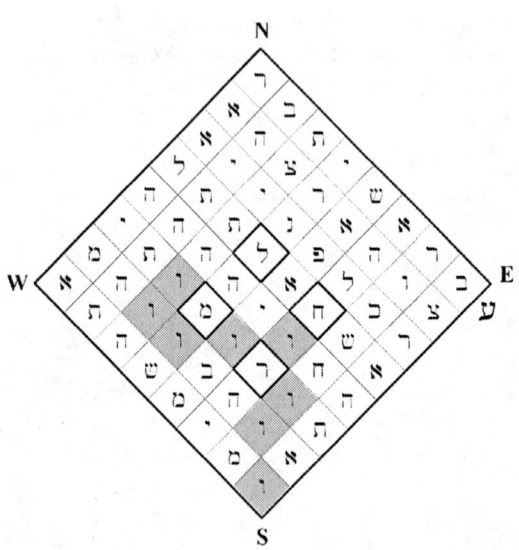

Figure 10.3

(when the lowest element is excluded) and רחם / *racham* / <u>a womb</u> (excluding the uppermost element). A distinct pattern is beginning to emerge. The womb that may properly represent the young mother of Jesus, but recently identified the Lady of the Lake, now does the same for the beautiful young woman who carries the Grail in the procession. Anyone familiar with Dan Brown's blockbuster bestseller *The DaVinci Code* will immediately recognise the juxtaposed symbols of the sacred feminine ( V ) and masculine ( ∧ ) – bread rising. The G2 square brings the same symbolism to life in language, with the beautiful young woman (womb) seen bearing the wafer of the sacrament (bread). This 'V' shape, when set atop the same stem as the Menorah (candelabrum) of G1 is the perfect explanation for why the Holy Grail has become synonymous with a cup or chalice.

Brown and other more serious authors[1] would have us believe the womb was that of Mary Magdalene, that she was pregnant and carried the blood-line of Jesus Christ to France and thence into the Merovingian dynasty. Chrétien of Troyes was less ambitious, merely creating a mythical world based, surely, on an even fresher understanding of the same source material. Knowing the background and courtly connections of Chrétien, it no longer appears a mystery that most of the Seal-based myths and legends are set or seem to have originated in France. The poet himself chose to develop French characters in an English setting. Perhaps, with an early form of nationalistic pride, he saw them acting in a missionary capacity.

There are a number of important facts we may disentangle from the writings of Chrétien. As we have already observed, the first is that in some way, mediaeval Europe had come to know of the rich content within the first few words of Genesis. That in itself is enough to make the point that the Seal can be recognised for what it is in any age and by any culture. Nor is it necessary to identify every aspect of the Seal to appreciate its enormous potential; for example, there is little evidence that Chrétien had any inkling of the vast numerical dimension underlying the text of the Seal.

Another lesson is in the range of concepts Chrétien was able to draw upon, from the same source. We can tell from his references to a sword in a stone, and a Lady in the Lake that he was aware of both the G1 and G2 squares. And this, in turn, tells us something about his conceptual understanding. That is because the transition from G1 to G2 is partly dependent on an awareness of kabbalistic concepts, most notably the Vast Face/Small Face duality of the creator. What is not entirely clear is whether all that knowledge came ready-made from the Holy Land, or whether it might have involved some subsequent analysis and interpretation. Comparison of Old Testament prophets' writings with the Seal could indicate that all its aspects were already known to them, and that the Knights Templar probably found documents in Jerusalem that revealed the full range of knowledge we have been considering. One way or another, we have good evidence that the G1/G2/G3 & G4 aspects of the text were all known by the time Chrétien wrote about the Fisher King and the Grail mysteries.

One thing is, however, quite clear. Present day writers do not mention even briefly the phenomenon I call the Author's Seal. No-one admits to knowing about this miraculous artefact that has been the unwilling accomplice in so much familiar myth and legend. It is high

---

[1] Notably Michael Baigent, Richard Leigh and Henry Lincoln, authors of *The Holy Blood and the Holy Grail*

time the true nature of the Seal came into the light of day, so that many blind speculations may give way to a more informed kind of study.

-oOo-

Jewish Kabbalah would seem to share the same provenance, as already implied by Chapter 5 in several ways. Kabbalah posits the separation of the Creator into Small Face within his creation, and Vast Face on the outside. The Author's Seal on the start of Genesis mirrors this belief in no less than four ways:

1. The transformation of the G1 aspect of the Seal into G2 was accomplished by the migration of the sole letter *ayin* to a position just outside. Kabbalah regards the letter *ayin* as the proper symbol for Vast Face.

2. As a prefix on the start of the Torah, the migrated *ayin* completes the word ארבע / *arba* / <u>four</u>, which begins with the letter *aleph*, the symbol for Small Face in Kabbalah. This letter *aleph* is, of course, within the word B'reishith on the inside of creation, yet intimately linked to the external Vast Face.

3. The insertion of Genesis 1:2 into the G1 and G2 aspects of the Seal truncates the text in the middle of the word *Elohim* (ie God). So that God is simultaneously both within and without.

4. Another consequence of 3. is that the 'face of the deep' is retained on the inside, but a 'face of the waters' is excluded. Why else could Kabbalah have chosen the word *face* to represent this otherwise mystifying concept?

The first documented stirrings of Kabbalah concepts emerged in the late 12th Century, around the same time that Chrétien was adding to the Arthurian legends. And there are enough points of contact between the Seal and the concepts listed above to suggest that Kabbalah is also founded in the same manuscripts discovered by the Knights Templar beneath the Temple in Jerusalem.

About one century later, a certain Moses de Léon in northern Spain wrote an enigmatic book called the Zohar, which was destined to become the central text of subsequent Jewish Kabbalah. This Moses wrote the Zohar in Aramaic, a language that is similar to Hebrew, but virtually unknown in mediaeval Europe. However, Aramaic had been very much alive in First Century Israel when the Templar treasure is most likely to have been buried. So it is reasonable to surmise that Moses de Léon had access to copies of those very manuscripts. And the timing of his work suggests they had come to him via Troyes. For obvious reasons modern commentators, lacking awareness of the Seal, have attributed the inspiration of Moses de Léon to nothing more than his own vivid imagination. However, that view is now evidently due a radical overhaul.

Before I go on to expand on the direct links between the Seal and Kabbalah, it is appropriate to recall that the length of the whole Torah also connects them indirectly. As described in Chapter 5, the total number of Torah letters (ie 304,805) bequeathes a geometric shape (two intersecting pentagons) that has a numerical affinity for the 8×8 square Seal, and a graphical resemblance to the same Tree of Life of Kabbalah seen at Figure 10.4. This Tree of Life is often described as the Ten Sephirot, and four of the names of the Sephirot can be recognised from the G3 aspect of the Seal.

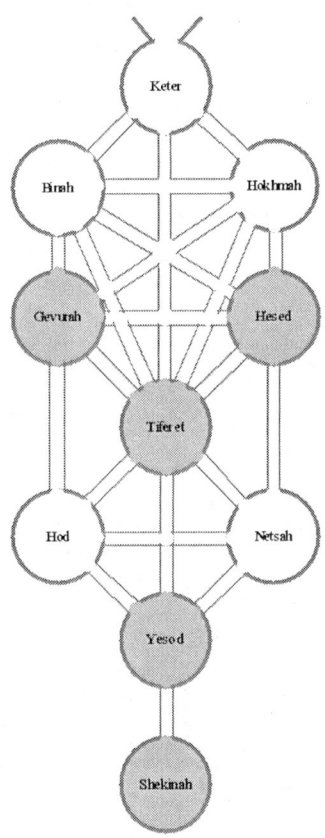

Figure 10.5 (overleaf) draws attention to the western quadrant of the G3 square, with a thumbnail sketch alongside to indicate the positions of letters that are especially relevant. Notice that this quadrant fully incorporates the immensely important *exultant man clothed in linen*, seen as a 'Y' shaped configuration of the letter *aleph* (א). And the same general shape is visible in Figure 10.4 as the shaded elements. Nor should we forget that *aleph* is the symbol of Small Face in Kabbalah. Now, with reference to Figure 10.5, consider the letters that correspond to positions 5-10-15 in the thumbnail sketch. This linear sequence spells כתר / *keter* / a crown, and is the name of the first *sephirah* (singular of sephirot) at the very top of the Tree. Recall that this uppermost component was missing from the overlapping pentagonal numbers mentioned above. The only other component of the Tree of Life that was missing from the overlapping pentagons was the lowest, called שכינה / *Shekinah*.

**Figure 10.4**

Therefore, note that these five letters are also seen in the topical quadrant, at positions 9-5-4-3-6 in Figure 10.5. Recall also from Chapter 7 that both Shekinah and *Mishkan* (The Tabernacle) derive from [ן] שכנ / *shakan* / <u>a dwelling</u> (9-5-3 in Figure 10.5), which links the G3 square to the following passage:

> *And he* [Japheth] *shall dwell in the tents of Shem.*
>
> (Genesis 9:27)

The expression 'he shall dwell' in this verse is rendered by *vayishkan*, grammatically based upon *shakan*. It is, therefore, highly significant that the linear באהל / *b'ohel* / <u>in a tent</u> (1-6-11-16) is a diagonal of the topical quadrant, and יפת / *Japheth* (10-2-4) is found at the corners of the included 3×3 group that contains a cyclic [ן] הארנ / *ha'aron* / <u>The Ark</u> (of the Covenant).

The same quadrant of G3 also contains the names of two more of the Sephirot (in addition to *Shekinah* and the linear *Keter*). The word בינה / *Binah* / <u>Understanding</u> is spelled with elements 6-3-4-16; and

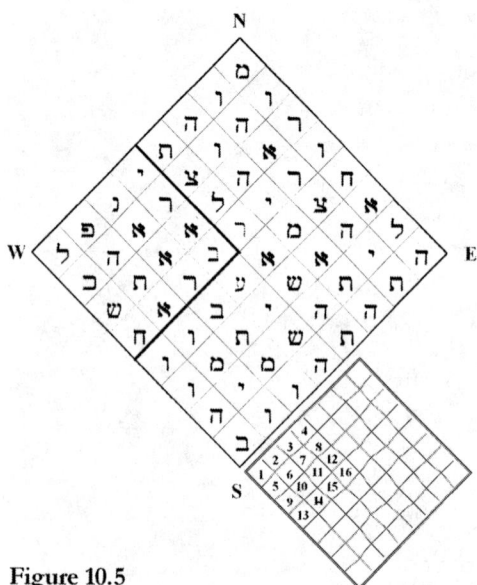

**Figure 10.5**

תפארת / *Tiferet* / <u>beauty</u> is spelled with elements 10-15-(7, 11, 12 or 14)-2-10. Here the same letter is utilised in both first and last positions.

To be quite realistic, none of the above will determine whether or not Kabbalah is a valid form of Torah study, since we may see this analysis in two ways. On the one hand, there are reasons to believe that Kabbalah derived some of its core concepts from the four square views of the Seal. That would help to explain the design of the Tree of Life and some of the names given to the Sephirot, not to mention the Small Face/Vast Face duality. It also says something about the vivid imagination of Moses de Léon. Couple the above possibilities with the dating of the emergence of Kabbalah, and it becomes more likely that knowledge of the Author's Seal came to light through the agency of the Templars.

On the other hand, the links made by the topical quadrant between *dwelling*, *tent*, *Japheth* and *Ark* (of the Covenant) show only that the Author intended his Seal as a blueprint for the Torah and all his temples. These associations are largely in addition to connections we examined in chapters 1 to 7.

Seen from this perspective, Kabbalah is undoubtedly a commentary on the Torah, albeit an indirect, esoteric commentary perhaps befitting the nature of the Seal. That does not necessarily make Kabbalah a legitimate commentary; but it is a major improvement over its previous status of having no certain pedigree.

In common with many other examples from history, the writings of both Chrétien and Moses de Léon still survive, while the source manuscripts that inspired them have been lost to us. However, it is not just the timing that points to their having both been inspired by the Author's Seal. The fact that the Seal demonstrably has been able to provide two such writers with so much choice of material is just as revealing. The two barely overlap at all with one another, but both do overlap significantly with my own descriptions of the Author's Seal on the Torah. As with the books of Ezekiel and Revelation, their differences reveal just as much as anything they share in common.

-oOo-

The transition from Hebrew documents held in Troyes in the north of France, to Kabbalah in northern Spain seems at first too long a step to have happened all at once. As yet we have seen no obvious mechanism to account for a leap of that distance with no intermediate influence. In such circumstances, recorded history often gives way to a free-for-all of speculation, in which romantic literature and conspiracy theories thrive. So, it is reassuring to find that history itself provides a fairly detailed background that fills the apparent vacuum.

It is interesting to ponder how 12th and 13th century Christendom might have responded to knowledge of sacred wisdom encrypted in the Bible. The Seal on the Hebrew Torah self-evidently confirms many of the narrative episodes in both the Old and New Testaments. Yet the Church itself either *is* ignorant or feigns ignorance of this mystifying artefact. The Church moreover, for whatever reasons, has declined to acknowledge the existence of the Seal, even when opportunities have arisen.

Certain free-thinking individuals (rare in those times) therefore must have worked independently to adapt the established Church doctrine to take account of this divine message from the Creator. Who knows how many alternative interpretations may have been considered

- perhaps as many as the number of different Christian denominations that exist today. But there was one in particular, known by several names, which had an enormous impact at the time.

The new-style Christianity of the Cathars[u] developed a presence in many parts of Europe, including Flanders and the Rhineland in the north, Aragon and Catalonia in Spain, and Lombardy and Tuscany in Italy. But the principal centre of Catharism is recognised as having been the Languedoc (from 'Langue d'Oc', language of Occitania) in what is now southern France. And, as with many such innovations, the timing of its emergence is especially significant. Catharism sprang into being in the mid-to-late 12th century, again coincidental with the time that the Templars' 'treasure' had recently reached the court of Champagne. It was also not very long after the confrontation in 1139 between Robert of Craon (the then Templar Grand Master) and Pope Innocent II, which had led to unprecedented fiscal and pastoral concessions for the Templars. So, if we are looking for a reason why the secret knowledge should have escaped its northern European custodians, the crisis and confusion caused by Robert's disclosure to the Church just might have provoked the right conditions. But that is merely circumstantial, and does not prove that the Cathar religion was one of the outcomes. There are, however, four other facts that point to the Seal being at the root of the development of Catharism.

For one, Abbot Bernard of Clairvaux is known to have used the term 'Albigensian' of the Cathars, although he need not have invented that name himself. This is the same Abbot Bernard who had been instrumental in installing the Poor Fellow Soldiers of Jesus Christ in the Temple in Jerusalem. And it seems odd that he, of all church representatives should have taken a direct and, it seems, active interest in so remote an issue. Odd, that is, unless he had a personal stake in the background circumstances, having been a key custodian of the knowledge the Church hoped would remain secret.

Second, the new sect often called themselves *Bons Hommes*, *Bonnes Femmes* or, collectively, *Bons Chrétiens* (Good Christians). This could, of course, be a straightforward statement of their self-image. Or it might be a pointed reference to a specific source of the leaked secret – Chrétien of Troyes.

Perhaps the most intriguing fact about the Cathars is that they, like the Templars, were reputed to be in possession of a great treasure. If

---

[u] **Cathar** - from the Greek: καθαρός (catharos) meaning pure or clean. Whoever coined this Greek name may have been among the first to suspect the much-loved Latin language as having become the Church's smoke-screen to mask an inconvenient truth.

we accept that the Cathar treasure was the same secret knowledge – the Seal, and God's blueprint for the Temple of Zion – it would help to explain not only their origin, but also a later mysterious event. By the latter end of the 12<sup>th</sup> century, the rapid spread of Catharism came to be seen as a serious challenge to the Catholic Church. So much so that, from 1205, the new Pope Innocent III called for a Crusade to be preached against them. The so-called Albigensian Crusade turned into a particularly bloody affair in which as many as a million people are believed to have died. And, like the Templars a century later, many of them were accused of heresy and burned at the stake. While these executions did not fully peter out until 1329, the serious military campaign had already ended with the siege of Montségur. And it is here that we encounter the suggestion of a Cathar treasure.

Montségur is a large steep hill or small mountain in the northern foothills of the Pyrenees, and was already equipped with a hill-top fortress. The last really significant, organised group of surviving Cathars took up their final refuge at Montségur in May 1243, and held out against 10,000 French troops for nine months. In the final days before their surrender, it is recorded that a small group of about three Cathar *Parfaits* (Perfects) slipped quietly out of their hilltop refuge and through the French lines, carrying their precious treasure. What that treasure was or how, in those circumstances, it could have been carried by so small a party has never been explained. Speculations on the nature of the treasure include esoteric or Gnostic literature, or the Holy Grail. And it is this latter suggestion that may hold the key to the Cathars' origins, since the first ever mention of a Grail came from Chrétien of Troyes. And that was around the same time that Catharism arrived on the scene. But that was a deviant mythology; whereas the Cathars themselves, we may assume, were in possession of the pure knowledge of the Seal. They may even have acquired original manuscripts retrieved by the Templars from beneath the Temple in Jerusalem. That could certainly account for the importance of their 'treasure', when there were no doubt plenty of faithful copies of the Seal in existence. The Church may have considered the original documents more of a threat than contemporary replicas.

Fourthly, aspects of Cathar beliefs provide hints as to which parts of the Seal influenced them most. We do, however, need to be ultra-cautious about drawing too many hard and fast conclusions. This is partly because the Cathar religion was a human interpretation and, inevitably, subject to possible mis-interpretation. In fact, it is quite possible that some of their interpretations had been adopted specifically to counter particular tenets of Catholic dogma. It is widely accepted that the Cathars were openly critical of the established

Church for its institutionalised corruption in almost every sphere of its activity, including the spiritual. Another reason for circumspection in assessing Cathar beliefs is, of course, that history records mainly the Church's views on the subject.

What we do know is that the Cathars believed our material world to be a false creation by a lesser and perhaps evil god. In effect, God's original, more perfect spiritual creation had become corrupted by the coarse material world. Then life in our physical existence is tantamount to the soul being imprisoned in an imperfect body. The aim of a Cathar *Parfait* was to overcome the vices that bind the soul to the body so that, upon death, the soul might escape an endless cycle of reincarnation. The nearest equivalent concepts in the Seal are:

(i)     In G1, the אור / *aur* / <u>light</u> displaced from the 666 stem of the crucified man, seen ascending in opposition to the descending עור / *aur* / <u>skin</u>. Here, Christ the pioneer is demonstrating how to exchange garments of flesh for perfect garments of light.

(ii)    In G2, the *lamed* (ל)-shaped river ascending, passes through the word [ם] רחם / *racham* / <u>a womb</u>; new birth in a perfect body, as opposed to resurrection in the old body.

(iii)   The 4×7 matrix of qatan letter values obtained from Genesis 1:1 contained the image of the cunning serpent almost identical in shape to the lamed-shaped river. And, as we know, the encounter with the serpent in the Garden of Eden is what led to the primordial Man and Woman being given garments of skin (Genesis 3:21).

Unlike in the Church, on the strength of point (ii) both men and women Cathars could become parfaits, and be entitled to teach with authority.

Given that Church doctrine is founded on resurrection of the physical body, the alternative Cathar beliefs derived from canonical scripture (ie Genesis 1:1-2), simply could not be tolerated. This scenario must have been even worse for the Church than the one time existence of alternative gospels, which were assumed to have been driven out of existence by the 3rd Century.

The historical record suggests that the Cathars, like certain Gnostic gospels, saw the perfect creator God only in the New Testament. The god of the Old Testament was the imperfect demiurge that had succeeded in corrupting the original perfection. But even if this *was* their belief, it is still possible that the Cathars may have recognised an initial perfection in the early part of Genesis, where God is known as Elohim. This God made every herb bearing seed, and every tree bearing fruit to be meat for man to eat. So the Cathars shunned only flesh for meat, and animal products like milk, cheese and butter, that are connected with the reproductive process (this is because reproduction produced more prisons of flesh in which to trap souls). In most of the Old Testament, 'God' is designated YHWH; and it may have been only YHWH that the Cathars believed to be a false and often capricious god.

Clearly, it is not necessary to agree with all the Cathars' interpretations while still accepting that they had knowledge of the Seal on the Hebrew Torah – maybe the only part of the Torah that seemed acceptable to them. In any case, not all Cathar communities arrived at identical conclusions in their beliefs. What is important from our point of view is that Catharism may have unknowingly fulfilled an incidental purpose. They may have provided the cultural bridge linking the court of the Count of Champagne, where the Seal gave rise to a literary mythology, and northern Spain where it gave rise to the alternative Jewish Kabbalah. But notice that the spread of Catharism merely provides a bridge for the transmission of something we believe already exists. It is only our new knowledge of the true nature of the Seal that now allows us to recognise the common origin of Kabbalah, Catharism and the Arthurian Legends. And as usual, the Seal links them more by their differences than by their similarities. In fact, the Seal gives us fresh insights into aspects of human history and literature that could even extend back as much as four thousand years. By itself, this would not *prove* that the Seal is a supernatural revelation; but it does suggest it has been recognised as something very remarkable by societies that are as far apart as they possibly can be, culturally, geographically and temporally.

-oOo-

Apart from Kabbalah and the surviving works of Chrétien of Troyes, once the Knights Templar and the short-lived Cathar religion had been eliminated the short period of enlightenment gave way once more to ignorance. Nothing more was heard about the existence of the Seal for several centuries. Then, in the 19th century a parody of the Seal emerged in England, in the form of occult studies and practices including Wicca (and other neo-pagan beliefs) and the more sinister Satanism.

One common factor shared by many of those reborn beliefs was a recognition of the importance of the pentagram, which we examined in Chapter 8. What set the Satanists apart from the others, however, was the way they linked the pentagram to some of the charges that had been levelled against the Templars more than five centuries before. At a stroke, the earlier false accusations were resurrected and adapted to latter-day black symbolism and ritual that are now a matter of clear record.

The satanists' version of the pentagram has two points uppermost, and a goat head seen within it, as shown in Figure 10.6. And to complete the Templar association, the Satanists named this emblem The Sigil of Baphomet. The word 'sigil' means a seal, and Baphomet is the name coined during the Templar heresy trials, and may have been derived from a Hebrew transliteration of the Greek Sophia (ie wisdom), using the atbash cipher. But note that the inventer of the satanic Sigil of Baphomet would not have needed any mystical, arcane wisdom, just a little classical geometry and the records of the Templar trials.

**Figure 10.6**

Incidentally, at one time the pentagram had been revered as a symbol for good in both Judaism and Christianity. I have seen this symbol made into the stone frame of a church window in Tomar[v], in central Portugal. However, the rise of Satanism led to the symbol being dropped by the Roman Church as recently as the 20th Century. How is it possible to explain such a display of fragile insecurity?

Wicca is more benign than satanism. Alongside the unadorned pentagram (no goat head) there sits a belief in the sanctity of the divine feminine as the equal of the divine masculine. A union of the two is symbolised in Wicca by the dipping of a sharply pointed knife into a chalice of wine, representing a womb. As we now know, both Christianity and the Seal substitute bread for the knife; but otherwise the correspondence is exact and unmistakable.

-oOo-

Outside of Judaism, Freemasonry in its many forms may be the last institutional custodian of knowledge obtained from the Seal. There is much in Masonic symbolism that we should recognise from our earlier analysis of the Seal. There is also a legend relating to the construction of an ancient temple, that freemasons hold as evidence of

---

[v] For a time, Tomar was the main centre for the Knights Templar in Portugal, later re-formed by King Diniz I as the Knights of Christ. And Tomar is still the site of the oldest surviving synagogue in Portugal.

their roots in antiquity. And it is possible to see how that legend too could have sprung from knowledge of the Seal. But let me start with the more common Masonic symbols.

There are many examples of Masonic symbolism in the public domain; though many of them will be subject to Copyright restrictions on their reproduction. In the normal course of events, the Copyright on Masonic emblems is rarely enforced. However, a publication such as this book, which may undermine the *status quo* of secrecy, would be unlikely to go unchallenged. Therefore, I choose not to include any illustrations of Masonic symbolism in my book. Instead, I shall simply list some of the more common symbolic elements and let my reader verify the facts from the ample available literature. The elements I describe here may often be seen in Masonic badges, tracing-boards and ceremonial aprons, as well as in the trappings of Masonic premises where ceremonies are held. They include: a stone-mason's square and compasses; the All-seeing Eye within a 45° right-angle triangle; a handshake; a letter 'G'; a chequered design, similar to a chessboard; two sturdy pillars; and the Sun, Moon and stars. The most surprising thing to note about these symbols is that every one of them is recognisable as a notable characteristic of the Seal in its first two aspects (ie G1 and G2), thus:

1. At the simplest level, the stone-mason's square could represent the many striking square attributes of the Seal, both numeric and graphic, but especially the numerous 45° right-angle triangles it reveals.

2. In the same way, the compasses represent the many ways in which the first Hebrew verse of Genesis, makes known the value of Pi. That is, the ratio of the circumference of any circle to its diameter. But note very particularly that, from Chapter 5 when the first letter *ayin* was migrated to become the prefix to Genesis, it created the three-letter word רבע / *raba* / <u>a square</u>. And the same three letters confer a qatan sequence of 227, suggesting the well known 22/7 approximation for Pi.

3. The All-Seeing Eye often seen overlooking all other symbolic, masonic elements is especially important. Initially, it might be assumed to be a concept borrowed directly from Jewish Kabbalah, the Vast Face aspect of God that remained outside his creation, looking in. But since *ayin* literally means 'an eye', it seems clear that the aforementioned migration of ayin is the single explanation not only for the square and compasses, but for the All-Seeing Eye too.

4. The large letter 'G' ought to be straightforward to explain, except that Freemasonry clouds the issue by suggesting it refers either to God or to Geometry. Whilst either of those suggestions might be credible, together they convey a sense of ambiguity and uncertainty. This is despite the fact that the use of the 'G' is undoubtedly a human contrivance, since the Seal does not include the equivalent Hebrew letter *gimmel*. In any case, it is at least as plausible that the 'G' represents the book of Genesis, the source of the Seal.

5. A hand-shake is undoubtedly symbolic of the unfailing bond between Small Face and Vast Face. The Seal reveals this link in two ways. One is 'the face of the deep' that is always within the Seal, and 'the face of the waters' that is always excluded. The other is the word *arba* (four) that straddles the start of Genesis when the letter *ayin* has been migrated. Arba starts with an *aleph* and ends with the *ayin*, the symbols of Small Face and Vast Face, respectively.

6. A chequered pattern is perhaps the most obvious allusion to the Seal, since every square facet of the Seal shares the same 8×8 chessboard layout. Masonic symbolism again reminds us of the mediaeval illustration of two Templar knights engaged in a game of chess. Especially since Freemasonry sees itself as an hereditary offshoot of the Knights Templar.

7. The two sturdy pillars represent the strength of perfect symmetry, which masons rightly admire. Symmetry is crucially important in the building of temples and cathedrals, and is evident in every aspect of the Seal. A less abstract interpretation is that the pillars are the particular ones built by King Solomon to stand at the inner entrance of the Temple. And the Seal is undoubtedly representative of every aspect of every one of God's temples mentioned in the Bible. It is also important that the biblical books of Ezekiel and Revelation both present their authors with a vision of a temple. And each author is instructed to measure its layout, one with a rod and the other with a reed. Therefore the measuring of Temple architecture must be considered by the Bible to be a legitimate activity in the pursuit of wisdom.

8. The Sun and Moon extend the emphasis on symmetry, as they are created in the fourth day of the Bible's creation account. That is the pivotal mid-point of creation, and includes previously un-recognised symmetrical attributes that I describe in Chapter 5. Genesis pointedly does not name the

Sun and Moon, calling them simply 'two great lights'. This is normally taken to be a polemic against neighbouring cultures' tendency to revere the Sun and Moon. However, it now seems just as likely to be linked to the presence in the G1 square of two emergent copies of the word אור / *aur* / light. Therefore, by depicting Sun and Moon, freemasonry is acknowledging the two lights within the Seal.

9. The use of stars in Masonic symbolism acknowledges the presence within the Seal of geometrical hexagram or Star of David numbers 13, 37, 73, 121 and 35113. It is highly significant that the product 37×73 generates the gematria of Genesis 1:1. And the largest of those numbers is equal to the product 13×37×73, so is composed of stars, within stars, within stars. Also, the distinctively juxtaposed, intersecting square and compasses in Masonic emblems are undoubtedly meant to resemble a Star of David hexagram.

10. Finally, the centre of the G2 square bequeaths the pseudo-history of the notional founder of Freemasonry, as described next, at length.

Freemasonry posits an original founder of their 'Order', known as Hiram Abif, who oversaw the building of Solomon's Temple in Jerusalem. This Hiram is not to be confused with the Lebanese King Hiram who supplied timber from the legendary cedars of Lebanon for use in building the Temple. It is well to recall the many conceptual points of contact between the Seal and all biblical temples, since it is the sacred Seal that is the true foundation of Masonic concepts.

The masonic Hiram was reputed to possess great skill and wisdom. And the basic story goes that one day, at the end of the day Hiram was preparing to leave the Temple when he was set-upon by three ruffians hoping to learn his wisdom. When he refused to divulge his knowledge, Hiram was struck by the first assailant on his right side (or right temple) as he tried to leave by the south gate; but he held onto his secret. Then he was struck on his left side by the second assailant as he tried to leave by the west gate; and again he succeeded in holding onto his secret. Finally, as Hiram tried to leave by the east Gate, the third ruffian struck a fatal blow full on his forehead. But Hiram's secret, sometimes said to be known by two others, did not escape his lips. There are occasional variations on the same basic theme, and one recent alternative even has Hiram in the role of a priest-king in the Temple of Thebes in ancient Egypt.

It should not need repeating how the Seal on the start of Genesis makes numerous cryptic references to the six alternative forms of God's temple. These are: (i) the tabernacle in the desert, (ii) the temple of Solomon, (iii) the second temple in Jerusalem, (iv) the body of Christ, (v) God's temple in heaven and (vi) the new Holy City. The key new fact we may recognise is that the name חירם (Hiram) can be found in the same small area at the centre of the G2 square, where we have just seen a 'womb'. In fact, the three letters of that *racham* are all included in the name Hiram, along with the letter *yud* (י), which is at the very centre of the cluster. This derivation of 'Hiram' is probably better understood as a reference to biblical narrative, and the name of the Lebanese king. The alternative Hiram Abif is a contrivance that we are obliged to recognise only reluctantly, along with the more legitimate artefacts bequeathed by the Seal. However, given that the masonic Hiram was assaulted at the gates of his temple, we should note that the emergent word שער / *sha'ar* / a gate is seen in the G3/4 squares (see Chapter 7, Figure 7.11) precisely where G2 has three of the letters of 'Hiram'.

All of this constitutes evidence that Freemasonry has been aware of all the square aspects of the Seal described in this book, but not that they accept its fundamental, underlying message. For all-round recognition of Seal characteristics, Masonic symbolism and its pseudo-history are uniquely comprehensive. The Seal is indeed the blueprint for all five biblical temples. Yet Freemasonry signally fails to acknowledge the Hebrew Bible's central role in its foundation.

-oOo-

There are now excellent reasons for believing that the treasure discovered by the Poor Fellow-Soldiers of Jesus Christ under the Temple Mount in Jerusalem was not gold, nor a physical head, but the long-lost sacred knowledge of the Author's Seal on the start of the Hebrew Torah. Luke 8:10 records that Jesus would speak to his closest disciples about the deeper secrets (of his kingdom), but to others only in parables, so that they might have only a partial understanding. Certain other gospels that were not adopted into the New Testament canon make further reference to the deeper mysteries, the mystical knowledge or wisdom. And it is now widely believed that the 1st Century AD community of Essenes, driven underground by political pressures and disputes with Jewish orthodoxy, may have been the last of the legitimate guardians of the same Jewish mystical tradition. That is, unless we accept that the first proto-Christian Apostles also secretly carried the same knowledge, which Luke 8:10 suggests we should.

It was, however, the Essenes who secreted documents we now know as the Dead Sea Scrolls, in caves near Qumran. This was not a single cache but several, distributed over a considerable area, no doubt to limit the risk they might all be discovered at once and destroyed. If the Essenes had hoped to recover their property at some later time when more favourable conditions might arise, they under-estimated the dogged persistence of their Roman overlords. The last of that generation of Jewish mystics were driven out of existence, and the Qumran scrolls remained undiscovered until 1947, nearly two thousand years later.

Curiously, among the Dead Sea Scrolls was one in which an ancient form of Hebrew text (with a sparse smattering of Greek letters) was etched on a sheet of copper. The literary content of the so-called Copper Scroll has been likened to a cryptic treasure map, which speaks of sixty-four treasures. That is certainly not the number of hidden scrolls, of which there are known to be over 900. And it is probably not the number of burial sites, of which only 11 have been found at Qumran. On the other hand, 64 *is* the number of letters in the Seal, which the Essenes may have considered both a temple and a priceless treasure. A typical cryptic clue translated from the Copper Scroll reads: *In the mouth of the spring of the Temple: Vessels of silver and gold for tithe and money, the whole being six hundred talents.*

It is now several decades since any new finds have been made at Qumran. But we need not assume that Qumran was the only place of safekeeping chosen by the Essenes. And it would be only natural that they should wish, if it were possible, to site their most precious knowledge within the confines of the Temple in Jerusalem; always presuming they could obtain access and that there was a suitably secure hiding place. If we accept that the Essenes were successful in that endeavour, perhaps with help on the inside, it would offer the most plausible explanation for the 'treasure' found by the Templars in the 12th Century. In the end, however, it matters more *what* the Templars found than who had put it there. What happened next is now a little easier to imagine.

While the Poor Fellow-Soldiers were undoubtedly 'knights' and, at the start, barely literate, they were also a religious order of soldier-monks. If, in their allocated quarters on the Temple Mount, they had come upon the Essenes' most prized possession, they could probably have been trusted to act sensibly and with discretion. The first of the Templars still had good communications with their home base and founder in Troyes in northern France and, therefore, with European scholars of biblical Hebrew. They also quickly developed a respect for other peoples of the Holy Land and no doubt established good relations with indigenous Jews. If anyone at that time could have made the most of the discovery of ancient Hebrew texts, the Templars were more favourably placed than most. Their subsequent history and other events in Europe attest to those documents having included a number of facets of the Seal on the Torah, and probably some accompanying analysis. If the analysis had been absent, then it would no doubt soon have been re-constructed, just as the material for this book has taken only five years to assemble.

Somehow, the re-emergence of the Seal after a thousand years did not have any noticeable long-lasting impact in the Holy Land. Only in Europe can we see evidence that knowledge of the Seal became the seed for several subsequent historical developments and literary outgrowths. This priceless inheritance for all mankind has long ago been unwittingly uprooted from its proper origin and, after the Templars' demise, treated falsely by several undeserving beneficiaries. The greatest need is to rescue the most sacred Torah Seal from its many unworthy usurpers, to afford it the honour it properly deserves but has seldom enjoyed.

To be realistic, I do not expect the established generation of biblical scholars and theologians to embrace these ideas, which are largely at odds with mainstream opinions. However, theirs are deductions that have been forged in a partial vacuum. But the next generation are already among us, representing an opportunity to reassess those deeply entrenched assumptions.

On the other hand, a large number of mainly Jewish and Christian traditions may claim the Seal as their rightful heritage. But no single claim should be allowed to override the legitimacy of any other, at least until a full and open debate has taken place. The organic integrity of the Seal itself does not favour one specific point of view. Everything it shows is the result of the same 64 letters, which introduce an ancient text adopted by a number of alternative traditions. But what it does reveal can be seen to overlap with and partially validate more than one of those competing beliefs. It is plainly apparent that no single faith has either the whole truth, or a monopoly on any one part of the truth. For this reason, I appeal to the followers of all belief systems, and of none, to come together under the banner of the Author's Seal. In fact, it would probably be advisable to include representatives of other subjects, since it is evident that the functions of the Seal extend beyond the normal bounds of religious thought. Their declared aim should be to seek a universal understanding that is as coherent as the Seal itself.

An ideal venue for a first gathering would be Jerusalem, given that legend suggests the Temple will one day be re-established there. However, considering the generally harmful role of Troyes in the history of the Seal, perhaps that city too might be given a prominent part in the healing process. Indeed, Troyes in northern France may be deemed the more suitable, if the streets of Jerusalem are not yet considered safe enough.

> *The secret things belong unto the Lord our God: but those*
> *things which are revealed belong unto us and to our children*
> *forever, that we may do all the words of this law.*
> Deuteronomy 29:29

תמם / *taamam* / <u>It is accomplished</u>

# Postscript – Beyond the Seal

At an early stage in this book, I reviewed some of the accepted opinions concerning the structure of the Bible's creation account in Genesis 1:1 to 2:4. Then, in Chapter 5, I showed that there is an underlying, parallel structure that places a particular emphasis on the names of God and Abraham.

In Chapter 6, I suggested that the end of the Torah may be meant to loop back onto its beginning. And I showed that the beginning and end text, with the displaced letter *ayin* (ע) interposed, bequeaths a family of closely related words, including *master*, *head*, *betrothed* and *heir*. They also confer overlapping gematria values of 611 and 613, where the first is also the gematria of 'Torah', and the second the number of commandments the Torah imparted to the children of Israel.

Then, in Chapter 8, I showed detailed evidence that the Author's Seal contains rich allusions to human genetics. And I might have added that the remaining parts of the Torah – the majority – may correspond to the vast tracts of human DNA for which no purpose has yet been determined. In effect, therefore, I have suggested both plainly and implicitly that there is much scope for further analysis of the Torah along similar lines.

Up to now, however, I have not presented much evidence that the elaborate structures seen within the Author's Seal (ie the first 64 letters of the Torah) may extend to the whole of the Five Books of Moses. This postscript is, therefore, included to address that omission, and so provide motivation for further research. It is based upon a provisional analysis that I have carried out on a data file that consists of all 304,805 Hebrew letters of the current 'definitive' Torah. That is, the cleaned-up Masoretic text that has been accepted by Orthodox Judaism since the middle ages. I briefly mentioned my own research in Chapter 2, where I showed that the mere presence of two emergent copies of the word אור / *aur* / light in the G1 square defied negative odds of about 25:1. I was able to say that, because the entire Torah text, when arranged like the G3/4 aspects of the Seal in a very much larger square, reveals only 937 emergent copies of the word *aur*. It is that 553×553 square of letters that forms the basis of this postscript.

In the rest of this section, the Torah text is assumed to be set out in a square having 553 horizontal rows and 553 vertical columns. The given text (ie the first letter *ayin* is not migrated) is inserted from the middle of the square, and proceeds outwards, clockwise in the now familiar square coil. Each concentric layer of the square is filled before the text breaks out into the next layer. The generalised structure is seen here as Figure P.01. Notice that all rows and columns are numbered from the top-left corner; so the 64 letters at the start of Genesis are found in a square bounded by columns 273 to 280, and rows 274 to 281. It will be seen from a comparison of the relative lengths of the intervals 1 to 272, 273 to 280 and 281 to 553, that the internal structure in Figure P.01 is not drawn to scale. The original 8×8 Seal at the centre should appear very much smaller.

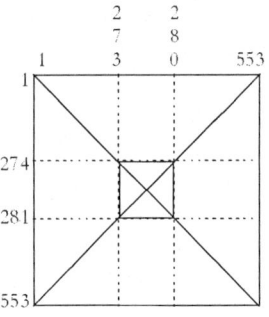

Figure P.01

The diagonals of the square are shown in the diagram because they have a prominent role in demonstrating deliberate, extended structures. The first letter of Genesis 1:1 is entered in position 277:277, at the origin of the diagonal that extends to the top-right. Note that this diagonal, and the next two (moving clockwise) mark positions where the regular Torah text makes a right-angle turn in the direction of insertion. However, the diagonal that ends at position 1:1 is where the coiling text breaks out of each layer into the next. So here, the text makes its right-angle turn one position higher, just above the diagonal.

It is perhaps worth pointing out that the letter at position 273:274 is the 64th letter of the Torah. That is the last letter of the Seal, before the text breaks out into the wider square. I mention this because the number 273 happens to be the gematria of the influential word אַרבע / *arba* / <u>four</u>, and 274 is 2×137. We know that 137 occurs at only three places in the entire Bible. All three are within the Torah, and all are the ages of important biblical personalities at the time each of them died. Had the length of the Torah not been 304,805 letters, but less than 304,705 or more than 305,809 then the 64th letter would not now be seen at position 273:274. Also, recall that these two numbers are found as the diagonals of a 3×3 group at the centre of the G3/4 aspects of the Seal (see Chapter 7). And now, the last letter of the Seal is at the point where column 273 crosses through row 274.

The first evidence of a planned structure beyond the Author's Seal is to be seen in the locations of transitions from each day of creation to the next. Figure P.02 shows the relative locations of the words *first, second, third, fourth, fifth* and *sixth* where the text reads: *And the evening and the morning were the* [number] *day*. In the Hebrew text, the number follows the word 'day', making it the last word of the verse.

# In the Beginning

What is immediately obvious from Figure P.02 is that the first four numbers all overlap a diagonal. The fifth number merely touches a diagonal. Then the sixth day – the day in which man is created – completely fails to reach a diagonal; which could be understood as confirming what I said in Chapter 3, that the creation of man is an ongoing work-in-progress.

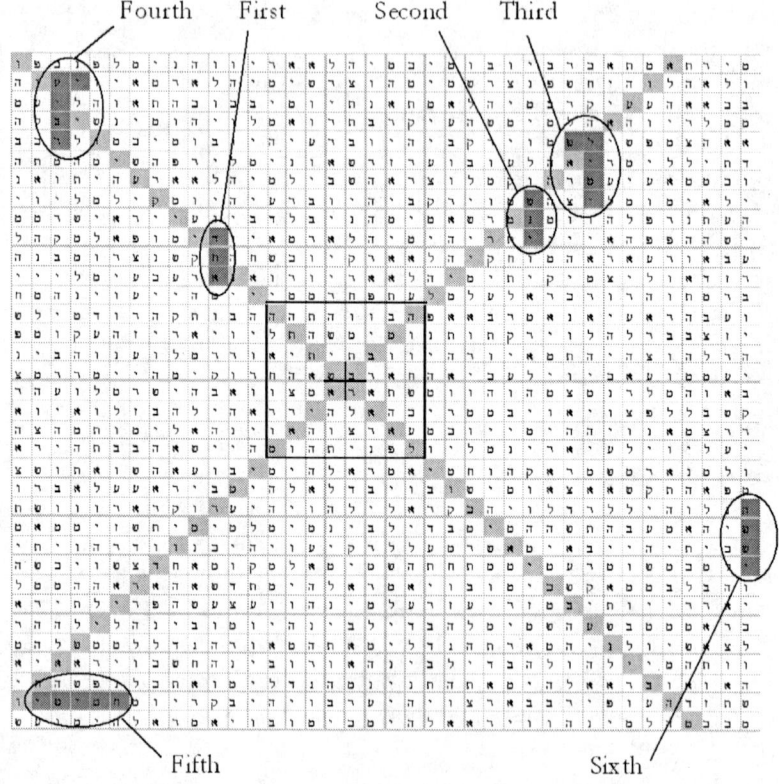

Figure P.02

The coincidence of the early days of creation with the square's diagonals is certainly visually arresting. But it would also be useful to know just how significant this is. Fortunately, we can easily express the significance as a calculated probability, based on the number of positions each word might have been located that either do or do not coincide with a diagonal. The calculation will, of course, depend both on the length of the word and on the width, or height, of the layer in which it is found. It is convenient to perform the calculation in relation to the length of a single side of the layer in which the word is found, as this makes the calculation easier, with no loss of accuracy.

In the case of the word אֶחָד / *echad* / <u>one</u> (or <u>first</u>) it could overlap a diagonal on any one of its three letter positions, in a layer having a side of 13 letters. So there is a 3/13 chance that this word, in the layer where it happens to fall, would coincide with a diagonal element. In the case of שְׁנֵי / *sh'ney* / <u>two</u> (or <u>second</u>) the fraction is 3/19; for שְׁלִישִׁי / *sh'liyshiy* / <u>third</u> it is 5/25; and for רְבִיעִי / *revi'iy* / <u>fourth</u> it is 5/29. According to the rules of probability (see Appendix C), we may multiply these four fractions to obtain the overall probability that the text that marks the ends of the first four days of creation will all coincide with a diagonal, thus:

$$\frac{3}{13} \times \frac{3}{19} \times \frac{5}{25} \times \frac{5}{29} = 0.001256$$

(or one chance in 795)

If we wish to include the fifth day, which does not overlap the diagonal but only touches it, then we need to relax the criteria for the first four days also. Then the probability that all of the first five number words will either touch or overlap a diagonal is given by:

$$\frac{5}{13} \times \frac{5}{19} \times \frac{7}{25} \times \frac{7}{29} \times \frac{7}{33} = 0.001451$$

(or one chance in 689)

These are still compelling odds that the underlying structure of the creation account is not random but following an elaborate pre-conceived plan. The natural, provisional conclusion is that the underlying design in the early Torah runs much deeper than the well-known superficial structure, based around the number seven. Another and more telling question might be: Does this deeper arrangement have anything to do with the other, parallel structure we observed in Chapter 5? It was there we noted that the first explicit use of the four-letter Name, יהוה / YHWH, occurs at Genesis 2:4. But we also found an earlier, concealed occurrence of the same Name in Genesis 1:14, underlined here in the expression ...הַלַּיְלָה וְהָיוּ... / *halaylah v'hayv* / ...<u>the night, and let them be</u> (for signs, etc). We shall now look at these particular occurrences of the divine Name in the context of the enlarged square. Both turn out to be associated with diagonals, and each is more elaborate than just its interesting location.

First, the hidden occurrence of יהוה in Genesis 1:14 was seen to overlap the final letter of the palindromic הלילה / ha'laylay / the night. Figure P.03(a) shows the location of the relevant text in the expanded Torah square, slightly below and to the left of centre. While (b) shows the actual text as it appears there. Note that the tiny square in the centre of Figure P.03(a) is the 8×8 Seal at the start of the Torah, now drawn to scale.

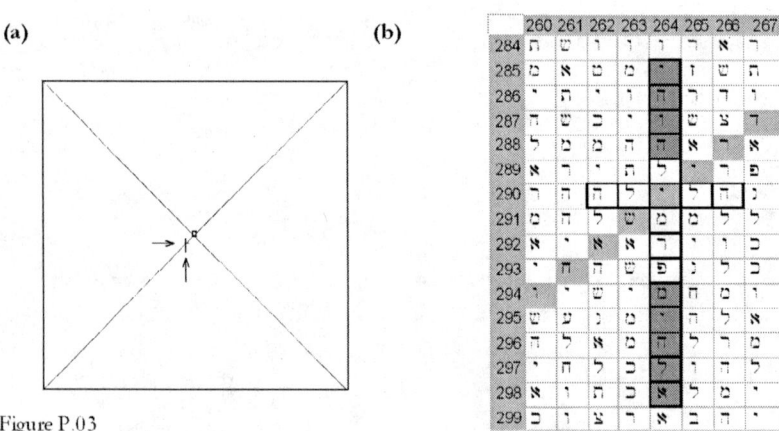

(a)                                                    (b)

Figure P.03

In Figure P.03(b), הלילה enters from the right, with its middle letter falling precisely on the diagonal. To the left, the letters לה appear to complete the linear word. However, they are an illusion, perhaps included to add to the appeal of this configuration. The regular word הלילה actually makes a right-angle turn at the diagonal. So the horizontal continuation is an emergent variant with contributions from two other words, one in Genesis 1:16 and the other in Genesis 1:18. Given that הלילה is palindromic about its central letter *yud*, this is already a most intriguing formation. But, of course, the hidden copy of יהוה also belongs to the same group, being in the reverse text descending from above (grey shading). What is more, an emergent copy of אלהים / Elohim / God (also shown with grey shading) is seen ascending from below, where the regular text is entered horizontally. Note that this Elohim is in the same column as יהוה, presenting an unexpected joint occurrence of the two names, even before their first explicit appearance at Genesis 2:4. Since the entire Torah square contains only 12 emergent copies of Elohim, the presence of this one here is all the more astounding. And it is rather curious that the two names of God are found so close together in column 264, since that number is the gematria of יֵרְדֵן / *Yardan* / Jordan.

Finally, there are two further emergent components that fill the vertical space between [ם] אלהים and יהוה. One is the word מילה (Milah), which overlaps three letters of הלילה / *ha'laylah* / the night and, like יהוה, terminates at its final letter. Recall that this last component is part of the expression *Brit Milah*, meaning the covenant of circumcision, by a token separation of flesh. Compare this with the other interposed word, פר / *par* / a young bull. All in all, we are dealing with a most astonishing cluster of letters, which utilises the plain-text palindromic *ha'aylah* mainly as a point of focus. Indeed, the middle letter of *ha'laylah* that is sited in the diagonal of the Torah square is the precise focus. So, recall also that *ha'laylah* was once seen within a 2×4 cluster in the G1 square, such that it defined an axis of bi-lateral symmetry there.

The Torah's first explicit occurrence of יהוה, in Genesis 2:4, is seen in Figure P.04(b), where part (a) illustrates its general location with respect to the Torah square.

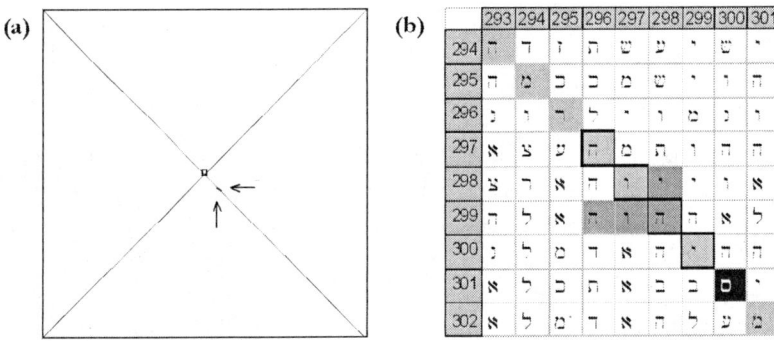

Figure P.04

Before I identify the plain-text copy of יהוה, it is useful to consider first another phenomenon that we met in Chapter 3. It was there we noted that the last of the 22 Hebrew letters to make its first appearance in the Torah was samech (ם), at position 2210, where it is squeezed between the square $47^2$ and triangular $T_{66}$. And in Figure P.04(b), this first occurrence of samech is the one now seen in the diagonal as a white letter on a black background. Recall especially that it was the position of the first samech that once alerted us to the fact that a 553×553 square is the smallest that can accommodate all 304,805 letters of the Torah. All of which adds to the surprise of seeing the same samech at the corner of a sizable square of the Torah text. Also, this letter happens to be contained within the word הסבב / ha'sovev / compasseth in Genesis 2:11. Note especially that the text I am describing is concerned with the first of four rivers, from:

> *And a river went out of Eden to water the garden; and from*
> *thence it was parted and became into four heads.*
>
> (Genesis 2:10)

So, maybe we are to understand that each of the four radial, diagonal lines in the enlarged square is one of those river heads.

In a sense we have now come full circle. It is at this point we encounter not one, but two copies of the divine Name יהוה. First, notice that there is an emergent copy of יהוה (heavy borders) lying entirely within the diagonal, starting adjacent to the first samech in Figure P.04(b). And the second letter of this יהוה is shared with the second letter of the first explicit copy of the same Name in the plain text. The Name in the plain text comes down to meet the diagonal, then turns the right-angle to continue towards the left. Oddly, there is also an emergent מלך [ך] / Melek / King running parallel to and just above the emergent יהוה.

The last artefact in the extended Torah square I want to describe takes us a long way from the start of Genesis; in fact to a section of the Torah that is more than halfway through the book of Numbers, the fourth of its five books. Here we find an emergent word ויקרא / vayiqra / and [He] called that is not uncommon in the plain text. For example, *vayiqra* happens to be the first word of the fifth verse of Genesis 1. And it is also the first word of the book of Leviticus and is, therefore, the name of that book in Judaism. In Chapter 5, we examined the text at the start of Leviticus, and found that the second letter of *vayiqra* is the start of an E.L.S. copy of יהוה that intersects with a plain-text copy of the same Name (which is precisely what we have just seen again in the lower-right diagonal, next to the first occurrence of the letter samech).

In contrast, as an emergent artefact, *vayiqra* is vanishingly rare. The relative frequencies of its five letters in the Torah lead to a prediction that only a single emergent copy will be found in the entire 553×553 square. And there is indeed only one emergent *vayiqra* to be seen. So the real surprise is not its rarity, but the fact that the one and only emergent vayiqra lies entirely within the same diagonal as the earlier יהוה, and the first letter samech but very much further downstream (see Figure P.05).

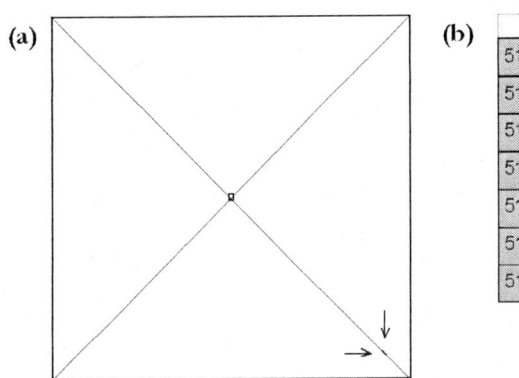

Figure P.05

Given the fact that there are 1106 letters that lie within diagonals in the Torah square, we can estimate that there is about 1 chance in 304805 ÷ 1106, or a 1 in 276 chance that the sole emergent *vayiqra* will intersect in any way with a diagonal. But the odds against it being oriented so it lies entirely within a diagonal are only about 1 in 1100. Which makes its coincidence with a diagonal a very improbable event.

What are we to make of the fact that so many notable words fall on diagonals of the Torah square? And is it even reasonable to calculate the odds as I have done? In other words, why should we choose to focus on these particular artefacts, in preference to thousands of other emergent words?

Part of the answer is in the wording of the first question. These are all especially notable words that are already prominent by virtue of their context. The day numbers of the creation account are associated with an iconic, strategically placed text that is already well-known for its conspicuous structure. The two copies of יהוה we elected to examine are, in one case, the first explicit use of that Name in the Torah, and the other is the very first concealed example. And together they define a portion of the creation account that warranted our prolonged consideration in Chapter 5. Likewise, the word הלילה / *ha'laylah* / <u>the night</u>, which is a palindrome (a form of symmetry), is first seen in the fourth (ie middle) day of the creation account, and was found in the G1 square precisely on an axis of symmetry. So its balanced position on a diagonal of the Torah square – itself an axis of bi-lateral symmetry - is particularly worthy of special attention. Last, but not least, the unique emergent *vayiqra* also merited our particular consideration in Chapter 5, because it associates people's names with the concept of 'preciousness'. So the unique emergent copy deserved close examination when it was also found to coincide with a diagonal of the vast Torah square. It is, surely, fair to say that the artefacts we have examined in this postscript have been especially deserving of careful consideration; that they are self-selecting on the strength of both their previous and continuing rich histories. And it is surely fair to ask why any word or group of words that is favoured in one context should also be favoured in another. The answer cannot always be 'coincidence'.

As for the first of the above questions, it should be obvious by now that the extended Torah shows evidence of the same kind of coherent structure that we previously saw only in the Author's Seal. But these are mere hints and clues that the Torah, as a consistent whole, is ripe for the kind of close examination I have applied to its first 64 letters. There is an interesting technical parallel that might also lead us to expect a much wider sub-structure. In 1963, a mathematician named Stanislaw Ulam was doodling with the set if natural numbers (ie 1, 2, 3, 4, ... etc), entering them into an expanding square spiral similar to our own G3/4 squares. He then highlighted those numbers that happen to be prime (having no whole number divisors), and he noticed a visual pattern emerging. Subsequent investigation has revealed that the further the square of natural numbers is extended, the more evident it becomes that prime numbers tend to form continuous, oblique, linear sequences, many of which hug the diagonals of the square. The merest hint of this behaviour is seen in Figure P.06, which

| | | | | | | | | | |
|---|---|---|---|---|---|---|---|---|---|
| (73) | 72 | (71) | 70 | 69 | 68 | (67) | 66 | 65 | 100 |
| 74 | (43) | 42 | (41) | 40 | 39 | 38 | (37) | 64 | 99 |
| 75 | 44 | 21 | 20 | (19) | 18 | (17) | 36 | 63 | 98 |
| 76 | 45 | 22 | (7) | 6 | (5) | 16 | 35 | 62 | (97) |
| 77 | 46 | (23) | 8 | (1) | 4 | 15 | 34 | (61) | 96 |
| 78 | (47) | 24 | 9 | (2) | (3) | 14 | 33 | 60 | 95 |
| (79) | 48 | 25 | 10 | (11) | 12 | (13) | 32 | (59) | 94 |
| 80 | 49 | 26 | 27 | 28 | (29) | 30 | (31) | 58 | 93 |
| 81 | 50 | 51 | 52 | (53) | 54 | 55 | 56 | 57 | 92 |
| 82 | (83) | 84 | 85 | 86 | 87 | 88 | (89) | 90 | 91 |

Figure P.06

oblique, linear sequences, many of which hug the diagonals of the square. The merest hint of this behaviour is seen in Figure P.06, which shows only the first 100 natural numbers. The pattern is not predictable (by any presently-known means), but is present nonetheless. Then the fact that the complete Torah square shows so many artefacts that hug *its* diagonals may be a clue to the Author's knowledge and understanding of prime numbers.

There is undoubtedly a lot more mileage in the search for hidden meaning in the Hebrew Torah. And I wish every success to those who follow me in the ongoing quest, in whatever directions it may lead.

# Appendix A. Mathematics in the Bible

(i) The written representation of numbers.

It is important to be aware that the peoples of the Ancient Near East would not have had the same understanding of numbers and mathematical concepts such as we have today. During the period in which texts were being written that would eventually be collected together as our familiar Bible, different societies at various times had alternative ways for representing numbers. Contrary to the practice of writing numbers the modern way in some translations of the Bible, as far as the Hebrew Old Testament is concerned the only way ever used to convey numerical values was by words. For example, at Numbers 1:21, the males of the tribe of Reuben are numbered as 46,500. In the Torah, this number is expressed (reading from right-to-left) as מֵאוֹת שֵׁשָׁה וְאַרְבָּעִים אֶלֶף וַחֲמֵשׁ which translated literally is 'six and forty thousand and five hundred'.

A much more useful method for writing numbers had already been developed in Babylonia by the time of the Jews' approximately 70-year exile there. That scheme shared one very important characteristic with our modern system, in that it employed positional digits. In the number 332 (three hundred and thirty two) the two 3s look alike, but in our decimal system the one on the left, in the 'hundreds' position is worth ten times the one to its right, in the 'tens' position. However, where the modern number system is based on 10 (hence the largest digit is a 9), the Babylonian system was based on 60, no less! Unfortunately for the Babylonians, their system suffered from having no symbol to denote a zero. The way the Babylonians expressed their equivalent of 'nothing in the tens position' was by leaving a gap between other digits. The equivalent today would be like writing the number 308 as 3 8. This inability to represent an explicit zero digit would have been a serious barrier to the development of more sophisticated mathematical concepts. Yet, for posterity, the Babylonians have left us a time measurement system based on 60 minutes in an hour, and a geometry that defines a complete rotation (eg a day) as 360 degrees. Consequently, the interior angles of an equilateral triangle are all 60°. This is also the historical reason why fractions of degrees may be expressed in minutes and seconds of arc.

Overall, in biblical times, number systems were better suited to use in trade and commerce than for serious 'scientific' purposes. But there were other developments going on elsewhere – most notably in India – that sowed the seeds of modern mathematics. Sometime in the period 400 BC to 400 AD (nobody knows just when), the symbols now known as Arabic numerals suited to base-10 arithmetic were devised on the sub-continent. And in parts of the Arabic-speaking world, the same symbols are still more properly called 'Indian numerals'. A substantial part of our modern form of arithmetic, using Hindu-Arabic numerals, had found its way into countries around the Mediterranean basin during the 12th Century. These ideas were collected together by the Italian mathematician Fibonacci, and published in 1202 in his *Liber Abaci*. The effect his book had on European thought should not be underestimated. It is no exaggeration to say that the development of modern mathematics began with Fibonacci. Yet this powerful system of writing numbers did not initially include a symbol for zero. And that continued to inhibit further development for some centuries to come.

It is not always recognised that there are two alternative concepts at stake when we talk about zero, one being more abstract than the other. The easier of the two concepts to understand is the use of a symbol as a place-holder in a positional number system. So, in the example of 308 I used earlier, the middle zero means 'there are no tens in this number'. And it is still much easier to understand 308 as a working number than 0 as an independent mathematical concept. Documentary evidence suggests that experiments with the zero symbol as a place-holder had been tried in parts of Europe by the middle of the Fifth Century AD, and in some central American cultures even earlier. But the use of zero as an abstract mathematical concept was delayed by about four more centuries. Nonetheless, being able to write numbers in our modern decimal (base-10 or denary) format, and especially large numbers such as 7,224,185 must have had a real impact in commercial circles. The arithmetic manipulation of decimal numbers is eminently more practical than, say, the addition of XIV and DXC in Roman numerals. In fact, the invention of the system of Roman numerals using letters of the Latin alphabet can now be seen as a return to the mathematical Dark Ages, compared with the earlier Babylonian system, or even the Greek and Hebrew systems (see next section).

## In the Beginning

### (ii) The numerology of biblical languages.

Bridging the time gap between the Babylonian positional number system and the one we use today, there have been many others, including two that utilised the letters of the principal biblical languages, Hebrew and Greek. The generic term for such systems is numerology but, regrettably, the use of this word has become ambiguous. The confusion arises because the same sets of letter values (see Table A.1 for the Hebrew values) have been used both in a practical, day-to-day way, and for more esoteric purposes. The esoteric Hebrew case is given the specialised name of gematria. Greek numerology also incorporates an arcane branch, from which the well-known value 888 of the name Ιησους (ie Jesus) is obtained. The essential difference between the two branches is that gematria is concerned with the numerical values of whole, *bona fide* words, while basic arithmetic is all about constructing practical, every-day numbers using letters as the basic building blocks. It will pay to concentrate first on the non-esoteric case.

Table A.1

| Ord. | Symbol | Name | Std. | Qatan | Ord. | Symbol | Name | Std. | Qatan |
|------|--------|------|------|-------|------|--------|------|------|-------|
| 1 | א | Aleph | 1 | 1 | 12 | ל | Lamed | 30 | 3 |
| 2 | ב | Beyt | 2 | 2 | 13 | מם | Mem° | 40 | 4 |
| 3 | ג | Gimmel | 3 | 3 | 14 | נן | Nun° | 50 | 5 |
| 4 | ד | Delet | 4 | 4 | 15 | ס | Samech | 60 | 6 |
| 5 | ה | Heh | 5 | 5 | 16 | ע | Ayin | 70 | 7 |
| 6 | ו | Vav | 6 | 6 | 17 | פף | Peh° | 80 | 8 |
| 7 | ז | Zayin | 7 | 7 | 18 | צץ | Tzadee° | 90 | 9 |
| 8 | ח | Chet* | 8 | 8 | 19 | ק | Qof | 100 | 1 |
| 9 | ט | Tet | 9 | 9 | 20 | ר | Reysh | 200 | 2 |
| 10 | י | Yud | 10 | 1 | 21 | ש | Shin | 300 | 3 |
| 11 | כך | Kaf° | 20 | 2 | 22 | ת | Tav | 400 | 4 |

To use Hebrew arithmetic as a case study it is, first of all, possible to identify an important advantage it has over the later Roman system. For example, in Roman numerals IV means 5 − 1 (ie 4), but VI means 5 + 1 (ie 6). This is a positional system of sorts, but one that is impossible to codify in a way that would make possible a useful arithmetic. The Hebrew version on the other hand, is entirely additive; there is no question of a letter value being added in some circumstances, but subtracted in others. Some simple numbers may be represented by a single letter (value), whereas compound numbers are composed from a sequence of letters of decreasing value, in Hebrew written from right to left. The actual values used are the standard values ('Std' in Table A.1, which is repeated above from Table 3.1 of Chapter 3).

For example, the decimal number 837 would be constructed as תתל"ז. Notice the " symbol interposed before the final digit (ז), indicating that a number is intended rather than a word. Notice also that two copies of the letter *tav* (ת) are needed to make 800; it is only the hundreds component of a number that may employ composite letters in this way, since 400 is the highest available letter value.

There is a practical limit of about 1000 for numbers that can be represented by Hebrew letters. Biblical numbers that are larger than the practical limit for gematria combinations are expressed in combinations of words, such as אלף / *alaph* / a thousand (see Appendix A(i)). In certain very restricted circumstances, numbers greater than a thousand may be contrived as letters. For example, in early 2008 AD, the current Jewish year is 5768, which is expressed as תשס"ח (ie 768), the thousands being understood from the context.

Some other examples of Hebrew numbers are:

(i)      ה"     5

(ii)     כ"     20

(iii)    ר"     200

(iv)    ר"ח    208    (Note that the decimal zero, meaning 'no tens', is not explicitly represented by the Hebrew digits)

(v)     י"ד    14

(vi)    ט"ו    15

(vii)   ט"ז    16

Examples (vi) and (vii) are included as special exceptions. Most of the numbers from 11 to 19 are composed from a letter *yud* (י) to represent 10, followed by the appropriate units. However, in the two cases of 15 and 16, the standard letter combinations would result in the spelling of two abbreviated names of God. Therefore, these numbers only are formed from the non-standard combinations 9+6 and 9+7. There is here just the merest hint of an overlap with the esoteric concept of gematria.

# In the Beginning

Scholarly advocates of the so-called Bible Code report having found the names of historically famous Jews associated with relevant dates encoded in the above format, in the form of Equidistant Letter Sequences. The relevant date is often a date of birth or of death. The lives of famous people whose names have been sought by this method were far in the future from the point of view of the authors of biblical books. The jury is still out on those findings, the greatest obstacle to credibility being the very nature of the subject, and the staggering implications if those results are shown to be correct. The subject of gematria also causes the same sort of unease (or studious indifference) in other scholarly circles and for similar reasons.

Dating the introduction of Greek and Hebrew numerology is difficult, using only archaeological finds and documents that are believed to be copies of earlier documents. But using these sources, it appears that the Greek version came into use around 600 BC. Hebrew numerology on the other hand may have been introduced about two to three centuries later. Accepting the legitimacy of the method described earlier for composing numbers from standard Hebrew letter values is not a problem, and shows evidence of simple, pragmatic ingenuity. It is easy to see it as a rational development to make life easier and perhaps based on the earlier Greek model. What is much more difficult to explain is when and how gematria emerged. There is no hard evidence that gematria was practiced in biblical times; so we are left to assume it is a relatively recent innovation. But if we accept the existence of an elaborate numerical sub-structure in the Torah, such as that described in this book, then it presents a rather profound paradox. It is as though the Hebrew alephbeyt, the language itself, and the Torah had all been designed together as a coherent suite; and that Hebrew numerology was more a discovery than an invention.

In mainstream academia, numerology is still seen as a fringe activity, rather than a subject for serious study. The relationship between numerology and acceptable scholarly endeavour is put on a par with the comparison between alchemy and chemistry, or astrology and astronomy. Where alchemy and astrology are concerned, such dismissal seems entirely justified on the grounds that neither has contributed any concrete, worthwhile knowledge. The same criticism may not, however, be valid for Hebrew gematria. For one thing, the use of Hebrew letters to represent numbers is not an entirely esoteric activity. As we have seen, Jewish society uses the numerical values of Hebrew letters in many everyday situations, and has done so for at least 2300 years; the earliest recorded use was on Maccabean coinage. So the use of Hebrew letters as numbers is by no means a matter of fringe belief. On the other hand, there is some extraordinary numerical information to be found interwoven with the text of the Torah. And, once we accept the presence of numeric sub-structures in early Genesis, we cannot but ask how they came to be there. At the very least, we should question the assumed 3rd Century BC dating for the earliest invention (or discovery) of gematria. And it is surely now incumbent on biblical scholars to accept knowledge of sophisticated numerical concepts in the makeup of the author(s) of at least Chapter 1 of Genesis.

As a subject for serious study, Hebrew gematria is at about the same stage that the geological branch of plate-tectonics found itself before the 1960s. In the half-century from 1915 Alfred Wegener, the first advocate of continental drift, and his supporters had only circumstantial evidence that some continents appeared to have drifted apart over time. There was neither understanding of the earth's internal processes to explain that movement, nor specific measurable data to show it happening. We now have a well-developed science of seismology to explain the processes. And we have samples of sea-bed rocks from near to creative margins, showing locked-in magnetic inversions that correspond to equivalent periodical inversions of the earth's magnetic field. So, we now know not only that continental drift does happen, but also the why and the how. What Wegener could see with his own eyes was largely scorned by his contemporary colleagues, because seeing and believing are not always comfortable bed-fellows. Also, at that time the very idea that continents might wander around must have seemed absurd. What is ludicrously implausible is, nonetheless, true! And make no mistake, it can be just as unwise to accept a proposition without good supporting evidence as it is to reject one for which the evidence does exist. What is important for gematria is that there is now a substantial body of supporting evidence that needs to be explained.

# In the Beginning

(iii) Figurate numbers.

By definition, a figurate number is one that can be formed into a basic geometrical shape using objects all the same size and shape (usually a disc). The definition should also stipulate that the discs etc must be distributed evenly and, if possible, touching all their neighbours. The basic geometrical shapes that concern us most are triangles, hexagrams and squares, the second of these being the formal mathematical name for a Star of David. Also of interest to a lesser extent are hexagons. Figure A.1 illustrates (a) the triangular number 10, (b) the hexagram number 13, (c) the square number 16 and (d) the hexagon number 7.

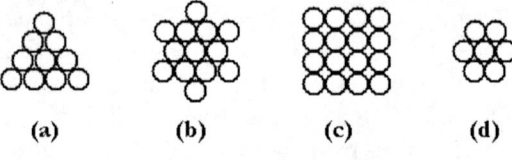

| (a) | (b) | (c) | (d) |

**Figure A.1**

These are all plane figures, meaning they can be drawn on a flat page. We are not, of course, dealing with the outlines of the shapes as they might be drawn using straight lines, but with numbers (or a number of identical objects) which may be formed into those shapes.

It is a simple fact that figurate numbers are always integers; that is, whole numbers with no fractional part. These are the counting numbers: 1, 2, 3 ... etc, also known as Natural Numbers. An important point about figurate numbers is that they have a visually self-evident existence that does not depend on us having a sophisticated system for writing numbers. They would, therefore, have been recognisable from time immemorial.

## (a) Triangular Numbers

In math-speak, the $n^{th}$ triangular number ($T_n$) is equal to the sum of the first n integers. For example:

$$T_3 = 1 + 2 + 3 = 6$$

The graphic shows clearly that it is composed of a top row of a single circular disc, a second row of two discs, and a third row of three discs. It is plainly evident that the $T_3$ triangle could be converted to $T_4$ by the addition of a new base row of four discs, and that this process could be carried on indefinitely.

Some of the triangular numbers that have special significance in this book are:

$T_3 = 6$ : The length of the first Hebrew word of Genesis, and first Perfect Number.

$T_6 = 21$ : The position of a word-break in Genesis 1:1, marking the end of the 3rd side of the G1 and G2 squares.

$T_7 = 28$ : The number of Hebrew letters in Genesis 1:1, and second Perfect Number.

$T_{31} = 496$ : Third Perfect Number and twice the gematria of Abraham.

$T_{36} = 666$ > Important characteristics of the gematria of

$T_{37} = 703$ > Genesis 1:1 (see Figure 3.7 in Chapter 3)

$T_{66} = 2211$ : One of the family group (along with $T_6$ and $T_{66}$), and associated with the last of the Hebrew letters to make its first appearance in the Torah.

$T_{666} = 222111$ : Prominent in the G3/4 aspects of the Author's Seal, and in the 7×4 matrix of Genesis 1:1, all as qatan letter values.

(The triangular numbers listed here are just the ones that occur most often in descriptions of the Author's Seal)

Of course, it would be awfully tedious if we always had to add up consecutive integers to find a given triangular number. So it is useful to have the following formula to do the calculation quickly:

$$T_n = \tfrac{1}{2}n(n + 1)$$

In this form, however, it appears that we may create a fractional element with the ½n term, when n is an odd number. So it is clearer what is going on if the formula is re-cast in this alternative form:

$$T_n = \frac{n(n + 1)}{2}$$

Here, we are guided to find the product n(n+1) in the numerator, before dividing by 2. Since the numerator includes both n and n+1, we know that one of them will be odd and the other even. And the result of multiplying any integer by an even number is always even. So, in the second version of the formula, it is easier to see why the final outcome will always be a whole number. For an example of this formula in use, we can find the value of $T_{100}$. In this case, n = 100 and n + 1 = 101. Therefore:

$$T_{100} = \frac{100 \times 101}{2}$$

$$= 5050$$

This is obviously a much quicker process than adding together every integer from 1 to 100.

The reverse process may be used to test whether a given integer is a triangular number. Say we are presented with the number 2926, and want to know if it is triangular. In the above formula, the final step is to divide by 2; so the reverse is to multiply by 2 (ie 2×2926 = 5852). In the formula, 5852 would be the result of multiplying two consecutive numbers (ie n and n + 1), which is slightly more than the square of n. So the reverse step is to find the square root of 5852, which is 76.498366. The fact that the fractional part of this square root is only slightly less than .5 is a strong indicator that the original number is triangular, with n = 76 and n + 1 = 77. This is easy to check using the formula to find $T_{76}$, and it is found that $T_{76}$ = 2926, as expected.

After triangular numbers, we shall be looking at square numbers. And for that, it will be helpful if we first look at two alternative ways in which the same triangular number may be graphically presented. Figure A.2 shows $T_7$ in two configurations.

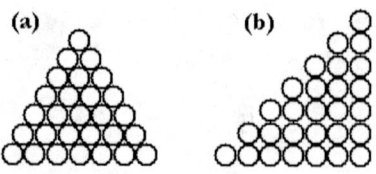

**Figure A.2**

In A.2(a), the 28 components are packed together as closely as possible, thus forming an equilateral triangle. Whereas A.2(b) illustrates a looser arrangement, in which the 28 elements are distorted into the shape into a 45° right-angle triangle. A purist might insist that only the equilateral triangle meets all the criteria for a triangular figurate number. Yet the right-angle version still makes most of the essential points, is feasible for any triangular number not just $T_7$, and is the one that helps to illustrate an important property of perfect squares.

(b) Square Numbers

The smallest non-trivial square number is 4; that is 2×2. Every set of figurate numbers includes 1 as its first member; but this is so trivial that, for most practical purposes it ought to be excluded. After all, if we see a single construction element in isolation, how do we know it is trying to be a triangle, a square, a hexagram, or some other shape?

To be truly faithful to the strict definition of figurate, a 'square' number should really be described as a rhombus such as version (b) in Figure A.3, which is undoubtedly more compact that version (a).

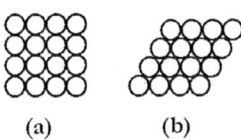

(a)          (b)

**Figure A.3**

However, arithmetically they are absolutely equivalent, so I will continue to follow accepted practice and call them square. They do after all obey the simple general formula for any perfect square number ($S_n$), so:

$$S_n = n \times n \text{ (or } n^2\text{)}$$

Note that we cannot transform one square number to the next as we did for triangles, just by adding an extra row. For reasons that should be self-evident, squares must grow in width at the same rate they grow in height.

The first few perfect squares: 1, 4, 9, 16, 25, 36 … show that the difference between consecutive ascending terms is the sequence of odd numbers. That is, the consecutive differences are: 1, 3, 5, 7, 9, … and so on.

In the context of the Author's Seal, an 8×8 square has the unique property that its outer layer (28 elements) and inner zone (36 elements) match the two consecutive triangular numbers from which it is formed. This is seen clearly in Figure A.4.

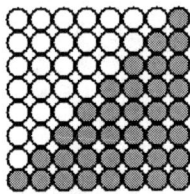

**Figure A.4**

Here, the grey-shaded triangular group represents $T_8$, and the white area is $T_7$. All perfect squares are the sum of two consecutive triangular numbers. But no other perfect square besides 64 consists of triangles that match its outer layer and inner zone in that way.

(c) Hexagram numbers.

A hexagram or Star of David (also Mogen David) is the overlap of two equilateral triangles, one of which has been rotated through 180° relative to the other. Apart from 1, which is the trivial first member of all figurate number sets, the first three hexagram numbers are 13, 37 and 73, all of which are also prime numbers. The next hexagram is 121, which is not prime, but $11^2$.

Figure A.5 uses the number 73 to illustrate some of the properties of hexagram numbers generally.

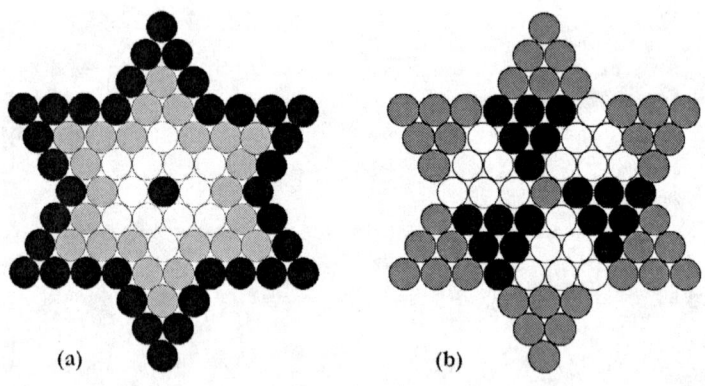

(a)        (b)

**Figure A.5**

First, A.5(a) shows that one hexagram number may be transformed into the next by the addition of a complete new outer layer. The single black central element is the trivial first hexagram, the number 1. The addition of a new white layer converts this to 13, the grey layer converts 13 to 37 and the outer black layer converts 37 to 73. The consecutive differences (ie 12, 24 and 36) suggest that successive hexagrams may be constructed by adding consecutive multiples of 12. And this is indeed the case.

Alternatively, Figure A.5(b) shows that the 73-hexagram may also be segregated into the single central element surrounded by twelve $T_3$ triangles. This overall format is preserved for all hexagram numbers, except the trivial single element. So, the 37-hexagram is $12 \times T_2 + 1$ (where $T_2 = 3$); and the 13-hexagram is $12 \times T_1 + 1$ (where $T_1 = 1$).

Using this principle, a general formula for $H_n$ (ie the $n^{th}$ hexagram) is therefore possible. So:

$$H_n = (12 \times T_{n-1}) + 1$$

When n = 1 in this formula, $T_{n-1}$ must be understood as 0 (zero).

(d) Hexagon numbers.

Descriptions of hexagon numbers closely parallel those for hexagrams, both graphically and arithmetically. Figure A.6(a) shows that hexagon numbers may also be described as a nested set, in which one is converted to the next by the addition of a new outer layer.

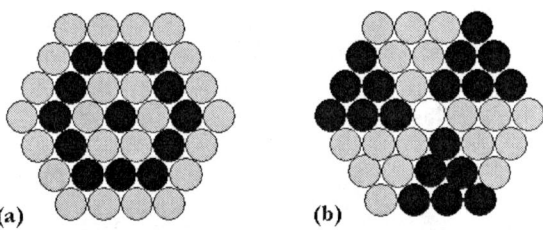

**(a)**      **(b)**

**Figure A.6**

Figure A.6(b) shows that a hexagon number consists of a single central element, surrounded by six equal triangles. The formula for the nth hexagon number ($P_n$) is, therefore:

$$P_n = (6 \times T_{n-1}) + 1$$

Note. The symbol 'P' is adopted for the hexagon (ie 6-Polygon) because 'H' has already been sequestered to represent hexagrams.

The various figurate number sequences have additional underlying numerical attributes that are described at **Appendix B(ii) – The signatures of common number series.**

## Appendix B. Number reduction and the signatures of common number series

(i) Number reduction.

The principle of number reduction lies in adding together the separate digits of a multi-digit decimal integer. There is no reason why the same process should not be applied to integers expressed in any other number base, should the need ever arise.

The very idea that decimal digits might be added may seem bizarre, but the expression 'should the need arise' used above is helpful. All forms of arithmetic, including the familiar addition, subtraction, multiplication and division, are in use today because a specific need arose. It just happens that those more common forms of arithmetic find frequent application in our daily lives. Number reduction is rarely needed, except in very specific circumstances, so it is unfamiliar to most people. But before I can expand on the rationale for number reduction, and possible uses, it will be helpful to work through the process and examine its special characteristics.

Consider the number 25. It consists of just two digits of which the smaller happens to be worth more than the larger; the 2 represents 20, which is greater than 5. This is a difference that is important in most day-to-day situations. There are, however, some situations in which the two digits should be taken at face value, and number reduction is one of them. The reduction process requires that the 2 and the 5 be added together to make 7. That is a very straightforward example. But what should we do with a number like 86, from which the reduced value (ie 14) is also a 2-digit number? And the answer is that it depends on one's purpose. There is an age-old version of number reduction called *fadic* in which the 14 obtained from 86 is regarded as the end-product. However, in this book, the required end-product of number reduction will always be a single digit. Therefore, the number 14 obtained from 86 by a first reduction is further simplified to 5 (ie $1 + 4$). In practice, it is rarely necessary for a number to require more than three iterations of reduction to arrive at a single digit (see the examples of 1999 and 3251342512 below).

One of the key properties of decimal number reduction is that the number 9 has no effect on the outcome; adding 9 has no more effect than adding zero. All 9s and multiples of 9 just cancel out. For example:

$18 \rightarrow 9$

$99 \rightarrow 18 \rightarrow 9$

Then:
517 → 13 → 4
19 → 10 → 1
91 → 10 → 1
92 → 11 → 2
98 → 17 → 8
1999 → 28 → 10 → 1
3251342512 → 28 → 10 → 1

The last two examples demonstrate that the absolute magnitude of the starting number is not always a good indicator of the required number of iterations, or of the final outcome.

So, what are the practical applications of number reduction? One that this writer has found useful from time to time, especially before pocket calculators became available, is the test for whether a number is divisible by 3. Take the number 245688; its digits reduce initially to 33, then to 6. The fact that 6 is divisible by 3 indicates that the original number is also divisible by 3. If the original number had been 245682, which first reduces to 27 then 9, we would know straight away that the starting number is divisible by 9. But this test only works for 3 and 9; not for 6 or any other single-digit number (Note. If the outcome is a 6, the original number is certainly divisible by 3, and may be divisible by 6, but the latter is not guaranteed).

A better known variation on number reduction is known as radix-9 arithmetic, used extensively in digital computers. The principle involved in radix-9 is simple integer division by 9, in which the required result is the remainder. For example, if 53 is divided by 9, the result in 'normal' arithmetic is: '5 remainder 8'. But in radix-9 division, the 5 is discarded and the result is the 8 remainder. The effect of radix-9 division is almost the same as in number reduction, but with one important difference. In radix-9, if the starting number is exactly divisible by 9, the result is 0 (zero), whereas number reduction will return a result of 9 from the same initial number. In radix-9 division, 0 is a valid result, but 9 is not. In number reduction, the opposite is true. But all other outcomes (ie the digits 1 to 8) are identical in both processes.

In the context of Hebrew numerology, a simple example of number reduction is seen in a comparison between the standard values of the 22 letters, and their qatan (ie small) values. All the standard values contain only a single non-zero digit which, in some cases, is followed by one or two zeros. It follows that the reduction of a standard value will eliminate any zeros, and leave just the one non-zero digit as result. The highest standard letter value in Hebrew is 400 (qatan 4); so the qatan values 1, 2, 3 and 4 are shared by three letters each. While the qatan values from 5 to 9 are shared by only two letters each.

#### (ii) Characteristic signatures of common number series

A particular application of number reduction that is not yet widely used is in recognising the underlying coherence in important number sequences and series. It is customary in mathematics to derive and apply formulæ with important number series so that, for example, a specific member of the series may be calculated easily. It is also customary to regard the formulæ as the main defining characteristic of the series. But this is not the only way to characterise many important number series.

The purpose of this Appendix is to identify distinctive patterns as a characteristic of certain number series, using only the method of number reduction. The results are found to fall into two clearly recognisable formats. There follow three self-contained analyses.

#### (a) Powers of 2

In effect, the sequence of powers of 2 starts with 2 itself, and continues with each term being doubled to make the next term. The first few terms are 2, 4, 8, 16, 32, ... and so on. The following table shows the first 15 members of this sequence, with their reduced values below them.

| 1 | 2 | 4 | 8 | 16 | 32 | 64 | 128 | 256 | 512 | 1024 | 2048 | 4096 | 8192 | 16384 |
|---|---|---|---|----|----|----|-----|-----|-----|------|------|------|------|-------|
| 1 | 2 | 4 | 8 | 7  | 5  | 1  | 2   | 4   | 8   | 7    | 5    | 1    | 2    | 4     |

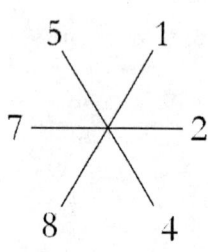

Figure B.1

Six entries in this table are emphasised by bold text to highlight the 1-2-4-8-7-5 sequence of reduced values, which repeats endlessly throughout the entire series. A distinctive characteristic of the repeating reduced values is seen in Figure B.1, in which they appear clockwise, in order in a hexagonal arrangement. It is of special importance that pairs of values at opposite ends of each axis add up to 9. Notice that the three totals of 9 are obtained just the same if the addition is formatted in the traditional way, so:

$$
\begin{array}{r}
124 \\
875 \quad + \\
\hline
999
\end{array}
$$

It is the combination of repeating reduced values, and their cyclic triple-9 sum that justifies calling the six-digit sequence the characteristic signature of the powers-of-2 sequence. This is a form of outcome that can be seen in the characteristic signatures of other number sequences, but not in all of them.

(b) Squares

As with the powers of 2, the first 15 square numbers are set out in the following table, with their reduced values below.

| 1 | 4 | 9 | 16 | 25 | 36 | 49 | 64 | 81 | 100 | 121 | 144 | 169 | 196 | 225 |
|---|---|---|----|----|----|----|----|----|-----|-----|-----|-----|-----|-----|
| 1 | 4 | 9 | 7  | 7  | 9  | 4  | 1  | 9  | 1   | 4   | 9   | 7   | 7   | 9   |

Again a repeating sequence of reduced values is emphasised. In this case it does not reveal cyclic triple-9 sums, but is a 9-digit palindrome; it reads the same forwards as backwards. Notice that the nine digits may be separated into three groups of three, in which each group reduces to 2. The sequence 7-9-4-1-9-1-4-9-7 repeats endlessly and is the characteristic signature of the sequence of square numbers.

(c) Triangular numbers

The first 17 triangular numbers are set out in the following table as with the previous two sequences.

| 1 | 3 | 6 | 10 | 15 | 21 | 28 | 36 | 45 | 55 | 66 | 78 | 91 | 105 | 120 | 136 | 153 |
|---|---|---|----|----|----|----|----|----|----|----|----|----|-----|-----|-----|-----|
| 1 | 3 | 6 | 1  | 6  | 3  | 1  | 9  | 9  | 1  | 3  | 6  | 1  | 6   | 3   | 1   | 9   |

Here, we find the characteristic signature is another 9-digit palindrome, this time centred on a 1 digit. This palindrome, however, exhibits some interesting extra attributes. For one thing, consecutive groups of three digits from the sequence 9-1-3-6-1-6-3-1-9 always add up to 13, and reduce to 4. In fact, by looking at separate groups of three digits in this way we discover two in particular that have additional significance for the topic of this book. The central 616 is immediately recognisable as the alternative to 666 found in Revelation 13:18 in some early manuscripts. And 616 is the same number that is seen explicitly in the G3 and G4 aspects of the Author's Seal, and is twice bestowed cryptically in G1 and G2. We know that 666 is itself a triangular number, and we now see that 616 is intimately related to the triangular number series.

The initial 913 group is, of course, the gematria of בראשית / *B'reishith* / <u>In the beginning</u> – the very first word of the Torah.

It is particularly evident that the author of the first Chapter of Genesis and the book of Revelation took into account both the triangular numbers and their characteristic signature. So it is especially noteworthy that when those books were written, there was not a decimal number system in use in which to add the digits of triangular numbers. So we ought to wonder how he knew the relevance of 616 and 913.

It will be found that many, if not most common number sequences succumb to number reduction to demonstrate characteristic signatures. For example, the signature of the hexagon numbers is just 171, and that of the hexagram numbers is 141. The well-known Fibonacci sequence has a rather lengthy characteristic signature, consisting of 24 repeating digits. Like the powers of 2, the digits of the Fibonacci signature may be written as a carousel, in which each pair of opposite digits sums to 9. Or the first and second halves may be added with the same effect, so:

| First half:  | 1 | 1 | 2 | 3 | 5 | 8 | 4 | 3 | 7 | 1 | 8 | 9 |
|---|---|---|---|---|---|---|---|---|---|---|---|---|
| Second half: | 8 | 8 | 7 | 6 | 4 | 1 | 5 | 6 | 2 | 8 | 1 | 9 |
|              | 9 | 9 | 9 | 9 | 9 | 9 | 9 | 9 | 9 | 9 | 9 | 9 |

The two 9s on the right are a special case. They first sum to 18, which then reduces to 9.

## Appendix C. The probability of underlying design in the Torah – A case study

The *raison d'être* for this book rests mainly in a two-fold argument. First, that the start of the Hebrew Torah intentionally contains an elaborate though largely unknown sub-structure beneath its plain text. And second, that the planning and design of that sub-structure is too complex to have been conceived by a human agency. The aim of this Appendix is to show, by a single example, that some aspects of that complexity are amenable to a statistical evaluation, to calculate the odds against them having arisen as a random effect.

This proposition will not be universally popular. Inevitably, there will be those who will persist in appealing to the agency of randomness, because that is preferable to the other two alternatives. Either that the text in question is an entirely human contrivance, or that it really is a bequest from God as some sections of Judaism hold it to be. For some, uncertainty will be preferable (or more comfortable) to knowing one way or another. Also, I am perfectly aware that this Appendix, by focussing on one small facet of the said sub-structure, risks becoming a hostage to fortune. That it may become the focus for sceptics who will employ the filibustering tactic of debating any peripheral issue that diverts attention away from the far more important overall coherence. But the evidence for coherence is plain to see throughout most chapters of this book. Equally telling are the literary signs (biblical and extra-biblical) that the same structures have been recognised on several occasions throughout several millennia, demonstrating that the Seal phenomenon is not a figment of one fevered imagination. However, the subject of this Appendix is the statistical type of evidence.

Our core topic will be the distribution of the nine copies of the letter *vav* (ו) that occur in the first 64 letters of the Torah. And the rationale for conducting this analysis is the stunning way these nine letters align with one another in the four square aspects (ie G1, G2, G3 and G4) of the Author's Seal. As described in chapters 2, 5 and 7, those nine letters appear to be a metaphor for water, in a number of its common situations. To recap, in the G1 tilted square, all nine copies of vav were found on or below the horizontal diagonal. That was interpreted as water collecting into the bottom of a receptacle, which could be a sea, a lake, or a laver of the Tabernacle or Temple. Their overall low location was in addition to five of them assembling into a 'Y' formation placed symmetrically within the square. Then a tiny modification converted the G1 square to G2, with the significant effect that eight out of the same nine letters became re-aligned into an unbroken chain, like a meandering river, but all still in the bottom half. In the G3 and G4 squares, the same nine letters (or water) became distributed between the upper and lower corners of the tilted square, again with discernible internal structure.

In a real sense, the internal structures just mentioned are just as important as the more general distributions of the nine copies of vav. However, it is probably not realistic to try to model those detailed structures mathematically; so this Appendix will concentrate on calculating the likelihood of random chance being responsible for the more general distribution. The analysis will focus on the shared characteristics of G1/2, in comparison with the distribution in G3. That is, all the water found in the lower half of G1/2, but divided between the extreme top and bottom of G3.

Ultimately, calculating these odds is a simple matter of applying the principles of probability, and the appropriate theorem may be stated as follows:

> *The probability that all of a set of independent events will happen in a single trial is the product of their separate probabilities.*

But before we can apply this principle, there are two obstacles that must be overcome. At some stage we will have to model the problem so that it can be expressed and evaluated mathematically. But we also need to address a small matter of perception, which can blind observers to the applicability of probability modelling techniques.

The usual difficulty with perception lies in accepting that we are dealing with a case of probabilities at all. That is, does it make any sense to ask whether the first letter vav, or any other, is likely to occur in one of the valid but restricted zones of the squares? After all, we are dealing with a given text in which the 64 letters are in known, fixed positions. The real issue is, however, whether the author of the given text had an eye on its detailed structure as much as on its literal meaning. It is true, of course, that the text is pre-determined; so we are not dealing with the casting of lots. In other words, we have no alternative texts with which to compare the one text we do have. So how can we possibly say that the distinctive distribution of nine particular letters out of 64 is anything but a happenstance? In all honesty, on that basis we can't; but there is a simple way out of this impasse. What we *can* do is make a plausible assumption that there must be many thousands of alternative ways the given 64 letters could be arranged into valid sentences, including unfinished sentences. Then the appropriate question becomes: What is the probability over all those alternative cases that the nine copies of vav will fully meet the eye-catching general criteria we have observed within the Seal?

Unfortunately, life is too short to search for all those thousands of potentially valid anagrams, so we shall have to make another plausible assumption. We will assume that, in the preceding scenario, the proportion of valid to non-valid letter distributions will be approximately the same as they would be for all random square arrangements of the given 64 letters. That is, with the given set of 64 letters, we shall allow any and every possible linear combination of them. On that basis, we are in a position to model the problem in a way that makes it possible to calculate the required probabilities.

Figure C.1 shows, in two alternative ways, the criteria that would have to be met in order to arrive at an acceptable distribution of the relevant nine letters. The two tilted squares indicate, (i) using numbers, the order in which the letters of each combination must be entered, and (ii) by a black background, the zones within which the nine copies of vav will meet the necessary criteria. The two horizontal rows of 64 small, black and white squares (the 1st on the left and 64th on the right) model the same text in its pre-insertion linear form. The black elements in each row indicate positions that would fall within black zones in the corresponding square. The actual positions of the nine copies of vav at the start of Genesis are indicated by the ◊ symbols between the two rows. It is clear, therefore, that these letters do meet the specified criteria, since they coincide with black elements in both the row above and the row below.

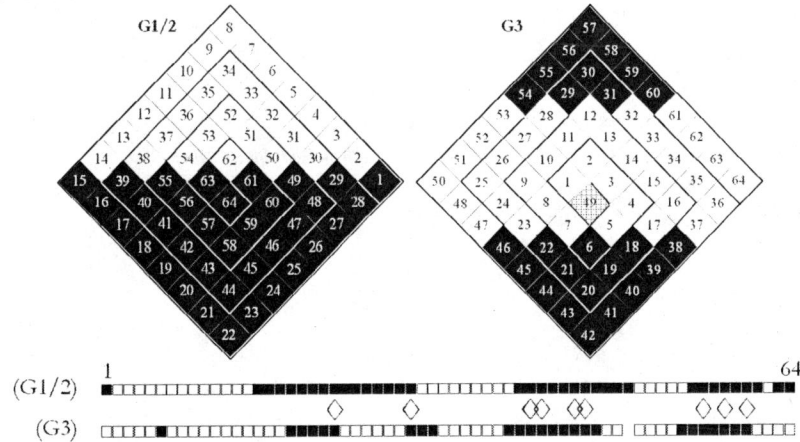

**Figure C.1**

Ostensibly, both rows represent the identical text, which is here assumed to be entered from left to right, from 1 to 64. But remember that in the G3 square the letter ayin from position 49 has been migrated to the centre of the square. So the letter numbers in the G3 square jump from 48 to 50; and in the linear equivalent, there is a gap at position 49.

The next question is: In how many positions within the 64 could the relevant nine letters be located in order to meet the stringent conditions of the exercise? And the answer is that there are just 20 linear positions that would coincide with the black zones in both aspects of the Seal. That is, in Figure C.1 there are 20 black elements in the upper linear row that coincide with black elements in the lower row. And this observation gives us the basic information we need to perform the appropriate probability calculation.

The actual calculation is even easier than might be supposed. In reality, all we have to do is account for the nine occurrences of the letter vav and ignore the other 55 letters. So, in any particular random arrangement of the given 64 letters we ask, what are the chances that the first vav will fall within a black zone? Since there are exactly 20 valid positions in the linear text – that is 20 acceptable positions out of 64 – the probability can be expressed as the fraction 20/64. If the first vav strikes lucky, we proceed to consider the next vav in sequence; otherwise the criteria are not met, and we abandon the test and proceed to the next possible string of the 64 letters.

Assuming the first vav is valid, we now need to know what the chances are that the second vav will also be valid. But there are now only 19 acceptable empty locations remaining out of 63 altogether. So the chances the second vav will also strike lucky are now 19/63. As we consider the linear position of each letter vav in turn, both the numerator and the denominator of the resulting probability ratio decrease by 1. The next question is what to do with the resulting nine fractions. And the answer is in the probability theorem given earlier. That is: *The probability that all of a set of independent events will happen in a single trial is the product of their separate probabilities.* In other words, we need to multiply all the fractions together, so:

$$\frac{20}{64} \times \frac{19}{63} \times \frac{18}{62} \times \frac{17}{61} \times \frac{16}{60} \times \frac{15}{59} \times \frac{14}{58} \times \frac{13}{57} \times \frac{12}{56} = 0.0000061$$

(or 1 chance in 163971)

This result looks very significant indeed, and allows us to say with confidence that the observed distribution of the nine copies of the letter vav in the G1, G2 and G3 squares (ie the appearance of water) almost certainly did not arise by accident. But let me put this specific case study into perspective.

First, it only addresses the general zoning of the topical nine letters. Their further organisation into eye-catching configurations within those zones should also be considered, but cannot so easily be calculated. Suffice to say, that the criteria for defining the more detailed configurations would have to be very much more stringent than those assumed in the above calculation.

Second, the zoning of nine letters is the least of the spectacular artefacts revealed by the Seal on the Torah. There are scores, if not hundreds of others to be satisfactorily explained. However, it would be unrealistic to try to express more than a small proportion of them in a way that can be numerically evaluated. For many of them, the best we can say is that they are exceedingly unlikely to have arisen by chance alone.

Third, whatever the odds may be against each additional feature being a random illusion, the rules of probability state that the overall probability is the product (ie multiplication) of the individual probabilities. So if, for instance, the Seal displayed just 20 striking features, each with a similarly low likelihood as our 'zoning' case study, then the overall probability of randomness being the creative agent would be only about 0.000(…)005% where the ellipsis (…) represents a further 100 interposed zeros. In reality, there are not just 20 striking features revealed by the Seal, but several times that number.

Fourth, it would be remiss of us to ignore the immediate message of the given text, which starts: *In the beginning God created* … Surely this declaration in itself has an important bearing on the nature of the phenomenon with which we are dealing.

One final observation is in order. Once we concede that the amazing complexity within the Seal is an entirely deliberate construct, we must also consider just how difficult that might be to contrive. In terms of the current case study, we have just calculated that the odds against the agent being randomness are very remote indeed. But what does that say about how difficult or easy it might be to fix the positions of nine specific letters? The answer turns out to be 'very little'. Once we know the best positions to place the nine copies of vav, we could do that first then arrange the other 55 letters around them. We even have some latitude to apply further fine-tuning adjustments within the known constraints. So, it seems that orchestrating a single feature, even a complex one, may be relatively straightforward compared with what would then appear to be the odds against it being a random illusion. But to then incorporate a second and a third must be incredibly difficult, because the plain text into which they are woven must not only make sense but convey the right message. It is difficult to be sure, but intuition suggests that as more and more subtle features are to be added into the same meaningful text, the difficulty will increase exponentially. What starts out as a fairly simple exercise quickly becomes all but impossible, as the index of difficulty (for the artificer) quickly overtakes the estimated probability of deliberate design (as seen by the detached observer).

## Appendix D.

**Table 3.1** (repeated from Chapter 3)

### Table 3.1 : The letter values used in Hebrew numerology.

| Ord. | Symbol | Name | Std. | Qatan | Ord. | Symbol | Name | Std. | Qatan |
|---|---|---|---|---|---|---|---|---|---|
| 1 | א | Aleph | 1 | 1 | 12 | ל | Lamed | 30 | 3 |
| 2 | ב | Beyt | 2 | 2 | 13 | מ,ם | Mem⁰ | 40 | 4 |
| 3 | ג | Gimmel | 3 | 3 | 14 | נ,ן | Nun⁰ | 50 | 5 |
| 4 | ד | Delet | 4 | 4 | 15 | ס | Samech | 60 | 6 |
| 5 | ה | Heh | 5 | 5 | 16 | ע | Ayin | 70 | 7 |
| 6 | ו | Vav | 6 | 6 | 17 | פ,ף | Peh⁰ | 80 | 8 |
| 7 | ז | Zayin | 7 | 7 | 18 | צ,ץ | Tzadee⁰ | 90 | 9 |
| 8 | ח | Chet* | 8 | 8 | 19 | ק | Qof | 100 | 1 |
| 9 | ט | Tet | 9 | 9 | 20 | ר | Reysh | 200 | 2 |
| 10 | י | Yud | 10 | 1 | 21 | ש | Shin | 300 | 3 |
| 11 | כ,ך | Kaf⁰ | 20 | 2 | 22 | ת | Tav | 400 | 4 |

\* This 'ch' is pronounced rather as in the Scottish loch, not as in church. The use of a letter h rather than a plain 'h' indicates the deeper guttural sound.

ø These are the five letters which have normal and final forms. Some schemes of numerology assign different values to the alternative forms.

## Appendix E.    A challenge to sceptics.

The phenomenon of the Seal on the start of Genesis will inevitably be disputed for any number of reasons. But the most valid counter would be some kind of visible proof that the number of emergent words it contains is nothing special. That is why I have elected to define a test that might be used by any would-be sceptic.

My challenge takes the same form as the Seal, and requires the contender to compose a short, meaningful and grammatically sound text that is to be entered into an 8×8 matrix in a coiling formation (see below), both forwards and backwards. The text may be on any subject and, like the Seal, may be longer than 64 letters, the last word entered then being truncated. Only the letters of the text should be entered into the matrix, not the spaces and punctuation within or between words. The challenge is to include as many emergent words as possible, say six or more with the text entered in each direction. The words must all be relevant to the topic of the entered text.

One potential criticism of the Seal hypothesis is that it may be relatively easy to accommodate short Hebrew words (which do not include explicit vowels) in the available space. But there are plenty of short English words with vowels making the task potentially just as easy. For example, if the entered text is on the subject of wildlife, the emergent words might include any from: ASP, ASS, BEE, CAT, COD, COW, EMU, FLY, FOX, GNU, HEN, HOG, JAY, OWL, OX, PIG, RAM, RAT, SOW, YAK. These words are only examples, and might also include characteristics and behaviour such as FUR, LEG or SWIM. Words of more than three letters are of course also valid, just so long as they are pertinent to the chosen topic.

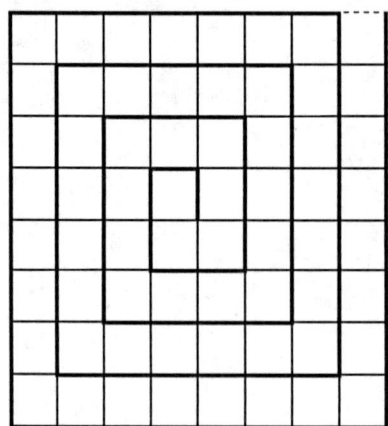

# References

Jenkins, V. (1999) *NEW for OLD*
(http://freespace.virgin.net/vernon.jenkins/NewForOld.htm)
Accessed 8 July 2008)

Jenkins, V. (2003) *The Ultimate Assertion*
(http://homepage.virgin.net/vernon.jenkins/Evidences.htm)
Accessed 8 July 2008)

Jenkins, V. (2004) *THE BEGINNING OF WONDERS*
(http://homepage.virgin.net/tgvernon.jenkins/Spectacular_1.htm)
Accessed 8 July 2008)

Read, P. P. *The Templars* (Phoenix Press, 2001)

Satinover, J. T*he Truth Behind the Bible Code* (Sidgwick & Jackson, 1997)

Wenham, Gordon J. *Word Biblical Commentary Volume 1, Genesis 1-15*
(Word, Inc., 1987)

# Glossary

Alephbeyt
: The set of 22 Hebrew letters, of which the first is Aleph and the second is Beyt.

Atbash
: A Hebrew substitution cipher in which each letter of a word or text is replaced by another according to a simple rule. Every occurrence of the first letter of the alephbeyt is replaced by its last letter, and vice versa. The second letter of the alephbeyt is replaced by its penultimate letter, and vice versa, and so on.

Baphomet (Sigil of)
: The first recorded use of the word Baphomet was in the early 14th Century, during the trials of the Knights Templar on charges of heresy and blasphemy. The name was at that time applied to a mysterious head that the Templars were accused of worshiping. No such head was ever found, nor its true identity uncovered.
The Sigil of Baphomet is a depiction of the head of a goat, superimposed on a pentacle having two points upwards. This is a 19th Century invention of Satanism, and has subsequently led to the Roman Church retreating from its one-time acceptance of the pentacle as a Christian symbol.

Bible Code
: A hypothetical encoding of words in the Hebrew Torah text, such that valid words are spelled with letters at equidistant intervals. Any starting point and skip interval is permitted; the greater test of veracity being that related encoded words should be found close together in a rectangular matrix representation of the source text.

Biblical Scholarship
: The academic pursuit of knowledge concerning the origin(s) and meaning of the Judeo-Christian scriptures, from a Christian or pseudo-Christian point of view. The analytical techniques that are acceptable can be described as rational and logical in the scientific sense that has come down from Greek philosophical origins. The techniques include 'Source Criticism', 'Form Criticism',

'Redaction Criticism' and 'Literary Criticism'. This approach is quite different from Jewish rabbinical modes of analysis (eg Midrash), in which veneration and the subtleties of the Hebrew language play much more prominent roles.

| | |
|---|---|
| Books of Moses (see Torah) | These are the biblical books of Genesis (*B'reishith*), Exodus (*Shemot*), Leviticus (*Vayiqra*), Numbers (*Bamidbar*) and Deuteronomy (*Devarim*). The words in parentheses are transliterations of the equivalent Jewish name which, in each case, is the first substantive Hebrew word in the corresponding book. |
| Creed | A set of rigid articles of faith that define the acceptable beliefs of a religion, or religious denomination. |
| Cipher | A method for hiding information in a message, often using symbols or other substitute text to replace the operative letters. |
| Divine Proportion | A precisely known number (approx. 1.618) that is often found in nature as the ratio of two closely-related numbers or lengths. This infinitely long decimal number is considered by mathematicians to be so interesting that it has been assigned its own symbol: Phi ($\Phi$). Phi may be found exactly from the formula $5\text{^}.5 \times .5 + .5$<br>It is sometimes suggested that the relative dimensions of the Ark of the Covenant (ie $3 \times 3 \times 5$) were meant to approximate the Divine Proportion, and is the reason it acquired this name. |
| Emergent (word) | In the context of a square or rectangular matrix populated with grammatical prose, an emergent word is one that is composed from letters that are not adjacent in the original text, but become adjacent in their new context. |
| Equidistant Letter Sequence (ELS) | A sequence of non-consecutive, yet regularly spaced, letters in the Hebrew scriptures, which are found to spell a valid word. This principle is the foundation of the so-called Bible Code. |

| | |
|---|---|
| Fibonacci Sequence | The infinitely long sequence of integers starting (by common consent) with 1, 1, ... in which each subsequent term is the sum of the previous two. The ratio of any two consecutive terms in the sequence is an approximation to the Divine Proportion. |
| Figurate number | A positive integer (whole number) which may be represented as a geometrical shape (eg triangle, square, Star of David) by the alignment of that number of identical objects (usually discs). The characteristics of figurate numbers that are important to our context are described in Appendix A(ii). |
| Form Criticism | A technique employed in modern biblical scholarship to try to understand the social background and oral traditions (myths and legends) that eventually led to the written forms of the Bible. |
| Gematria | The analysis of biblical Hebrew words on the basis that each letter is associated with a numeric value of supernatural origin. |
| Golden Ratio (see Divine Proportion) | Just one of many names for the same mathematical concept. |
| Graph Theory | A branch of mathematics that describes ways in which one or more nodes may be joined to one another by connecting lines, called edges. The properties of such graphs and the associated language can be helpful in expressing many real-world problems, especially in the fields of Operational Research and combinatorics (eg. finding the shortest of many routes between two towns). |

| | |
|---|---|
| Hexagram | Also known as the Star of David (or Mogen David). It is formed from two overlapping equal-sized equilateral triangles, one point-up and the other point-down. As a symbol of Judaism, the edges of one triangle are often drawn as though weaving in and out of the other triangle. |
| Leitmotif | A term used especially of music that includes a recurrent theme. Also applicable to literature (and history) in which a repeating pattern is discernible. |
| Literary Criticism | Literary Criticism is almost the antithesis of Source Criticism, Form Criticism and Redaction Criticism. It is a refreshing approach in biblical scholarship which aims to understand a text and its contemporary context together, without denying that it might have been the result of a literary evolution. |
| Midrash (or Drash) | The third and best known of four increasingly deep levels at which the Hebrew scriptures may be understood. The others are Pshat (plain reading), Remez (allegorical and metaphorical) and Sod (deeply mystical and esoteric). These techniques, along with unswerving reverence, are the foundation of the Jewish alternative to biblical scholarship. |
| Numerology | A generic term for the analysis of biblical Greek and Hebrew words on the basis that each letter has an intrinsic numeric value. |
| Outremer | The mediaeval European name for the Holy Land, during the times of the crusader wars. |
| Pentacle | The generic name for any line-drawing that depicts a star-shape having an odd number of points. The term is most often used to refer to the five-pointed star, assuming (incorrectly) that the word derives from the Greek word *pente*, meaning 'five'. The five-pointed star should more properly be called a 5-pentacle, though this epithet now tends to be restricted to 'expert' discussion. |

| | |
|---|---|
| Pentagon | In principle, any enclosed figure formed from five straight lines may be called a pentagon. A regular pentagon is formed from five straight lines of equal length, such that its vertices (the point where the ends of two lines meet) coincide with the circumference of the circumscribed circle. |
| Pentateuch (see also Torah) | The first five books of the Bible (ie Genesis, Exodus, Leviticus, Numbers and Deuteronomy). |
| Pi (Symbol: π) | The ratio of the circumference of any circle to its diameter (approximately 3.1415926). When expressed in decimal form, the fractional part of Pi has an infinitely long number of digits that do not repeat. Although Pi is transcendental and is not rational (it cannot be expressed exactly as one whole number divided by another), it is definable as an infinite progression of rational numbers. Therefore, the value of Pi is not dependent on the structure of our particular universe. |
| Redaction (...Criticism) | Redaction is the process of combining multiple texts that may or may not agree or overlap, along with some judicious editing. The starting point for modern biblical scholarship is the belief that some of the biblical books we know today are the result of splicing together two or more sources. Redaction Criticism is the process of untangling the text in an attempt, first to understand the motives of the redactor, and second to try to reconstruct the separate parts. |
| Rosetta Stone | A large (760kg) stone on which is carved a single text in three languages: classical Greek, Egyptian demotic and ancient Egyptian hieroglyphic. The stone was discovered in Egypt in 1799AD, during Napoleonic occupation. By 1822, comparison of the three versions of the text had led to the first 'modern' understanding of hieroglyphic writing. |

| | |
|---|---|
| Source Criticism | A technique employed in modern biblical scholarship to try to deduce where different parts of the Bible came from. It is assumed that differences in structure, vocabulary and style are indicative of multiple authors. |
| Star of David | Also called the Mogen David (see also Hexagram). |
| Talmud | An evolving Jewish compilation of analyses of, and commentaries on the Hebrew scriptures, but the Torah in particular. Two versions exist: one is the enormous Babylonian Talmud which was initiated during the Babylonian exile of the Jews; and there is the smaller Jerusalem Talmud which was compiled later. It is a fundamental principle of Talmudic analysis that a contribution, once accepted, is never removed; alternative understandings of scripture are always possible and valid, even though they may appear superficially contradictory. |
| Tetrahedron | In principal, any 3-dimensional shape that is enclosed by four flat surfaces, all of which will be triangular. Every tetrahedron has exactly 4 faces, 6 edges and 4 vertices. In practice, the word is most often applied to a regular tetrahedron, in which the six edges are of equal length and the faces are all equilateral triangles. A regular tetrahedron could be described as a three-sided pyramid, which is inherently more perfect than the sort that sits on a square base. |
| Tetragrammaton | The four-letter Hebrew name of God; revealed first to Moses at the burning bush on Mt.Horeb (or Sinai). Within the Bible, this name is translated as 'The Lord'. Outside the Bible, it is often transliterated as YHWH (or JHWH), which gives rise to the popular term Jehovah. However, the true pronunciation was lost at the time the second temple in Jerusalem was destroyed by the Romans. |

In the Beginning

Torah

The original Hebrew text of the Five Books of Moses. Known outside Judaism by the Greek name Pentateuch.

Transliteration

A useful way to describe how a word in a foreign language should be pronounced. Clearly, the spelling of the transliteration will need to reflect the rules of pronunciation of the language with which the reader is familiar.

ISBN 142517071-4